D0025363

PRIVACY

STUDIES IN SOCIAL
AND CULTURAL HISTORY

PRIVACY

STUDIES IN SOCIAL AND CULTURAL HISTORY

BARRINGTON MOORE, JR.

M. E. SHARPE, INC.
Armonk, New York
London, England

Copyright © 1984 by Barrington Moore, Jr.

All rights reserved. No part of this book may be reproduced in any form
without written permission from the publisher, M. E. Sharpe, Inc.,
80 Business Park Drive, Armonk, New York 10504.

Library of Congress Cataloging in Publication Data

Moore, Barrington, 1913-
    Privacy: studies in social and cultural history.

    Bibliography: p.
    Includes index.
    1. Privacy—Cross-cultural studies. 2. Privacy—History.
I. Title.
GT2405.M66   1983   306   83-23524
ISBN 0-87332-266-5
ISBN 0-87332-269-X (pbk.)

Distributor's ISBN 0-394-53819-6 Cloth
                0-394-72494-1 Paper

Distributed by Pantheon Books, a division of Random House, Inc.

Design: Angela Foote

Printed in the United States of America

To E.C.M.

|Contents

PREFACE AND ACKNOWLEDGMENTS

This book is a set of exploratory studies about the nature and meaning of private concerns in several societies. Though ideas are not neglected, the emphasis is on behavior and especially the social and cultural context of behavior. At the outset I took seriously the possibility that in some societies there might be nothing at all that corresponded to our conception of private. As the reader will see, there are some societies where that is very nearly the case. More generally, in looking for the meaning of private concerns in societies very different from our own I have deliberately cast the net as widely as possible. Thus the book discusses privacy, both in the sense of refusing access by other persons in specified situations, and as private rights against holders of authority or other members of the same society. Personal privacy and private rights are linked by the notion of intrusion. Social rules protect what is private from intrusion and interference by other people.

Certain problems of definition recur in all forms of inquiry that draw upon the recorded experience of societies other than our own. To make an inquiry manageable it is necessary at the start to block off some area of human behavior for intensive scrutiny. One cannot look into everything thoroughly. But one cannot make this preliminary definition of the subject matter too narrow or too strict without severe risk of omitting vital evidence. It is not the investigator's definition of privacy and private rights that matters in this case; it is what members of other societies have felt about these issues and what they have done about them—if they have even been concerned about them at all. One can learn what their conceptions were only by patient examination of evidence that is frequently limited and fragmentary. Sharp definitions become possible only after an investigator has acquired great familiarity with the evidence. By that point, on the other hand, precise definitions are likely to be superfluous.

Though the book closes with a few brief observations on contemporary societies, nearly all of it is about societies remote in time and space from our own. To the extent that these studies may make any contribution to understanding contemporary aspects of privacy and private rights, it is by setting them in a wider context, indicating the range of variation in private concerns and providing evidence about their early history. Such knowledge is necessary in assessing the prospects for desirable as well as dangerous trends in our own times. It is, however, by no means the only necessary kind of knowledge. For the curious reader I have therefore included in the bibliography a brief selection of works on privacy in the modern world.

The book begins with an examination of some anthropological evidence. This is the best kind of evidence for discovering the range of known human behavior. For the most part I have concentrated on very simple societies without chiefs or priests. Though such societies are of course in a strict sense our contemporaries and anything but ancient, with their primitive technologies and relatively simple social structures they may well reflect some modes of behavior that antedate "civilized" societies with a written language. The second chapter analyzes ancient Athens, one of our cultural ancestors. With some knowledge of ancient Greek I had long planned to study the nature of public and private concerns in Athenian society as soon as the leisure of retirement made this possible. Though I had thought this would be a long undertaking, even a moderately thorough investigation took much less time than anticipated. At that point I decided to add two more studies, one on the Old Testament because the ancient Hebrews were also one of our most important cultural ancestors. The other study is ancient China during the age of the philosophers, selected in order to take one sounding into a civilized society outside the orbit of Western civilization. In each case I have relied mainly on primary sources, today accessible in quite good translations.

Two considerations led to the choice of privacy as a topic for research. I have always had an unusual fondness for privacy, especially the privacy necessary for intellectual work. Hence I wanted to see how other cultures treated this problem and if they were even aware of it. At the same time I have always set a high value on social mechanisms that protect the individual against arbitrary political and economic demands. The less one believes in the prospects of a perfectly just society the more one is likely to value protections against injustice. Both considerations may strike some potential readers as a reflection of "late bourgeois" attitudes and values and therefore subject to immediate dismissal. But injustices and intrusions are not necessarily easier to bear because they come with a socialist label.

Though I have tried to indicate the nature of the evidence in the course of discussing specific practices and ideas, a few general remarks will be helpful here. In the case of anthropological evidence a great deal depends on the quality of the anthropologist. One gets a sense for this quality, or the lack of it, mainly from reading a great many monographs and noticing the amount and kind of detail an author presents, the length of time the anthropologist has spent in the field, the internal consistency of the author's claims, and similar matters. There is no escape from some element of subjectivity in the anthropologist's report and the reader's interpretation of that report. But there is a bedrock of hard facts to work with. In general I have tried to find good anthropological monographs with detailed accounts of daily life, the only kind likely to contain evidence relevant to privacy, and feel fortunate in having come upon several from widely separated parts of the world.

In the case of ancient Athens, the ancient Hebrews, and ancient China one can work from documents that report more or less directly the actual words of individuals in those societies instead of an anthropologist's report of what they did and said. There are some advantages in this situation. But there are disadvantages as well. The documents often fail to deal with aspects of social life about which we would like detailed information. Second, the documents may for a variety of reasons be unreliable or at least partly misleading.

There are the fewest difficulties of this sort with Athenian sources. In most cases scholars have succeeded in identifying the author and the date of any given text. In addition there are many kinds of texts such as historical accounts, forensic speeches, political speeches, and works in social philosophy. The situation is very different in the case of the Old Testament, our main source for the life of the ancient Hebrews. It appears that there is scarcely a clause in the Old Testament about whose date there has not been at some time a scholarly dispute. Nevertheless there does appear to be considerable agreement on the main stages of ancient Hebrew history. For the most part I have tried to cope with this difficulty by indicating the specific historical stage to which a specific type of behavior seemed to belong. But at times I have also treated the Old Testament as a unit representing the crystallization in writing of a unique cultural tradition. The result is admittedly a bit of an awkward straddle. The justification is that the cultural tradition does exist and that in a set of soundings like this book what comes to the surface is more important than its detailed interpretation and assessment.

The materials from ancient China present still another problem. Most of them are texts in social philosophy. Most can be dated with reasonable accuracy. But they have not been preserved nearly as well as the classical texts from ancient Greece. There are gaps, probable interpolations, and in some cases ancient forgeries. In addition the meaning is often very hard for a translator to decipher. In using the texts I have therefore tried to heed the translator's warnings about difficult passages and avoid using them. There are also two sets of materials that are roughly similar to Western medieval chronicles, the *Tso chuan* and the *Chan-kuo ts'e*. I hoped at one time to use these to get more data on actual behavior than was available in the writings on social philosophy, revealing though these often were. But after I had finally managed to locate translations that were modern and seemed adequate, I found that these prolonged accounts of court intrigues yielded very little usable for this inquiry. Therefore I set them aside, contenting myself with a few valuable nuggets quoted by Burton Watson in his *Early Chinese Literature*.

Despite these difficulties there is in each case enough material to draw what I believe to be an adequate sketch of social institutions and the place of private concerns therein. In all cases I have tried to show the social context of whatever forms of privacy and private rights existed. To the extent that there is any explanation for what is private, it is, in my judgment, to be found in this context and its historical background.

Of all the books I have written, this one has been the most enjoyable to write. I hope that readers may share at least some of this pleasure with me.

Acknowledgments

As a working scholar I have for over three decades drawn intellectual sustenance from the rich holdings of Widener and other Harvard University libraries and the learning of colleagues. By not asking busy colleagues to read the manuscript I no doubt have included misstatements which might have been reduced (though it seems they can never be eliminated). Such mistakes are of course my own fault.

From various parts of the university I have received a great deal of help, for which I wish to express my gratitude publicly. Dean Henry Rosovsky not only showed interest in this study in its early stages but encouraged me to keep at it, with compassion and generosity, when the wrench of retirement was taking its toll on me. Many doubts began to fade away, and the work moved forward. I owe him as old friend and wise mentor an inestimable debt.

Among those colleagues whom I did not ask to read the manuscript are some who have given me very useful advice, usually over the luncheon table or while walking along the street between classes. For the anthropological chapter Professor David Maybury-Lewis begged me not to include certain ideas of mine, although he approved of others. On another occasion Professor Zeph Stewart, on hearing what I might say about ancient Athens, advised me to read the ancient orators. His suggestion led to a complete recasting of my research for Chapter 2.

The Russian Research Center has for years generously provided me with working space and typing services, all along displaying great tolerance for my idiosyncracies, favors for which I am very grateful. When the first draft of the manuscript was finally ready for typing, the job was done quickly and well by Mary Towle, Administrative Assistant at the Center, and by Rose DiBenedetto, who for years has taken care of my secretarial needs with cheer and despatch. The strong and spontaneous expressions of interest in the book's ideas by these two women gave a great lift to my spirits. Theirs was the first "public" response to this work, suggesting that it might find favor in other quarters. In addition I want to express publicly my thanks to Professor Edward Friedman for an instructive and entertaining letter about the term "private" in current Chinese usage.

My wife, Elizabeth C. Moore, has worked as home editor and first reader of whatever I write. In addition to making editorial suggestions she has verified all the references and prepared an index that will enable the curious reader to pursue selected themes through all the chapters. Somehow she has managed to be a marvelous and affectionate companion as well. With such supportive and intelligent help this book should be flawless. I know perfectly well that it isn't. The responsibility for its defects should be laid at my door.

PRIVACY

STUDIES IN SOCIAL
AND CULTURAL HISTORY

ANTHROPOLOGICAL PERSPECTIVES

CHAPTER 1

Privacy, Anger, and Dependence:
Notes on an Eskimo Community

Occasionally a good ethnographic report can reveal unsuspected yet elementary aspects of human feelings and behavior. They are elementary in the sense of being psychological and social processes that recur very widely as essential components of more complex human relationships. There seem to be several ingredients in such a discovery. One is a reader with a moderately but not too narrowly focused curiosity on an issue with which the anthropologist is not explicitly concerned. Unintentionally revealed evidence is less likely to be contaminated with what an author hopes to prove. Another ingredient is the simplicity of the society under investigation because simplicity strips away confusing considerations to reveal elementary ones. A third ingredient may be a society that displays some extreme or unusual features. If either the physical environment or certain aspects of behavior, such as an *apparent* lack of aggression, are near one end of the currently known spectrum of human variability, the resulting emphasis can render visible unsuspected causal relationships.

To see how half a dozen people can get along together inside an igloo through a long arctic winter can, as I hope to show, tell us a good deal about human needs for privacy and autonomy as well as the psychic and social costs of politeness and cooperation. One last ingredient is an anthropologist who is a candid and accurate observer, able to communicate findings in lucid prose, not pseudoscientific mush.

All these qualities come together in a study by Jean L. Briggs of a remote Eskimo community of twenty to thirty-five people living at the mouth of the Back River in the Canadian Northwest Territories, northwest of Hudson Bay and well inside the Arctic Circle. These

3

people call themselves the Utkuhikhalingmiut, which the author merci-
fully abbreviates to Utku.[1] Like other Eskimos they live in a physical
setting that the extreme cold renders harsh and dangerous for anyone
who is not an Eskimo and on occasion even for them. For this reason it
is appropriate to regard their situation as extreme, despite their generally effective adaptation to it, an adaptation that, at least while food is
plentiful, can produce expressions of contentment and preference for
their own way of life over that of the nearest mission and trading
settlement, several days away by dogsled. On the other hand, their
recent history also includes famine.[2]

Toward the end of August 1963, a prospective member of this
society, the Radcliffe graduate student in anthropology Jean L. Briggs
stepped out of a small airplane with but a rudimentary knowledge of
Eskimo and a great deal of trepidation. There was to be no more
contact with civilization, not even by radio, until the winter months
when the Eskimos made an occasional journey to the mission-trading
center by dogsled. The only Eskimos who knew some English, two or
three schoolchildren, were to leave on the plane's return trip. She
would have to survive the arctic winter on the basis of Eskimo
technology without Eskimo skills and barely knowing the language.
And she was far from sure that she could.[3]

Immediately on her arrival she found herself in a trap of forced
sociability, as visiting the white woman became a major diversion for
the Eskimos. Her tent was never empty from the time she awoke in the
morning, and sometimes before, until, frayed to exhaustion, she re-
treated to the warm protection of her sleeping bag, leaving departing
visitors to tie the tent flaps shut as they went out. She felt wooden
within and without, her face from smiling, her mind and tongue from
struggling with unaccustomed and meaningless sounds. To be sure, she
recognized her visitors as extraordinarily benign and considerate. They
performed many little favors, such as noticing when her fish was all
eaten and then bringing her more. If she was slow in attacking the slimy
raw flesh, they assumed she did not know how to cut it. So they filleted
it for her. They lit her lamp when her fingers were too stiff with cold,
fixed the Primus stove when it clogged, sharpened her knife when it
was dull—all without asking.

In a word, Briggs was not competent to participate in their society,
at least not yet. But she had to take part. She felt their anticipation of
her needs as immensely warming, as if she were being cared for like a
three-year-old. She recognized the Eskimos' constant visits as a sign of
friendly acceptance as well as hunger for the luxuries of tea and
bannock, a native fried delicacy. But as she reports, "I could not help
seeing them as an invasion of privacy. I felt trapped by my visitors."
Nothing depressed her more than inactivity, she adds, and when the

site of inactivity was a tent permeated with the dank chill of autumn, the situation rapidly became unbearable. The fact that the Eskimos when they felt cold could go out and do some warming work or chase each other around the tents while she had to attend the next relay of visitors aroused her resentment.

This entrapment and tremendous yearning for privacy lasted for six days. Only later did she learn that Eskimo etiquette did not impose the obligation of constant attendance on a visitor's wants.[4] The essence of the entrapment was the imposition of a social obligation (1) from which there appeared to be no escape, (2) that she was not competent to carry out and which therefore (3) produced severe psychological and even physical pain. The privacy that she so dearly wanted would have amounted to escape from or protection against the obligations imposed by the surrounding society.

There is a fourth element in this situation: her sense of dependence or feeling "like a three-year-old." It was through an intensification of this sense of dependence and then a partial surrender to it that she was able to overcome or at least anaesthetize her longing for privacy and a degree of personal autonomy. As we shall see in due course, a competent adult Eskimo does not have to surrender so much. Adequate participation comes much more easily. But the conflict between the desire for independent and even "selfish" behavior and the objective need to depend on others remains a central aspect of Eskimo society—and in *any* human society with *any* painful obligations.

After six days the steady stream of visitors to Jean Briggs's tent stopped for a moment. She seized this break to flee from her tent to spend the day alone, wandering in the tundra, memorizing Eskimo vocabulary, and feeling homesick. Coming upon two women picking berries as she retraced her steps in the late afternoon, she wondered guiltily if they had sensed the rebuff underlying her flight that morning. But they welcomed her warmly, giving the impression that they had overlooked her hostile withdrawal. Not until a year later did she learn that Eskimos never overlook such behavior; they merely conceal their disapproval for a time. "At the time," she writes, "secure in my innocence, I felt the giddy hope of being . . . accepted. More, for the first time I really enjoyed the company of my new acquaintances. And it dawned on me how forlorn I would be in that wilderness if they forsook me. Far, far better to suffer loss of privacy."[5] She had become aware for the first time how important her Eskimo neighbors were for her survival and how dependent she was on their favorable response and personal reassurance. The conflict between her need for privacy and for the material and psychological support from her hosts was to recur, though in a somewhat less intense form, as she developed more resources to cope with her situation.[6]

For the purpose of this inquiry it does not matter a great deal that Briggs, who describes herself as a middle-class American, may have had a stronger culturally induced need for privacy—in the quite specific sense of barriers against intrusion and ways to cut short undesired sociability—than did her Eskimo hosts. Since Eskimo culture has its own set of circuit breakers for shedding social overload,† it would be unwise to assume that middle-class Americans generally put a higher value on privacy.

So far the inquiry has focused on the conditions that intensify the desire to be left alone and those that extinguish this desire, to replace it with one for responsive human contact and social support. We can assume that both desires are part of the general repertoire of human responses to the social and physical environment, at least in a latent form, and that they are emphasized or deemphasized in a generalized fashion by different societies and cultural norms. To repeat what can be learned so far by generalizing from the Eskimo data, the need for privacy amounts to a desire for socially approved protection against painful social obligations. The desire for privacy can be extinguished by a need for dependence that comes from an awareness of helplessness and isolation.

In the hope of gaining further insights we may now explore the connections between obligations and dependence among the Utku themselves. To do that, it is necessary to understand how they lived.

For the adult males, getting food appears to be life's predominant concern. For the adult females it is taking care of the males, a division of labor that is felt as fair since the males are perceived to take the risks and do the hardest work.[7] Fishing and hunting are the principal sources of livelihood. There is also some trapping of furs to exchange for those white man's goods such as Primus stoves that make Eskimo life easier.

Both their winter economy of ₁a compact settlement of igloos and their summer economy of widely scattered hunting camps and tents appear to be quite individualistic, or more accurately familistic, though Briggs does not provide a detailed account. Among these Eskimos at any rate I found no report of any economic activity that required the cooperation of all adults in the community.‡ Such activities do exist in other simple hunting bands, such as some African pygmies, and have far-reaching effects on social life. But among the Utku, decisions about where and how to fish and hunt are made by the head of the household.

---

†For instance the Eskimos rarely adapted their activities to the presence of a visitor. Visitors either joined in family activities or sat quietly in the periphery. "If the host had business elsewhere he simply announced the fact and went out, whereupon it was incumbent on the guest to leave also": Briggs, *Never in Anger*, 26. Perhaps that is one reason guests usually appeared unannounced.
‡Cooperation was greater in the summer camps, which according to Briggs, *Never in Anger*, 88, came to resemble a communal unit.

Where there is a cooperative group, it is likely to be a pair of males from the same kin group.

More generally, the "real family"—an elastic term that can stretch from the nuclear family to an extended one including genealogical or adoptive siblings—is the main social unit for both production and consumption. As Briggs writes: Whenever possible, it is with their "real family" that people live, work, travel, and share whatever they have. Moreover, it is only with their "real family" that they appear to feel completely comfortable and safe.[8]

In a manner that accords with their atomistic economy, the Utku cherish independence of thought and action as a natural prerogative and look askance at anyone who shows signs of wanting to tell them what to do. There are no formal chiefs whose authority transcends that of the separate householders.[9] Briggs also found them a people reluctant to answer questions. They displayed "an extremely strong sense of privacy with regard to their thoughts, their feelings, and motivations; and I feared to offend it."[10]

Though Briggs reports no instance of an Utku unburdening his or her soul to her in the course of her seventeen-months' stay, that is quite understandable in the light of her circumstances. Living in very close quarters with an Eskimo family, there were few opportunities for a *tête-à-tête*. In this sense privacy was an almost unattainable commodity among the Utku. Furthermore, toward the end of her stay, when her command of the language might have been enough for more extensive and intimate talks, due to circumstances beyond her control her Utku hosts came to distrust her.

Against what danger then is this strong desire for privacy directed? As becomes increasingly clear in the course of Briggs's account, both the capacity and desire to control feelings, especially hostile feelings, are part of a desire to maintain an atmosphere of social harmony. It would be misleading to label this air of smiling politeness and consideration for others as a façade, with the implication that it is a decoration without structural function. In a society with no formal institutions for the exercise of authority and with an individualistic or familistic economy, and where all members are exposed intermittently to risks of drowning, freezing, and running short of food or other supplies crucial for survival—not to mention comfort by Eskimo standards—it makes excellent adaptive sense to create and sustain an ethos of social harmony and considerateness alongside one of sturdy self-reliance.

Utku society was also one without specialized crafts or occupations and the forms of cooperation and hierarchy that such specialization frequently produces. The division of labor followed the lines of age and sex, and manifested itself within the kin group and household. Nevertheless, living as they do in a potentially dangerous environment where individuals are liable to run short of specific supplies, the Utku like other Eskimos soften their individualism with a strong emphasis on reciprocity and responsiveness to the needs of others. In practice this emphasis takes the form of a strong obligation to share, especially to share food, and to lend a helping hand or do small favors.[11] This sharing and mutual assistance was in large measure a safeguard against inconveniences and more serious misfortunes to which all were liable. Hence adult Utku were quite dependent on each other.

Dependence can be a very attractive situation, especially in a social group with an ethic and etiquette of warm, friendly concern. It is a pleasure to be able to relax from time to time, secure in the awareness that someone will be smilingly helpful. But for the adult there are costs. There is an obligation to share and to help, an obligation that is liable to be inconvenient if not burdensome on occasion. Then comes the temptation to stint one's own performance of an obligation, to avert one's attention from the existence of the obligation. When that happens, if not sooner, the neighbors begin to talk. The air will become poisoned with gossip and recrimination; the easy friendly politeness that seems so natural and attractive will turn out to be a mask that covers and but partly controls a slowly churning cauldron of resentment.

This was the situation among the Utku as Briggs came to see it on learning the language and getting to know her hosts. The attitude was clearest in connection with one deviant couple, Nilak and his wife Niqui, a woman of apparently subnormal intelligence. For reasons that are not altogether clear, this couple seemed rather less effective than others in providing for its own needs and a bit negligent about obligations to share. It lived somewhat apart from the others. The family with which Briggs lived, and into which she accepted adoption as a daughter, always maintained superficially cordial relations with Nilak and his spouse. But in private they were very critical and hostile. Nilak's warm Eskimo smile, which his wife somehow could not manage to produce, concealed bad temper, stinginess, and unhelpfulness, Briggs was told. These are three of the most damning traits one Eskimo can ascribe to another.[12] His unhelpfulness took the form of failure to offer food or assistance. Nevertheless he shared meals on occasion with the family in which Briggs lived without any overt penalty for his failure to contribute.[13]

If Nilak's behavior was extreme it was not unique: the same reluctance to carry out obligations occurred at times within the kin group. So of course did the gossip and verbal aggression. They were widespread enough to lead Briggs in time to comment on the Eskimos' "malicious tendency to cast others' behavior in the worst possible terms."[14] Fear of hostility and other people's moodiness, she remarks elsewhere, is endemic. A moody person may be planning to knife you in the back when out fishing, to claim on return that you had drowned.[15] These observations shed a revealing light on the famous Eskimo smile whose absence is evidently rather ominous.

Thus these Eskimos display their full share of the normal human hostility toward individuals unwilling or unable to perform obligations defined as socially necessary. What does distinguish the Eskimos is the extent to which they denied this hostility through their code of politeness.† The strength of the denial may be a consequence of the rather strong fear of personal hostilities. Such fear seems quite realistic. Severe personal antagonisms could be a mortal danger for a small band of isolated hunters living in a dangerous environment. In this context there is a certain irony in the fact that beyond gossip the only weapon that the Utku have to cope with individuals who put their private interests ahead of those of their neighbors is to give such persons an extra dose of privacy. As a form of tacit punishment the Utku reduce to a minimum social contact with a deviant person. To use an old English expression they send such a person to Coventry. Probably the sanction is effective: loneliness is a central concern for the Utku, as well as other Eskimos. Their word for it carries overtones of a dropping off of human and natural activity, a loss of meaning and purpose in daily routines, and conveys in Briggs's judgment the essence of unpleasantness.‡

At this stage of the analysis it is possible to discern a clear linkage among these features of Utku society and culture: (1) an individualistic or familistic economy in a setting of severe hardship and potential danger, (2) a system of reciprocal obligations to help and to share, (3) a code of politeness and social harmony that helps to control aggressions arising from intermittent failures in the system of reciprocal obligations, and (4) a heavy emphasis on privacy that prevents unseemly curiosity about the feelings that lie beneath the polite and friendly exterior. The rules about privacy also provide occasions for intimate relaxation away from social pressures as well as a system of circuit breakers to prevent social and psychological overloads.

The study of such safeguards takes us into a new area of investigation, the rules of modesty that control the visibility of physiological functions. Most of what we have found out about privacy so far is explicable in terms of the economy and the system of social obligations arising therefrom. Such considerations have an important influence on

†Briggs, *Never in Anger*, 131, in discussing their denial of hostility mentions an English-speaking informant who, when asked to translate the word "hate," flushed and denied that there was such a word in Eskimo.

‡Briggs, *Never in Anger*, 202–203. Her own experience of ostracism is described on pp. 285–291. I suspect that there is more to this kind of loneliness than the threat to physical survival that ostracism can entail in other cultures. So far as I can see, there is no reason why an able-bodied Eskimo household could not make out on its own in winter as well as summer. The lone individual is another matter.

the satisfaction of the sexual drive and on other physiological needs in Utku society as in any other. But at this point these physiological needs and other psychological ones begin to appear as distinct causal factors in their own right even if they operate in a distinct social setting.

As Briggs had a unique opportunity to notice, the Utku are extraordinarily modest. Their rules make good sense as an adaptation to the forced intimacy of the igloo. For a large part of the year the outdoors was simply not available for excretion or for sexual intercourse. For the sake of social harmony sexual arousal had to be very carefully controlled, and excretion managed in a way to minimize discomfort and inconvenience for all concerned.

The Utku strictly avoid the exposure of the genitalia.[16] Sexual intercourse in the igloo apparently took place silently. Before going to bed at night each person uses the urine can beneath the covers or sleeping bag and then puts the contents in a drum outside the dwelling.[17] One odd gap in Briggs's otherwise candid account concerns defecation: from her report one would never know that Eskimos did this. It must be quite an undertaking during a severe winter storm. There are also some signs, especially among children, of a generalized fear of intrusion into private bodily spheres.†

At one point Briggs's father by adoption tried to introduce a Western folkway about privacy and intrusion. "Have you heard?" he said once on return from a trading trip to the mission-trading post, "Jesus says we should knock on igloo doors before entering when we go visiting." On inquiring later at the post about the origins of this notion, Briggs was told that people were beginning to be shy about having others see them when sitting on the urine pot; with a knock beforehand they could get ready. But the community failed to adopt the practice. Within six weeks the only sound that announced a visitor was the familiar creak of feet on the hard frozen snow.[18]

As mentioned earlier, Utku society provides a number of other circuit breakers with which to shut off the current of unwanted social interaction. Both the summer tent and the winter igloo have a division between the family's sleeping and living area in the rear and the general utility area containing the kitchen larder and general storage space. Guests ordinarily sit or stand in the general utility area. Only specially privileged guests such as old people, close friends, or whites are invited to sit in the family area. Within the family area in turn, each individual has a sleeping space allotted according to a standard order.

†Briggs, *Never in Anger,* 150. On the other hand, Inuttiaq, Briggs's father by adoption and an unusually assertive and rough person at times by Utku standards, had the habit of grabbing playfully at adolescent penises while clowning. On such occasions he would also boast about his excretory prowess (p. 46). Nor did Eskimo conventions about modesty inhibit occasional exchanges of ribald comments within the family circle about the anthropologist's farting in the night or jokes about a little girl's lack of testicles (pp. 93, 96).

Into this space no one intrudes without permission. Briggs reports the sense of security she gained from having her own spot:

> I possessed my spot, and from it I always looked out on the same view. The sameness of it gave me a sense of stability in a world of shifting dwellings, a feeling of belonging in a family; it even gave me a sense of privacy, since no one encroached on my space without permission, and sitting there I could withdraw quietly from conversation into an inner world, reading or writing, or observing the rest of the family and their friends without disturbance.[19]

Though no doubt less frequently, the Eskimos used their sleeping spots in the same way. Although her father by adoption was ordinarily the most active and energetic member of the household, there were hours and occasionally whole days when he lay silently in his quarters apparently insensible of those working, talking, and playing around him. In these aloof moods he turned his back to society and his head to the wall, apparently a somewhat unusual form of withdrawal.[20]

It is also worth noticing that a child's reaction to the pains of learning proper Eskimo self-control was sullenness in the form of passive but total resistance to social overtures. A child's resistance, on the other hand, did not earn adult respect. Teasing or other attempts to penetrate the child's retreat into a private world were the usual adult reaction.[21]

With the alternation of the seasons, essentially a short summer and a long winter with brief transitions between them, both the opportunities for sociability and ways of escaping from it changed markedly. In the summer camps, made up of scattered small groups, there was a great deal of cooking together for more than one household, in order to save labor and fuel. This was also a period of more or less obligatory sharing of fuel. Life was lived largely outdoors in what appeared on the surface as a happy communal manner, especially for the women and children.

In the winter the Utku came together and set up their igloos. Each household became a monad, though the women did a certain amount of inter-igloo visiting. It was mainly the children, however, who flitted in and out of the various igloos, to be cross-examined by their fathers whenever they came home, the main way the fathers kept track of what was happening. For women and children winter was a period of relative confinement and restricted social space. For the men, on the other hand, social and physical space expanded enormously. They could and did travel for hundreds of miles with their dogsleds over the snow-covered tundra.[22]

Let us now review the social and psychological processes revealed by these observations of an Eskimo community in such a manner that it will be possible to assess and extend them with evidence from other societies. Since Eskimo life cannot be expected to display all aspects of privacy, other questions and other relationships will turn up in other cases. But this one will provide a good concrete starting point.

The need for privacy appears as one segment of the range of human "fight or flight" responses to stress and danger. We may posit its most probable occurrence as a response to a painful but socially approved obligation where the individual feels unable to carry out the obligation. Thus the character of a society's obligations will determine its needs and opportunities for privacy. In turn these obligations derive from the nature of the social and physical environment, the state of technology, the division of labor, and system of authority.

Even a strong yearning for privacy can evidently evaporate in the face of an acute awareness of one's dependence on other human beings. Dependence in the sense of having one's wants correctly anticipated and met can be a very pleasant state for a short period of time. But for adults it cannot last. (For a good many adults, I suspect, it would not be pleasant if it did promise to be permanent.) Sooner or later the obligations reassert themselves. Dependence can also be combined with privacy as in situations when the individual relaxes with a small group of trusted friends or relatives. We can expect to find alternating cycles of private dependence and public performance of demanding roles in a good many societies. These cycles, however, are likely to be much more prominent for adult males than adult females. For women the domestic role is more or less continuous, though its demands may slacken when the males are off hunting or engaged in some other predominantly male activity.

Since it is highly unlikely that all persons in any given society will be willing and able to meet all obligations, there is an overwhelming probability of frustration and hostility due to such failures. Such hostility is important and necessary as a source of sanctions against failure to meet social obligations. On the other hand, this aggression can also take socially divisive forms and has to be kept under control by various devices such as codes of politeness. The simplest sanctions are gossip and the refusal of supportive social contact. In simple societies lacking any extensive repertoire of sanctions, temporary ostracism may be the strongest one available. Among other Eskimos, not the Utku, we do hear of examples of socially sanctioned murder of individuals defined as dangers to the community.[23]

Since there is bound to be some friction between social obligations and individual reluctance or inability to meet them in just about any society, we may also expect to find in most societies cultural mechanisms for switching off a social overload at least temporarily. I also suspect that there will usually be implicit rules about the time and place for resorting to these mechanisms. It seems highly unlikely that an individual can symbolically or actually absent himself from a social gathering at his or her own whim. There are likely to be conventions about when one is expected to be "at home" and able to receive visitors and when one is not. It is also highly likely that access to these culturally defined circuit breakers will vary according to social status. In the case of as simple a society as the Utku we saw that adult males could resort to them far more easily than women and children.

Under certain circumstances these circuit breakers take on the character of real rules of avoidance. Sexual access to other persons is subject to some limitations in every known human society. There may possibly be a desire, which cannot always be gratified, to keep the human body inviolate, to prohibit or prevent intrusion in times of weakness or great emotional excitement, such as excretion or sexual intercourse. Menstruation is another instance, and one about which Briggs does not provide information. Such an hypothesis must remain purely speculative at this point.

As another theme for subsequent investigation we should also notice the absence of any articulated distinction between public and private spheres and concerns in Eskimo society. Lacking chiefs and any division of labor beyond that by age and sex, Eskimo society may be too homogeneous for the distinction to put in an appearance. The only sign of it that I have been able to discern in Briggs's account is a tacit awareness of the human qualities necessary to make a good Eskimo and the ways in which parents try to instill these qualities into their children. While generally permissive and gentle, Eskimo child-rearing can at times be very painful for a young child.[24] In this conflict between discipline and impulse we can perhaps discern the seeds of a distinction between what in more complex societies becomes one between social or public interest and that of the individual. Then again, complexity as such may not be decisive. Among the Mbuti Pygmies of the Ituri forest in the Belgian Congo, whose society is no more complex than the Eskimos, there is one band (the Epulu) that engages in group hunting with a net, a custom requiring skillful cooperation among all adults. Here there are some quite clear signs of an incipient "public interest" and institutions to make it effective. These we shall discuss in due course.

Subsequent essays will investigate the ways in which such an awareness develops. We shall also examine the different perceptions and definitions of public and private spheres that emerged in ancient civilizations. In all forms of civilization the relationship between the individual and the larger society has been a major concern for religious, political, and ethical thought. This issue has also been the source of some of the most passionate and bloody conflicts in human history. It is impossible for a single scholar to map the variety of practice and belief that has grown up around this issue. But preliminary sketches of some historically crucial areas may bring to light some of the decisive causes of both similarities and differences in this body of thought and behavior.

The Origins of the Public

The most prominent theme to emerge from the description of Eskimo life is the ambivalent reaction to social obligations, especially the obligation to share food and utensils. On the surface all is harmony and cooperation. Beneath the surface there is a considerable charge of resentment. Privacy thus appears as an escape from the demands and burdens of social interaction. But a conception of public as opposed to private scarcely appears. There is no sign of anything we can recognize as "the public," certainly not "the public interest" at the level of overt verbalization, and not even, so far as I can tell, at the level of action. There are no forms of society-wide cooperation and no system of organized authority.

In this section, through a series of soundings into anthropological data, I shall try to describe and explain how a distinction between private and public aspects of human behavior can develop in nonliterate societies. Through the actions of nonliterate peoples and their feelings, insofar as I have been able to find evidence about them, I hope to ascertain their own explicit and implicit conceptions of what was private and what was public, if they made the distinction at all. There is no reason to assume in advance that all of them did make such a distinction. Especially in simple societies of hunters and gatherers, generally living in small bands, every adult knew all the other adults. Opportunities and even the desire to withdraw from the human group that was the source of sustenance and security cannot be presupposed. Modern Western conceptions of the distinction between private and public spheres of human behavior are the outcome of long and often violent historical struggles and debates, conflicts that continue today and are likely to continue as far into the future as we can see. To impose our own categories on the very wide range of behavior and ideas displayed by "primitive" societies would obviously be misleading.

At one end of the range we find a society even simpler than the Eskimos in terms of technology, culture, and social organization, the migratory Siriono Indians of eastern Bolivia. We can somewhat arbitrarily set the other end of the range to include the League of the Iroquois. The League was clearly an institutional creation for the furtherance of a public interest. But we will exclude the Aztecs and the

Incas, theocratic empires closer to ancient Egypt and Sumeria than to any society generally regarded as primitive.

We shall examine first the way certain societies with very primitive technologies produce and distribute food, the most important social product and, in a society of hunters and gatherers with hardly any domesticated crops, just about the only social product. Differences in the social arrangements for getting and sharing food show a clear connection with conceptions of public and private. Individualist patterns of hunting accompany reluctance to share the product of the chase and a very feeble conception of the public sphere, if any at all. Cooperative arrangements, on the other hand, can lead to at least an incipient distinction between public and private or individualist interests. Quarreling and wrangling are common enough in societies, whether based on self-help or on a more developed system of cooperation. But in the societies with individualist patterns of hunting the conflicts are among a series of individual or household interests all of which are equally valid or nearly so. Where cooperation is more prominent we find a sense of the importance of maintaining cooperation as a socially important goal in its own right and a tendency to censure those who allow self-interest to threaten collective existence. Such an attitude is one major source of a distinction between public and private affairs.

What we do not find in the societies with a primitive technical base is the creation of a substantial surplus over the amounts regularly consumed. Without such a surplus there is of course no dominant segment of the society such as a priesthood or warrior caste to appropriate the surplus. There are also of course no disputes over how the surplus should be distributed. Therefore this aspect of public concern does not yet exist. In slightly more advanced nonliterate societies, priests, shamans, sorcerers, and chiefs do occur. But their powers, perquisites, and capacity to embody the public interest remain limited in comparison with literate societies.

In their stress on self-help and lack of concern for others the Siriono Indians, as described in Allan R. Holmberg's classic monograph, present us with an extreme case. They are a hunting and gathering people without domesticated crops, numbering perhaps 2000 in all at the time of his field work in South America in the early 1940s.[25] With no means for making fire, they carry firebrands from camp to camp. They make only rude pots, possess bow and arrow as their only weapon, live in hastily constructed leaky houses, and use almost no clothing.[25a] Hunting is far and away their most important activity. Each morning the naked males leave the camp to hunt, some alone, some in pairs, a few in groups of six or seven to search for peccaries or a band of spider monkeys.

There is some limited cooperation among hunters as one may signal to another by whistling to signal the existence of a bird out of range of his own bow but within the range of another. Or two hunters may work a tall tree together; as one climbs partway up a tree, the man on the ground shoots his arrow up into the tree. The hunter in the tree grabs the arrow in flight, inserts it into his own bow, and shoots the animal. This practice is, however, rare and can be used only against animals unlikely to move. Hunting for peccaries requires the most cooperation, as they are approached against the wind and then encircled in order to bag as many as possible. Though the tapir is the greatest prize of the chase due to its large size and abundance of meat, bagging one is a rare event. Those that are killed are usually shot while asleep by a lone but lucky hunter.[26] Thus the degree and frequency of cooperation in the hunt is quite limited. Mainly it is an affair of one or two men, occasionally a half-dozen. There are no reported occasions in which all adults in the band† team up together for a hunt, a common practice among the Mbuti Pygmies of the Ituri forest whose way of life contrasts sharply with that of the Siriono.

Though the Siriono's food supply is always insecure, they do not actually starve because they collect edible products growing in the forest. All participate in collecting such foods. With a digging stick and fire for clearing the forest, they also practice a limited amount of desultory cultivation of maize, manioc, and other products. Since with these primitive techniques the amount of labor relative to yield is enormous, and also because game may become scarce and force a move before the rewards of agriculture can be reaped, they strongly prefer collecting to cultivating.[27] In collecting as in hunting there appears to be little division of labor and hence little cooperation. More people collecting means more food collected simply by the addition of extra hands for picking, not through the performance of separate yet related tasks yielding a larger social product.

As might be expected from a system of supply that alternates in an unpredictable fashion between occasional gluttony—meat cannot in any case be preserved beyond three days[28]—and long periods of hunger, the Siriono system of distribution is erratic and liable to intermittent breakdown. In turn the undependability of the system contributes to an atmosphere of mutual suspicion, especially between the sexes, that renders cooperation and a sense of mutual social obligations very difficult to achieve at even the most elementary level of the household.

At one time the Siriono seem to have had rules requiring the distribution of food within the band. There is in theory a taboo on

---

†Holmberg, *Nomads*, 102, reports that few tasks require the cooperation of all members of a band. In several readings of his text I failed to notice *any* such tasks.

eating the flesh of an animal one has killed oneself. Breaking the taboo supposedly entails the consequence that the animal so eaten will not return to be hunted by this hunter again. But few hunters now pay any attention to the taboo. When they do, it is only in connection with big animals such as the tapir that they seldom bring down anyway.[29]

There is marked reluctance to share food. This is hardly surprising in the light of its erratic supply and the apparent decay of rules for sharing. Large amounts of food are consumed at night in order to avoid the crowd of nonfamily members that is liable to gather and beg for morsels in daylight hours. Even though the Siriono pay little attention to such importunate claims, they find them a nuisance. The distribution of food rarely goes beyond the extended family and then only in times of abundance.[30] Frequently sharing does not go beyond the nuclear family, the basic unit of cooperation in work.[31]

In this society most quarrels break out over the distribution of food or over sexual gratification. Complaints and quarrels about the distribution of food and especially the allotment of meat are common. Within the extended family there is usually someone who feels he is not getting his share. Men accuse women of hoarding meat, eating it when the men are not around, and consuming more than their share. "Women even push meat up their vaginas to hide it," according to one of Holmberg's informants.[32]

The behavior of a returning hunter clearly reflects this suspicious attitude. The bigger the catch, reports Holmberg, the more sullen the hunter. Sometimes the man does not even carry the game into the house. Instead he leaves it behind not far from the house. Then he enters empty-handed, aggressive, and angry. That is the signal for his wife to bring a pipeful of tobacco which he smokes without uttering a word. It is her job to go out and retrieve the game, bring it home, and cook it. The hunter maintains his unapproachable air until after the game has been eaten.[33]

Except in the realm of food, theft is unknown among the Siriono. It is hard to discern any form of property they could steal from each other. Even the theft of food is rare because people rapidly consume their own supplies. Premeditated murder is unknown and accidental homicide unpunished. Flexible standards of sexual morality reduce the possibility of socially recognized offenses in this area of human behavior, though indiscreet and excessive adultery will lead an irate husband to cast out his wife.[34]

Without disputes to settle there is hardly any function for society to perform and acquire a sphere of "public" action against "private" interests. In the case of the Siriono, society is the hunting band. The band that Holmberg describes in some detail contains five extended families, composed in turn of seventeen nuclear families. Every individual in the band is supposedly related to every other one, though

Holmberg was never able to determine the actual relationship. Each band has a single dwelling, within which cluster the extended families. The chief, who has little or no formal authority but is one of the best hunters and exercises a very limited degree of personal leadership, takes the center of the house. The band serves to provide sexual and marital partners. Other economic or ceremonial functions it seems to have either lost or never possessed in the first place.†

Though Holmberg does not say so explicitly, living in bands may also make possible a wider choice of hunting partners and thereby contribute to survival. He reports no signs of pleasure at the sociability offered by common residence in the band. Rather the opposite is the case, with frequent complaints each morning about sleep being disturbed by noise from farting and copulating neighbors. These, however, may be dismissed as some of the universal gripes that with the help of laughter make living together possible for human beings.[35]

The band may also offer some protection against dangerous nocturnal animals. Even that protection is slight. As an instance of the Siriono's extreme lack of concern for one another, Holmberg reports what happened to an unmarried cripple who lost his way back to the camp a few hundred yards off, on a night black as ink. The cripple began to call for help—for someone to bring him fire or guide him back by calls. No one paid any attention. After about half an hour his cries ceased. His sister remarked that a jaguar had probably gotten him. When the cripple did make it back to the camp next morning, he told Holmberg that he had spent the night sitting on the branch of a tree to avoid being eaten by jaguars. The sister's only reaction to his safe return was to complain bitterly about the small part of the catch she received from her brother.[36]

Beyond a few indications of shared conceptions of proper Siriono behavior,[37] the band hardly provides a public for the individual Siriono. All in all, this society appears to be one with scarcely any distinction between public and private spheres. The Siriono manage their lives with a minimum of cooperation and shared interests. For males at any rate there is hardly any possibility of entrapment in a social group from

†Holmberg, *Nomads,* 130–131; see also 220–221 for ceremonial blood-letting, certifying adulthood, which may have been an all-band affair. Earlier in the account (47–48), Holmberg briefly mentions seasonal variations: the band is a cohesive group during the sedentary rainy season, a loose social unit in the nomadic dry season. Among other hunting and gathering peoples (such as the Hare Indians, some Eskimos, the Pygmies of the Ituri forest) these accordianlike expansions and contractions of the band produce fundamental yet recurring changes in the relationship between the individual and the social order with important consequences for ideas, feelings, and behavior about the distinction between public and private. To oversimplify somewhat, society with all its demands is there for part of the year and absent during other parts, leaving a household on its own. Both situations evidently impose severe strains. Something similar may have existed among the Siriono but with less marked a contrast and so escaped more than passing notice by even so acute an observer as Holmberg.

which they cannot escape on very short notice. The most serious social obligation is to hunt. But an empty stomach provides as much of a prod to go hunting as does pressure from relatives, while memories of fruitless hard labor on recent unsuccessful hunts may incline him to stay in his hammock a while longer.[38] Thus the obligation to hunt is as much physiological as social. There is no serious possibility of resisting the obligation on the grounds of some private right or legitimate private interest. By way of summing up, I would suggest that Siriono society lacks all but the most minimal distinction between what is private and public—and suffers the disadvantages of both. There is neither protection against intrusion nor the advantages that come from cooperation and the recognition of a collective interest. For them, life is indeed "nasty, brutish, and short."†

In comparison with the Siriono the existence of the Mbuti Pygmies may at first glance seem idyllic. The Mbuti Pygmies inhabit the Ituri rain forest south of the Sahara. It is a forest dense with vegetation and game, with an almost daily rainfall producing an average of seventy to eighty inches a year. The temperature varies little from 80° F. For the Mbuti, with their hunting and gathering economy, the forest provides a rather benign environment, though to other native cultivating tribes it is a threatening and mysterious one. Throughout the year hunting is generally adequate. Hunger occurs sometimes but starvation not at all. Sickness though not uncommon is rarely serious.[39]

Possibly the African rain forest provides the Mbuti with a somewhat less demanding environment than the South American rain forest does for the Siriono. But it is reasonably plain that the Siriono and the Mbuti present us with two very different human responses to similar environments and with a similar level of technology. Both peoples live in nomadic bands, moving about their forest. There the main resemblance ends. The structure and meaning of the band is very different in the two societies.‡

Whereas the Siriono's method of hunting based on the bow and

---

†Cf. Holmberg, *Nomads*, 203, 222–224 on the undisciplined character of these people, the poverty of their culture, their harsh, drab life almost wholly taken up with the pursuit of basic necessities. Sex after a full stomach appears to be their only unalloyed pleasure.
‡The information about the Mbuti presented here comes almost entirely from Turnbull, whose fieldwork was limited to the Epulu net-hunters. I have also looked through Paul Schebesta, *Die Bambuti-Pygmäen vom Ituri*. Schebesta's account differs in important respects from Turnbull's, mainly in stressing kinship as the basis of band organization. The difference may be due to the fact that Schebesta did not study the Epulu, which he rather summarily dismissed on the basis of very brief contact as an overacculturated group. (See his "Colin M. Turnbull und die Erforschung der Bambuti-Pygmäen," *Anthropos*, 214.) From Turnbull's account it is plain that the Epulu were *not* overacculturated. I have therefore accepted his account as essentially accurate, just as Shebesta is probably accurate in reporting the groups he studied at length. For further discussions between Turnbull and Schebesta see the references given in Turnbull, *Wayward Servants*, 7, n. 1.

arrow was highly individualistic, that of the Epulu Mbuti who hunted with nets, required the cooperation of all adult members of the band.† In the Mbuti hunt each net, owned by a nuclear family, is set up as part of a long semicircle. The women act as beaters, forming a long semicircle opposite the nets and driving the game toward the nets. Each net is therefore utterly dependent on all the others, as is each beater.[40] As the game is driven into the nets, the hunters spear the animals. Here too the men have to work together speedily and carefully to dispatch the struggling animals without accidentally hurting one another.[41] Thus the net hunt imposes a cooperative life-pattern on the Mbuti.[42] It is an unforgivable crime to place one's net in front of the others during a hunt; to the Mbuti this is true theft.[43] Any form of magic that might give the individual hunter an advantage, a common practice in many hunting cultures, the Mbuti reject as an antisocial practice. Any display of prowess, even in hunting, arouses distrust or ridicule.[44]

Despite the cooperative pattern of hunting, the distribution of the social product does not take place without friction. Though the division of spoils stresses band rather than family values, both men and women, and especially women, are prone to cheat by concealing meat under the leaves of their roofs or in empty pots. There are numerous petty squabbles over the division of food. On the other hand, the participants settle these squabbles among themselves and do not allow them to come before the whole band for discussion. They are far less serious than "hunting crimes," such as placing one's net ahead of the others.[45] If anything, such disputes may provide both a pretext and safe outlet for all sorts of petty personal hostilities arising from other causes. By making the dispute seem to relate to the hunt the Mbuti keep it within bounds, since they feel that no dispute can be allowed to threaten the cooperation of the hunt upon which their subsistence depends.[46]

As we have noticed from Briggs's account of Eskimo life, an ethic of sharing and cooperation can impose very high and at times unbearable social costs. There are grounds for suspecting that the Mbuti ethic might also impose quite unbearable costs were it not for certain structural features of band life that permit or rather even require "private" choices enabling the individual, if not to escape these pressures, at least to change residence so that the social shoe will then pinch in another spot.

Mbuti bands continually undergo a process of fission and fusion. At its maximum a band contains some thirty nuclear families. It is continually dividing into small segments, whose minimum size is three

†Some Mbuti are also archers, who generally work in groups of three and once a year engage in a beat hunt, the *begbe,* requiring the cooperation of all band members, like net-hunting. See Turnbull, *Wayward Servants,* 28, 107, 153–155, 161–164, 270–271. Thus although the technological factor has an important influence on the choice between individualist and cooperative hunting techniques, it is not by itself decisive.

families, each with its own hunting territory, and then reforming again into a large band. In the course of this accordionlike transformation a few segments will drop out to join a different band while new segments that have dropped out from other bands will replace them.[47]

At its maximum size the band is a function of the available resources in game and the "economy of size" in net-hunting. As soon as a band establishes itself at maximum size, cleavages along lines of faction, friendship, and hostility show up in the residential pattern of whose hut is next to whom and the direction the doors face. Since a change of campsite occurs about once a month, there are frequent opportunities to alter the residential pattern.[48]

The advantages of covering an area in order to find game pushes the band toward division into segments. This fragmentation is most apparent during the honey season when the band scatters in search of bees' nests. The opportunity to live apart also dissipates much of the animosity and moral disapproval that collects while band members are in a single camp. After the honey season is over, the band reforms and the process begins once more.[49] Thus Mbuti society provides for periodic withdrawal from the burdens of collective living—or, in a word, privacy. But it remains a collective version of privacy, not an individualist one. Due to their cooperative hunting practices the Mbuti, in contrast to the Siriono, have created a clear if rudimentary distinction between public and private concerns. The existence of a public sphere, in this case the net-hunting economy, is a necessary precondition for the appearance of privacy. Without the public, nothing can be private.

The seeds of public institutions appear vividly from a case of ostracism. The victim was a man called Asuku who had earned the dislike of his campmates by his presumptuous behavior in attempting to step into the shoes of his absent uncle, a respected hunter. On one occasion he accused his campmates of being too lazy to hunt. When they shouted him down, he claimed to be the son of his uncle and that the camp was therefore his camp. This move failed. On another occasion he claimed the net and central position in the hunt of his uncle instead of his current position on the fringe. That claim aroused vehement objections from the man whose net would then be next to Asuku's. The objection temporarily checked Asuku.

That evening Moké, a highly respected senior hunter, gathered the senior hunters around him, raised his arm, pointed to Asuku across the camp, and speaking quietly as if only to the other hunters, uttered a powerful indictment of Asuku. After the evening meal Moké stood in the middle of the camp, pointed to the hearth of each great hunter and male elder in turn, named them, and said "This is my man, this is my hearth, for it is his hearth, but it is not Asuku's."

Despite this near excommunication, Asuku remained a band member, partly because the band members were reluctant to do more than ignore him out of respect for his uncle. After some three months, however, Asuku began to frequent the non-Pygmy cultivators' village for long periods.

> When he refused a summons to return to the hunting camp old Moké once again stood in midcamp, an honored position from which any Mbuti, young or old, is free to claim the attention of everyone. He said that since now Asuku had become a villager, he was no longer a Mbuti, no longer "ours"; he belonged far away, very far away indeed. Pointing to the central fire in the section of the camp that included Njobo's [Asuku's uncle-father's] wife and three great hunters, and divers others both related and unrelated, he said, "This is a matter of the forest. This is our hearth. It is not Asuku's hearth. He belongs in the village or completely and absolutely far away." Murmurs of assent came from everyone. Moké looked to each hearth asking, "Is my spirit right?" Agreement was unanimous if subdued. Moké simply announced, "It is finished." The next day a messenger departed to report the event to Asuku. Asuku never returned to the Epulu band.[50]

This account is particularly instructive because it shows how public institutions can arise spontaneously out of a crisis that threatens the harmony of the group. That can happen only where harmony is itself important for other reasons, as was true of the Mbuti but not the Siriono. The role of the hearth as the center of camp existence, and the expression of opinion in terms of one's individual spirit while the issue is formulated as a "matter of the forest," are also revealing.

The forest served as a generalized expression—symbol would be too abstract a term—of Mbuti existence. As a projection the forest constituted an idealized public, the source of social morality and good hunting. Many societies make the source of morality into a source of pain and suffering as well. Not so the Mbuti, for reasons that are obscure, but may have something to do with the fact that their daily lives, if far from idyllic,† were seldom tragic or afflicted with catastrophe.

In Mbuti society there are no chiefs or headmen, no councils of elders, not even ritual specialists such as diviners or prophets. Instead the forest is the only recognized authority, one that on occasion expresses its judgments with ummistakable clarity. Severe storms, falling trees, poor hunting, and ill health are signs of displeasure. Good weather, good health, and good hunting are indications that all is well. But often the forest remains silent. Then the Mbuti have to sound out its opinion through discussion. Though there is diversity of opinion and great freedom of expression—for the Mbuti are individualists for all

---

†Note Turnbull, *Wayward Servants,* 212, where they appear as routinely crabby and rather pleased with their own ill nature.

their cooperation—prolonged disagreement they regard as "noise" and as such offensive to the forest. Unanimity, on the other hand, is the opposite of noise, that is "quiet"—a sign of the forest's pleasure and approval of a band's decision. The justification for any proposed course of action is that it would please the forest. Anyone not associating himself with a band's decision is therefore likely to be considered "bad" and "displeasing to the forest."[51]

Unlike the Homeric view of the gods, the forest is for the Mbuti both benevolent and impersonal in the sense that it does not owe special allegiance or favors to one Mbuti more than to another.[52] Laziness, aggressiveness, disputatiousness, traits that interfere with the cooperation necessary for the hunt, are all displeasing to the forest.[53] Finally, the *molimo,* a festive ritual of crisis, such as the death of a member of the band, reaffirms the social order and virtues of the forest. Significantly, all adult males are expected to take part. Failure to take part, the Mbuti say, is punishable by death.[54]

The existence of the death penalty, as an idea if not as a verified practice, demonstrates that severe conflict between public obligation and private inclination was at least quite conceivable in this very simple society. In ordinary daily life this conflict, as we have already had occasion to notice, surfaced most frequently in connection with sharing game brought in by the hunters. Since women were in charge of the household as the social unit for consumption, they were especially prominent in attempts to cheat and cut corners when there was a distribution of meat.[55]

It is also worth noticing that mealtimes were the only occasions in the course of the day when there was a definite emphasis on the nuclear family.[56] Otherwise, age and sex divisions with their respective activities constituted the natural groupings within the band. These were complementary and cooperative units within the larger structure of the band. Too great an emphasis on kinship, Turnbull repeatedly argues, would have threatened the cohesion of the band on which all depended for survival.[57]

In theory at least, the most insignificant and routine activities of the nuclear family were matters that could concern the band as a whole. A man seeking to borrow his brother's pipe could trigger off petty jealousies that would divide the brothers if not the whole camp.[58] The elders, or males past the age of strenuous hunting, are also in theory able to intervene in the most private and domestic affairs of any individual. An older male will concern himself with questions about bringing up children, their puberty, and marriage. In times of crisis he is expected to provide a resolution.[59] All this begins to sound if not like totalitarianism, at least like the oppressive *volonté générale* of the small community. But the absence of organized institutions through which the band could enforce its will allows a great deal of scope for individual choice and the free play of strong personalities, forms of freedom upon which the Mbuti place a high value.[60] If the permission of the band is required for marriage, there is also great concern for the feelings of the pair. If private life is everybody's concern and leaf-covered dwellings make it hard to conceal private matters, residence patterns enable individuals to choose and reject their neighbors as well as to maintain some barriers of privacy among the sections of the band.[61]

Marital disputes that are overheard but not deliberately forced on the band's attention are for the most part ignored. If the arguments keep people awake, there may be complaints and ridicule. A real fight between husband and wife inside a hut is an event for youths and younger married couples to follow with zest. They may watch the hut shake, prepared to catch the partner that comes flying out first and so prevent further damage.[62]

Thus Mbuti culture did not generate any conception of private rights as necessary institutional safeguards against undue or unjust public demands. In Mbuti society, without chiefs, priests, castes, or classes, there was no possibility for class egoism to wrap itself in the robes of public interest and the general welfare.

As the last case to be discussed in some detail, we may now turn to a society that has developed the private sphere to a pathological degree but displays no more than hints of a public realm. The Jívaro Indians of the Ecuadorian Amazon rain forest have long enjoyed some notoriety as the original headshrinkers. Instead of bands they live in dispersed, fortified, polygynous households. Residence in scattered households is due to their dependence on cultivated plants for nearly two-thirds of their diet. The rest comes from hunting, the principal male activity. Since cultivation is by the primitive slash-and-burn technique, the household does have to move every few years.

Beyond hunting the activities that set the tone for Jívaro culture are headhunting expeditions against neighboring tribes and raids for revenge and assassination against other Jívaro. This is a society organized around private revenge. For the Jívaro males the thrill of the hunt for human victims is what makes life worth living. Women are domestic servants, brood mares—and the object of competition and conflict among males. As a whole, Jívaro society and culture recall the Western European world of Gregory of Tours. Both were suffused with unpredictable violence and lacked effective means, or even much desire, to put down the violence. Still the Jívaro world does seem simpler and more straightforward in its cruelties, perhaps because it lacked the Christian cant of barbarian Western Europe.

Four clusters of related but distinguishable causes provide a serviceable explanation of the Jívaro emphasis on privacy and self-help and the correspondingly stunted growth of the public realm.

The pattern of dispersed households makes sense as a way of maximizing the available food resources within a given territory. The Mbuti system of shifting campsites for whole bands would not be possible with slash-and-burn agriculture that requires more than one growing season in one spot. The series of independent households also requires individualist methods of hunting. This the Jívaro had in the blowgun, later superseded by rifles obtained through long-distance trade. The lone stalker, usually alone but sometimes with one male companion, was the characteristic figure on the hunt.[63]

In a peccary hunt, on the other hand, all the households in a given area would cooperate, some as beaters, others as hunters, turning the event into a festive occasion.† But peccary hunts were quite clearly unusual undertakings and not part of the ordinary hunting routine. Similarly, in agriculture at the beginning of the slash-and-burn cycle there may be an occasional community-wide effort (that is, by several households in the same area) to make a large clearing for one household. But the general rule is for one man to make his own small clearings at different times.[64]

In the absence of cooperative networks tying the scattered households together into an organized community with a sense of public interests, it is easy to see that they might come into sustained conflict with each other and develop a pattern of feuding should there be any source of antagonism or competition. That is exactly what has happened.

Competition for women is the major source of disputes, despite a two-to-one sex ratio in favor of women. Sexual offenses, except for wife stealing, it should be pointed out, do not ordinarily lead to homicide. Women are a valuable commodity in this society because the more wives a man has the more land he can farm and the more beer and general hospitality he can offer neighbors, with an increased probability of gaining their support in a feud. Feuds begin as an attempt to avenge a wrong. Hostilities continue for long periods partly because neither party feels that the opponent has been sufficiently punished.[65]

Other factors intensify and prolong feuds. The Jívaro *do* have relatively clear-cut and consensually approved rules concerning offenses and sanctions regarding human life, sexual relationships, the inheritance of women, and other less prominent sources of dispute. In this very limited sense there is a notion of public morality. But their society lacks any corporate unit, beyond the household, capable of enforcing these rules. There is not even a corporate kin group to which

†For an eyewitness account of 1930–31 see M. W. Stirling, *Historical and Ethnographical Material on the Jívaro Indians,* 105–106. An indication of at least temporary solidarity comes from the fact that the observers were unable to purchase any meat since as a community venture no one was entitled to receive payment for it. But they received a share for their participation.

an injured individual can appeal. Instead, their system of bilateral descent provides only the most ambiguous clues as to what person belongs where. Only by adroit manipulation of the available categories can a visitor avoid having his beer poisoned or being ambushed on leaving the house.[66] Hence, in the absence of formal political or kin organization, the Jívaro resort to sanctions against the violators of social norms through informal partisan action. The party with a grievance finds supporters and takes upon himself the responsibility for punishment.[67]

Jívaro religious beliefs provide both a form of assurance against anxiety about being murdered and support for the system of feuds leading to repeated murders. The possessor of one kind of soul, the *arutam,* cannot, according to the Jívaro, be killed by any form of physical violence, poison, or sorcery, though he is not immune to death from contagious diseases.[68] This soul is acquired through ritual, making use of hallucinogenic drugs. By repeated killings one can acquire new *arutam* souls. This "trade-in" mechanism is important for two reasons. With two such souls one is immune to both disease and murder. In the second place, *arutam* souls have a tendency to wander off after a few years. Hence it is desirable to obtain a new one before the old one wanders off.[69] Another kind of soul, the *muisak* or avenging soul, is complementary to the *arutam* soul in that as the soul of a murdered man it seeks vengeance for the murder.[70] The well-known practice of headshrinking is connected with this belief. The members of a headhunting expedition shrink the heads in order to force the *muisak,* hovering alongside the retreating expedition, back into the head trophy or trophies and thus thwart the mission of vengeance.[71] Such expeditions occur only against people who speak differently, that is, non-Jívaros.†

In local feuds and assassinations the practice prevails of seeking out a famous strong man with one or more *arutam* souls to take charge of the expedition. There is a regular procedure for making such overtures to an enemy for this purpose. It is also common to try to shoot him in the back while on the trail.[72] Jívaro feuds and assassinations may well constitute the highest elaboration possible of behavioral patterns for coping with disputes in the absence of a superior public authority.

There are some clues to suggest that the state of affairs among the Jívaro at the time Michael J. Harner studied them may have represented pathological degeneration in a social system with less internal violence, greater cohesion, but also very likely even greater violence

---

†Harner, *Jívaro,* 183. As an indication of the level of suspicion prevailing in this society it is worth noticing that on expeditions to take heads it is the custom for pairs of close relatives to "cover" one another from assassination by another member of the expedition. See Harner, *Jívaro,* 185.

against other non-Jívaro tribes. According to Harner, whose field work occurred in 1956 and 1957,[73] over the preceding half-century there had been a shift away from large-scale headhunting wars with other tribes in which men, women, and children were all killed, to an increased emphasis on individual assassination within the tribe, directed primarily at adult males.[74]

M. W. Stirling has combed the writings of the Spanish explorers to provide further bits of evidence. One from the year 1549 carries the intriguing mention of *buhios,* identified in a footnote as community houses.[75] No such community structure occurs in Harner's study. Its possible existence in the sixteenth century suggests the existence of collective efforts and perhaps public institutions that may have died out subsequently. An account of 1571 reports the absence of any head chief but mentions that each "town" had a chief and captains. They were a "warlike people fond of fighting and killing and cutting off heads and plundering"[76]—enough to suggest that the principal cultural traits are four centuries old. Finally, a more detailed account from 1682 reports the practice of building separate houses in the wilderness and relates it to the high level of mutual suspicion and frequent treachery.[77] Fragmentary though it is, such evidence is enough to establish that the main features of Jívaro culture antedate the coming of the white man. If recent changes have been pathological, they are also within the framework of a long-established cultural pattern.

The creation of a public sphere comes about through the creation of a wider sphere of social networks. A private matter is one where another person's actions don't matter. The other person's behavior may be good or bad. But it is no concern of ours. A public affair, by contrast, is one where the other person's behavior matters. It is difficult to imagine an ordinary Siriono or Jívaro caring very much what happens to other Sirionos or Jívaros. They could be killed by a member of their own tribe or by a wild animal without the incident causing much concern. This is not the case among the Mbuti. What happens to another person makes a difference to the extent that it affects cooperation in work or the exchange of values—both material values and nonmaterial ones such as affection. Thus public concern implies the capacity to put oneself in another person's position, to identify with other persons. The public is a generalized self in the form of the other. Its existence presupposes shared moral standards and a sense of moral community.

The creation of wider social networks can come about through the division of labor and the sharing of the social product, as we have seen from the example of Mbuti net-hunting. But that is not the only way and may not even be the most important. In nonliterate societies kinship often provides the framework that supports a wide variety of cooperative networks. Among Indians in North America the League of the Iroquois represented an ingenious and effective extension of kinship ties to create a federation of tribes that approaches the form of a modern state. There is no doubt that the Iroquois had a sense of the public sphere and the public interest very close to modern Western conceptions. It came into existence despite the lack of economic cooperation. Hunting and settled agriculture—the latter the main source of subsistence—were centrifugal rather than centripetal forces. The purpose of the League was to control warfare in the sense of (1) suppressing internal conflicts among members of the League, (2) avoiding the dissipation of collective military energies by preventing members from engaging in warfare on their own, and (3) by thus centralizing foreign policy to concentrate the League's collective force on appropriate and profitable targets.†

Despite the achievements of the League of the Iroquois, there appear to be limits to the possibility of creating public organizations through allegiances based on kinship. The League was an oligarchical federation with very limited executive authority or functions. Based mainly on their African studies, Meyer Fortes and E. E. Evans-Pritchard have suggested some of these limitations and possibilities. They distinguish social links established through the family and a system of bilateral descent. Such links are, they hold, relatively transient. A second form is the segmentary system of permanent unilateral descent groups, which they call lineages. Only the second form can, they claim, establish corporate units with political functions.‡

As the Mbuti conception of the forest shows, primitive religions often create a supernatural social authority that in effect constitutes a public authority. Seldom, however, is the authority so benign as it appears to be in the case of the Mbuti. Nor do all nonliterate societies do this. Siriono religious beliefs do not go much beyond a belief in ugly, black, and hairy monsters that lurk outside the house at night to carry their victims off into the forest and strangle them.[78] The social utility of

---

†The sachems (or tribal chiefs) of the League assembled each autumn to legislate for the common welfare, according to Lewis Henry Morgan, *League of the Iroquois,* 66. For an analysis of the League's structure and workings see chaps. III, IV, V, still a good exposition of essentials according to the Introduction (p. xii) by a modern authority, William N. Fenton. Buell Quain, "The Iroquois," in Margaret Mead, editor, *Cooperation and Competition Among Primitive Peoples,* 240–281, provides a more recent account that corrects Morgan on significant points such as the role of agriculture in the hunters' state, and stresses issues under consideration here.

‡Meyer Fortes and E. E. Evans-Pritchard, editors, *African Political Systems,* 6. A lineage can be the group to whom a person turns for support in cases of injury, leading to a feud or vendetta, though as the Jívaro case demonstrates, lineages need not be the basis for such alignments. The feud is both source of and obstacle to the formation of wider public allegiances. The upper limit to kinship as a basis for public authority and public

such beliefs seems minimal, unless one is prepared to believe in the need to inhibit some innate propensity to wander about in a dangerous forest at night.

Perhaps the first major step toward the creation of external social authority through religion comes with the belief that antisocial behavior which is a threat to the group—such as murder—is a source of threatening pollution. As Mary Douglas has written about pollution: "The whole universe is harnessed to men's attempts to force one another into good citizenship. Thus we find that certain moral values are upheld and certain social rules defined by beliefs in dangerous contagion. . . ."[79] Among the Cheyenne Indians in North America, "murder within the tribe is the most horrendous of crimes and sins. Not only does the murderer become internally polluted and begin to rot inside, but flecks of blood soil the feathers of the Arrows [the supernaturals' great gift to the Cheyennes and their central insurance for survival]. Bad luck dogs the tribe, and all game shuns its territory until atonement is made in the Renewal. . . ." The Renewal of the Sacred Arrows is a great ritual attended by the entire tribe, a ceremony that affirms the unity of the tribe and its moral order.[80] Beliefs about pollution are likely to occur where more practical sanctions against antisocial behavior are weak and the risk of such behavior considerable. Where the sense of moral outrage has effective primitive outlets of another kind, pollution is unlikely to occur.[81]

Religion provides human beings with an opportunity to cope with their problems in the realm of fantasy. Relatively free from the checks and limits of reality they can express both their hopes and their fears in more intense form than when confronting real dangers. The conception of "the public" may well have begun as a religious conception of the universe. The religion of the North American Hopi Indians shows clearly how this could have occurred. Crowded into their pueblos for security against their enemies, the Hopi Indians still live in a theocratically tinged garrison community. The restraints necessary for living in such a society, one with a minimum of privacy, generate a high level of hostility. There is a great deal of malicious gossip in this overtly calm and peaceful society.[82] Relatively powerless themselves, they conceive of the universe as an ordered system functioning under a definite set of rules known to them alone. By regulating their behavior, emotions, and thoughts in accord with these rules, the Hopi believe they can exercise a measure of control over their environment.[83]

The universe, with humanity as an integral element, thus appears

---

allegiance derives, I suggest, from the fact that kinship has to be an ascribed status and cannot be an achieved one. In other words, the obligations of kinship derive from inherited position in a system of descent. They cannot derive from the merits, attainments, and performance of an individual, nor is it easy to withdraw from the obligation in the case of demerits and failures.

as "public" and external while at the same time something to which humans belong and can control. If the efforts at control, mainly magical, fail to work, if rain does not come and the crops do not yield a rich harvest, the Hopi conclude that one or more individuals have failed to follow the Hopi Way. Since such behavior brings misfortune on the whole community, gossip blames specific individuals and severely censures them. When failure assumes the proportions of disaster such as drought, pestilence, disease, and death, the Hopi believe that certain individuals have not only failed to work for the common good but have worked actively against it. Such individuals are taken to be witches with death-dealing powers.[84] In this manner the whole universe is brought into play as an expanded form of public morality whose violation accounts for human disasters.

Though nonliterate societies do not distinguish religious and secular spheres of human action in the same way as modern Western ones, the distinction exists. They have a fund of secular knowledge about cause-and-effect relationships in growing crops, hunting, and fishing, and use this knowledge to good effect. Many have secular political institutions such as chiefs and councils, alongside of, as well as intertwined with, the religious institutions of priests and shamans. Thus secular aspects of the polity also contribute to the notion of the polity. War and politics are often enough male affairs and part of the *res publica* as in ancient Rome, while the management of the household at least in its more routine aspects is "private" and left more in the hands of adult women. Hence the polity too, and especially its military aspects, can become a source of the conception of public as opposed to private affairs. We shall look at this aspect more closely in discussing feuds and warfare.

At this point we should notice that even in nonliterate societies the conception of a public realm has several sources and can take a number of forms. Each is a form of moral community with obligations resting upon the individual. The main forms are (1) the nuclear family, (2) the lineage, (3) the band, (4) the tribe, (5) the village or permanent settlement, (6) the occupational grouping such as the caste or guild of canoe builders, smiths, etc., (7) religious communities or subcommunities, and (8) the political unit, often a tribe writ large, such as many African kingdoms, and others as well.

Not all of these occur in all societies, as has already been apparent from the analysis of societies where the band was the most inclusive unit. Nor in larger and more complex societies do these various forms of the public nest neatly into one another like a set of Chinese boxes, though there may often be an ideology or official doctrine that proclaims the existence of such a patterned fit and overall social harmony. Instead of a series of publics in ascending order of inclusiveness we find that the forms of public compete with one another for the individual's allegiance and acceptance of their obligations. In the course of time some publics grow in importance while others dissolve.[85]

The largest and most inclusive publics—band, tribe, and kingdom—generally perform three functions, or more concretely, provide three types of service that contribute to collective survival. One is to furnish a permanent, self-replenishing reservoir of individuals for the division of labor, along with some measures for distributing individuals among their allotted tasks and seeing to it that people actually do their jobs. A second function is to provide protection against external threats to the group from other human groups or the forces of nature. A third function is to settle disputes according to prevailing conceptions of justice and injustice.

From the examples of the Siriono, Mbuti, and Jívaro it is plain that the public function of settling disputes may display no more than the most rudimentary development. Nor does leaving people to settle their own disputes as best they can necessarily and inevitably lead to a crude form of *Faustrecht* or right of the stronger to do as he likes. *Faustrecht,* such as in France in the time of Gregory of Tours or among the Jívaro Indians, represents extreme cases. Therefore it is worthwhile to pause for an examination of the conditions that make it possible for some societies to manage somehow without organized systems of public authority before looking more closely at how such authority can come into existence.

In the first place, the potential for conflict among individuals in the society may be low because there is nothing much worth fighting about. Among the Siriono, theft is unknown except in the case of food, apparently because there is hardly anything else worth stealing. Even the theft of food is rare because it is consumed before anyone can steal it.[86] A second factor is that the level of popular wants is necessarily low in such a simple society. For other disputes, such as those arising from sexual jealousy, a similar situation applies. In practice males generally have a considerable choice among available females. If quarrels arise anyway, there are informal ways of settling them. Shame and "public opinion"—whose existence implies consensus if not formal public institutions—are often powerful forces sufficient to keep most adults in line. Deviance is not the problem that it presents in more complex societies.[87]

In nonliterate societies, for this reason and others, most individuals meet their social obligations adequately, that is, according to the standards of their own culture which have guaranteed survival for a long enough time to enable anthropologists to find them. Many such societies, though by no means all (the Mbuti and the Kalahari bushmen are well-known exceptions) tolerate considerable loss through violence and hunger as well as the less severe forms of social friction—which are just about universal—and still keep on reproducing themselves and their specific way of life.

Since even talk can hurt, the power of public opinion—or better, gossip—does exist in even the most fluid societies and situations. The early stages of its crystallization into more regular and effective institutional forms are likely to escape notice a great deal of the time because in part they are apparently minor modifications in what is happening all the time. Public opinion or group opinion exists only in latent form prior to behavior that violates it. Public opinion does not come down ready-made from heaven, though it is often socially useful to believe that this is the case.

For effective existence public opinion requires a spokesman in the form of a catalyst. In turn the spokesman needs a body of latent sentiment derived from collective experience to back him up. (In some situations the spokesman may in fact be a woman.) If the sentiments are ambiguous or confused, a skilled spokesman may be able to crystallize them at once in favor of his own view. But there is also the possibility of confusion, quarrels, and inaction. To have an impact the spokesman must be someone whose words carry weight in the community. In the case of ostracism from Mbuti society it took an old and widely respected man, Moké, to make known the will of the forest. Even then, the decision did not come until after repeated tries and provocations.

Among the Karimojong of East Africa, spokesmen are likely to arise from among the men who own a large herd of cattle, since such a man can give cattle for many marriages and through marriages gain the support of a large body of kinsmen. The spokesman is not deliberately chosen. It is simply taken for granted that people will look to his lead in any collective action. "Essentially a 'spokesman' is a persuasive talker whose views have been proved wise by experience." If there is strong opposition, he may cease to be spokesman or the neighborhood may divide. Among these people there appears to be, " . . . explicit recognition that a programme cannot emerge from the collective consciousness of a meeting, even a small one; it must have taken form in someone's mind."[88]

Resort to the authority of specific individuals is unavoidable and provides a crystallization point for the growth of institutions through repetition and habit. But that is by no means all. Crisis both brings out latent structure and transforms that structure. Ostracism among the Mbuti was a rare event. No great perspicacity is necessary to see how the authority of a man like Moké could have grown through a series of crises as long as he remained able to resolve them in accord with popular sentiment. The mixture of habit, crises, and creative innovation by powerful individuals constitutes the source of effective public institutions. They are not inevitable.

The feud with its systematic retaliation for injury, especially the social injury of homicide, appears to be the earliest form of effective collective punishment. It is rare in hunting and gathering societies where the main unit is the small band. As pointed out, in such societies the potential for conflict is generally low enough to allow informal methods to take care of disputes.† Among nomadic herders and settled agricultural people the feud occurs frequently. Within a group small enough for all members to know each other well through daily routine contacts, the feud is unlikely to occur. For the feud to take root, the society must be large enough for two or more subdivisions to lead a separate and territorially distinct existence.‡

The feud is a form of self-help or, more precisely, self-protection. But it is group self-protection instead of individual. The killing of a member of one's own group creates the obligation of vengeance. In many feuds it is not necessary to take vengeance on the actual murderer. Any victim from the murderer's group will do. Though the weight of the obligation to seek vengeance may rest more heavily on certain individuals such as the brother or son of the victim, this obligation too is collective. It is this aspect of collective obligation that forms a decisive step in the direction of obligation to "the public," or even public interest. Vengeance is a social obligation. By its nature the feud unifies but also divides. It strengthens the cohesion of those who seek vengeance and those who fear it, at the same time that it sunders these two groups.

The range of reactions to the obligation of vengeance varies from the sense that it is an unpleasant and frightening chore[89] to the thrill of the hunt for a human victim. Thus vengeance can become as much of a right—defended tenaciously against those who would destroy it in the name of progress, peace, and humanity—as an obligation.[90] In fact, we have no way of knowing for sure whether it was mainly a right or

---

†The Siriono do not have the feud, and Colin Turnbull makes no mention of it in his account of the Mbuti Pygmies. See, however, Paul Schebesta for indications that both feud and war may have existed in the past in his *Die Bambuti-Pygmäen vom Ituri,* Institut Royal Colonial Belge *Mémoires,* II, chap. VIII, Section 6, "Krieg, Blutrache, Anthropophagie," 538. The index to Richard B. Lee and Irven DeVore, editors, *Man the Hunter* contains no entry for "feud" or "vendetta" but mentions (p. 158) earlier feuds among the Tiwi, Australian aborigines. Among the Kaingáng, a tribe in the forest highlands of Brazil, feuds had almost succeeded in destroying the tribe by the time Jules Henry described it in his *Jungle People.* Perhaps one should say that *currently surviving* hunting and gathering peoples lack the institution of the feud.

‡The Kaingáng live in extended families numbering from fifty to three hundred individuals. The families exist in a state of nearly perpetual feud with one another. The main

mainly an obligation in its earliest appearance on the historical stage. From recorded practice, on the other hand, one point stands out. The notions of personal honor and shame become strong enough to threaten any conception of the general welfare. Nevertheless it would be unwise to accept this bluster at face value. The would-be hero may be inwardly quaking and very glad of pressure to take things a bit easy because the last thing anybody in the victim's group wants is another murderous feud on its hands.†

Among the Kalingas, a rice-growing tribe in a mountainous sector of the Philippines, before the coming of the Americans the route to positions of leadership lay through multiple killings. First a youth would kill somebody in order to get his tattoo and the right to voice his opinions among men. "Then seeking dominance he would kill more people and thus inspire fear among the folk." Next he would intervene to settle disputes between kinship groups, something he was expected to do as a powerful individual. If he were successful and acted for "the good of all the people" and otherwise behaved in accord with Kalinga ethics, he would become accepted as an official leader.[91] It is hard to imagine a clearer example of the emergence of public spirit out of homicide. In this society a whole kinship group is responsible for the wrong committed by one of its members.[92] Private vengeance took the form of a headhunting expedition, usually made up of a band of a half-dozen males who would lie in wait in ambush in the enemy region until a member (male or female) of the enemy kinship group appeared. Then they would take the head, hack off a few parts of the body, and take them home.[93]

Kinship and private vengeance were, however, not the sole public institutions of the Kalingas. They had also begun to graft a territorial principle onto the kinship principle. A few of the leading killer officials became what was known as pact holders. A pact holder held a dual office of (1) spokesman for his own region in its relations with another region and simultaneously (2) the agent of the other region. In the latter capacity he was the man who righted and often avenged wrongs committed by his own people.[94] This was a tiny step in the direction of eliminating or controlling feuds and toward the creation of a larger public.

---

activities in this society, hunting, housebuilding, and raiding do require cooperation. Henry regards the culture as displaying a marked emphasis on cooperation. See *Jungle People,* 50, 172–174. But the cooperation appears to have been among rather small numbers of people and, so far as I can tell, did not have to cross family lines. Nor are there signs of the band or any permanent group transcending the extended family.

†Cf. Max Gluckman, *Custom and Conflict in Africa,* chap. I, "The Peace in the Feud," esp. 12–14, where he points out that some marriage rules can create divisions of purpose in the vengeance group since a man who has relatives by marriage in the opposing group will wish to remain on good terms with them.

The Kalinga pact holders lead us toward a brief consideration of international relations and war as they are found in nonliterate societies. Nearly three-quarters of a century ago William Graham Sumner coined the expressions "in-group" and "out-group" to distinguish human attitudes toward their fellows. Law and order of a sort prevailed within the in-group while members of the out-group were legitimate targets for hostility—to the extent that they were considered human at all. The distinction now strikes me as a misleading oversimplification. Instead there is often a series of gradations beginning with the (formal) peace group of the nuclear family or the household and extended family and spreading outward in concentric circles through members of different groups to include all sets of human beings known to a particular society. Different forms of and occasions for hostility receive different degrees of legitimacy as one passes through each concentric circle. The feud passes imperceptibly and gradually into open warfare while even warfare contains built-in checks and limitations.

All of these gradations appear among the highlanders of eastern central New Guinea. They live in villages or hamlets, occupied by one or more patrilineages and their adherents. These villages are in turn members of districts, the largest political units. The district is endogamous, the village exogamous. These districts wage war with one another continually. Though retaliation is an element in this systematic conflict, the pattern of warfare is not that found in feuds, where retaliation swings back and forth between the same enemies for long periods of time, often for generations. Instead the New Guinea pattern resembles the rapidly shifting configurations of alliances found in the international politics of states claiming to be civilized.

As endogamous units in perpetual conflict these New Guinea districts recall Sumner's in-group–out-group distinction. But Sumner's term fails to bring out the fact that despite warfare—indeed perhaps even *through* warfare—the districts create and sustain a collective identity. "All districts other than one's own are potential enemies as well as friends; it is only strangers with whom one does not fight." Hostility is a necessary component in a relationship that is actively sought. Sometimes victorious districts send pleas to neighbors they have driven away: "Come back to your own ground: we have no one here to fight!"[95]

As we have just seen, the feud shades into warfare. Both have been a major source of discipline and authority external to the individual. In the course of human history war has probably been *the* main source of painful social discipline, of public obligations that override private pursuits and obligations. The role of war in strengthening the state is so familiar that it is easy to forget that there have been many occasions when the destruction of human and material resources has severely damaged the social fabric of both victor and vanquished. On balance it remains true that war has provided a major impetus to the creation of more effective and disciplined forms of social organization for both offensive and defensive purposes and thus to the creation of different kinds of public interests. That not all such public interests coincide with the welfare of the underlying population goes without saying.

By intensifying the need for an effective central authority, war has promoted the transformation from private justice, exemplified most clearly in the feud, to systems of public justice. To follow through this development would rapidly take us beyond anthropological data and require an extended discussion quite out of place here.[96] Subsequent chapters will discuss specific aspects of this process in particular societies.

Some general observations are nevertheless appropriate here. One very important aspect is the decline of conceptions of collective responsibility with the decline of kinship as a major principle of social organization. The "private justice" of the feud, it is important to recall, is private only in relation to an overall political authority, where and if one exists. In relation to the individual who is part of a system of collective responsibility and set of obligations, his responsibility is definitely a public matter. A key aspect of the transformation to "public justice" is the definition of offenses, such as murder, as threats to the society as a whole, not just as offenses against a segment. Notions of pollution can provide the crystallization point for such a redefinition. There are other possibilities to be discussed later.†

Finally, the key to the whole process is the acquisition of rights to settle disputes by some leading segment in the society. The Kalinga killer-leaders show one way in which the process can start off. The history of the consolidation of the English and French monarchies[97] shows one way in which the process can continue. It is likely to involve a great deal of cruelty and violence. The lawgiver is not merely a Solon—or a sanitized Solon turned into a copybook hero. At times he can be a quaking and bloody despot, such as China's also semilegendary first Emperor Shih-huang-ti. The differences between a Solon and a Shih-huang-ti—and the difference in circumstances that made them possible—has a great deal to do with the conceptions of public and private that become rooted in social practice and put their mark on a civilization.

Thus the feud through its creation of obligations and loyalties to a tribal segment was a step on the long road that led to identifying the public with the overriding public authority of the state. Within the state

---

†Pollution and patriotism combined in ancient Athens, as we can see from the *Eumenides* and *Persae* of Aeschylus.

there remain of course numerous smaller publics. For that matter there are strong reasons for holding that some conception of public, in the sense of a generalized notion of other human beings as a source of obligations and authority, has been a universal aspect of human culture.

The experiences of infancy and childhood are sufficient to implant a conception of generalized others since no human being can grow up without facing some frustrations imposed by other human beings: parents, parents' surrogates, and, in most cases, many other persons. Whether the Oedipus complex is a universal aspect of this experience is not relevant to the point under consideration, though I will not conceal my highly skeptical attitude toward such claims. It is enough to observe that no human child can gratify all of its impulses all of the time. At some point an adult is bound to intervene—and, in nearly all cases, other children too—in a way that frustrates instincts, drives, or impulses.

Child-rearing in nonliterate societies is often quite permissive if not highly indulgent even by liberal middle-class Western standards. That is partly because there is not a great deal to learn in the way of skills and general knowledge that the child cannot pick up by watching adults and imitating them to the extent the child is able and permitted to do so. The Shavante, Brazilian Indians, are a rather extreme case where toddlers soon become small tyrants who react violently if occasionally thwarted and fly into tantrums that can last as long as half an hour. David Maybury-Lewis reports the comical instance of a small boy offended by something or other who leaned on his toy bow, just as he had seen the mature men do when making an important speech in the men's council, and wailed for a half hour.[98] This youngster's anger and disappointment had already begun to express itself in the ready-made forms of his society.

Among the Mbuti in camp at midday the never-ending voice of the forest with its sounds of birds, monkeys, and bees may or may not "continually whisper[s] assurances that all is well, that the forest is looking after its children." But if a baby crawling around this warm friendly world gets into a bed of hot ashes or a column of army ants, the camp comes to life with shouts and yells. Angry adults surround the baby, give it a sound slapping, and carry it back unceremoniously to the safety of a hut. As all adults in the camp are in a sense the child's parents or grandparents and share responsibility for its welfare, it matters little to which hut they bring the baby. With its games that are both fun and a preparation for life in the forest, lack of confinement, and close supervision, Mbuti childhood sounds enjoyable. Colin M. Turnbull characterizes it as a frolic interspersed with a healthy sprinkle of spankings and slappings that sometimes seem unduly severe.[99]

The diffusion of responsibility for the care of the young is a striking feature of this society. When a Mbuti child gets into a scrape, a "generalized other"—at least a set of adults (not necessarily including parents)—punishes and comforts the young person. It is easy to see how the distinction between self and other people and a generalized conception of the latter can emerge in this society.

Even among the undisciplined Siriono, where young children in temper tantrums beat their parents as hard as they can—sometimes in response to momentary teasing or neglect by their parents—without making their generally affectionate and proud parents angry,[100] there are rules the children cannot break with impunity. The Siriono appear to have made some connection between contact with feces and common ailments such as hookworm and dysentery and therefore watch infants carefully to prevent them from playing with feces. Quite frequently the children will do this anyway. Then the mother will grab the baby, scold it, and give it a rough cleaning up, sometimes sticking her finger into the baby's mouth and cleaning out the excreta if the infant has been putting them there.†

There are food taboos with no obvious physiological basis that apply specifically to children. Though enforcement is flexible to the point of breaking the taboo rather than let a child continue to whimper with hunger, these dietary rules are among the first patterns of behavior every young child must learn.[101] Another more painful and frustrating experience that every infant undergoes about twice a month is the regular removal of eyebrows and hair from the forehead. Infants often howl at this treatment which does not seem to have any rational basis. Not until about the age of three does the child submit without whimpering.[102]

Thus by no means do all the rules that exist within a generally indulgent context serve the welfare of children or adults. Older Siriono children, including the girls, fairly often tease and torture younger ones by pinching genitals, poking fingers into eyes, scratching, and in other ways. Younger ones retaliate and defend themselves with a brand of fire, or a digging stick, sometimes inflicting severe blows and burns on their tormentors. Then adults will put a stop to the fray by preventing the older children from retaliating in their turn.[103] In this manner the children presumably acquire some sense of acceptable and unacceptable forms of aggression against members of their own society and a knowledge that these forms may well be enforced by other adults. That seems to be about as far as the sense of public pressure or public obligation goes in this loosely organized society.

In a large number of nonliterate societies the experience of child-

†Holmberg, *Nomads,* 198. Since in the case observed by the author, the mother after cleaning up the baby went back to eating her own meal without washing her hands, it is safe to infer that the empirical lessons in sanitation have been learned imperfectly if at all.

hood includes rites of passage signifying the transition to adulthood
and the assumption of adult status and responsibilities. Generally these
initiation rites include episodes intended to impress upon the mind of
the young the major ideals, religious beliefs, and moral precepts of the
culture.[104] Where they exist, such rites create an awareness of belonging to a public community with specific privileges and obligations for
the adults in their status. Particularly in the case of males, the rites
often include the infliction of intense suffering, partly as a test of
manhood but more as a way of dramatizing the transition, since just
about every young male is expected to pass the test and acquire full
status. I will describe only one such rite, to my limited knowledge a
rather extreme one, that comes from an excellent modern account
focusing on the problems of social control and social order among
some of the New Guinea highlanders, mentioned above in connection
with the feud.[105]

Penis bleeding is the culmination of initiation rites for males
among some of these people. It occurs around the age of eighteen to
twenty and will be repeated periodically during subsequent years. To
the accompaniment of flute-playing, the candidates on the first occasion are taken to a nearby river. Leaning backward across the lap of a
brother—his own or another—several persons grasp and hold him
securely. Then an elder inserts into the penis duct a length of "spear"
grass treated with ashes, pushing it in as far as possible as the novice
cries out. The next stage is to withdraw the "spear" grass and replace
it with a special twig together with a length of wild orchid grass. The
procedure is to twirl the twig until the youth, crying in pain, urinates.
The next stage is to remove the twig, spray it with salt, and reinsert it
until the youth "defecates crying in great pain; but there are no cases
reported of fainting."†

The highlanders use the seminal fluid and blood that emerges to
anoint special arrows, kept above the fireplace in the men's house. In
cases of serious fighting these arrows are distributed among members
of the lineage and, according to their belief, always find their mark.
After a few weeks the penis operation is repeated a second time. A
similar operation whose details need not be recounted follows this one.
After recovery and healing of the penis, men of the lineage prepare a
banana cake and give it to the candidate to eat and strengthen his body.

By this point the initiation is complete. Presumably, during the
period of his initiation, the youth has also killed a man, the last hurdle

---

†The language at this point in Berndt's account cited above (98–99; also 86, n.2) indicates
that this evidence came from informants rather than direct observation. Though Berndt's
careful attention to detail and frequent use of concrete examples generally inspire
confidence, I cannot repress the hunch that in this instance informants may not have
refrained from imaginative exaggeration. Nevertheless, how many males in any society
would regard a lesser version of this ordeal as anything short of a traumatic experience?

in acquiring adult status. He can now eat the banana cake, an act signifying rights of sexual intercourse with the wife promised to him.[106] The intermingling of the themes of male sexuality, warlike prowess, and public honor, in which females concur enthusiastically, is especially striking in this society though hardly a unique feature.

Moral instruction as such does not appear to take place as part of the penis-bleeding ritual. It is prominent at an earlier nose-bleeding part of initiation when the men harangue the novices thus:

> You must not steal food from another man. You must not abduct the wife of another man. You must not steal another person's pig, nor his fire. . . . But you may shoot men; you may use your bow and arrow. . . . You must grow strong, you must be big so that you can do these things. You must look after your gardens. . . .[107]

Through childhood experiences that vary in intensity and pain from those just described to simple imitation and brief admonition, the individual in nonliterate societies, and indeed all societies, learns at least the rudiments of self-control and responsibility toward others. That the lesson is often very imperfectly learned goes without saying and there are huge differences among societies and, at least in large societies, among the individuals within these societies. Nevertheless it is easy to perceive through an examination of such experiences the germs of a distinction between private and public, between self and others, between acceptable and unacceptable behavior and therefore the seeds of public opinion and public authority.

These considerations make plain the connections among privacy, social control, and social disorder, and shed light on the linkage between such apparently trivial and, in our society, private acts as going to the bathroom and the political issues of freedom and unfreedom. All come together in a society's attitude toward intrusion and protection against intrusion in connection with control or lack of control over instincts, drives, or impulses.† The protective shields against intrusion that have been commonplace among the comfortably situated in Western societies, in such personal aspects as the privacy of physiological functions and the political ones, such as private rights against the state or even the right to choose one's friends, may seem bizarre and unnecessary or indeed highly suspect and antisocial to men and women of other times and places.

The widespread social suspicion of what goes on in private is not purely pathological. It has a basis in the control of our inclinations and instincts and suspicion about those who may be getting away with not controlling theirs. The impulses that we have learned to control at the greatest emotional cost are likely to be the ones whose free expression

---

†There is no need here to consider the thorny problem of distinctions among these terms and their "real" meaning.

in other people we resent most angrily. The resentment may be thoroughly justified or a dangerous delusion, depending on circumstances. In any event such feelings are a source of both the desire for intrusion and resentment against it.

Looking back over the ground traversed in this chapter, we can see the variety of forces and situations that have given rise to a conception of the public. Economic cooperation for the sake of goals that are widely accepted because they are obviously essential to social survival is one possible source. Practices among the Mbuti net-hunters are a clear illustration. But it is also apparent that conflict, so long as the conflict can be settled, has been an equally important source of public institutions. From the decisions of a petty chieftain to those of the most powerful monarchs, the main concern of rulers has been to settle disputes and the main concern of subjects to obtain justice. The settlement of disputes and the administration of justice have been the main concrete manifestations demonstrating the existence of public institutions. Both kinship and religion have in many times and places provided the original structures out of which public ones could grow or upon which they could be grafted.

To return once more to conflict, the feud has been a major cause of the growth of a public interest through the imposition of a collective obligation for vengeance. At the same time, the continued existence of feuds inhibits the growth of larger public powers. The public in the full sense of the term cannot exist before punishment for murder becomes the task of some central authority and ceases to be that of some social subgroup such as the lineage. In turn, as we have seen, the feud shades off into social practices that resemble ordinary warfare among sovereign states. Among some nonliterate peoples and also in ancient Greece and other civilizations there may exist, despite chronic warfare, an awareness of belonging to a larger community, an idealized but inefficient public.

Finally, in all human societies, even the simplest and least integrated, ways of rearing children exist that impart, however imperfectly, an awareness of what it means to be a member of a specific human society. By inculcating a sense of obligation to others and a keen awareness of the obstacles to immediate gratification, child-rearing practices create a sense of society as something greater than the individual, the key element in an awareness of the public.

Retreat to and
Escape from Intimacy

In very many societies there exist small intimate groups to which the individual may retreat from time to time for protection and relief from the demands and obligations of the larger society. Within such groups there is no need to maintain the kind of self-control, deportment, and costume required "in public" by the larger society, though other demands are likely. The emotional atmosphere is warm and supportive, encouraging trust and a relaxation of one's guard.

Among the Fulani, a tribe of African cattle-raisers and agriculturalists inhabiting parts of the Upper Volta, adult males constitute in effect a leisure class. Public Fulani behavior, as befits their warlike past, requires that one put forth an image of strong self-mastery that amounts to a denial of emotional and physiological needs.[108] There are situations where such behavior is not required. The anthropologist describes them as one where people are together "en famille," carefully noting that the French expression apparently lacks a precise equivalent in their language. Nevertheless, "it evokes accurately the atmosphere of secure human warmth where people feel close and where there is no need to maintain any façade because they feel able to behave together 'naturally.' " In other words, the brakes are taken off certain impulses. In general these impulses have to do with eating, drinking, and sex in either sublimated or unsublimated forms. That there is no complete freedom for the satisfaction of impulses, that such satisfaction may be highly stylized and restricted in intimate groups, is well known. Among the Fulani the most common form of this situation occurs when a man is with the mother or mother's brother. In front of these persons a man has no need for shame.[109]

The mother-son relationship may be prototypical of a major form of intimate escape. In its ideal form it combines affection, protection, and the meeting of personal needs such as nourishment. The father-daughter relationship, on the other hand, is liable to be somewhat strained due to the elements of authority and potential sexual exploitation inherent in the paternal role. Another main prototype could be that of clandestine lovers where erotic attraction brings together two human beings in defiance of social rules and conventions. Where a wide choice of casual sexual partners is openly available, as among adolescents in many societies, such a clandestine relationship is rare. For its full development the rule of monogamy is necessary. But other forms of clandestine love are possible and are likely to arise everywhere since all human societies put some obstacles in the way of sexual gratification.

Among intimate groups and even loving couples common experience shows that friendly warmth can with the passage of time turn into highly charged hostility. Protection can turn into oppression. One reason for this transformation is sheer boredom and satiety. Another, as we shall see in more detail shortly, is the breakdown of cooperative relationships within the small intimate group. When that happens, there may develop a desire for solitude, or even for escape from intimacy into public affairs and public life. In several societies we find a rhythmic oscillation between privacy and a more publicly oriented existence.

In some societies the rhythm is a function of the annual cycle of economic activities. The cycle has been the subject of careful study by Joel S. Savishinsky as he lived among the subarctic Hare Indians. Its features reveal the essential dynamics that apply in other societies as well.

For about half the year, during the summer months, these Indians live in villages of more than a dozen households containing some sixty-five to seventy-five people. During the winter months households separate and live in dispersed bush camps, trapping furs for the market.[110] The nuclear family constitutes the main locus of economic cooperation and emotional support. Within this unit the bonds of interdependence and mutual aid are strongest. But it is not the only cooperative unit. The system of bilateral kinship permits a choice of residence and cooperative affiliations. Kinship is only one of several factors in the formation of close group ties. Others include age, sex, personality, and allegiance in local quarrels.[111]

There has already been occasion to mention some of the main causes for disputes and tension among families off camping in the bush: they come down to the fact that no strategy for hunting and trapping can possibly guarantee continuing success. In addition there are liable to be disagreements over contributions to camp supplies, the use of these supplies, and the share in the work load.[112]

While out in the winter camps these Indians do have some ways of coping with these stresses. The work of trapping, hunting, fishing, and wood-cutting takes the men out of the camp for substantial periods each day and enables them to dissipate some of their accumulated anger. For the women, life is in some ways harder, though they do not have to face the physical dangers and effort of outdoor work to the same degree. Savishinsky reports that the women occupy a high rung in a pecking order of safe aggression. Men pick on their wives. When the husbands are out, the women yell at their children. The children turn on each other and the dogs. Even the dogs, Savishinsky claims, had their own hierarchy of aggression.[113]

With the passage of time the families in the bush camps come to look forward to the summer reunion of the village (as well as shorter ones at Christmas and Easter) as a release from the tensions of life in the bush. They are as eager to get back to the amenities and strains of village life as they had been to escape from them into the "real Indian" life of the camps.[114]

Village life of course creates its own tensions. The village is the place where one has to create a favorable self-image. That possibility depends on the success one had while out trapping in the bush.[115] On the other hand, the village appears to be the place where strained cooperative social networks can be renewed or replaced, perhaps the most positive aspect of village existence.[116] Village life requires more contacts among people and thereby generates more gossip. The gossip gets into the cabins, the single-room dwellings characteristic of the village, and poisons relationships that may be in bad shape anyway, due perhaps to someone's refusal to do domestic chores. The doors to these cabins are never locked.[117] People enter each other's houses freely without knocking and without asking permission. Only at night are doors locked and curtains drawn as a sign that people are asleep and not to be disturbed. But drunks pay no attention to these signals, and there is a great deal of festive drinking during these ingatherings of the village community. In turn, the drinking encourages the release of all sorts of aggression.

As the absence of locked doors suggests, these people lack socially accepted defenses against unwelcome intrusion. The only form of total individual privacy occurs during a trip to the family outhouse. These Indians do not have such devices as turning one's back or refusing to acknowledge the presence of others. There is, however, a certain amount of spatial privacy, such as the area of one's own bed in the village cabin.[118] Hence it is hardly surprising that after the euphoria of the return to the village wears off, many people become conscious of gossip as an overload of information and find it painful to be the object of rough humor.† In short, there is too much human society. Once again they hanker for the release of life in the bush.

Among the Fulani, the cattle-raising leisure society of the Upper Volta in West Africa, the men have at their disposal two regular ways of escaping from their society. Neither way can be permanent. Only one recurs on a regular basis when men must take the cattle to a salt lick.

The other is a visit to a village of former slaves. According to Fulani stereotypes, captives or ex-slaves display all the traits that are the opposite of Fulani qualities. Captives or former slaves are supposedly black, fat, coarse, naive, irresponsible, uncultivated, shameless, and dominated by their needs and emotions.[119] Thus a visit to an ex-slave village constitutes an opportunity to escape from the decorum that rules Fulani community life. Yet it is not an escape into a private area; it is an escape into a neutral form of public area. Riesman compares it to the café in French social life. Men can meet there who would never dare enter one another's village. The local Fulani administrative officer never goes into the villages of his subjects in the course of his rounds. Instead he meets them in a former slave village.[120]

The key elements in this arrangement are (1) the relaxation of the

---

†Savishinsky, *Trail of the Hare*, 131. In this society too the men have an easier time due to greater mobility.

official code of decorum and (2) the definition of the area as both neutral and external to the essential social order. Only those Fulani who have a strong interest in the outside world and who feel ill at ease at home visit these villages frequently. Most go but rarely, and feel the same discomfort when visiting the ex-slaves as they would feel if the ex-slaves came to visit them.[121] In this rank-ridden and uncosmopolitan society this kind of escape from a private and provincial existence is somewhat of an anomaly, perhaps no more than a tiny entering wedge. The salon and the café as public meeting places and escapes from private life are unimaginable for this society. Yet one can see in Paul Riesman's account one possible form of their origin.

The other safety valve in Fulani society is transhumance or the taking of the cattle to the salt licks. This choice is available to vigorous young men only and has some of the characteristics of a camping expedition in our society. On the other hand, Riesman, when he joined these young men, perceived transhumance as manifesting more clearly than any other behavior those values that the Fulani consider most characteristic of themselves, something one could hardly say of American camping. The tending of the herd and watching out for the needs of the cattle completely overshadowed human needs and comfort. Moments of rest, hours of rest, and speed of travel were completely determined by the animals. But this dependence on the cattle meant complete escape from habitual social pressures. It was also a completely legitimate escape because it was socially necessary.[122]

Taking the cattle on transhumance means going into the bush. The bush is the metaphor for solitude, for that which is outside society. The bush gives off overtones of fear. A place one leaves becomes bush when no one is there, an idea expressed in the formula used to persons about to depart from a village: "You will make us bush." At the same time it is from the bush that men obtain their sustenance and they must bow to its demands. In turn this necessity not only makes men aware of their weakness in relation to the bush, it also gives each man the opportunity to realize his own individual capacities and qualities insofar as he takes responsibility for meeting his own needs.[123]

Thus transhumance represents an opportunity for self-reliance and self-expression, at least in comparison with the routines of village life. It is a form of private self-realization in the service of a public necessity, perhaps a preliterate version of Engels's famous leap from necessity to freedom, inasmuch as freedom for Engels as much as for the Fulani implied the recognition of necessity. Here too the subarctic Hare Indians join the tropical Fulani in setting a high store on socially necessary and legitimate escape to their respective but very different forms of bush life, where individual freedom and independence amount to dependence on the behavior of animals instead of other human beings.

Now we may turn to the analysis of the social structures that provide intimate retreats from social pressures. There are two main types, those based on ascription and those based on free individual choice. Ascriptive groups are those based on kinship, age, and sex. Membership in such an intimate group as the nuclear family, age set, boys' clique or girls' clique, and corresponding groups among adults, comes about from birth and the passage of time. There is little or nothing that the individual can do to obtain membership, though in some cases it may be possible to refuse membership in cliques.

At the opposite pole from these are such group as clubs and networks of intimate friendship created by the participants. Ascriptive factors are at work in such groups too insofar as social class and sex restrict opportunities for intimate contact. The ascriptive factors determine the population whose members will be able to form clubs and networks of friendship through their own efforts. Social opportunities are seldom if ever distributed in a completely equal fashion. But the use made of given opportunities depends on the individual character and personality.

The structural forms of legitimate and intimate escape from external social pressures also serve at times to transmit these pressures. That is obviously true of the nuclear family. It is a major agency for the transformation of raw human nature into socially acceptable human beings. The same is true of personal affinities that arise in the place of work. From them the individual learns the real nature of the job. Different intimate groups, depending on their location and function in the society as a whole, serve to transmit and sustain different aspects of a society's culture. All of them develop some standards of behavior. Therefore escape into such a group is never a complete escape from social demands. That is one of the reasons for continuing individual ambivalence toward such groups, a tendency to retreat into an intimate protective group and then to escape from it. Solitude itself provides no permanent solution.

Taking the biological differences of sex and age as their starting points, kinship systems have elaborated upon them in different ways to define obligations of protection and supervision and to mark off areas of intimacy and affection. Many kinship systems specify a set of persons with whom the individual is expected to remain on formal terms of respect and another set with whom informal intimate relationships are the norm or even required. Thus kinship limits and establishes rights of intrusion or control over the individual's living space, as well as providing protection for this space. Among the Shavante, grown-ups come and go freely in and out of the huts of their relatives by blood, but they avoid those of their relatives by marriage.[124] The custom is not an arbitrary peculiarity but part of a larger set of political and social arrangements centering on competing factions organized around lineages.

The possible mingling of aggressive and affectionate motifs in intimate groups defined by kinship appears in a striking manner in Fulani rules about insults. In this instance it is the opposite of privacy that has been institutionalized in rules emphasizing the superiority of age and masculinity. Elder brothers have the right to insult their juniors, and parents their children. All these insults refer directly or indirectly to the sexual organs or anus of the individual or his parents. According to one informant, the individual uttering these insults would have previously had the right to see the things he is talking about. Thus the results are verbal rights of intrusion held by older people.

Younger individuals may not return insults. That is the case even though the insults are often deliberately wounding. But among age-mates there is another pattern of mutual insult similar to the kidding, roughhousing, and horseplay familiar among males fond of each other in our culture. Among the Fulani, as among ourselves, a young man who is not insulted in this manner feels left out. It is a sign that his age-mates do not trust him because he is in some way different.[125]

Though there is a general tendency for authority to carry with it rights of intrusion that often have aggressive overtones, there are also reverse currents that deserve brief mention at this point. In many hierarchically organized societies house slaves and servants—not to mention secretaries in a bureaucracy—get to know the most intimate and secret details of the masters' behavior, while the dominant stratum finds the private life of the lower orders impossible to penetrate, or not worth penetrating, prior to the invention of sociology. Where patriarchal relationships are fully developed, on the other hand, as can occur at times even under plantation slavery, the patriarch and more especially the patriarch's wife may assume considerable responsibility for the welfare of subordinates and learn a great deal about how they live outside of working hours.[126]

Due to its wide distribution in time and space the nuclear family of biological parents and offspring may seem at first glance a respectable candidate for the most important social structure in providing privacy in the sense of intimate escape. There has already been occasion to mention the mother-son relationship as the prototype of such a relationship. A closer look at the evidence, however, reveals numerous obstacles to the performance of this function by the nuclear family.

Among hunting bands such as the Siriono and Mbuti, the desire for escape may be weak because the collective pressures of the band weigh lightly on the individual and life outside the band is too dangerous to be considered seriously. Flimsy residential structures, collective or individual, combined with wandering, curious children can render the notion of domestic privacy meaningless or ridiculous.

The demands of the lineage or other larger social unit in slightly more complex societies may make individual decisions difficult or pull the spouses apart through obligations to parents belonging to distinct and perhaps competing social units. In a matrilineal society the wife bears children for her own blood kin and the bond to her husband is liable to be weak. Women are liable to side with brothers against husbands, and divorce is likely to be frequent. Speaking of African systems in general, including patrilineal ones, Max Gluckman quotes as an illuminating exaggeration the remark of an unnamed observer: "A man seeks companionship with other men, loves his sister, and sleeps with his wife."[127]

Then there is the extended family. Whatever the theoretical structure, in practice it is likely at some point in its own life cycle to become a tyranny presided over by an elderly valetudinarian female who wields her bouts of illness with the timing and precision of a professional athlete to extract services from sons and daughters' husbands for the sake of the family's female members.†

Where for one or more of these reasons structural conditions do not permit the nuclear family to become the social unit for intimate protection against a larger world, I suspect that smaller units of personal affection within the family may often play this role. A brother may form a sustained attachment with a sister or another brother, parents with each other or one child, and so on. Since by definition intimate escape goes somewhat against the grain of every social order—or at least against its proclaimed principles—evidence on these connections is hard to come by.

Since the nuclear family is not always the main social unit to provide privacy, it is appropriate to ask under what conditions it may become such a unit. Powerful biological forces work in this direction. So far in human history the human child has required a female parent and a male one. Though the identity of the mother is easy enough to establish, all known societies have required an identification of the father as well.[128] There is also reasonably good evidence for the existence of something we can call parental affection as a normal human inclination. Infanticide has of course existed on a widespread scale. But so far as I am aware it is always a reluctant acceptance of apparent necessity. Cruel treatment of children also exists, and more information about it becomes available daily. Like other pathologies, it sheds light on the normal by emphasizing the sources of aggression built into the parental function. There is no reason to deny that parental affection may be fused with dangerous and powerful currents of hate. Yet the affection is there. It is the source of comment in numerous ethnographic monographs on societies in all parts of the globe. With the exception of such an obviously mortally wounded culture as that

†For the atmosphere of such a family see the novel by V. S. Naipaul, *A House for Mr. Biswas.* At least for this reader it made an alien kinship system far more comprehensible than many a scientific treatise.

Turnbull describes in *The Mountain People,* nonliterate peoples generally treat children affectionately if not indulgently.

To the extent that these observations are correct, there is justification for the position that the nuclear family with certain characteristic bonds of affection does constitute the basic building block upon which different human societies have worked to create different rules—and characteristic patterns of rule-breaking—about the ways in which human beings should relate to each other. The bonds of intimacy and affection, or at least powerful impulses in that direction, are there to start with. They can be emphasized, inhibited, or deflected in various directions. But it is impossible to ignore them. For the family to develop from this starting point toward becoming the major social unit of intimate escape from disagreeable or painful external pressures, certain other conditions, I suggest, are necessary.

In the first place, there have to be disagreeable pressures or obligations. That point I shall try to elaborate more systematically later. Here it is enough to observe that any human society is bound to display some such obligations in connection with growing up and learning to live in human society and in some aspect of the division of labor. But the actual and perceived weight of these obligations, and the real and socially defined opportunities to do something about them, all vary enormously.

So does the tendency to make the family, or some other social formation, into a unit of intimate escape and protection. Other conditions are necessary. For reasons already hinted at, a patrilineal system with a substantial dose of patriarchal authority appears to be much more favorable to the establishment and legitimation of private concerns, including some of their oppressive features, than the opposite combination of matrilineal descent and emphasis on maternal authority. The passage of property and authority down the male line from one generation to the next bonds the female to the male, removing the possibility of a succession of husbands or lovers as the fathers *seriatim* of her children.

This stabilization of the parental relationship seems to be necessary for the creation of sustained cooperation and collaboration of husband-wife and growing children. Though the cooperation might start up on some other basis including love and congeniality, purely voluntary cooperation without any element of authority or material incentives and penalties is notoriously unstable. Thus sustained cooperation constitutes the key to the whole process since it is the source of the sentiments of affection, trust, and mutual dependence that together with the drawing of a social boundary constitute the essence of intimate withdrawal.

The boundary and self-limiting aspect is of course an essential element in the whole psychological and social process. Purely as a matter of time and energy it is impossible to be on intimate terms with more than a very small number of people. The gushings of the cocktail party and the camaraderie of the radical or religious social movement are both correctly suspect as forms of pseudointimacy, attacks on the individual's social space masquerading as efforts to preserve it.

The social boundary has to have some physical expression to be meaningful. Hence arises the significance of technological factors that permit some degree of residential segregation, especially from the prying eyes—not to mention the noisy cries—of wandering children, to judge from the anthropological evidence. First comes the separate house with sturdy walls and real doors, oddly prefigured in the Eskimo igloo, and then very much later the modern middle- and upper-class home with separate rooms for distinct household activities and individual members of the family.

But, to repeat, it is not the physical accoutrements but the cooperative activities that generate the emotional atmosphere under discussion. For such an atmosphere to be created and sustained there must be a set of related roles that contribute to the well-being of the family as a whole. The father's place of work must be in the home; the wife and mother must have an economic role to play that is clearly related to household production, and transcends strictly domestic chores. The nature of economic activity must be such that children can learn to make a contribution at an early age.

Taken together, these considerations indicate a level of social and economic development well beyond that of most but perhaps not all nonliterate societies. Certain types of peasant societies—but not those with a powerful, intrusive, and inquisitorial village community—might accord with these requirements. So would a simple level of urban crafts and town life. Though the necessary mobility of nomadic herders would inhibit the development of residential privacy, the cooperative aspects could develop there. More developed urban life leads to the separation of the place of work from the home and thus undercuts one of the main prerequisites.

To turn for a moment to considerations that go beyond the family, it is important to keep in mind the ambivalent character of social units for intimate escape. If they are to flourish, they have to carry out some socially necessary task, as the family does in child-rearing and the legitimation of procreation—that is, placing new members of the society within a given network of social relationships concerning property and authority. At the same time to the extent that such units provide privacy they insulate individuals from the larger society, especially from the organs of authority. Yet, as studies of informal organization and private networks within both capitalist and socialist†

---

†It is revealing that Soviet authorities constantly complain about "familism" as corrupting and undermining Communist authority and socialist morality. The Chinese Communists likewise criticize systems of mutual protection and informal patronage.

bureaucracies have often shown, without these informal networks and practices the bureaucracy almost certainly could not function at all. Without breaking some rules, and getting protection for having broken them, it is impossible to get any job done, or more precisely what is socially defined as the most important part of the job done on time. To work strictly by the rulebook is the most effective form of strike.

Hence the social arrangements that undermine authority are simultaneously those necessary to make it effective. Though the balance between these two components varies from situation to situation, it may be that the inevitable growth of these recalcitrant cells in any large social organism provides the most realistic basis for hope that some aspects of privacy may continue to survive in the world to come.

By this point it has become obvious that the taste for privacy as well as the ability to satisfy this taste are very unequally distributed among human societies and within them, even in simple unstratified societies. The suspicion may easily arise that women pay the social cost for whatever privacy men obtain in and through the nuclear family. Does the nuclear family carry with it the inherent burden of what modern feminists call the trap of domesticity? Do women generally have to perform all the menial tasks connected with maintaining the household and rearing children? Are these tasks in some essential sense menial, or is their boring and even stultifying character a matter of cultural definition and socially induced attitudes?

As might be anticipated, anthropological evidence demonstrates the possibility of a wide range of practices and attitudes on this score. Among the Yanomamö, the "fierce" people inhabiting remote jungle areas on the borderlands of Brazil and Venezuela whose menfolk pursue continuous warlike feuds with one another, the domesticity trap would appear to be the least of the woman's worries. Indeed there is little domesticity to escape from. Food preparation is simple and rarely requires much labor, time, or equipment. Both sexes participate although women do the greater share.[129] Though the houses are fairly complicated structures built at the cost of much cooperative effort from poles, vines, and leaves, they only last a year or two because the leaves begin to leak and the structures become so infested with cockroaches, scorpions, and other vermin that the far-from-squeamish inhabitants find it necessary to burn them to the ground.[130]

The women's real problems in this society come from the brutality of the men. When the men return from a hunt or a visit, they march slowly across the village and retire silently to their hammocks. Women are expected to drop whatever they may be doing, hurry home, and quietly but speedily prepare meals for the returned husbands. "Should the wife be slow in doing this, the husband is within his rights to beat her." Most reprimands take the form of blows with the hand or a piece of firewood. A good many, however, chop their wives with the sharp edge of a machete, shoot them with a barbed arrow in the buttocks or leg, or hold the hot end of a glowing stick against them. It is not rare for a man to injure his wife seriously. Some men have killed their wives.

The women do have some protection provided by their brothers, who will protect them from a cruel husband, sometimes taking the woman away and giving her to another man. But this protection is far from generally effective. By and large, and for obvious reasons, the women have a vindictive and caustic attitude toward the world around them. At the age of thirty a woman has "lost her shape" and developed an unpleasant disposition. They seek refuge and consolation in the company of other women, sharing their misery with their peers.[131]

In this sense, it appears, they seek surcease and escape from what domesticity there is in this society. Though male brutality among the Yanomamö is extreme, it is by no means uncharacteristic of societies where the male role carries with it an emphasis on the manly virtues of the fighter. One might construct a good case for the domesticity trap among the Jívaro. There the wife appears as a far-from-glorified servant necessary to the male self-image of a munificent host, the breeding mechanism for an unusually didactic and disciplined manner of child-rearing, and of course a key cause of feuds.[132] Among Ronald Berndt's war-loving New Guinea highlanders, the domineering and aggressive aspects of male sexuality are very striking. So is the extent to which women encourage and require the male to assume and play out the role of the manly warrior.[133]

The connection between manly, warlike qualities and brutal treatment of females, however, does not hold everywhere. Lewis Henry Morgan, to be sure, claimed that among North American Indians the Iroquois regarded women as the servants of men, and that the woman accepted this position. Like the Yanomamö and others, the Iroquois woman was expected to serve up food to her husband at any time of day he returned.[134] But Morgan makes no mention of brutality. In any case, with marriage customs permitting easy separation and the woman's important role in politics among the Iroquois, brutality would be incompatible with the male's dependence on the woman for the food she raised by farming.[135] Among the Cheyennes, too, husband and wife generally constituted a close working team and as a rule relations were affectionate even if cases of jealous and brutal treatment of wives did occur. The Cheyenne attitude toward sexuality was one of fear and distrust. Male and female economic roles were strictly separated but complementary.[136]

The Iroquois male was accustomed to prolonged periods of absence from home, which gave the women considerable independence and made their agricultural contribution more obvious, while in the Cheyenne case, the fear of sexuality, including, we may assume, its aggressive component, combined with carefully defined yet complementary economic roles to produce broadly similar results. Hence it is not only the objective economic performance of the female but the cultural perception and definition of this performance, and of the female role in general, that distinguishes the North American Indian examples from the other societies with legitimized brutality against women.

Looking now at the men, it does not appear that their brutality against the women represents some innate aspect of sexual aggressiveness that has to be held in check by social prohibitions in those societies where we do not find it. Instead this form of brutality appears to be a spilling over into the conjugal relationship of a generalized norm of fierceness. This connection is clearest in the case of the Yanomamö. Frustrations intentionally or unintentionally inflicted by the wife when the husband returns, hungry and tired from the hunt, frequently trigger off the aggression. It is reasonable to suppose that many cases of extreme violence against the wife occur against the background of a large reservoir of male aggression due to sexual jealousy or the wife's previous inadequacy in performing her domestic chores, or both.

If sheer brutality constitutes more of a threat to wives than the burden of domestic chores under conditions I have tried to specify, reports on other nonliterate societies (except for the Mbuti) do describe situations resembling the domesticity trap as well as several ways of coping with it. This evidence shows rather plainly that child-rearing and housekeeping have inherently unpleasant and burdensome aspects, though there are rewards as well. One way of coping with the unpleasantness is to shift the burden onto someone else. It is rather surprising to come upon this device in so simple a society as the Siriono. Polygyny occurs in about one-quarter of Siriono families. In these the first wife dominates the other wives, who do more of the domestic work and all "menial tasks such as bringing in firewood and water."† Hopi women, it seems, on the basis of incidental remarks, are expected to be both disciplinarians and housekeepers, a burden for them that can on occasion be physically and psychologically crushing.[137]

It is among the arctic-dwelling Utku Eskimo and subarctic Hare Indians that the nuclear family most clearly constitutes the unit of intimate protection and escape, partly against the elements but also against social pressures. In her monograph on the Utku Eskimos Briggs conveys effectively the contrast between behavior in daytime hours and in the evening or on stormy days. In the daytime when the houses were full of visitors, men and women usually ignored each other—except when men required services such as boiling tea or

---

†Holmberg, *Nomads,* 131, 125–126. Holmberg does not spell out the term "menial," but the context suggests that it applies to repetitious, physically somewhat arduous tasks requiring little or no skill, and, perhaps most important, performed for someone else.

picking lice out of an undershirt. In the evenings or on stormy days when family members were alone together, the separate circles of men and women meshed. "The division then was not between men and women but between Family and Outsiders."[138] The evening was also a time of storytelling and the recollection of shared family experiences, some of happiness, some of extreme hardship. These memories, including private jokes, were, as Briggs remarks, "threads in the intimacy that I felt binding and giving security to the members of Inuttiaq's family in these private hours."[139]

Within the domestic circle the Utku husband dominates the wife. Inuttiaq, Briggs's host and adoptive father, may have been more peremptory in his commands than other Eskimos. But the practice of making major and minor decisions and giving orders to make tea, make bannock, fetch a pipe, help feed the dogs, or chip stalactites off the walls are evidently part of routine daily living. If snow came through a hole in the wall and began to pile up on the bedding or if a dog broke loose from its chain in the night, it would always be the soundly sleeping wife and not her wakeful husband who had to go outdoors and repair the damage.[140]

The women accepted their situation with overt good cheer. To do otherwise, it seems to me, to display resentment and throw a frying pan at a domineering husband, might have been to court collective suicide. They had to get along in very close quarters, just to survive. Perhaps this necessity lies at the root of the famous Eskimo politeness and consideration for others. Yet this obvious imperative somehow does not do full justice to the emotional tone reported by Briggs.

Male behavior was for an Utku wife part of the natural order of things. Men, the women observe correctly, have the hardest and most dangerous work to do. The wives want to help them for this reason and also because the husbands are seen as taking care of them. The *desire* to help in a difficult situation, not merely the necessity to help, seems central to the emotional atmosphere.[141] Even a husband is capable of this emotion. Without it, intimacy and human society generally might not be endurable. To feel that one's efforts and sacrifices are both needed and appreciated may be one of the general human capacities that render human society not only possible but quite often a source of real pleasure.

Even granting these observations on the desire to be helpful, I do not think it is possible to deny the existence of a domesticity trap among the Utku and a component of self-control verging on self-repression in the standard female adaptation to the wife's role. She does carry much of the burden of making the family dwelling the locus of intimate escape from the surrounding world.

Among the Mbuti Pygmies in their benign forest (benign for them and their culture), on the other hand, I have not been able on several close readings to turn up any situation that resembles or recalls domestic entrapment. The forest that makes it possible for these inhabitants to meet their simple needs without prolonged immersion in physically demanding yet confined and routine tasks may provide part of the answer. But only part.

The diffuse character of the nuclear family is an important aspect. The nuclear family does not seem to be a significant private refuge in this society. Any small child in trouble, the reader may recall, can run to any mother for solace. Parental authority is shared and diffused. Though members of the family generally take their meals each at their own hearth, for mealtime is the only time of emphasis on the nuclear family, males from youth to old age may take their food to a central fire and eat with their fellows there.[142] (As an escape from even mild domesticity the men's club appears among the simplest human societies.) Unlike the Cheyennes, the division of labor by sex is not strictly marked out. A good many tasks can be exchanged if the situation calls for it. Finally, adult women play an indispensable part as beaters in the cooperative net hunt. Men, as befits their strength, do the dangerous work of killing the animals as these thrash about in the nets. But without the women no animals would go into the nets.[143]

To sum up, a strong sense of collective unity in the band—all the society the Mbuti know—a correspondingly weak development of familial bonds, an equalitarian division of labor between the sexes rendered possible by an undemanding environment, and a simple technology have apparently prevented the wife's entrapment in a domestic role. How much of this complex could be transposed into social arrangements that might work in a modern society is a worthwhile query that I shall leave to others. Even among the Mbuti, it is worth noticing, more options are open to the male role than to the female.

In somewhat more complex societies the difference is even more noticeable. Males exercise whatever authority may exist within the family, larger kinship unit, or society as a whole, though de facto and de jure sharing of authority in kin and family matters is quite common. Males have the opportunity to retreat to domestic intimacy as well as to escape from it rather more than females. For the females the main escape comes with legitimate errands away from the dwelling or periods when the husband is off to work in the fields or on the chase. Then the wife can mingle with other women, gossiping, commiserating, exchanging advice, and in general creating a distinct feminine subculture. Only at a later stage do we come upon the distinction so sharply drawn in classical civilization between domestic affairs as essentially the private and predominantly feminine sphere and the exclusively male and public sphere of war and politics.

If men have more opportunities to escape from intimate social relationships, there must be something to escape from. It is a matter of common observation that the warm, supportive atmosphere of intimate groups can change to latent and even explosive hostility. This change can occur in such different groups as a family, a village or small town, the crew of a small ship, a team of explorers or mountaineers. A novice entering such a group with euphoria may suddenly come to the realization that volcanic forces have been below the surface for some time. One student of the Alaskan Eskimos has recently claimed that "instead of the smiling, friendly, non-aggressive mask presented, Eskimo life in reality is a seething cauldron of angers and violences, emotional abandonments and impulsive acting-out defended against, in some, by rigid and uncreative personalities and, in most, poorly defended if at all."[144] The person who discovers or feels this latent hostility is liable to find the formerly warm and supportive atmosphere suffocating and to seek escape or at least temporary surcease from it. Indeed this desire for escape can arise without so extreme a shift in the apparent emotional atmosphere.

Now we may explore some of the sociological and psychological reasons for this change. First let us try to analyze the ways in which cooperation can break down, under the broad rubrics of (1) production of goods and services, defining this activity broadly to include goods and services obtained through fighting and/or through movements for religious, political, and general social change; and (2) the distribution of such goods and services, again defining them broadly enough to include erotic rewards. It is easier, I suggest, to approach this problem indirectly by asking first how cooperation is sustained and strengthened.

The answer to that question seems to be straightforward and simple. Success in accomplishing a chosen task, in meeting an unexpected or deliberately sought challenge, strengthens the bonds of respect and affection *to the extent that all members have made a contribution*. One can see this happen when a group of secretaries finishes up a rush job or the crew of a ship brings a vessel through a bad storm or a team of mountaineers scales a difficult peak. But if the success is only due to one person, especially the leader, or comes about despite the negative contribution or slack efforts of one or more team members or finally if the rewards, including praise and social esteem, bear no relation to individual contributions, success will not bring about this strengthening of cohesive bonds. Instead there will be disaffected mutterings and grumblings in dark corners. But a genuine collective success produces a mood of euphoric fellowship. The memory of this success and the efforts behind it become part of the collective memory and subculture that gives the group a distinct identity. As these individual memories accumulate, they make the group private or at least exclusive. *Esprit de corps,* which can exist even in a family circle, by its nature excludes other groups.

As we turn now to the sources of dissension and conflict, we can locate them most easily by noting the decisions a group must make in the course of production and distribution. Among the Hare Indians, let us take the case of the nuclear family, which is here the main unit of economic cooperation. During the winter season each family goes off to its winter trapping grounds. We know it is an event they look forward to eagerly as an opportunity to escape from the gossip and competitive pressures of community life. But once in camp the family members have to make decisions about where to set the traps and other aspects of winter hunting. No amount of lore and tradition can guarantee the success of any given decision. The behavior of the game animals always displays unpredictable features that the Indians' culture can neither predict nor control. Therefore whenever the hunting is mediocre to poor it is always possible for some adult member of the family to claim that it would have been better to set the traps somewhere else. In this way recriminations start and bitterness spreads to other issues such as the allocation of the food supply.[145]

To generalize from this plain but vivid example, the first thing a group has to decide (as Lenin argued in a famous polemic) is what it will do. To the extent that the existing culture cannot provide a ready-made answer, disagreements and recriminations are liable to occur. They are of course a major source of factional conflict in religious and political movements, where they are likely to fuse with rivalries over who is in charge of the group as well as what persons are entitled, and on what grounds, to take part in the big decisions about strategy and tactics.

If there is no disagreement about major policy, there can still be disagreements and bitterness about the division of labor within the group. Objections can arise to doing disagreeable jobs, those that are both confining and arduous, or whose nature implies a degree of subordination to other persons or dependence on others that the prevailing culture defines as unacceptable. There are the problems of inadequate performance: the man who will not or cannot pull his oar, or among fighters the rash or cowardly individual who brings unnecessary risks and danger upon the whole group.

In connection with the distribution of the social product there can be quarrels over what criteria should be used, such as need or the value of an individual's contribution to the group's product, as well as discontent about the concrete application of the criteria in individual cases. In groups containing both males and females there is always the latent issue of the distribution of erotic favors, one reason for the widespread preference for exclusively male or female membership in many working groups in all cultures. Without claiming that this list is complete, it points to enough potential loci of conflict to reveal the serious difficulties facing any form of social coordination.

Now we may turn once more to the psychological price of comforting intimacy. The individual who seeks an opportunity to drop the public mask, find sympathy, warmth, and emotional support in a small walled-off group, is liable to find another mask necessary. If it is a working group, there will be the requirement to cooperate. At a minimum there will be the need to share some goods and services and to echo group opinions. If the individual begins to find any of this burdensome, he or she may begin to wonder if others may not find his or her presence burdensome. What then lies behind the polite smile, the carefully phrased hint? The new member finds it necessary to control aggression generated by the frustrations of sharing. If the group is one with achieved membership, there will be anxieties about the reality and depth of one's acceptance. Indeed this anxiety can occur even with ascribed membership, as in modern families where the parents discipline the children by withholding affection and approval.

Among isolated groups, such as the crew of a ship, a small military outpost, or explorers marooned in a distant land, boredom is likely to set in. Repeated stimuli and repeated rewards, as is well known, eventually lose their effectiveness. Minor foibles in one's associates that would pass unnoticed in a different situation become increasingly annoying. The well known "cure" is work, even work that is imposed for no very obvious reason by outside authority. The pain of constant and fairly intense work somehow deadens the awareness of other pains. Work is the great narcotic; it can even render bearable the agony of grief at the loss of one's beloved.

All in all, the price of intimacy at its worst may include pretended affection, the control of one's own hostilities, anxiety over one's acceptance and status in the group, and with the passage of time boredom with the whole situation.

One form of escape from both private *and* public pressures is that taken by the loner, a form of inner emigration. Especially where the group is the source of both security and anxiety, as can often be the case for adolescents in the nuclear family, an individual can try to cope with these pressures by building a wall of defensive seclusion around himself or herself.[146] Such a person tries to avoid emotional commitment to any one person or ideal. The consequence may be an appearance of great control and the capacity to avoid immediate reactions, in some cases even a certain emotional deadness. But this rigid control is liable to be deceptive, since the individual lacks social support in coping with emotional stress. Hence under certain kinds of stress or severe emotional overload the result can be a damaging general collapse. In the end there is no prospect of escape from the bonds of human society.

Human Physiology and Privacy

For those with some intellectual agility there is no very perilous leap from the discussion of intimacy and emotional commitment to an analysis of the place of privacy in the "intimate" physiological functions of the human body. Are certain physiological functions intimate and private in other human societies the way they are supposed to be in modern middle-class Western circles? What are the reasons for the variations we are reasonably sure to find, and what is their larger meaning? We will now seek answers to these questions.

A few general observations will help to get our bearings. The intake of food and drink among members of the human species takes place by and large in the presence of other persons. It does not of course take place in the presence of just any other persons. Eating and drinking are central among the activities through which human beings draw social boundary lines to include some individuals and exclude others. When a rule of privacy does apply, it applies not to the absorption of nutrients but to secretions and excretions. The discussion here will be limited to defecation, urination, and copulation, omitting sweat, tears, and runny noses despite the fact that these are widespread and trying features of the human condition.

For defecation, urination, and sexual intercourse human beings tend to draw social boundary lines in a different way from that used for eating and drinking. The acceptance of another person as observer or participant in the major secretions and excretions is likely to imply a high degree of intimacy. (The habits of the army latrine, however, are enough to show that the connection is not universal.) Conversely, an expectation of privacy in this situation implies that all other persons should be excluded—not merely strangers, nonrelatives, or some other broad category. In this area of human behavior privacy tends toward solitude.

Defecation, urination, and copulation display two characteristics that bear upon an inclination toward privacy. They are biological urges in response to internal and external stimuli, which go through a specifiable series of physiological states to culminate in a strong sensation of relief or joy.† Since the interruption or blocking of the

†The analysis of instinctive behavior by the psychologist John Bowlby in *Attachment*, esp. 148–150, 153–157, is helpful here for the connection between instinct and processes of growth and maturation.

sequence of physiological states that culminate in relief or joy in these physiological acts is liable to cause considerable distress, there are biological grounds for positing a desire to be left undisturbed while performing them. The second characteristic, shared in different degrees by these three activities, is that they are capable of arousing disgust. This feature is more complex and quite puzzling.

Disgust is a broad but useful concept that for our purposes can include the ideas and practices associated with ritual purity and pollution but is not limited to them. In its more extreme forms disgust becomes nausea, a state that can be in a quite literal sense incapacitating, as anyone knows after a bout of severe seasickness or airsickness. Defecation and urination and the smells associated therewith are widely though not universally regarded as disgusting. To a lesser degree, the same is true of sexual intercourse; it can be messy and threatening as well as alluring. Disgust becomes an aspect of moral disapproval for all physiological acts carried out in the "wrong" place or the "wrong" way.

The origins of disgust are very hard to discern. Psychologists and other social scientists, so far as I have been able to discover, have not undertaken any sustained empirical inquiries into its causes. Small babies appear to lack the feeling altogether. As is well known, babies often play with feces, treating them in a neutral or somewhat pleasurable manner like any other nonthreatening object they encounter. Observant parents have told me that although babies can of course have strong negative reactions to food and vomit frequently enough, they recover from such bouts almost instantly and without indications recognizable as nausea, loathing, or disgust.

Evidently disgust is no simple instinctive reaction like sucking, breathing, or excretion. Instead it appears to be a learned response acquired mainly in connection with toilet training. From this standpoint, disgust would arise originally from the blocking or social control of excretions, particularly defecation and also sexual impulses. At later ages children in our society often react with disgust to foods that suggest feces or sexual activities. It is also clear that through the simple methods of conditioning it is possible to extend the reactions of disgust to a huge variety of objects and situations. Likewise as is evident from the behavior of parents, hospital orderlies, and others who have to clean up disgusting messes, human beings have the capacity to bring their feelings of disgust under control and get on with the day's work.

Disgust therefore appears to be in large measure an acquired distaste. Turning from a psychological to a sociological standpoint, we can easily perceive that behavior that is unavoidable but which society defines as disgusting has to take place in a way that will not offend others. Defecation is the one most subject to control. I know of no society in which adults are permitted to defecate in the living and cooking area. If there is such a society, it seems rather surprising that it has not attracted attention, indeed notoriety. But to my knowledge the data are not conclusive.†

If there is nothing inherently disagreeable or disgusting about human feces, it becomes very hard to explain the widespread prohibition against defecation in intimate living spaces. For that matter the prohibition is not a universal one. In 1665 the court of Charles II took refuge from the great plague of London in the Oxford colleges. After their departure their excrements were found in every corner, in chimneys, studies, coal houses, cellars. In the seventeenth century men and women lived in the constant sight and smell of human feces and human urine.[147]

An explanation in terms of enhanced prospects of survival due to the unintentional adoption of superior sanitary practices is hardly tenable. Enough obviously counterselective practices exist in many societies to make the concept of survival value very hard to apply to specific cultural traits. By way of positive explanation I can only offer a pair of outright guesses.

The simplest explanation might be the best. Even if the odor and texture of human feces are in no way inherently objectionable—how many people could discriminate blindfolded between healthy feces and some strong cheeses?—they are messy underfoot and around cooking pots. From this standpoint, teaching small children to defecate elsewhere does not differ from teaching them not to spatter mud, leaves, twigs or other odd objects into the evening meal, especially when the food supply is precarious. Among nonliterate peoples such teaching is often astonishingly patient and slow by our standards. But it does take place. Another consideration is the possibility that there may be something strange and potentially threatening in bodily needs that present themselves as imperious demands that result in substances coming out of the body. In defecation we are all temporarily immobilized and helpless. Some form of protective isolation might be a natural response to these circumstances.

There is of course considerable variation in the extent to which different societies have required or facilitated protective isolation for excretory functions. The main determinants of these practices are, I suggest, a socially created tendency toward concealment, a tendency

†John W. M. Whiting and Irvin L. Child, *Child Training and Personality*, 63, remark that in all societies the freely evacuating infant has to be changed into a responsible adult. Out of the total of 75 societies selected on the basis of having necessary information on various aspects of child-rearing the authors found it possible to give ratings on excretory behavior to only 22. Most of these treated children much more indulgently than in American middle-class circles. See pp. 48, 73.

that in any given individual begins as an obligation but becomes a desire, which has to match up at least roughly with the socially available space for privacy.

"Socially available space" is a useful shorthand expression for the way a social group treats its physical and social environment. For any group the socially available space is a function of technology, social attitudes and institutions, and the character of the environment itself. Socially available space is not the same as population density since societies with low population densities such as the Siriono, Jívaro, and Eskimo may be unable, for quite different reasons, to use the land area available to them. Modern American society is almost certainly unique in the extent to which it has created space for the privacy of physiological functions through bedrooms, bathrooms, and their associated equipment.

It is easy to see and to smell the limitations of social space among the nomadic Siriono, who live in a threatening physical setting, with a limited technology, rudimentary systems of cooperation, and weak impulse control. They have no latrines. Though adults usually go a respectable distance away from the home for defecation during the day, at night they stay near their dwellings due to the intense darkness, the annoyance of insects pests, and the fear of evil spirits or wild animals. Thus a Siriono hut usually has innumerable piles of excreta around it, freshly deposited each night. Only rarely are the excreta removed the next day. As a rule, they are left to attract flies, dry up, or be washed away by the rains. The immediate environs of the house may become in a few weeks' time unbearable to the unaccustomed.

For the Siriono themselves the situation is presumably tolerable but not particularly pleasant, because they do have some rules. One avoids defecating directly in the house, on the trails leading out from the house, and within about ten yards of a water hole. Further evidence that feces and even urine are equated with dirt, in the sense of "matter out of place"—though there is no sign of beliefs about pollution—comes from the habit of cleaning oneself by backing up to a sapling after defecation and the women's way of urinating, to spill as little as possible on their legs. A person who must defecate in the night, however, may not take the trouble to clean up before going back to the hammock.[148] As there was occasion to point out earlier, Siriono mothers try with limited success to prevent infants from playing with feces and very gently and gradually teach their young not to defecate in the house. About urination, on the other hand, they take little or no trouble.[149] If privacy seems too strong a term to apply to Siriono excretory behavior, there is nevertheless a clear tendency to isolate such behavior.

Skimpier data on Jívaro habits, mainly limited to toilet training, reflect a somewhat similar form of social space. When toddlers start to defecate or urinate in the house, they are just taken outside without scolding or punishment. "The mother simply digs up the soiled portion of the dirt floor and throws it out." Adults too may urinate on the floor at night to avoid exposure to possible attackers outside the house. Whether they also defecate on the floor at night is not reported. But the general rule is to do these things outside the house when it is not too dangerous.[150] Since the Jívaro, unlike the Siriono, who congregate in bands, live in widely scattered separate households, primitive fecal accumulation is presumably less malodorous. At least Harner does not mention it.

Among the Fulani, as we have already noticed, there is a sharp distinction between the domain of public and private life. The domain of public life, a strictly masculine domain, is one of idealized self-control in the presence of others. The private domain, which includes women, especially the mother, is an area where the expression of "natural" feelings is appropriate and expected. In public one must not express any discomfort, "whether it be a pain, physical or moral (such as grief), or a need (like hunger, thirst, or defecation), and one must not break wind."[151] This public rejection of emotion and physical necessity makes sense in what was once a warrior caste, dominating slaves who seem to have done all the physically necessary work. By consistently applying the principle of the stiff upper lip, a dominant stratum can both distinguish itself from the subordinate strata and impose a sense of its own superiority. The requirement of public self-control among the Fulani does not, on the other hand, apply to urination. Both men and women urinate in public. They merely go off a few yards and turn their backs.[152]

For a grown-up, it is extremely shameful to be seen defecating. This one does literally "in the bush," though the expression also has the meaning of "away from regular human society." A person who needs to defecate may say "my bush has come." A young toddler may defecate anywhere except in the house. Eventually a child is expected to go to the bush without adult assistance or supervision. Since in the dry season the bush does not begin for some two hundred to five hundred yards away from the dwellings, children cannot achieve this independence until the age of four or five.[153] Out of fear of loneliness, a strong sentiment among the Fulani, children and young people sometimes keep each other company as they go to the bush to defecate. But the act itself normally takes place in solitude, as the young hide from each other behind trees and bushes. To be discovered defecating is the source of great shame.[154]

The Fulani use the same word for discovering a person defecating as they do for coming upon a person eating—if he is one of those who should not eat in front of you[156]—or doing anything else regarded as shameful. I do not think this evidence from linguistic categories means that the Fulani have any more difficulty in distinguishing between a person eating and defecating than we do. But it does show that, except for urination, they have a strong sense of shame about meeting physiological needs, considerably stronger than ours. Though I have suggested a connection with warfare and slavery, the origin of the Fulani sense of shame is lost in the mists of unrecoverable history.

Fulani rules about privacy and bodily functions are especially interesting because they reveal the connections between social status, shame, and ideals of self-control, a connection that occurs in many cultures. Whatever their origins, the Fulani sense of shame and consequent desire for privacy are the exact opposite of treating defecation as an ordinary "natural" function requiring no special social definition or attitude.†

One authority claims that just such a naturalist attitude prevails among the Hopi. Mischa Titiev writes:

> There seems to be some correlation between the scatalogical habits of the Hopi and their attitude towards sex. They exhibit so much indifference towards bodily excretions of all sorts that there is an attendant carelessness regarding the organs involved. Toilet facilities are completely wanting and but little trouble is taken to conceal performances of the natural offices. Men and boys especially, urinate at will in the presence of the opposite sex, and women may often be observed in the act.[157]

Such an attitude is somewhat surprising for the crowded conditions and strongly socialized inhabitants of a theocratic garrison state. Titiev, it is worth noticing, says nothing specific about defecation.

A search of the literature on this much-studied society yields little more on this topic. But the fragmentary evidence is consistent with remarks made above about the role of social space. As soon as children are able to move about under their own power, they are taught to defecate outside the house. For a beginner this means just outside the door. Here too there is a rule against defecation in intimate living quarters. But with advancing age, stronger rules apply. Older children go to a corner of the plaza. Adults go outside the village. A child who fails to go out of doors at the proper time can expect a spanking.‡ If Wayne Dennis is correct in those observations the attitudes are not so

†For the Hare Indians, while living in the villages, according to Savishinsky, *Trail of the Hare,* 122–123, use of the family outhouse provided the only form of complete individual privacy. But all this sounds very much like a borrowing from white culture.

‡Wayne Dennis, *The Hopi Child,* 36. Despite the title, this is the only work I have found that reports adult behavior. Some additional details on toilet training for defecation may be found in Esther Goldfrank, "Socialization, Personality, and the Structure of Pueblo Society" in Douglas G. Haring, compiler, *Personal Character and Cultural Milieu: A Collection of Readings,* 251; Ernest and Pearl Beaglehole, "Hopi of the Second Mesa," 40; Titiev, *The Hopi Indians of Old Oraibi,* 65. The last-named work is a field diary, not to be confused with the monograph cited in the preceding note.

casual as Titiev's statement would lead one to believe. If not strictly private, a point on which I have found no evidence, defecation among well-trained Hopi is not supposed to be socially visible. In the end their attitude, if not their facilities, resembles ours.

In reviewing the evidence on this aspect of human physiological functions, clear indications appear of a desire to arrange matters so that excreta are deposited away from other people, at the very least away from the intimate living quarters. In this sense and for this reason defecation constitutes unacceptable public behavior. The forms of social concealment and how far away from others one should go depend in turn on the amount of social space available to a particular society.† Two motivating forces are apparent behind the search for privacy in this particular context. One is the adults' desire to keep messy and generally unpleasant substances away from the immediate living quarters so that they do not interfere with household routines such as cooking. The other is the individual's sense of temporary helplessness while defecating and, at a minimum, the wish not to be mocked. No human being can be dignified and impressive when engaged in this particular act.‡

Sex is much more interesting than evacuation. That is the case partly because sexual attraction brings into play a much wider span of emotions and behavior than those which occur in the act of copulation itself. Like the urge to evacuate, the sexual urge has to be brought under some degree of social control. But the need for the social regulation of the sexual urge is much easier to perceive because sexual activity can result in new members of society instead of waste products or, at best, fertilizer. To start off the discussion I shall take some observations from Bronislaw Malinowski's classic, *The Sexual Life of Savages,* that apply far beyond the Trobrianders.

The first point that Malinowski makes as he comes to focus on the personal details of erotic behavior can be translated into the suggestion that behind specific cultural idioms and emphasis there are powerful constant features in both erotic attractiveness and erotic repulsion or disgust. At one point he summarizes the essential conditions of per-

---

†If for some reason the space is not available, the act may be public but socially invisible, as reportedly occurs in parts of India. See Douglas, *Purity and Danger,* 124, citing V. S. Naipaul, *An Area of Darkness.* My interpretation differs from the more general one put forth by Douglas in *Natural Symbols* where the author classifies societies according to social structure and, she claims, certain corresponding attitudes toward organic behavior (see esp. pp. 16, 174, 195). Where she sees variety, I perceive a single tendency with various possibilities of fulfillment, depending on concrete circumstances.

‡At the court of Louis XIV attendance on the monarch's nightly visits to the *chaise percée* was the privilege of Gentlemen of the Bedchamber who could afford to pay some 15,000 *louis d'or.* But on these public occasions the monarch merely went through the motions and did his real business at another unspecified time. See W. H. Lewis, *The Splendid Century,* 47, 57.

sonal charm: "normal bodily build, health, absence of mental and functional disorders, strong growth of hair, sound teeth, and a smooth skin—all signs of vigour and of a good constitution."† Even if this list may not fully specify the erotic attributes necessary to obtain the title of Miss or Mister Universe, health, vigor, youth, and freedom from abnormalities are almost certainly the major components of erotic attraction across time and space.

Malinowski's discussion also leads to a second and more significant suggestion. Romantic intensification of erotic attraction—the idealization of a single person and only this person as the fulfillment of love—can occur only where there are strong obstacles to erotic satisfaction. Where several sexual partners are available and the failure to obtain the joys and services of one partner may be no more than a prelude to success with another, this form of intense passion will not occur.[158]

At this point I want to raise the question whether there may be some panhuman desire to cast a veil of privacy over the sexual act itself, to make it a union of two persons and *just* two persons, even when the union enjoys social approval. Or is such a notion no more than a projection of a culture-bound (and now perhaps antiquated) Western romantic idealism and "possessive individualism"?[159]

Since dwelling arrangements in a great many cultures render this form of seclusion impossible, at the most it can represent no more than a desire. Clearly human beings can dispense with privacy in the sexual act. By itself, that would be merely one more proof of human adaptability, not of human preferences. Fortunately some quite good evidence exists that does demonstrate quite clearly a widespread desire for seclusion during sexual intercourse. A doctor and an anthropologist examined twenty-five societies about which adequate information on such matters existed. The results could be divided into societies where people have intercourse indoors and those where people repair to the bush; and the indoors category divided further into those with private dwellings or partitioned rooms as opposed to unpartitioned houses with many families. This analysis gave the following results:

†Bronislaw Malinowski, *The Sexual Life of Savages in North-Western Melanesia,* 292; see also 308–309. Ugliness, physical deformity, age, and disease are a source of physical repulsion or disgust among the Trobrianders as with us. Nevertheless Malinowski discovered it is commonplace for persons with such afflictions to have sexual partners, especially if they or their spouses enjoy high rank; see 288–295. The Trobrianders' disgust at ugliness and deformity differs from the kind that arises from a more general rejection of sexuality as such. This general rejection has at times been a major theme in Western culture. Puritanism and Pauline Christianity in their attempts to block and control the sexual impulse can lead to the feeling that sexuality as such is sinful, threatening, and messy, a notion that Trobrianders and many others would find absurd. Thus the apparent uniformities behind sexual attraction do not preclude a wide range of culturally induced variation.

Preferred Location for Intercourse in 25 Societies as a Function of Type of Living Quarters

	Private family dwelling or partitioned rooms	*Unpartitioned multiple dwelling*
Outdoors	3	9
Indoors	12	1

SOURCE: Clellan S. Ford and Frank A. Beach, *Patterns of Sexual Behavior*, 70–71. Originally published in 1951.

Thus of the ten societies with unpartitioned multiple dwellings, nine displayed a preference for intercourse out of doors, where seclusion was presumably to be found. Of the fifteen whose dwelling arrangements afforded privacy, twelve preferred intercourse indoors. The preference for seclusion appears to be overwhelming.

In this connection the authors mention the case of the Kiwai in Oceania. Formerly when they lived in long unpartitioned houses, intercourse regularly took place in the bush. In modern times, as they took to living in small one-family dwellings, intercourse in the house started to become the regular pattern. A very similar transformation has been taking place among the Hare Indians. In 1971 a group of young adults converted their shared quarters into six multiroom dwellings because they wanted privacy, that is, their own rooms and their own places where they would not be bothered by their parents.[160]

This anthropological evidence, I submit, is enough to dispose of any thesis to the effect that a desire for privacy during the sexual act is no more than a projection of a historically provincial Western ideal. The ideal quite clearly transcends Western culture. To be sure, the building of private dwellings among the Hare Indians, and very likely similar arrangements among the Kiwai, reflect Western influences. Nevertheless, one has to take into account the obvious appeal of Western arrangements for personal privacy to these peoples.

In the light of this conclusion it will now be useful to look more closely at some of the ethnographic evidence in the hope of uncovering some clues about the nature of this desire for privacy. Among the Siriono the preference for privacy is obvious. Since in this society there is a wide choice for both sexes of socially approved sexual partners, up to eight or ten potential spouses in addition to one's real spouse,[161] during daylight hours there is abundant opportunity for sexual intercourse in a secluded location. A man ordinarily whispers his desires to a woman and the couple steals off into the forest. Between married couples sexual intercourse frequently takes place in the late afternoon in the bush near a water hole or stream by which the band has made its camp.

Much less intercourse takes place at night or within the hut, where privacy is almost unavailable, since as many as fifty hammocks may be hung in the space of five hundred square feet. Young children also commonly sleep in their parents' hammock, with the result that as many as four or five people may be crowded together in a single hammock. In addition to these obstacles, people are up and down most of the night, quieting children, cooking, eating, urinating, and defecating. Yet coitus does occur despite the fact that the hammock itself is hardly conducive to amorous dalliance:

> Sometimes during the height of the act a man's knees slip through the strings of the hammock and his whole emotional set is disturbed.
> Informants frequently made jokes about their fellows in this respect. I even know one man who injured himself rather seriously when his knee struck the ground.[162]

If passion can overcome serious obstacles among these people, there is also a preference for its release in more traditionally romantic circumstances. The same preference for romantic solitude appears among the Mbuti and the Trobrianders.[163]

The secrecy that surrounds even legitimate sexual intercourse among the Fulani comes from different sources (though these are found in many other societies). Women are special creatures, excluded from the men's councils and public affairs. During menstruation they are also unclean.[164] Sexual attraction suggests if not dirt or matter out of place, at least behavior that is out of place in public, where the true Fulani is expected to appear immune to physical needs and emotions. In the first stages of a marriage the man makes love to his wife in the bush, not the village. They do not even live together because the couple do not yet own a separate hut.[165]

When they do have a hut of their own, children sleep on their parents' bed up to the age of three or four. Up to that point the children supposedly do not understand what is going on. After that, a husband returning home late in the evening to find a heap of children sleeping all over his wife's hut will often chase them out with harsh words and even blows.[166] The sexual act itself carries overtones of impurity: if a couple has had "sexual relations during the night they must wash their sexual parts in order to be able to pray in a manner acceptable to God."[167]

Hopi dwelling arrangements render complete privacy impossible for sexual intercourse as well as for other domestic matters though, as we shall see, there is a clear desire for privacy and modesty. Sexual desire should be concealed, while modesty takes a very different form from that which recently prevailed in Western middle-class circles. Pueblo houses contained two to four rooms with no toilet facilities, at least before the coming of the whites and for a long time thereafter. Daughters bring their husbands into the house. After a few children are born, the houses are felt to be too crowded and the husband may come under pressure to build a house nearby for his family.† Since there is a religious taboo on intercourse in the fields, at a shrine, or at a spring,[168] it seems likely that legitimate intercourse nearly always takes place in the house.

Under these crowded conditions it is hardly surprising and perhaps quite "natural" that small children should witness the sexual activities of their parents. They sleep no more than a few feet from growing children and are reported to make little effort to conceal their marital activities.[169] Adults and older children casually play with the genitals of young male children. A young child who gives a public imitation of what he saw in the sleeping room creates no disturbance among his elders.[170] When one adds to such behavior the unconcealing nature of native Hopi garments and the freedom of certain aspects of their language, it would be easy to jump to the conclusion that among the Hopi "things of the body arouse none of the shame that they do in other cultures."[171] In other words, we seem to have found at long last in Hopi society a completely "natural" (or naturalistic?) matter-of-fact and "healthy" attitude toward sexuality, far removed from the crippling taboos and pathological concern with privacy that have so long plagued our own culture.

Nothing could be further from the facts of the matter than this version of Rousseau transposed to meet late twentieth-century concerns. As Titiev, in the best anthropological tradition of emphasizing concrete reporting over premature generalization, goes on to show, the Hopi do have restrictions on the open display of sexuality and, except for urination (as indicated earlier), a clear sense of modesty. In contrast to widespread Western customs, Hopi men who brag about their conquests or who gaze at women in public are very much despised. Young Hopi girls strike some Western observers as exceedingly coy. When a girl is called upon to don a short kilt in one of the religious ceremonies, she often exhibits "a painful sense of shame" at being exposed to male stares. Women who frankly enjoy watching the obscenities of clowns in their own village may refuse to witness their performance in another village "because they feel it is indecent." An excessive taste for sexual indulgence can arouse scorn.[172] To these observations we may add that there is no indication that anyone except very young children may witness marital intercourse. For the Hopi, as for others, the sexual act is no casual biological routine whose setting is a matter of indifference. There are fear and reluctance about exposure, basic ingredients of privacy, even if privacy—not to mention secrecy—is itself beyond reach.

†Alice Schlegel, "The Adolescent Socialization of the Hopi Girl," 451. Building a new house is probably a modern practice: there could hardly have been room when the pueblo was a garrison community. Lack of toilets is mentioned in Titiev, *Old Oraibi*, 205.

Before discussing the sources of this desire for privacy, it will be worthwhile to glance briefly at the types of occasion where copulation is a public act carried out with some degree of social approval.† Two elements appear to be present in such situations, either together or separately. One is that of a moral holiday from ordinary restraints, a holiday that justifies or encourages extra sexual activity as in a fertility rite or wedding ceremony. The other component is aggressive and sometimes punitive. Collective rape of a helpless female is one wide-spread example. In such cases the public may be confined to other male participants and the behavior may be subject to general disapproval. In other cases the aggression may have social sanction and the plural copulation takes the form of punishment of the female.‡ With some uncertainty about its actual existence, Malinowski reports the practice of sanctioned collective female sexual aggression combined with especially disgusting humiliation of the male victim.[173] Such evidence indicates that public sex can be especially exciting and that one of the sources of excitement may be the fusion with legitimate aggression. Therefore one reason for privacy may be to keep these explosive and socially dangerous impulses under control.

Another source of the preference for privacy is jealousy or, more precisely, sexual possessiveness. There was a time when a fair number of anthropologists believed that sexual possessiveness was no more than a culturally induced trait, a viewpoint that has from time to time prevailed in "advanced" Western circles. But, as Malinowski tartly observed, the ethnographers' evidence consisted of nothing more than the simple fact of license: the connection between license and the absence of jealousy is anything but self-evident.[174] No doubt feelings of jealousy can be repressed. In a good many societies situations occur where either men or women or both have to repress feelings of jealousy and on the surface manage to do so quite successfully. But the fact that human beings can control certain impulses does not mean they lack these impulses. The human psyche is no blank slate upon which social training can write any message. Even in older anthropological accounts, the reports of conflict due to jealousy are abundant. In more recent literature they are ubiquitous. It is safe, therefore, I believe, to regard it as a panhuman trait—which does not mean that we under-

---

†The first result of such a glance is the discovery of how little reliable information exists. A check of the index entry "Feasts with sexual license," in that curious treasure-house of ethnographic cases, Edward Westermarck's *The HIstory of Human Marriage,* failed to turn up any clear-cut examples observed at first hand. But see II, 436, where in one instance witnesses must attest to the male's potency.

‡Cf. Malinowski, *Sexual Life,* 258, where copulation takes place in the sight of persons with regard to whom the strictest taboos are ordinarily observed.

†Both forms are reported in considerable detail in Berndt, *Excess and Restraint,* 167–173. In this Papuan society there is a very noticeable fusion of sexual and aggressive impulses.

stand it. As part of our biological and precultural equipment, controllable within limits like the rest of this equipment, jealousy helps to account for the reluctance to permit the intrusion of prying eyes into the most intimate of human actions.

Indeed the interruption of coitus by any intrusion or distraction is liable to be distinctly unpleasant, to say the least. By itself this aspect may be enough to explain the preference for privacy, which after all is no more than a preference, widely unsatisfied in practice. Very likely there is a biological reason behind this dislike of interruption. But in the light of the widespread use of *coitus interruptus* as a deliberate method of preventing conception, the biological and psychological costs do not appear sufficiently high to provide a very powerful explanation.

Thus, even if we add the factor of an aesthetic preference for romantic solitude, a consideration that turns up often enough in the available evidence to warrant fuller discussion than is possible here, something seems missing from the explanation. So far it has taken the form of a search for the individual's preference for privacy, with society perceived mainly as an obstacle. Now this form of explanation is quite suitable to clandestine sexuality, something that presumably exists in some form in every society and as such presents no serious explanatory problems. But, if forbidden sexuality is secret and private, why is not legitimate sexuality public? Indeed, why is it not generally required to be public? (Public proofs of consummation of a marriage do exist in some parts of the world.) May there not be some social and collective interest in defining copulation as a private act?

To adapt one of the explanations of the incest taboo, the answer may be that sexual passion is inherently threatening to cooperative human relationships and must therefore be kept out of sight. This does not mean that human beings are potential sex maniacs whose passions require a continuous powerful curb. It does mean that erotic attractions can interfere with getting a job done and that human societies have to find ways to limit the flaunting of sexual attractiveness—to teach one another that there is a time and place for everything—hardly our most successful pedagogical effort. One of the ways to get this lesson across, and only one, is to make the sex act itself private. Even if this is not the best of all possible worlds, individual inclinations may from time to time coincide with social necessities.

The Need for Privacy and Some Alternatives

Is there such a thing as a need for privacy? If there is, it can hardly be a compelling one like the need for air, sleep, or nourishment. Every human activity, from working through praying or playing, has been carried out somewhere in the company of other human beings. Nevertheless human beings do not always want to do things that way. In seeking privacy, what precisely does a person want, and why does he or she want it? The answer seems reasonably plain. Such a person seeks at least temporary escape or surcease from contact and conversation with other human beings because their presence has become overly demanding, oppressive, or simply boring.† This seems to be something that can happen in any society or cultural milieu. The victim feels trapped in a particular social situation and is unwilling or unable to continue the human exchanges required by that situation. He or she wants to withdraw, at least temporarily.

The situation that triggers the response represents a disagreeable or threatening obligation. The obligation may be no more than to keep on talking, or it may be to share what one does not want to share or perform a task one would rather not perform. There is an important distinction between legitimate and illegitimate obligations. A person feels guilty about avoiding legitimate obligations, but righteous resentment or outright anger when facing illegitimate ones. Only where the social order defines an obligation as illegitimate do we find a right to privacy. But this situation can occur in a very simple society. Briggs reports that the Utku Eskimo resent any sign of bossiness. Among the Utku nobody has the right to tell other people what to do, and everybody has the right to reject an intrusion on his or her freedom of action. The feeling seems to be so strong that such intrusions hardly ever take place.

Generalized rights against authority develop much later. Their beginnings appear in the immunity of the free males in stratified societies to obligations and punishments imposed on the servile sector of the population. The concept of immunity is basic to all notions of rights against society. Medieval society in Europe was based on a complex system of immunities and obligations. That may be one reason for the greater stress on privacy in Western society than in China.

Behind the desire to escape from oppressive companionship or to evade a threatening obligation we can generally discern a resentment against intrusion and the threat of offensive exposure. A person trapped in disagreeable company must hide certain feelings and simulate at least a minimum of amiability. One feels exposed or threatened in unwelcome intimacy. The same is true about unpleasant obligations. They are intrusive demands upon time and energy we would rather put

---

†The fusion of sex and escape is explicit among some Brazilian Indians. Small clearings in the forest, known as "alligator places," serve both as areas allowing privacy in sexual intercourse, and as temporary refuges from fellow villagers when social pressures become intolerable. See Thomas Gregor, *Mehinaku*, 93.

to other uses. In short, the basic element in a violation of privacy is intrusion: the need for privacy is a need for protection against intrusion.

From these considerations it is evident that the need for privacy is a socially created need. Without society there would be no need for privacy. The need is a consequence of the fact that in order to survive, indeed to be or become human, men and women must live in society. For that purpose they are imperfectly endowed by their natural or physiological and psychological equipment. Inevitably life in human society imposes frustrations even if it is also on occasion a source of satisfaction and even great happiness. Since societies differ, the desire or need for privacy will vary historically, from one society to another and among different groups in the same society.

The notion of the well-integrated individual and harmonious life in nonliterate and premodern societies is a romantic myth, as is plain from the analysis of anthropological materials presented above.[175] Though some societies, such as the Mbuti, resemble this model, many others at the same level of technology such as the Siriono, the Jívaro, and even the Eskimo certainly do not. There are also grounds for skepticism about the thesis that all cultures possess mechanisms to enable people to achieve desired levels of privacy.† As we shall see later, human societies can vary the intensity of the need for privacy that they generate among their members.

By and large, privacy appears to be much less of a social necessity, as well as much less of a social possibility, in nonliterate societies than in those with a written language and some form of state.‡ To be sure, human beings can get on each other's nerves in nonliterate societies. Oddly enough, the Siriono seem to be among the most irritated and irritable about the ordinary mechanics of living together, while at the same time they display the least concern about the social threat from quarreling. Other very simple societies, such as the Eskimo or even the !Kung bushmen, seem to live in intermittent fear of explosive quarrels threatening the whole social order.[176]

The difference between the Siriono and the !Kung bushmen or Eskimo is traceable, I suspect, to the fact that among the Siriono, "society," in the form of the band, serves almost no purpose for the

---

†Irwin Altman, "Privacy Regulation: Culturally Universal or Culturally Specific?", 66–84; see esp. 70, 79. As is well known, many societies cope with crowded living quarters by creating arrangements through which the individual can signal a temporary withdrawal from the assembled company. Usually one does something like turning one's face to the wall. But not every society has managed to create such arrangements. For one that has not, see Gregor, *Mehinaku,* 219.

‡The existence of castes and classes cannot serve as a criterion for distinguishing nonliterate from civilized societies because they exist in many nonliterate societies. It is hardly necessary to add that civilized societies often display the most uncivilized behavior.

individual. Only at night does living in a common dwelling offer protection against wild animals. In the daytime, hunting is something the individual Siriono can do on his own or with the help of one or two friends. Cooperation and mutual protection is much more important in the other societies. Among the !Kung bushmen, the Eskimo, or the Mbuti it is hard to imagine any one person demanding rights *against* society, since the main problem is to preserve forms of cooperation that are a matter of life and death for everybody.

In a civilized society the situation is quite different. A civilized society has a capacity in "normal" times for repressing dissent and enforcing unity far more powerful than is the case in nonliterate societies.† It is only in civilized societies that the need for private rights against the social order can take on a clear form. That the need can exist without being satisfied goes without saying.

Hence the need for privacy or protection from intrusion is not explicable as an instinctive or reflex reaction. Instead it derives from the perceived difference between benefits derived from the social order, such as protection and an assured supply of food, and the costs of maintaining the social order in the form of social obligations like sharing food and performing labor. The nature of the balance between benefits and obligations varies from society to society and over time. In a stratified society it also varies according to social status. It is important to stress the perceived difference between social benefit and social cost because the criteria for assessing the difference can also vary. Within broad limits the criteria can vary independently of objective circumstances. Human beings can teach one another to value freedom and independence or to take pride in submission to authority for the sake of distant political and religious goals.

Societies with minimal privacy occur at both ends of human history as now known to us. Among the Siriono, for example, there is little or nothing to escape *from* in the way of social obligation. Hunger provides quite a sufficient drive to motivate the socially necessary labor of hunting. The dangerous and frightening situation is being left out of society (recall the case of the cripple who could not make his way back to camp at night)—not being subject to boring or painful social pressures. It is a safe inference that, on this score at least, the Siriono do resemble our earliest human ancestors.

The modern totalitarian state likewise minimizes the opportunities for privacy, but for the opposite set of reasons. In postrevolutionary totalitarian regimes the dictator supposedly represents the will of the mass of the population actively seeking to create a new civilization and

---

†Again an exception comes to mind with the case of terrorist rule among the Zulus under Shaka in the nineteenth century. Contact with the West, however, may have been a necessary ingredient in the establishment of Shaka's despotism.

a new humanity. In fact this mass seeks to protect itself as best it can against such remolding by secreting protective coatings and erecting walls around individual social cells in the place of work and at home. Modern dictators mortally fear privacy, not only because it permits the hatching of conspiracies, but also because it frustrates the main policies of social change to which the regime has made a commitment. A major difference between the Russian and Chinese variants of totalitarian control is that the Chinese have done far more than the Russians about penetrating and manipulating the informal social structure based on cliques and small groups.[177]

In order to understand the social meaning of privacy it will be helpful to attack the issue, so to speak, backward: that is, to ask when the violation of privacy is justified. More precisely, what situations justify intrusion into another person's social space? There are, I suggest, two. One appears in the need for protection. This occurs plainly enough in a large town or city when an adult suddenly grabs a child to prevent it from running out into the street in front of a car. More generally, the right of protective intrusion derives from the right *and* obligation of the stronger and more competent person to protect the weaker and less competent one. The right of supervision, especially supervision at work, showing a person how the job needs to be done and making sure that the task is carried out correctly, is similar but more continuous.

The rights of intrusion that derive from love and affection are more ambiguous. Friends and lovers often protest that they have no secrets from each other. In this case no right derives from superiority. *Both* are equal, and admission to each other's social space is by mutual consent. A close friend can enter one's presence in situations such as extreme grief or severe illness when a casual acquaintance would be unwelcome. Nevertheless the risk of unwelcome intrusion remains. Tact and judgment remain necessary. Without some degree of autonomy or the feeling of control over one's own behavior, affection can become a source of suffocation and resentment.

If protection and affection can under certain circumstances justify the invasion of privacy, we ought to turn the question around and ask what social interests, if any, privacy may serve. This question requires a much more historically specific answer than the preceding ones. Privacy of communications becomes possible only in a literate, complex society with strong liberal traditions—in other words, a quite modern society. For technological reasons this privacy is becoming increasingly precarious. In a liberal society privacy is essential for free and frank communication. The exchange of ideas and information requires the opportunity to express ideas about policies and persons at all levels in the society without fear that one's remarks will become public property or a source of embarrassment by falling into the wrong hands. With perfect judgment all around there would of course be no reason to fear unauthorized or undesired disclosure. Since perfect judgment is impossible, the need for confidential exchanges will remain. Society as a whole gains to the extent that information exchanged confidentially is more accurate and serviceable. (Though it is very hard to prove that it is more accurate, the probability is very high that such is the case.) Hence, any threat to the privacy of communications is a matter for serious social concern.

Modern societies have developed a social interest in privacy for another reason. The professions have come to play an indispensable role in modern life. Without the sciences and scholarship that support the professions, contemporary society would soon grind to a halt. Without the arts, it would also be a great deal more barren. Modern society demands intellectual talent to a degree that has no precedent in earlier times. As Goethe remarked when this demand had just begun to grow, the development of talent requires peace and quiet. Professional training requires time, money, and application, as well as opportunities for reflection. In a word, one needs privacy, both to acquire professional skills and to exercise them. Both socialist and capitalist societies are willing to devote considerable resources to this end so long as the skills serve the purposes of dominant elements in the society. Where the purposes are not obviously utilitarian, there is much greater reluctance to provide the resources and the privacy. Social utility is generally social utility for the dominant class.

In recent years there has been a reaction against the private aspects of professional training, particularly among politically "advanced" students in the West, because this privacy seems associated with an intellectually debilitating competitive atmosphere. To diminish this competition, students have experimented with various forms of cooperation in the process of learning. A highly competitive atmosphere can certainly be intellectually stultifying by inhibiting innovation and experiment. Hence these cooperative attempts display many constructive features and deserve encouragement from teachers. But in the end learning is a very private process. Somehow or other students have to put knowledge into their own heads. No one can do it for them. Therefore long hours of solitary labor, often quite tedious labor, are bound to remain an essential aspect of serious education. It is a social necessity.

In concluding I would like to raise the issue of whether or not there may be social mechanisms that can serve as alternatives to and functional substitutes for privacy.† It is a possibility that deserves

†This idea occurred to me after reading Margaret Mead, *Coming of Age in Samoa,* 43, 108, 124, 128, 161, where she discussed various forms of "entrapment" that are painful in our society, but allegedly do not exist in Samoa. After reading what I find to be the completely devastating criticism by Derek Freeman, *Margaret Mead and Samoa: The*

further investigation. Most but not all of the arrangements I have come upon are not so much substitutes for privacy as adjuncts to certain forms of privacy that for some reason are felt to be insufficient or burdensome.

One such type of arrangement could be called a system of multiple escape hatches or multiple caretakers. Among the Mbuti Pygmies, for example, a small child who is hurt can run to anybody in the camp who will pick up and comfort the child. In due course, we may suspect, the child will go back to his or her mother. But after the age of three or four, children sometimes change families.[178] Nevertheless, the more children can get help and comfort outside the domestic circle, the less chance there is of the household becoming an autonomous private unit closed to outsiders. In our own society the very high frequency of divorce is part of another system of multiple escape hatches. It is also a sign that the home as the major traditional locus of privacy is ceasing to be satisfactory—if, indeed, it ever was all that satisfactory. With children so often bearing the pain of the parents' separation, it is far from obvious that this particular transformation of private life has increased human happiness.

To return to nonliterate societies, we occasionally find arrangements that lighten the burden of intimacy discussed earlier in this chapter. Some of those for married couples among the Shavante appear to have the effect of greatly reducing the need for privacy, a need that would in any case be very hard to satisfy due to the material conditions of their life. Relationships between spouses are for the most part harmonious. One important factor reducing possible friction is the fact "that a man need not spend too much time in the company of his wife." From dawn to dusk he is likely to be away from the conjugal dwelling. This dwelling is nothing more than a partitioned-off section inside the household of the wife's kin. Ostensibly it serves to provide privacy for the couple. Actually the erection of a partition amounts to a public statement by the wife's kin that the marriage has been consummated. In fact, the Shavante seldom seek privacy. If on a rare occasion they do feel a need for privacy, they look for it outside the hut. Darkness or the cover provided by a sleeping mat will do.[179]

In this case one can perceive how certain social arrangements reduce the possibility of abrasive social contacts that in other societies drive individuals to seek solace in privacy or drink or both, and how the very desire for privacy may diminish when it is very hard to obtain.

Making and Unmaking of an Anthropological Myth (Cambridge, Mass., 1983), which appeared when this book was in press, the conclusion seemed inescapable that all evidence from this source was highly suspect. For that reason I have cut out a few passages and revised this one on alternatives to privacy. Yet it would be mean to omit all reference to her work by failing to acknowledge the source of an idea that might be fruitful.

Yet the fact that the partition is built "ostensibly" to provide privacy shows that among the Shavante at least the desire has not been completely extinguished.

Discretion in the sense of social rules against noticing or even discussing specific human actions may serve as both a substitute for privacy and a supplement to it, depending on the circumstances. Some forms of discretion are rules of social invisibility, customs that for a given reason assert that a person in plain sight is not really there. Among the Brazilian Indians called Mehinaku, to greet a man while pasing by his trash yard, the private part of the house as opposed to the front or public part, would be "a violation of an unspoken rule of 'civil inattention'—rather as if a boor in our own society were to lean through an open window to accost an acquaintance."[180]

Discretion is a highly developed virtue in this society, which depends heavily on informal mechanisms for the control of information to limit disruptive quarrels and assure cooperative economic activities. There is an elaborate code governing what one can say to whom and under what circumstances. Appropriate and inappropriate topics vary according to time and place as well as the age, sex, and kinship status of the person to whom one is talking. The most important general restrictions on free discussion concern sex and witchcraft, both of which are potentially explosive. Though sex is a much more open topic than witchcraft, there is a strong prohibition on speaking to a cuckold about his spouse's unfaithfulness. According to the Mehinaku code of politeness and discretion, "a Mehinaku does not reveal socially damaging information about himself, neither does he expose such information about others."[181]

Even in the case of theft, which is quite widespread, the victim who knows the identity of the thief must remain discreet about the situation. To confront the thief publicly will merely make the thief lie and produce a quarrel. Then the victim will have gained nothing but a reputation for being angry and sullen, a disagreeable and even potentially dangerous situation in this small community. In fact, no matter what strategy the victim follows, he is unlikely to get his property back.[182] Thus in this society it seems that even the thief gains the benefit of social invisibility. But perhaps that is not so far from our own situation.

Mehinaku society displays an unusually well-developed code of discretion. Gregor sums it up in observing that "personally intrusive questions are considered to be in bad taste and unless one has a good reason it is improper to inquire into a person's whereabouts, his plans for the next day, or his personal property."[183] Since most societies, and perhaps all, have some rules against intrusive inquiry, it is tempting to suggest that the greater the social control over human curiosity, the less will be the felt need for the forms of privacy familiar to us: walls, houses, individual rights, and untapped telephones. In this sense the control of curiosity would cease to be an adjunct to privacy but would be a substitute for it. If nobody wants to know secrets, there is little sense in going to the trouble of keeping secrets. That of course would be an extreme case and an unlikely one, utopian or antiutopian, depending on one's preferences.

We may set aside the presently unanswerable question of whether or not it might be possible to control human curiosity to that degree in order to point out other limitations on the possibility and desirability of such control. Certain forms of curiosity are socially necessary, especially in dangerous environments. In sharp contrast to the Mehinaku reticence about a person's plans and movements, Alpine guides, when they meet, nearly always chat about each other's plans and the whereabouts of other individuals. To a lesser extent small-boat sailors in casual conversation will ask one another where they are headed. Such information can save lives and often has.

The role of socially controlled curiosity or discretion under a tyrannical government—and nearly all governments have some tyrannical tendencies—is perhaps more interesting because it's more complex. The more extreme tyrannies, ancient and modern, display a tendency to create a monopoly of secrecy and of information about the whereabouts of individual members of the population, especially high-placed ones. To the extent that individuals become discreet about revealing information about themselves, their friends, and their associates, they hinder the collection of information by the government, whether it is done through informers or open officials. In practice discretion often turns into straightforward falsification of economic and other facts needed by the regime. On the other hand, the same tendency to lie low and keep quiet limits the possibility of organized opposition to the existing order, be it democratic or dictatorial. These considerations indicate that there are very clear limits to both the feasibility and the desirability of controlling human curiosity. Curiosity seems safe enough for the long haul even if privacy does not.

There remains a more inclusive alternative to privacy that prevails very widely in nonliterate societies: direct participation in decisions affecting daily life. Among bands of hunter-gatherers, where and whether the band will hunt on a particular day, when and to what place the camp will be moved, are matters decided by all adult males, with considerable informal participation by females. Especially in societies lacking the formal institution of chieftainship, as is often the case with hunter-gatherers, every adult member of the band has an "input" into such decisions, ranked according to the individual's prestige in the band. From the standpoint of the individual it is obviously better to be able to influence a group decision in the direction one wants than to have some kind of protection as a defeated minority. To be sure, the fission and fusion so common among hunting bands often provide exactly this kind of protection by offering legitimate choices for all parties.

Yet even in very simple societies there can be decisions where some are winners and some are losers. It is impossible for everybody to go hunting and stay in camp on the same day or to have war and peace at the same time. A split decision may fragment scarce human resources. With increasing size and complexity, direct participation in vital decisions becomes less and less feasible. The locus of decision-making tends to become more distinct and to move up the social and political hierarchy. As these transformations take place, the prospect of arbitrary decisions and the need to protect the interests of defeated minorities become more apparent. Since in the nature of the case it is often impossible to satisfy both parties to a dispute, human society at a certain stage of complexity arrives at its normal state of chronic low-grade conflict.

PUBLIC AND PRIVATE IN CLASSICAL ATHENS

CHAPTER 2

The Terms
Public and Private

Even in simple hunting and gathering bands, the distinction between public and private affairs is visible. In tribal societies, especially those with chiefs, it is considerably clearer. Yet it remains hazy, due to the rudimentary development of political and religious institutions with an impact on the lives of all the people. As pointed out in the preceding chapter, it is frequently necessary to turn to the child's experience of social life to gain a sense for the impact of outside forces, a public realm, affecting the life of the individual. In turning to classical Athens, we enter a different world where the distinction between public and private had for long been part of the language and was quite taken for granted.

Most of the analysis that follows will treat Athens from the end of the Peloponnesian War (404 B.C.) to its defeat by Philip of Macedon in the battle of Chaeronea (338 B.C.). The reason for choosing the Athens of Plato, Aristotle, and Demosthenes over the Athens of Pericles and the great tragic dramatists is very simple. For fifth-century Athens the materials for a study of privacy are relatively sparse and require greater interpretive ingenuity. A detailed description of the workings of Athenian society at the apogee of Athenian political and cultural attainments would certainly be welcome if it were possible. But there is no reason to reject the age of the philosophers and orators as somehow culturally and politically second-rate.

To be sure, the Peloponnesian War marked the end of an epoch in much the same way that the two World Wars of the twentieth century marked the end of the epoch of liberal parliamentary democracy as it had flourished in nineteenth-century England. Nevertheless Athenian democracy managed to survive and surmount a bloody white terror under the auspices of the Spartan victors, the rule of the Thirty Tyrants (404 B.C.). With the restoration of democratic institutions Athens managed to regain much of its naval and commercial eminence. Hence a great deal of the social landscape of fourth-century Athens resembled that of Periclean Athens. The resemblance may have been closer than that between the England of Attlee and Churchill and the England of Gladstone and Disraeli. In any case there is no doubt that fourth-century Athens was very much a functioning democracy; in fact, one where ordinary citizens had more power than under Pericles. As the first democracy with a written language—indeed, in every sense the first literate and civilized democracy—it has a sufficient claim on our attention.

We have no adequate record of the Greek language before Homer, when it bursts upon our attention as the instrument of one of the world's greatest literary masterpieces. From Homer onward, the language drew a distinction between public and private. Though it occurs only twice in Homer, according to the unabridged edition of Liddell and Scott's *Greek-English Lexicon,* the contrast is perfectly plain. The word for private is *idios,* meaning "one's own, pertaining to one's self," hence private or personal. Telemachus, bashfully asking Nestor for news of his father, says that his business is a private, not a public matter (*Odyssey* 3.82). The word for public here is *demios,* which means literally "having to do with the people." Later, Menelaus asks Telemachus if his quest is a public or a private one: *demion e idion* (*Odyssey* 4.314).

The noun form of *idios* is *idiotes,* from which comes the English word "idiot." Its main meaning is a private person or individual, or one in a private station as opposed to one holding public office or taking an active part in public affairs. It can also mean a layman or person lacking professional knowledge and, by extension, an ignoramus or raw hand. The old soldier and gentleman farmer Xenophon uses the adverbial form (*idiotikos to soma ekheis*) to tell a man that he looks in bad shape, as though he needed exercise—that is, that he was ignorant of athletic training.[1] Thus privacy in Greek carries negative overtones, implying lack of full participation in the approved social order.

To aristocratically minded Greeks the word for public, with its overtones of "common people from the countryside," also carried negative implications. Right through the age of Pericles the central issue of Greek politics was how to keep the common people out of politics. By the fourth century, however, and especially after the Macedonian defeat, the issue had been decided in favor of the common man.

There is another widely used word for public, *koinos,* which means "common," in the sense of shared in common, as opposed to private.† The neuter plural of *koinos* can indicate "what is shared by or among friends" but it can also mean "public affairs." Still another meaning of *koinos,* found in Thucydides, is "lending a ready ear, impartial, or neutral."[2] In this usage it comes closest to the idealized conception of a responsible public in modern English.

In English we often use the word "public" in a different sense when we say to a child, "Don't pick your nose in public!" Here it is part of a distinction between public and private that is used to classify forms of behavior appropriate to each of these spheres. The Greeks had a similar distinction. Though we cannot know in full detail just what sorts of behavior fell into each category according to Greek usage, which probably varied according to social class as it does with us, we know that in some important ways it was similar to our own. Thus, as discussed in more detail later on, copulation was ordinarily not something done in public. Aristophanes uses still another expression showing a distinction between private and public when he admonishes against using buffooning language "at the wrong time."[3] The distinction, we can assume then, was taken for granted by the fourth century if not earlier.[4]

The absence of a specific Greek term for "in public" does not, so far as I can tell, reflect in any way a lesser awareness of public pressure on behalf of proprieties, which as we shall see was quite strong in fourth-century Athens. The main differences between English and Greek usage that are apparent are (1) a certain bias in the Greek against what is private; (2) a greater stress on the element of sharing in what is public, combined, however, with (3) a negative identification of "public" with "common" in the sense of "vulgar and inferior."

Membership in the Polis

Given these distinctions between public and private realms of behavior, the first questions to which we need answers are these: who belonged to the public, that is, the polis? How did one become a member? What degrees of membership existed? Only with answers to these questions will it become possible to discuss those raised in the next two sections: What were the individual's obligations to the polis, and what, if any, were the obligations of the polis to its members?

---

†In the *Iliad,* according to the unabridged Liddell and Scott, *A Greek-English Lexicon* (1977), the word for "shared in common, general, public" was not *koinos* but *xunos.* In the three passages cited, *xunos* seems to me to carry a more abstract sense than the more specific and varied meanings we find by the fourth century in the term *koinos.* Did the sense of shared identity, always crosscut by other sentiments, develop a richer content as the city-state took shape and the struggles for democracy came to the fore?

What, in other words, was the public expected to do for the private individual?

The only full members of the polis were adult male citizens. As soldiers they were, from at least one point of view, enough by themselves to constitute a polis. A striking passage in Thucydides puts into the mouth of Nicias, the Athenian general desperately trying to encourage his troops just before the final collapse in Sicily, these words:

> . . . You should when you look upon yourselves and see what fine
> hoplites you are and what a multitude when marching in battle array
> not be too greatly dismayed; nay remember that wherever you establish
> yourselves you are at once a polis. . . . for it is men that make a polis,
> not walls or ships devoid of men.[5]

Nicias' speech is of course a rhetorical exaggeration uttered in a moment of crisis. For an Athenian, at any rate, there was more to a city than its soldiers. Yet they were its indispensable core and the only full-fledged members. Women were citizens too. But they could not attend the Assembly, where all political issues were discussed.

As we shall see in due course, women's lives were closely restricted to the household although an occasional individual, such as Aspasia, the mistress of Pericles, probably had more real political power than a substantial number of males working in concert. Other women may have influenced their husbands' political opinions, though, according to cultural norms expressed by both Pericles and, at much greater length, by Xenophon, they were not supposed to attempt this.

For both men and women, citizenship was based strictly on descent from citizens on both the paternal and the maternal sides.[6] If both parents were citizens, the *deme* (township) could confer citizenship on a child at the age of eighteen by registering its name on the rolls of the *deme*.[7] On occasion the Assembly granted citizenship to a foreigner for distinguished services to the polis. In some cases the grant was revoked when the recipient proved unworthy.[8] A minor orator, Andocides, goes so far as to claim that Athens frequently granted citizenship and generous gifts of money to slaves and foreigners from every part of the world if they had performed some service for the city.[9]

In addition to the body of citizens the population of Attica included free aliens or metics, mainly immigrants who had settled permanently, and slaves. The metics were voluntary immigrants who could leave when they wished except in time of war—which was most of the time. They enjoyed full civil as opposed to political rights except that they could not own land. Hence they were to be found mainly in commerce and artisans' workshops. They were subject to military and naval service and to taxation at a slightly higher scale.[10]

Among slaves there was a wide range of social statuses with

varying degrees of acceptance and incorporation into the larger society. At the bottom were those who toiled in the silver mines, quite literally out of sight of the rest of the Attic world. Farm laborers were somewhat better off, especially those who were in a status analogous to servants, working alongside their masters on relatively small plots. Slave craftsmen may have enjoyed an even more enviable position. Then there was a small scattering of overseers and even an occasional manager of a bank.[11]

There are no dependable figures for the size of the Athenian population. Though estimates of a sort can be patched together for citizens, metics, and slaves, the estimates become increasingly unreliable as one works down the social pyramid. Demosthenes casually mentions that there were about 20,000 citizens in all.[12] Since Demosthenes was greatly interested in Athenian resources in manpower and wealth, his figure is probably not too wide of the mark. The number of male metics between the ages of eighteen and fifty-nine has been estimated to be in the neighborhood of 12,000 for the period under discussion, with a total of 42,000 for the year 323 B.C.[13] The estimates for the slave population range all the way from 20,000 to 100,000.[14]

Thus the number of citizens came to something like that of a large American university community today. It was a community far too big for everyone to know everybody. Yet Athens was not so large that anyone with a fairly high social position would be unlikely to know most of those similarly placed. Nor does it seem likely that a citizen would feel qualms about making the acquaintance of another citizen if the situation called for it. To sum up, Athenian politics were small-town politics over pan-human issues. For the first time in human history the issues of justice, power, and freedom were the subjects of public argument by very articulate men influenced by a powerful current of secular rationalism.

Even the subordinate strata participated to some extent in public debate and contributed to the climate of public opinion. Demosthenes asserted that in Athens even metics and slaves were freer to speak their minds than were citizens in other city-states, though they were banned from the deliberations of the Assembly.[15]

On the other hand, full membership in the political community did require citizenship. One of the minor orators in an impeachment for treason defines in passing the meaning of citizenship in daily life: access to the cults and sacrifices, to the market, to the laws, and to the constitution (Lycurgus *Against Leocrates* 142). To be deprived of these privileges was obviously a severe blow, at least for many a city dweller. But farmers who lived some distance away were unable to take full advantage of these opportunities. Aristotle tells us that in his day participation in political affairs was at a maximum among the less well-to-do urban population, when pay for attendance at the Assembly had risen to three obols a day (*Athenian Constitution* 41.3), perhaps just enough to live on. Furthermore, he claims, the multitude had a great deal of leisure to attend the Assembly and to act as judges in lawsuits because they were not hampered by care for their private affairs. The rich, on the other hand, had such cares to a degree that they often took no part in the Assembly and in judging suits (*Politics* 4.5). Despite Aristotle's obvious disapproval of this situation, I see no reason to dispute his factual claim.

Obligations to the Polis

Just as membership in the polis varied according to social status, so did the public obligations of individual members. For free male members the primary obligations were military, and military needs formed the basis of economic obligations. The original form of these military duties was attributed to Solon's division of the free male population into a set of military classes based on the economic contributions of a farming community. Aristotle describes the four propertied classes as follows:

1. *pentakosiomedimnoi:* based on a minimum yearly return of 500 measures dry or liquid;
2. *hippeis:* a minimum of 300 measures, also reportedly restricted to those with enough property to maintain a horse;
3. *zeugitai:* a minimum of 200 measures, wet and dry combined (other sources indicate this to have been the main category of heavy-armed foot soldiers, hoplites);
4. *thetes:* the remainder of the population.[16]

Solon flourished in the early sixth century B.C. before Athens had become a naval and commercial power. But even in the fourth century much of the original classification remained in effect, though adapted to the new circumstances. In the navy, *thetes* served as oarsmen while wealthy individuals undertook to provide the ships. In the army the *zeugitai* continued to provide the hoplites, while the cavalry came from well-to-do sectors of the population. Metics served in the army in separate divisions and also as oarsmen in the fleet. In addition they probably contributed proportionately more than did citizens to the *eisphora,* "an extraordinary property tax," not unlike a capital levy in wartime.[17]

The importance and universality of military obligations were impressed on young males, beginning with their registration on the records of the demes at the age of eighteen. Since these arrangements reveal much about the intersection of public and private concerns, they deserve detailed description here. Every boy of eighteen, of *zeugitai* census or over, was entered in the hoplite ranks of the army. A list of *thetes* liable for service in the fleet was also kept.[18] After a possible challenge to registration and therefore to citizenship and verification of the lists, the fathers of the cadets took part in the selection and election of a set of disciplinary officers and athletic trainers to supervise drill and the use of weapons. Each disciplinary officer received pay from his own tribe, supplemented by a smaller amount granted to individual cadets for the purchase of rations. Cadets messed together by tribes, a way of breaking their connection with the home and thereby with private life. This stage lasted for one year.

The next year an assembly of the cadets took place in the theater. After giving a display of drill before the people they received a shield and a spear from the polis. Then they served on patrols in the country and were quartered in guard posts. This service lasted for two years, during which they were also sealed off from the demands of private life. In order that cadets might have no pretext for absenting themselves from their required service they were given exemption from all taxes and could not sue or be sued in the law courts. (Exceptions were granted if an issue came up about the inheritance of an estate, the marriage of an heiress, and the inheritance of a priesthood.) When the two years were up, the cadets became part of the citizen body.†

Well-to-do adult citizens and metics were subject to a series of special obligations known as liturgies. A liturgy was the compulsory carrying out of a public function by a private citizen, and involved considerable expense even though the polis supplied some of the necessary funds or equipment. The most important one was the trierarchy, whereby citizens provided triremes, and all food and pay for the crew. From the early fifth century onward the *strategoi,* or elected generals, chose from among wealthy citizens a number of trierarchs corresponding to the number of triremes to be manned.

After 411 B.C., two citizens, as a rule, shared each trierarchy. Subsequent reforms in 357 B.C. and 340 B.C. attempted to spread the burden more equitably.[19] But there is considerable evidence for the fourth century showing widespread evasion and abuse. The fundamental difficulties appear to have been an inability to collect sufficient public resources, along with an unwillingness to make the naval command a clear-cut public function. Hence public and private interests clashed to the detriment of both, a transitional situation character-

---

†Aristotle *Athenian Constitution* 42. This detailed description contradicts the remark in Xenophon *Memorabilia* 3.12.5, that "the polis takes no public care of military training," and that therefore the individual "must not make that an excuse for being a whit less careful in attending to it" himself. Perhaps the reconciliation lies in the absence of further special training for those past the age of cadets. Active service, in other words, was expected to be enough.

istic of this stage of political evolution. In due course we shall examine a very similar situation produced by the absence of a public prosecutor for certain kinds of cases and lack of an effective police force, with the consequence that private individuals had to cope with many aspects of criminal behavior.

Several forms of evasion of the trierarchy turn up in the orations of Demosthenes, although to a modern reader the techniques are at times obscure. By 350 B.C., when Demosthenes was beginning his career, the prevailing arrangement had become one of choosing twelve hundred citizens as joint contributors to a trierarchy. From these twelve hundred a shady character could exact a talent (unit of money) and then contract for the equipment of the trireme at the same price. If the polis then, according to established practice, provided the crews and the gear—which, as we shall see, frequently failed to take place— the shady contractor could get by with spending nothing and, by pretending to have performed one liturgy, enjoy exemption from the others.[20]

In another case Demosthenes accuses a man of being so rich that he gave his daughter a marriage portion of one hundred minae but never had performed any liturgy whatever. According to Demosthenes, he had managed this feat through secret banking profits, a feat perhaps no more difficult then than now. Simple concealment of wealth was evidently another way of evading a liturgy.† In still another case Demosthenes asserts that while those engaged in mining have been suffering reverses, owners of landed estates have been prospering more than they should. He goes on to accuse the owner of two such estates of avoiding the obligation of the wealthy to render service to the state and to fellow citizens by unspecified techniques of secrecy and evasion.[21]

The wealthy and public-spirited man who did accept a trierarchy might, on the other hand, soon find himself in a position where he had to pay out of his own resources not only for a crew to work the ship, but also for arms and for light infantry as well.[22] In general it appears that the polis left the duty of levying troops and raising money to pay for them at this time up to the naval commanders since money in the treasury was inadequate. The naval commander had to cruise about exacting funds and might have to hire himself out to a foreign power.[23] Sometimes the trierarch used his position for private gain by plunder

---

†Demosthenes *Against Stephanus I* 1.66. Some conception of what these amounts of money mean may be derived from the fact that the considerable fortune which Demosthenes lost through his guardians' mismanagement came to fourteen talents. One talent was worth sixty minae, and one mina, one hundred drachmae. One drachma in turn was worth six obols or roughly twice the subsistence pay given for attendance at the Assembly. See the Loeb edition of Demosthenes, Vol. I, Introduction, p. xi for Demosthenes' fortune and Vol. V, p. viii, for Table of Athenian Money.

and pillage. In the end Athenian citizens might have to pay for such damage.†

In at least one instance the trierarchy went to the man who promised delivery at the lowest cost, presumably lowest to both the polis and his own pocket. After defeat in another case, the Athenians decided to imprison the trierarchs for having betrayed their ships and deserted their posts. In commenting on these and other cases, Demosthenes asks why ordinary sailors who receive only thirty drachmae apiece should be imprisoned for deserting their ships when the trierarchs who do not even sail with their ships make thirty minae for so doing. "Where then is equality and democratic governance?" he concludes with characteristic rhetorical flourish.[24]

In the fifth century there was a powerful spirit of rivalry and display in the performance of a public duty such as a trierarchy.‡ This spirit had by no means died out completely in the fourth century. A man still could take pride in furnishing a ship entirely with his own equipment, taking nothing from public stores, making everything as beautiful and magnificent as possible, outdoing all other trierarchs.[25] But such presumably laudable behavior could cause still a different kind of demoralization by spoiling the crews. The man who did this was asked by the next one due to take over the ship and its equipment:

> Have you so far surpassed others in wealth as to be the only one of the trierarchs to have equipment of your own and gilded ornaments? Who could endure your madness and extravagance, a crew corrupted and accustomed to receive large sums in advance and to enjoy exemptions from services normally required on board a ship and able also to make use of baths, and marines and rowers rendered luxurious by high wages paid in full? Bad ways are these you have taught the army. It is partly your fault that the troops of the other trierarchs have become more unruly . . . .[26]

In assessing all of the evidence on the trierarchy, it is important to remember that extreme cases are the ones likely to be preserved in the records available to us and that Athens was struggling to recreate a naval and commercial empire after two crushing defeats and the destruction of her navy at Spartan hands. Yet extreme cases do reveal innate difficulties. The real puzzle seems to be that there existed such a public institution as a navy at all during this time, not that it faced severe operational problems.[27]

There were corresponding internal difficulties in the organization and supply of Athenian land troops, as appears from the widespread

†Demosthenes *On the Trierarchic Crown* 13–15. In this connection it is worth noticing that land troops engaged in private plunder on a campaign, apparently in order to replenish supplies. See Xenophon *Hellenica,* 1.2.5.

‡Thucydides presents a vivid picture of the enormous fleet and manpower garnered by such competition as the Athenians set sail from Corcyra for Sicily, *History,* 6.31.1–3.

use of mercenaries. Nevertheless the stated ideal of public obligations for the well-to-do male remained liturgies for the older men and military service for the younger ones.[28] The practice of using mercenaries was probably due in the main to the disorganization created by the Peloponnesian War, whose end may well have left behind it numerous unemployed soldiers for whom plunder was the main means of subsistence.[29] Athenian commercial development also created a preference for comforts and profit over armed combat.

Even if we discount heavily for rhetorical exaggeration, the frequent complaints of Demosthenes to the effect that the Athenians were unwilling to make the sacrifices necessary for the anti-Macedonian policy he advocated so strenuously, there is enough evidence to reveal widespread reluctance to fulfill military obligations. In the light of what we know about mercenaries on land and the workings of the trierarchy, we can accept the generalization that during the fourth century, if not earlier, private concerns had begun to erode the public edifice.

The other major liturgical obligation in addition to the trierarchy was the *choregia,* the production of a chorus at musical and dramatic festivals.[30] According to Aristotle, the king archon at the beginning of his term appointed three chorus leaders for the tragedies, the wealthiest men among all Athenians.[31]

When Demosthenes was *choregus* at the Great Dionysia in the year 351–350 B.C., a rich bully by the name of Meidias struck him in the face with clenched fist as he was sitting in state in the orchestra, awaiting the chorus' entry. Demosthenes attempted to treat the attack not as an ordinary case of assault but as an attack on someone holding an official position, and hence a public sacrilege profaning the festival.[32] According to Demosthenes, Meidias by his behavior inflicted wrongs not only on Demosthenes but also on the chorus of his tribe, the tenth part of the citizens, and the god himself to whose service Demosthenes had been dedicated. Citing a series of similar cases from the recent past, Demosthenes went so far as to claim that Meidias deserved the death penalty.[33] At least that is the way Demosthenes claimed to view the episode in the text of the speech attacking Meidias. We also know, however, that Demosthenes settled the case out of court for 30 minae.†

Demosthenes' behavior makes it necessary to discount his claims about the strength of the sentiments violated by aggressive behavior during the festival. Yet there is no reason to doubt that the *choregia* was a distinguished and burdensome honor. It is equally plain that the festival constituted an affirmation of the sharing of all Athenians in a sacred experience. For its duration, the ordinary quarrels about prop-

---

†See Introduction to *Against Meidias* in Loeb Classical Library edition, 4 citing Aeschines 3.52 and Plutarch 12. How the text, which was never delivered, came to be published is unknown.

erty and other matters of daily life had to be suspended. It was against the law while the Dionysian festival was in progress to distrain or seize the property of any debtor.[34] Demosthenes may have exaggerated this Durkheimian affirmation of community, but he could not have invented it. The sacred elements of shared belief and shared experience—which it was hoped would produce concord (*omonoia*) and security, though that never happened—were an integral part of the Athenian conception of the public.

An Athenian upon whom fell the obligation of a liturgy had the right to refuse it by requesting, at an officially fixed date, that another citizen either perform it in his stead or agree to an exchange of properties (*antidosis*). If the other citizen rejected the offer, a court decided which one should perform the liturgy. Three days after one citizen had formally laid claim to another's possessions, both men had to divulge under oath the extent of their entire estates (except for shares in the silver mines of Laurium, which were free from liturgy obligations). Such a procedure would seem to constitute a distinct invasion of privacy. (In modern times declaring the entire extent of one's worth has become common practice for presidential candidates and others aiming at high public offices in the United States and elsewhere.)[35]

In the absence of state support for a large portion of military obligations and for such a major festival as the Dionysian, we are led to ask what could have been the sources of public funds in Athens and for what purposes they were spent. By answering these questions we shall see much more clearly the differences between our modern conception of public institutions and those prevailing in classical Athens.

During the fifth and fourth centuries B.C., regularly recurring direct taxes on Athenian citizens themselves or on their property were practically unknown. Evidently taxing the body, labor, and land of a citizen was taken to be incompatible with the status of being free.[36] Furthermore in the earlier period there was scarcely any necessity for direct taxation. Prior to Pericles (495–429 B.C.) the chief item of the military budget, the pay of the soldiers, did not exist. Instead, the liturgies, the tribute of the allies, and generous gifts from the citizens sufficed to cover the expenses of the military expeditions, which were, moreover, of shorter duration in those times.[37]

Customs dues were a major source of what income existed under Pericles and later. The total, however, cannot be calculated. Smaller amounts were obtained by miscellaneous levies, such as a tax on harlotry; court fees—which were often large and amounted to confiscation for political purposes—and the purchase of various rights by metics.[38] Finally, the Athenian state obtained substantial revenues from the silver mines of Laurium. The mines were considered the property of the state which were rented out to private citizens by the *poletai* or "sellers." In Aristotle's time there were ten of these appointed annually by lot from the ten tribal divisions of the city. In the presence of the Council they held auctions for the sale or rental of these rights, as well as for the sale of noncitizens who had been enslaved as a legal penalty, and for the use of other state properties.[39] Taken together, these arrangements reveal the rudimentary state of public institutions at this stage of historical development.

In terms of its overall political consequences the tribute from the allies was the most important source of public revenue. Athens had obtained the right to collect this tribute from its position of leadership in the Delian League, organized for the wars against Persia. Until the death of Pericles the amounts levied were moderate. This moderation helps to explain why the allies did not object to Athens using a tax for national defense for her own adornment and glorification, and consented to subjecting themselves to the oppressive jurisdiction of Athenian law courts and giving up their right to coin money. But with the death of Pericles, power fell into the hands of more aggressive popular leaders such as Cleon. Both domestic and foreign policy changed. The Athenians more than doubled the tribute and increased the sums of money distributed in various ways to Athenian citizens.

After the disaster in Sicily (413 B.C.), they substituted for the tribute a five percent tax on exports and imports. When Athenian hegemony was partially restored after the Peloponnesian War, the tribute was for a time called "contributions." Within two decades, war broke out between Athens and her allies, which, according to one modern authority, ruined the finances of Athens and devastated the islands, though it also ended the autonomy of those who revolted. The tribute, which had reached about a thousand talents during the Peloponnesian War,[40] was by then very much less, though the exact amount is unknown.[41] In general, the tribute was used to support the Athenian populace.[42]

Hence it appears that Athenian democracy was heavily dependent on tribute from Athens' allies. Evidently the Athenian empire prior to its final defeat by Macedon had been headed in the same direction as Rome, that is, toward the creation of a parasitic populace in the imperial capital. Democracy depended on imperialism, which in the case of Rome undermined democracy. But in Athens such a connection is less clear, probably because Athenian imperialism was short-lived.

Two additional obligations and sources of money for the treasury require a brief discussion here. One is the *eisphora* (literally "bringing in"), the extraordinary property tax or capital levy mentioned earlier. Introduced at the beginning of the Peloponnesian War and resorted to more than once during the conflict, the *eisphora* became a regular institution in the fourth century. By that time full democracy had increased expenses while the reduction in tribute from the allies had made it impossible to accumulate treasure.[43]

The tax required an assessed valuation of the property to be taxed, which included not only immovable property such as real estate but also movable wealth, including slaves.[44] According to the assessment in 378–377 B.C., Athenian wealth came to 5,570 talents, a figure very close to that given by Demosthenes, 6,000 talents, in 354–353 B.C.† As the necessity arose, a certain fraction of the assessment—$1/100$, $1/50$, $1/12$—had to be paid.

It appears that all citizens who possessed some property were subject to this tax. The taxpayers were divided into units or fractions of the whole census list that were financially nearly equal to one another. Within each unit, a form of mutual control was established, for each member suffered a loss if another member paid less than his assigned share. Some years later the system was changed to collecting the tax from the three hundred richest citizens, on whom then devolved the necessity of collecting the "prepaid" tax from the rest of the citizens.[45] There was enough evasion all around to give rise to the creation of technical terms that occur frequently in the orators and mean "to put out of sight" and "to hide away."

Specialists have expended a substantial amount of ingenuity on the question of whether or not the *eisphora* was a progressive tax. That question may be impossible to answer with the available data. But if we set alongside the system of liturgies and the *eisphora* the last remaining form of taxation we will consider here, the *epidoseis*, which were voluntary gifts in money or in kind, usually for quite extraordinary and specific needs and generally arranged by a decree of the state appealing to the people, it then becomes possible to draw some firm conclusions. Though the demands of the Athenian treasury—one can hardly call them a system of taxation—may have been designed to have a progressive impact in the strict sense of taking proportionately more from the rich than the poor, there were too many loopholes for us to be certain about that.‡ But of one thing we can be sure: the public sphere *did* impose a proportionately much more severe burden on wealthy men of outstanding public spirit and patriotism than upon the rest of the population.§

†Oxford Classical Dictionary, s.v. "Eisphora." Demosthenes *On the Navy Boards* 19. Though the similarity of the two figures is striking, there is no way to judge their accuracy.

‡At one point Demosthenes remarked bitterly that the rich would make financial sacrifices only in the face of severe threat. See *On the Navy Boards* 25–26.

§In the text I have not enumerated and discussed *all* the obligations falling on a wealthy male citizen. Demosthenes *Against Leptines* 21 lists in addition to the trierarchy: chorus masters (discussed above), presidents of gymnasia, and public hosts, saying there were in all about sixty citizens who performed these annually. According to the Introduction to this speech in Loeb Classical Library, p. 487, the gymnasiarch supervised the public

Athens was a warrior society that by this time had developed marked commercial and plutocratic characteristics.† Just as a warrior society imposes extra burdens on the brave and uses up such individuals at a greater rate than ordinary people, so Athens used up its public-spirited elite at an especially high rate. Here lies, I suggest, one of the inherent weaknesses of the polis that made it a relatively short-lived social formation.

In addition to his obligations to the polis, a wealthy man faced a series of social burdens and threats. Xenophon's writings contain some passages that are revealing on this score even if one has to apply a discount for rather heavy-handed ironical exaggeration. Charmides in the *Symposium* 4.29–32, tells how much better off he is, now that he has lost all his property. When he was rich, he was afraid of someone digging through the walls to take his money or do him personal harm. He had to give in to blackmailers and informers. The government was forever ordering him to undergo some expenditure or other, and he never had the chance to travel abroad. Now that he was impoverished, he no longer felt subjected to threats but did the threatening himself. He had the free man's privilege of traveling or staying home. When rich he paid revenue to the body politic (lit. the *demos*); now the state paid tribute to him.

In Xenophon's *Oeconomicus* 2.2–9, Socrates points out to a prosperous interlocutor, Critobulus, the disadvantages of wealth. He had, Socrates observed, to make many large sacrifices. Otherwise he would get into trouble with gods and men alike. He would have to entertain on a large scale both strangers and citizens. The state exacted heavy contributions. Whenever he fell short, Socrates continued, the Athenians would certainly punish him as though they had caught him in a robbery.

The theme recurs in Xenophon's *Memorabilia* 2.9. There Criton complains about the perpetual legal harassment of the well-to-do citizen. Plaintiffs go to court not because they have suffered some injury but because they believe a man like Criton would rather pay than have trouble. The need for a private defender to frighten off such characters appears in this passage to be taken for granted.

Though Demosthenes remarks that in terms of willingness to grant

---

gymnasia, maintained the athletes' training for public contests, and was responsible for the expense and organization of the torch races. Public hosts feasted a tribe. Other officers financed the sacred embassies sent by the city to the Pan-Hellenic festivals.

†Lysias *Against Philon* 6 expresses contempt for citizens who regard any country in which they have business as their fatherland. Such men would abandon the public good of their city for private gain because their fortune, not their city, was their fatherland. See also Demosthenes *Against Aristocrates* 207–208 for the rise of ostentatious private houses among men in public life and the contrast between these and the dwellings of Themistocles or Miltiades in whose time the great public buildings, docks, etc., were constructed.

respect *(time)* and security of possession, democracy was superior to both tyranny and oligarchy,[46] for the prosperous the threat of legal harassment was a severe one. Acting as his own prosecutor, under Athenian law governing individual crimes against other persons, a private citizen with a grudge might find legal grounds, such as a man's alleged mismanagement of public funds, to sue for confiscation of the man's patrimony.[47]

Probably more serious consequences for the wealthy arose from the practices of *sykophantai,* literally "fig denouncers," though the origin of the expression is obscure. Such persons brought suit in order to gain money by blackmail, or to earn money from someone who had personal reasons for wanting a specified individual prosecuted, or even just for personal fame. Wishing to check the *sykophantai* without discouraging public-spirited volunteer prosecutors, the Athenians imposed penalties on a prosecutor who dropped a case after initiating it or whose case was so weak that he failed to obtain one-fifth of the jury's votes.[48] Nevertheless the practice flourished. More general ways in which Athenian law treated public and private offences we shall discuss later on.†

Obligations on the Polis

In return for obligations to the polis what did its members expect from the polis? What in other words were the legitimate obligations of the polis? The first and by far the most important answer to this question is defense and aggrandizement in war. To provide for the security and prosperity of its inhabitants by military means was far and away the most important function of any Greek city-state, including Athens. The remarkable thing about Athens is that it had so much energy, talent, and resources for other things as well.

The provision of security meant the delivery of justice, along with the development of institutions for the control of aggression and the peaceful resolution of internal conflicts. That was no easy task. We shall examine these features of the polis more closely in subsequent sections as we discuss the theory and practice of political debate in Athens, followed by the Athenian concepts of law and crime.

The next function of the polis in order of importance, to judge by the effort and resources devoted to it and the results of these efforts, was the satisfaction of aesthetic demands. They were not of course

†See Isocrates *Antidosis* for more details on the atmosphere of potential harassment. Though the *Antidosis* is an imaginary literary exercise, it must have been generally credible to be made public.

purely aesthetic: patriotic self-glorification and religious sentiments were major sources of aesthetic creation. The results are visible to this day in the temples, market place, the magnificent sculptures, the theater, and some of the plays themselves.

Finally, the government of fourth-century Athens was expected to prevent what the ordinary customer in the market place regarded as profiteering and thereby protect the interests of the consumer, especially through the regular and adequate supply of grain. Not only did the state take these measures to ensure an adequate supply of foodstuffs, but through state pensions for the disabled and payments for attendance at the Assembly and jury courts, the polis intervened to sustain effective demand.[49] The two policies together amounted to an assumption by the polis of responsibility for the welfare of the economically unfortunate. In the world's first civilized democracy nearly twenty-five hundred years ago the welfare of the poor was a matter of public policy and public responsibility.

It is a serious error, on the other hand, to regard this sense of public responsibility as a manifestation of some preindustrial sense of community later to be destroyed by the industrial revolution, the advance of capitalist individualism, the triumph of the acquisitive society.† The conflict between rich and poor was savage in Athens from before the time of Solon. The poor obtained a voice in Athenian politics only through bitter and at times bloody political struggles. More precisely, we ought to say that discontented individuals in the upper classes used popular discontents to advance their own factional purposes and thereby led the populace into the arena of political decision-making. And, as we have already seen in part, the whole system of Athenian welfare policy depended on the empire: first for tribute and second for grain.

Much of the grain came from the Chersonese and even as far away as Byzantium. Athenian law prescribed the severest penalties against any person residing in Athens who transported grain to any place other than the market in Athens.[50] In Athens itself and at the Piraeus there were grain wardens or market officials whose duty it was to see that unground corn was on sale in the market at a fair price with corresponding prices for barley meal and bakers' loaves of wheat. They were also in charge of weighing the amounts fixed by officials.[51] Lysias reports that the Athenians had often inflicted the death penalty on market officials for failure to prevent the villainy of grain dealers. Other commodities too were subject to market clerks in control of these commodities.[52] Thus, though energetically pursued, the policy of market control was far from universally effective.

---

†Classic presentations of the thesis rejected here are in Karl Polanyi, *The Livelihood of Man,* edited by Harry W. Pearson, and R. H. Tawney, *The Acquisitive Society.*

Disabled persons with insufficient means of support were entitled to a pension from the polis. After the restoration of democracy in 403 B.C. the pension was set at an obol a day, probably barely enough to live on. The Council examined pension claims of this type once a year. On this occasion any citizen could challenge the claim of any applicant.[53]

Other forms of relief payments included the drachma a day fee for attending the Assembly, in addition to which the individual received just short of four quarts of grain. There was also a payment of four obols a day for attendance at court. Finally, there was an allowance of two obols per head payable to registered citizens for attendance at the theater. Demosthenes compared these doles to the diets of physicians that neither put strength into a patient nor allowed him to die.†

Political Participation and Debate

The embodiment of the Athenian public was the *ekklesia* or Assembly of all adult male citizens. Though there was a great deal of political discussion in the marketplace and elsewhere, it was in the Assembly that the Athenians formally took part in politics by debating current issues and making decisions.‡ By the fourth century the Athenians had created a series of institutions and procedures to make political debates orderly while maximizing the opportunity for individual citizens to present their views.[54] Indeed, reconciling orderliness with wide popular participation was the central problem Athenians had to solve. They appear to have been quite successful.

For the Assembly, the *boule* or Council prepared the agenda and drafted resolutions. The Assembly debated the resolutions and could accept, reject, or amend them. It could not debate a matter on which the *boule* had not prepared a resolution, but could require the *boule* to prepare one for the next meeting. Certain matters came up on a regularly recurring basis ten times a year, such as continuation of the magistrates and the corn supply. Others such as ostracism and the

---

†Demosthenes *Exordia* 53.4; and *Oxford Classical Dictionary,* s.v. "Theorika" for payments to attend the theater. In the fourth century B.C. a regulation was passed requiring that all surpluses of the state should be used for the theoric fund. ("Theoric" comes from the word meaning "a viewing or beholding.") Demosthenes managed to get passed an enactment permitting military use of this surplus in wartime. But a law remained in effect, punishing with death any person even *suggesting* the use of this fund for the army in peacetime.

‡Presumably most informal political conversations took place among social equals. Theophrastus *Characters* 4 gives the following as a characteristic trait of the boor: "He distrusts his friends and kinsfolk but confides matters of great import to his servants, and tells all that went on at the Assembly to the hired laborers that work on his farm."

review of the laws came up annually. The issues of war and peace and even major military strategy came before the Assembly for debate and decision. Every citizen present had the right to speak. Magistrates enjoyed no special privilege. In each *prytany* (or tenth part of the year) one session of the Assembly was given over to petitions. Any citizen who chose to do so might address that body about any matter he wished, whether public or private, after observing the ritual of placing a suppliant's wool-laced olive branch on the altar of the Assembly.[55]

Demosthenes describes the procedure by which an individual may propose a law. There is, he says, a prescribed time for legislation. Even at the proper time a man is not allowed to propose a law just as he pleases. He is required in the first place to put it in writing and post it in front of the Heroes [near the Council chamber] for everyone to see. Then it is ordained that the law must be of universal application, that is, applicable to all Athenians and not directed against an individual. It is further directed that laws of contrary import must be repealed. Other directions exist, Demosthenes states, but does not repeat them. If a man failed to comply with these rules, anyone who chose to do so might indict him.[56] Hence a private individual had the right to propose legislation as long as he complied with certain not very burdensome regulations.

The *boule* had five hundred members, fifty from each of the tribes. Membership was open to all citizens over thirty. Members were appointed by lot. They met daily except on festive and unlucky days. Its business was prepared by a changing committee of fifty, the *prytaneis*. Ordinary citizens and most magistrates could communicate with the *boule* only through the *prytaneis*. Thus the *boule* was to a considerable extent shielded from popular and foreign influences.† On the other hand, ambassadors and heralds from foreign states were permitted to address the Assembly directly. In addition to preparing resolutions for the Assembly, the *boule* had wide-ranging administrative powers over the maintenance of the fleet, financial affairs, and other matters.

The word *"prytaneis"* means "presidents" or, as we would be more likely to say, "chairmen." Each tribe's group of fifty men chosen by lot for the *boule* served as *prytaneis* for one-tenth of the year. The *prytaneis* were on duty every day. They made arrangements for meetings of the *boule* and the Assembly, received envoys and letters addressed to the city of Athens, and conducted other day-to-day business. Each day one of the *prytaneis* was picked by lot to be their foreman. He remained on duty for twenty-four hours, along with one-third of the *prytaneis*. He had charge of the state seal and of the keys to

---

†Demosthenes *Against Aristogeiton* 1.23 remarks that the *boule* is "master of its own secrets, and no private citizen can enter it."

the treasuries and archives. In the fifth century he also took the chair at meetings of the *boule* or Assembly held on his day. (Socrates held this office on the day of the trial of the naval commanders at Arginusae.) Toward the end of the fifth century or early in the fourth, the system was changed, presumably because the foreman was thought to be overburdened. Under the later system chairmen *(proedroi)* were chosen by lot from one of the ten tribes other than those to which the *prytaneis* themselves belonged.

From this brief account it is plain that the press of business, and the need for an orderly procedure to conduct it, led to the creation of a committee system complete with chairmen that must have softened the impact of pure democracy. For that matter, the committee is a ubiquitous social formation that can blunt the thrust of an autocrat's will as effectively as that of a popular assembly. Nevertheless it is reasonably clear that the Athenian Assembly managed to retain firm control of major policy. It was able to do that partly due to the annual turnover in the membership of the boule and to the Assembly's right both to reject resolutions and, perhaps more significantly, to insist that the boule bring other business before it. But the Assembly could not and would not have been able to retain its authority without a vigorous desire on the part of a large segment of the citizenry to exercise it. Though Athenian democracy suffered from internal weaknesses, especially a tendency to destroy its own leaders, it did not succumb to internal decay. Overwhelming military force was necessary to halt it temporarily under Sparta and curb it for good under Alexander and his successors.

In regard to the quality of popular decision-making, it is much more difficult to make an objective assessment. The populace seems to have had a relatively limited role in the making of Athenian policy up to the time that Athens reached the apex of its cultural and political achievements under Pericles. In the subsequent period it is mainly the dramatic and disastrous popular decisions that stand out: (1) the Sicilian expedition, (2) the condemnation of the naval commanders at Arginusae, (3) the execution of Socrates. On the other side, there is the restoration of democracy itself and the amnesty granted its opponents. For this period, the most one can assert with any confidence is that nondemocratic or antidemocratic regimes could hardly be expected to have avoided comparable disasters and that the mass of the population was clearly better off under a democratic regime.

We may turn now from the institutional framework for political debate and popular decision-making to the more elusive topic of the tone and atmosphere of such debates. The surviving literature from the fourth century often gives the impression of an atmosphere of semipermanent crisis rather worse than that which prevailed in the 1950s in the United States when the figure of Senator Joseph McCarthy dominated the discussion of public issues. In Athens there are many signs of a pervasive fear of treason and the subversion of democracy. It appears that many citizens, very likely an overwhelming majority, were devoted to democratic institutions. But they were uncertain about the strength of their own support.

Hence the most fruitful question to pose at this point is: what were the implicit and explicit taboos governing Athenian political argument? One useful clue comes from the customary ritual that opened every meeting of the Assembly and the *boule*. It began with a form of prayer that included a curse upon enemies of the city. Evidently it included alleged enemies within the city also, because Demosthenes in a savage attack on his political rival Aeschines asserts: "To show you that this man is already accursed by you . . . recite the curse." Unfortunately the text, apparently read aloud by the clerk at that moment, has not been preserved. But its general tenor as a curse on the city's enemies is known.[57]

Our sources also contain a series of confused and confusing references to legislation against treason and efforts to overthrow or subvert the democracy. The Constitution of Athens, attributed to Aristotle, refers to the relatively mild penalty of disfranchisement, imposed upon Peisistratus (d. 527 B.C.), who had attempted to set up a tyranny.[58]

By the fourth century the laws seem to have become much more severe. In a speech delivered in 399 B.C. by Andocides, who had participated in the mutilation of the Hermae, we read of a law engraved on stone in front of the Council chamber. Supposedly it was based on a law of Solon, but it was part of the law of Athens as revised in 403 B.C. Part of the text reads:

> If anyone shall suppress the democracy at Athens or hold any public office after its suppression, he shall become a public enemy and be slain with impunity; his goods shall be confiscated and a tithe given to the goddess.[59]

Another speech delivered some time between 330 B.C. and 324 B.C. quotes from a law whose penalty was impeachment for treason (*eisangelia*). The quoted portions read:

> If any person seeks to overthrow the democracy of the Athenians, or if he attends a meeting in any place with intent to undermine the democracy, or forms a political society; or if anyone betrays a city, or ships, or any land or naval force or being an orator makes speeches contrary to the interests of the Athenian people, receiving bribes . . .†

---

†Hyperides *In Defence of Euxenippus* 6–8. See also the discussion of this passage in *Oxford Classical Dictionary*, s.v. "Eisangelia." It asserts that the law was passed toward the end of the fifth century B.C.

This law prohibited not only subversive and treasonable acts but also speeches, though it appears to have been necessary to demonstrate that the speaker had been bribed. A passage in Demosthenes directly contradicts this legislation and casts doubt on its existence: "Ours is alone among all cities in granting immunity to plead on behalf of our enemies, and where a man who has been bribed can safely address you in person . . . ."[60]

Still another speech, which modern scholarship claims to be falsely attributed to Demosthenes, quotes yet another law against conspiracy, bribery, and subversion:

> If any man enter into a conspiracy, or join in seeking to bribe the Heliaea or any of the courts in Athens, or the *boule,* by giving or receiving money for corrupt ends, or shall organize a clique for the overthrow of the democracy, or while serving as public advocate shall accept money in any suit, private or public, criminal suits shall be entered for these acts before the Thesmothetae.†

Even if the record of legislation about treason and subversion is confused and at points contradictory, it is enough to demonstrate a strong current of anxiety about such possibilities. The very language of the laws is both vindictive and anxious. Aristotle could discuss the virtues and defects of democracy along with other forms of government in a dispassionate academic manner. That does not appear to have been true of politically concerned citizens. The evidence just cited suggests instead that the Athenians were trying to place a taboo around this topic and at the same time feared they were not succeeding.

Against this impression it is appropriate to set that produced by the long record of debates over foreign policy from the time of Pericles (c. 495-429 B.C.) down to the Athenian defeat at Chaeronea (338 B.C.). Thucydides reports on a number of them in detail. For the fourth century, actual texts of Demosthenes and Aeschines are available. The level of political reasoning is remarkably high throughout. Advocates of a particular course of action tried to specify the advantages that would accrue to Athens and the resources necessary to carry out such a policy. If they were better at specifying the risks of their opponent's policies than their own, that is scarcely surprising, given the inherent uncertainty of the most informed political estimates. On many occasions these estimates were couched in strictly secular and amoral terms. On the other hand, moral considerations, especially obligations to allies, often did play a part in the arguments. At times, as any reader

---

†Demosthenes *Against Stephanus II* 26. The *Thesmothetae* were the six junior of the nine archons appointed annually. Acting together as a college, they were the magistrates responsible for many important types of cases, including impeachment. See the article on them in the *Oxford Classical Dictionary*.

of Thucydides knows, moral and political considerations were in dramatic conflict. Athenians knew this. Unlike the ancient Hebrews, they did not perceive the massacres they committed as part of their obligations to God. On this score the Athenians allowed their critical faculties free play. And Athenian audiences guffawed at Aristophanes' mockery of military bluster while their own soldiers were locked in a mortal struggle with Sparta.

The speeches of Demosthenes contain several brief passages indicating how he expected the Assembly to react to his arguments. They shed considerable light on Athenian attitudes toward freedom of speech. Though we cannot be sure that he anticipated correctly the audience's reaction, he was an experienced and very skillful speaker who knew the atmosphere of the lawcourts as well as the Assembly.

Early in one speech he makes some highly critical remarks about the conduct of Athenian foreign policy and the lazy, cowardly attitude of the citizenry that lay behind such a policy. Then he remarks that, "by Demeter," he could expect rougher treatment from his listeners for pointing out these faults than from the men who committed them. "For you do not allow liberty of speech on every subject, and indeed I am surprised that you have allowed it now."[61] Evidently Demosthenes felt that he had to appeal to the principle of freedom of speech (*parresia*) in order to get a hearing, perhaps even to save his own skin.

Another speech opens on a similar note: "Your duty, men of Athens, when debating such important matters, is, I think, to allow freedom of speech to every one of your counsellors."[62] Again the appeal to principle is a device for making the audience listen to some unwelcome advice. That, after all, is the general purpose of free speech. On the more ceremonial occasion of a funeral speech for soldiers killed in battle, he presented a variation on this theme. One of the many virtues of democracy, he asserted, was the impossibility of deterring freedom of speech from exposing the truth. It is impossible, he continued, for those who commit a shameful act to appease all the citizens. Hence even the lone individual uttering the deserved reproach makes the guilty wince. Even those who would never utter an accusing word on their own are pleased to hear someone else do so.[63]

In these somewhat disenchanted remarks, freedom of speech appears as the ally of prevailing morality. An even more disenchanted assessment appears in two of the *exordia,* brief set openings of a paragraph or two that an orator could use to start just about any speech as a device for capturing the audience's attention. One *exordium* begins with the cynical remark that the deliberations of the Assembly might not be any the worse for refusing to listen to the advice of the speakers. "Next you know in advance," Demosthenes continues, "not only what speeches each man will make, but also with what motives each one harangues you, and if it were not spiteful, I should also have said, for what price. I think you are prudent in reducing to a minimum the time for being cheated." The last sentence presumably refers to the use of the water clock for limiting the length of speeches.[64]

In another of the *exordia* he expresses a different opinion of the audience's impatience. There he asserts that the Athenians often allow themselves to be captivated by one side of an argument and refuse to pay attention to its critics. Hence their policies often run into trouble. On this account they should see nothing wrong in being willing to reopen debate and listen to the critics of measures already voted.[65] In these remarks, we should notice, Demosthenes is not criticizing freedom of speech. Instead he is asking for its more careful and critical application.

To a modern reader there is something sinister in the treatment of political opponents by Athenian orators. It is not merely the frequent personal vituperation. It is the presumption of bribery, treachery, and evil motives leading to the conclusion that the opponent represents a danger to the political community that should be rooted out by force. On several occasions Demosthenes expresses vindictive and threatening attitudes toward the Athenian partisans of Philip of Macedon, asserting that they deserved to be killed.† By this reasoning Isocrates should have been executed. But there is no evidence that he suffered for his Macedonian sympathies. There are occasional brief neutral references to him as a distinguished teacher in the surviving works of Demosthenes.

This savage attitude toward political opponents, which seems to me more intense in the fourth century than in the fifth, reflects a partial failure to cope with the general problem of political disagreement and opposition. On the positive side, the Athenians did create the concept of freedom of debate and in practice allowed very substantial latitude to the expression of different viewpoints. But they did not develop the theory and practice of a legitimate opposition or, as it was originally called, a loyal opposition. That came about much later. Possibly the unifying symbol of a monarch played a necessary part in its creation. Even in the course of this later development, factions remained in the minds of many intelligent political thinkers an unmitigated evil. It took a long time and special historical circumstances to tame factional disagreements and make them serve the purpose of constructive social change.[66]

For most of Greek history, on the other hand, factions smacked of violent disorder. Factions were something to be feared and avoided if at all possible. The only alternative the Athenians could perceive was an idealized consensus, a general will and sense of obedience shared by all, with the suffocating and indeed totalitarian overtones that such a

---

†Demosthenes *On Halonnesus* 45; *Third Philippic* 49, 53. Toward those advocating oligarchical principles he was only slightly milder, asserting that since they were bribed, they should be disqualified from giving advice. See *For the Liberty of the Rhodians* 30–33.

consensus necessarily implies. Aristotle, to his credit, refused to regard it as a virtue.[67] To criticize the Athenians for the failure to develop a working notion of legitimate opposition would be both unjust and ahistorical. In our own day the problem has hardly been solved. It plagues not only liberal democracies but also contemporary China.[68] Indeed it may be one of humanity's problems for which no completely satisfactory solutions exist, even if some solutions are much worse, in terms of human suffering, than others.

Law and Rule-making

Every human society lives by rules that limit the behavior of individuals and groups. In the form of law, such rules constitute the main feature of what is public. In the case of fourth-century Athenians we want to learn how they perceived and practiced the making of these rules. Then we shall need to understand the perceived purpose of law. Was it to protect society or the individual, or both, and if so, to protect them against what? If the protection of society and the individual was seen as the function of law, how were these considerations balanced?

Early forms of human society quite generally stress the divine origins of the society and the rules governing human intercourse. Athenian notions about the divine origins of their law appear very plainly in Aeschylus' *Eumenides*. It is a bloodthirsty play centered on the themes of murder and vengeance, ending, however, on the hopeful if dramatically artificial note that Athens will be able with divine help to bring these destructive tendencies under control. Throughout the fourth century a religious conception of the origin of law remained powerful.

From very early times, conflict and the resolution of conflict through law were prominent aspects of Greek speculation about their own institutions. But the really remarkable fact about such speculation is the early emergence of strictly secular notions about human society and institutions, including law, as purely human creations that were at least partly subject to rational human control. Such ideas surface among the pre-Socratics.† Again, in the famous choral ode of *Antigone*

---

†The notion of human laws as created by agreement, in contrast to laws of nature marked by necessity, occurs in a fragment of Antiphon the Sophist (5th century, exact dates unknown). In this passage Antiphon also says that it is most beneficial for a man to obey the laws of the city when he is before witnesses, the laws of nature when he is alone. The main idea appears to be that natural laws permit of no escape or evasion. See Hermann Diels and Walther Kranz, *Die Fragmente der Vorsokratiker*, II, 346–347. For general treatments of rational secular conceptions of human affairs among Greek thinkers, see Eric A. Havelock, *The Liberal Temper in Greek Politics* and J. de Romilly, *La Loi dans la penseé grecque*.

to the "wonder that is man," we find among his achievements "Language and thought like the wind, and city-laws *(astunomous)*."[69]

There was much more to this tradition than mere speculation. There were also the figures of the great lawgivers, Solon at Athens and the semimythical Lycurgus in Sparta. In the original accounts Solon appears as a political therapist who took it upon himself to cure through legislation the social and political maladies of the Athenian body politic.

By the fourth century B.C., the secular conception was well-established. Thus Xenophon, hardly a daring speculative thinker, has Hippias define laws as covenants that the citizens enact to determine what ought to be done and what ought to be avoided.[70] This is a statement of straightforward secular and manmade morality. A mixture of divine and secular elements, however, was more likely to find its way into any definition offered by a political leader who played an active part in determining what the laws actually were. Thus Demosthenes asserts:

> The law is that which all men ought to obey for many reasons, but above all because every law is a discovery and gift of the gods, a tenet of wise men, a corrective of errors voluntary and involuntary, and a general covenant of the whole city-state in accordance with which all men *(pasi)* in that city-state ought to regulate their lives. [The use of *pasi* a masculine plural dative form, seems to exclude women as active moral agents.][71]

In this passage law appears as (1) a gift of the gods *and* of wise men, (2) an expression of ideals capable of correcting human weakness and error, and (3) the outcome of a contractual agreement among male citizens about how to conduct their lives. Elsewhere Demosthenes describes the laws of all cities as responses to two sets of problems. First, laws reflect the principles under which human beings associate with each other, define the obligations of private life, and in general order their social relations. In the second place, laws define the duties that every man owes to the commonwealth if he chooses to take part in public life and professes any concern for the city.[72]

The awareness that laws and political systems were manmade contrivances that differed sharply from one city-state to another produced severe moral uncertainties. How was it possible to show that law and even the concept of justice itself were anything more than the right of the stronger and therefore just another tool of oppression? There were many attempts to answer this question and to define justice, of which Plato's *Republic* is the longest though not necessarily the most satisfactory.

When people talk about justice in general they are liable to be a bit woolly because what they really have in mind is injustice and usually some specific injustice that affects them or people like them. Though Greek literature from Homer onward is full of complaints about injustice, there is no need for a classical education to understand what the plain man and woman usually mean by injustice. It is something that a powerful person does to them that hurts. And it hurts without doing anybody except the perpetrator any good.

For the victim injustice takes the form of a painful intrusion upon one's private existence, an attack upon whatever limited autonomy the individual has managed to achieve. The man who sees his property or his wife taken by a rich and powerful neighbor needs no philosopher or political agitator to tell him he is the victim of injustice. Plain citizens are often willing to make painful sacrifices, to offer up life and limb for what they have learned to regard as the common good, whether it be that of the family, neighborhood, tribe, or some larger unit. Injustice, on the other hand, always has an arbitrary component in the sense that what hurts has no believable justification.

The Athenians had their own historically specific experience of injustice and attempts to remedy it. It is possible to get a sense of their own memories and traditions about these matters by reading the historical section (Part I) of *The Athenian Constitution,* attributed to Aristotle. It is the first attempt at social history in Western literature. But it is not history with the politics left out. Political institutions take center stage as they ought to.† It is a violent tale that requires no summary here. On the other hand, it is worth pointing out that most of the facts in it were reasonably familiar to Athenian citizens. In the orators' speeches the frequent polemical allusions to Athenian history presuppose just such a familiarity.

The two main institutional forms of injustice with which the Athenians were familiar were tyranny and oligarchy. In a strict sense oligarchy was not important as a direct part of Athenian experience, except for a brief and traumatic interlude following the Peloponnesian War. They were more familiar with the rule of a closed and at times oppressive nobility, whose power the populace was able to limit under the reforms of Cleisthenes (508/7 B.C.) and Ephialtes (murdered 461 B.C.). In other cities, whose experience was known to many Athenians, oligarchy tended toward the rule of the few, based on a fusion of the older landed wealth with new forms of urban wealth, such as trade and mining.

---

†C. Hignett, *A History of the Athenian Constitution,* 29, remarks that this historical survey "resembles a careful essay written by a modern research student who brings to his task much industry but no judgement." He concludes, I think correctly, that one of Aristotle's students wrote it and that the ancients attributed it to Aristotle because it was one of the series of constitutional histories of particular cities issued by his school. It is not widely recognized that among his other achievements Aristotle was the founder of organized research.

Tyranny in its early seventh- and sixth-century forms reflected in part a popular reaction against aristocratic and oligarchical rule. It took the form of an individual usurper who acted somewhat like a modern dictator in attacking the established forms of noble and oligarchical rule. In this way the early tyrants helped to prepare the way for democracy, a transition also favored by changes in military technology as the heavily armed foot soldiers, or hoplites, replaced the cavalry. In the turmoil that accompanied the defeat of Athens by Sparta at the end of the Peloponnesian War, however, the Athenian population experienced the worst features of both oligarchy and tyranny. Under the Thirty Tyrants (404 B.C.) there was what amounted to a white terror. Some fifteen hundred men are said to have been executed.

By and large, democracy was the remedy that the Athenians conceived and created for the injustices felt to be inherent in tyranny and oligarchy. Taking power away from the rich and powerful and giving it to the citizens seemed to many a workable and worthwhile precaution against the injustices with which they were familiar. By this I do not wish to convey the notion that Athenian politics came down to a programmatic class conflict. Popular leaders were often aristocrats using popular grievances to destroy the power of other aristocrats. No leader could foresee clearly the institutional consequences of the policies he tried to put into effect. Nevertheless democracy became the main remedy and was widely though far from universally seen as such.

Unlike modern Western democracy, Athenian democracy came to power without any carefully articulated ideas about the necessity for protecting the individual citizen against the arbitrary abuse of the state's power. That is explicable in the light of the fact that in Athens prior to the triumph of democracy there was no noble and popular struggle against royal absolutism. Royal absolutism itself did not exist. These differences in historical background make comprehensible the fact that Athenian democracy came to power without any Bill of Rights, though, as we shall see shortly, legal practice did generate some very important procedural protections. In Athens the emphasis was very much on public obligation, not on private rights. On the other hand, citizenship carried definite privileges in relation to the rest of the population. As will appear in the next section, there were certain things that the polis could not do to a free man.

Insofar as democracy itself was the remedy for correcting the abuse of power in the polis, there did not at first seem to be much reason to make special provision for the protection of the individual. Critics of democracy could be brushed aside as amounting to no more than covert defenders of oligarchy or the old nobility (much as many modern socialists continue to treat critics of socialism as covert defenders of capitalist oppression). Indeed, early Athenian democracy was in a position resembling socialism about a generation ago: there was not as yet enough historical experience to make it possible to discern its inherent structural defects.

As a cure for arbitrary injustice Athenian democracy created its own forms of injustice. Aristotle asserted that the kind of democracy where the masses were in charge and not the law was comparable to tyranny. The spirit was the same; both exercised despotic control over the better classes. Decrees of the Assembly resembled the commands in a tyranny. Demagogues and flatterers were the same people and played a similar role. "Where the laws do not govern," he observed in a famous passage, "there is no constitution."[73]

In this discussion Aristotle viewed laws as a protection for the magistrate against arbitrary decisions by the Assembly. His position comes close to an assertion that law protects the individual against the state.† The orator Hyperides likewise characterized law as a protection against the threats of a ruler, groundless and unproved accusations from any source, and the slanders of those who truckle to their masters.[74] Finally, Demosthenes expressed clearly the ideal of equality before the law: "Of private rights within a constitutional state the laws grant a common and equal share to all, weak and strong alike." For him the law was a general barrier against injustice.[75]

In the course of political debate among themselves and in the adversary procedure before the law courts the Athenians had, by the fourth century B.C. worked out a significant body of principles and procedures to protect the individual against arbitrary injustice. In his *Law and Legal Theory of the Greeks* J. Walter Jones has taken the trouble to collect them, and I can do no better than reproduce his important findings.

First of all, apart from occasional speculation by Plato and others, the protection of private property remained a fundamental principle of the Athenian polity. Similarly, with all its faults, democracy, according to Isocrates, does not put men to death without trial.‡ Thus there was protection of a sort for life, limb, and property. A citizen was not to be put on trial a second time for the same offense. He was not to be singled out for punishment by retrospective enactment unless six thousand of the people voted for the proposal. He was not to be subject to corporal punishment except in the last resort. It was also contrary to accepted principles for officials to enter a citizen's house against his

---

†Both Plato and Aristotle knew perfectly well that by themselves legal and ethical systems were weak and ineffective defenses against the "right of the stronger," the advantages of wealth, or the power of sheer numbers. That is one reason why Plato devotes so much attention to types of personality as determinants of the character of political regimes. Aristotle puts more emphasis on social and economic factors. Democracy, he asserts, works best in a society of small farmers because most of the population is too busy looking after private affairs to take part in political excitement (*Politics* 6.2.1).
‡J. W. Jones, *Law and Legal Theory*, 85, 89. About torture we will speak later. It does not seem to have been used against citizens.

will. A freeman in a democracy may not fall physically into the power of someone he has injured, or indeed of anyone else. He was to be subject only to the law, even after arrest by the complainant or the complainant's friends. Unless deprived of civil rights for some offence, the citizen had the power to initiate prosecutions against anyone. Except when charged with homicide he could be condemned to death only by the people in Assembly, which reserved to itself the final word in such crimes as treason and attempting to subvert democracy. There were statutes against assault, though in practice they appear to have been ignored frequently. Finally, Athenians felt that what distinguished them from slaves and barbarians was the right to say what they pleased, a right that under the name of *is-egoria* they came to identify with freedom in general.[76]

No doubt these principles were not always adhered to in practice. Nevertheless the Athenians did more than any civilized people before their time, and many since their time, to erect protective walls against arbitrary injustices by public officials and institutions.

Public and Private
Responses to Crime

In the definition and punishment of crime a society announces to all its members what forms of behavior it forbids. Those acts for which it prescribes the death penalty constitute the extremes of antisocial behavior as perceived and defined by the makers of the law. In a democracy such as fourth-century Athens the definitions of antisocial behavior are very widely shared. By successfully claiming the right to put one of its own members to death, a society asserts in the most emphatic way possible the supremacy of social interests over individual desires, of public concerns over private inclinations. Thus a list of capital offenses sheds a brilliant light on the nature of public and private concerns in any society.

Xenophon provides such a list in two passages about Socrates. In both of them he tries to contrast the behavior of Socrates with practices specified by Athenian law as deserving the death penalty. The two lists overlap but are not identical. Very likely Xenophon was merely stating in these passages what the ordinary Athenian citizen learned from experience about the application of the death penalty. Yet if Xenophon was summarizing common knowledge about the law rather than the law itself, that makes his testimony all the more useful sociologically. Combining the two lists of actions punishable by death, we find a series of threats: (1) to private property by thieves, highwaymen, burglars, and cutpurses; (2) to persons by kidnappers and by those who enslaved free men; and (3) to property involving sacrilege by temple robbers. Two other crimes meriting death involved more generalized harm to the society as a whole. Of these, one was (4) treason to the state. Still another (not included in Xenophon's lists) was of course the impiety or sacrilege (*asebeia*) for which Socrates was on trial and for which others had been tried before him.[77] Though we do not know how many people were executed under all these laws, the world's first civilized democracy does not seem to have spared the death penalty.

This impression gains strength from scattered references to the death penalty in other sources. Treason was evidently interpreted rather broadly, at least in times of crisis. Mere cowardice and flight were sufficient grounds. Aeschines mentions the case of a private citizen who undertook to sail off to Samos and was punished with death by the Council of the Areopagus on the same day. Another private citizen, he reported, was prosecuted for sailing off to Rhodes and would have been cast out of the country if the vote of the jury had not been a tie.[78]

Demosthenes reports that there was a law making death the penalty for any man who broke his promise to the Assembly, to one of the Councils (*boule*) or to the law courts.[79] According to another law, an informer could claim immunity if his information turned out to be true but was put to death if the information was false.[80] A person who laid a charge of impiety against someone and failed to gain one-fifth of the votes lost his rights of citizenship and was forbidden under penalty of death to set foot in the temples of the gods against whom the alleged impiety had occurred.[81] In these instances the death penalty served to prevent frivolous and untrue statements and accusations before public bodies.

The Athenians on occasion also put persons to death for offenses against morality. It is not clear whether these offenses were specifically prohibited by law. From the sources it seems possible that the death penalty was invoked in a fit of popular outrage. All that we know is that the Athenians killed one Menon the miller because he kept a free boy from Pellene in his mill. Likewise they put to death a man who assaulted the Rhodian lyre player at the Eleusinian festival and another man because he put "the Olynthian girl"—otherwise unidentified—in a brothel.[82] Two of these examples suggest illegal sexual exploitation. The other was a violation of the sacred peace of a religious festival, similar to that of the bully Meidias who struck Demosthenes when he was in charge of a chorus.

There is also at least one recorded case of execution in order to set a political example. After the defeat of the Thirty Tyrants, when someone tried to violate the agreed-on amnesty by stirring up grudges against the democratic returnees from the Piraeus, Archinos, an Athenian statesman, persuaded the *boule* to execute him without trial. This was the moment, said Archinos, for them to show that they wished to save the democracy and keep their oaths. By letting this man off, the councilors would incite others to break the amnesty. But if they put him out of the way, they would make him an example to everybody. According to the *Athenian Constitution,* from which this tale comes, after he was put to death no one violated the amnesty. The Athenians appeared, according to this account, to have behaved in public and private in the most completely honorable and statesmanlike manner of any people in history, blotting out all recriminations.[83]

The evidence discussed so far indicates that the major threats to public order feared by the Athenians were treason, deception and failure to keep promises made to public bodies, sacrilege, and felonious assault. Probably they resorted to the death penalty for this wide variety of crimes because public authority lacked other means to cope with them. There was only a very primitive form of police, and imprisonment seems to have been a method of holding the accused— and by no means all accused—for trial rather than a form of punishment. In that sense public authority was still rudimentary. Furthermore, as present-day experience makes plain, public systems for catching and punishing criminals are not very effective in the absence of generalized acceptance of public authority and respect for it. The death penalty was one way of insuring such respect.

So far, I have not said anything about the Athenian treatment of homicide, which might be regarded as *the* crucial aspect of public order. (It is curious that Xenophon omits it from his list.) A society that cannot secure the life of its members is hardly a society at all. It lacks the most elementary basis for public order. Athenian beliefs and practices concerning homicide are especially interesting in their differences from and resemblances to our own. The state's concern with homicide appears to have grown out of beliefs about pollution and efforts to control private vengeance.

Athenian notions of pollution arising out of murder were both a reflection and expression of shared fears about the consequences of such an act. According to one of the orators, the victim of murder was robbed of the gifts bestowed upon him by the god. Naturally he left behind him the angry spirits of vengeance, the god's instruments of punishment. Those who prosecute or testify unjustly bring these spirits into their own home and share in the sin of him who did the deed. Those who wrongfully cause the death of innocent people are themselves liable to the penalties prescribed for murder. On the other hand, by inflicting upon the real criminal a punishment proportionate to the injury he has done, the Athenians can cleanse the whole city of its defilement.

The whole city, says Antiphon, is defiled by the criminal until he is brought to justice. His sin becomes ours.[84] The polluted wretch passes on his defilement to the innocent by sitting at the same table as they. He causes death and public calamity. The jury therefore has a personal duty to avenge the dead.[85] In judging cases of murder the court sat in the open air in order that jurors might avoid entering the same building with those whose hands were unclean and also in order that the person conducting the prosecution (ordinarily a relative of the victim) might avoid being under the same roof as the murderer.[86]

By coming to the aid of a victim and punishing his murderer, the jurors in condemning the murderer to death were said to accomplish three good things for the city. They would reduce the number of deliberate criminals, increase the number of god-fearing individuals, and rid themselves of the defilement resting upon them in the name of the defendant.[87]

To sum up, pollution came from the unavenged anger of the dead victim. It threatened the whole city. Acting on behalf of the whole city, the jurors avenged the victim by condemning his murderer to death and thereby purified the city. Punishment was purification. It was also an expression of socially approved aggression, which helped to create a unified public opinion. Murder, which originally had been a threat to the social fabric, in this way turned into something that strengthened this fabric. In our own time it has been observed that nothing holds society together so well as a juicy case of murder. The Athenians hit on this discovery at quite an early date, in fact, long before the time of the sources upon which we depend for knowledge about their legal procedures.

Though revenge had been sublimated into punishment, it remained the task of the victim's kin to apprehend and prosecute the murderer. There were situations, to be discussed shortly, in which immediate vengeance was the expected norm. They involved attacks on a man's womenfolk or self-defense. But even slaves who murdered their masters and were caught red-handed were not put to death by the victim's relatives. Instead they were handed over to the authorities as ordained by ancient laws. In such instances revenge had to flow through public channels[88] and became a public obligation instead of a private joy.

The first obligation of the victim's relatives was to make a proclamation in the *agora* (market place), instructing the killer to "keep away from the things laid down by law," a reference to the murderer's capacity to pollute. They then went to the king archon, an official especially concerned with religious matters, and presented their charge to him. The king archon is said to have also issued a proclamation ordering the accused to "keep away from things laid down by law." Though we do not know precisely what things were laid down by the law, they included all temples and public religious ceremonies, the agora and the law courts (except the one for the trial of the accused), and presumably all public meetings.[89] The accused became a semi-outlaw, but was not ordinarily put in prison.

Athenian law distinguished between intentional and unintentional homicide, with various gradations in between that determined which court would try a particular case. These variations we may ignore. Most cases, it appears, were tried by the *Areopagus* or high Council, which came to consist entirely of former archons, or by the *ephetai,* a court of fifty-one men over fifty years of age, chosen by lot.[90] Thus juries for murder trials consisted of mature and presumably respected men. After listening to the speeches of the prosecutor and the defendant, both of which might be the work of professional orators, the jury voted and the king archon formally pronounced the verdict. The penalty for intentional homicide was death and confiscation of property; that for unintentional homicide was exile. Such a man—all rules seem to envisage only men though Greek drama presents some of the most powerful examples of female murderers in world literature— could keep his property and live a free life abroad. If, on the other hand, he entered Attica, whoever found him could either kill him at once or arrange for his execution.[91]

Finally, there were assaults on a man's womenfolk, for which the man was expected to kill the attacker without interference from the polis. In these cases vengeance remained the prerogative of the offended male. Passions were deemed too strong for the public authorities to intrude. A man overhearing slander of his sister was expected to strangle the slanderer on the spot.[92] Demosthenes quotes a law covering several other situations: "If a man kill another . . . in intercourse with his wife, or mother, or sister, or daughter, or concubine kept for procreation of legitimate children, he shall not go into exile on that account." Instead the slayer was to go scot-free.[93]

Curiously the law also specifies, in the portion omitted from the above quotation, that there was to be no penalty for unintentionally killing a man in an athletic contest, a fight on the highway, or unwittingly in battle. Presumably the last instance does not refer to killing an enemy but to killing someone on the same side in a period of confusion. Later in the same speech Demosthenes mentions the killing of another man in self-defense while being violently attacked as a further form of lawful homicide. This situation Demosthenes believed to be covered by the unwritten law of our common humanity, a belief still sometimes put forth in modern times as a defense for allegedly legitimate homicide.[94] Public authorities, so the belief runs, must not interfere with the individual's right to protect himself and his womenfolk.

A speech by Lysias sheds additional light on laws covering the protection of females. If anyone debauched a free adult or child, he would be liable for damages double the amount set for violating a slave. But anyone who seduced a woman could be killed with impunity. The lawgiver, Lysias claims, considered that those who use force deserve a lesser penalty than those who use persuasion. Those who use force are hated by their victims while those who use persuasion corrupt their victims' souls, making the wives of others more closely attached to themselves than to their husbands. According to this interpretation, the laws direct the husband to seek satisfaction.[95] Lysias, it is important to notice, in this case had written a defense for a man accused by the dead man's relatives of murdering his wife's seducer. In the concluding section of the speech Lysias has the husband assert that he did not regard vengeance as his own private affair. Instead he claimed to be acting in the interests of the whole city.[96] Private vengeance here becomes a public service. Or so Lysias would have us believe.

Thus the main features relevant to our concerns were the limitations on public capital punishment and the absence of a public prosecutor for crimes committed against individuals.[97] Prior to Solon it appears that only the victims of crime or, in the case of murder, members of the injured family had the right or the obligation to prosecute. Solon's reform of the constitution allowed anybody to prosecute for redress of injured persons. He also introduced the system of jury courts made up of ordinary citizens, a change that according to the *Athenian Constitution,* greatly increased the powers of the multitude.[98]

The right to prosecute exercised by a free adult male covered only offenses or injuries regarded as affecting no more than the individual parties involved. In contrast, a public prosecutor handled public cases, those concerning offenses regarded as affecting the whole community. Crimes against the state included treason, desertion from the army, embezzlement of public funds, and *hybris,* a generalized term for aggressive misconduct with no regard for the rights of others.[99] Though the lines between private and public cases might at times be blurred, as we saw when fears of city-wide pollution marked certain trials for homicide, legal rules for initiating trials were apparently well-known. In general then Athenian law and legal procedures recognized the distinction between private and public spheres of life.

The only police mentioned in the sources were "The Eleven." These were officers chosen by lot to superintend persons in prison and to punish with death persons arrested as thieves, kidnappers, and footpads if they confessed their guilt. Otherwise the latter were to be tried before the jury court and executed at the hands of The Eleven if found guilty. The Eleven also had the task of bringing before the jury court lists of farms and houses declared to be public property and handing over to the vendors those properties the court had decided to confiscate.[100] Scythians were also imported as slave archers to perform certain unspecified police duties under the direction of The Eleven.[101]

It is somewhat surprising that Athens with its large and heterogeneous population including numerous foreigners and slaves was able to maintain a satisfactory degree of public order with so limited a police force. Perhaps violent crime was so much a fact of life that it did not seem worthwhile to worry about it. Another possibility is that insecurities due to war and changes in political regime overshadowed the risks from ordinary crime to the point where it seemed trivial. For the well-to-do the risks of blackmail and prosecution by an informer loomed much larger than felonious assault.

Let us now examine the forms of protection available to the Athenian individual accused or suspected of a crime. Athenians were proud of these rights. The first one was the right to a trial in the case of capital crimes. "We condemn as unfit to live in," says Isocrates, "those states in which an occasional individual is put to death without trial."[102] The feeling that a trial was necessary was at least partly religious. The legislator in charge of a homicide case is displaying respect for the whole city, Demosthenes claims, by not specifying what penalty was to be meted out before the trial had ended. "I say of the 'whole city,' because it is impossible that all of you should know who the manslayer is." Hence the purpose of the trial was to convince all the citizens that the accused actually *was* guilty so that "conscience permits us to inflict punishment with knowledge, but not before."[103]

The laws forbade the same man to be tried twice on the same issue no matter what type of case was involved.[104] Even in the most trifling cases the laws did not admit the use of hearsay evidence.[105] In cases of murder, as we have seen, retribution was to be carried out by the public authorities. Anyone who captured a murderer was required to turn him over to the judges. The law forbade mistreatment of the captive by scourging, binding, or similar actions or by attempting to extort blood money.[106] When a private individual faced a trial and was unable to conduct his own defense it was customary to allow any citizen to come forward and help by giving the jury a fair statement of the case.[107]

The right to a trial if accused of a crime was of course basic. But there is evidence of an even wider form of protection. The Council of the Areopagus was guardian of the laws and kept a watch on magistrates to make them govern in accord with the laws. A person unjustly treated might bring a complaint before the Council stating the law in contravention of which he was treated unjustly.[108] In addition, private individuals had the right to lay an information of illegal procedure against any official they wished. In such cases, on the other hand, an appeal was possible to a jury court if the Council of Five Hundred passed a verdict of guilty.[109]

Demosthenes once prosecuted an official for illegal behavior that, according to his assertions, included the following gross violations of privacy: with police magistrates (The Eleven) and other officers in tow, the official invaded private houses, demolished front doors, dragged the bedclothes from under the inhabitants, and if a man was living with his maidservant, levied distraint on her.[110]

According to what appears to be an ancient tradition, the citizen's home was inviolable. Demosthenes remarks that even under the Thirty Tyrants ". . . . no man forfeited the power to save his life who could hide himself at home; what we denounce the Thirty for is that they arrested men illegally in the market place."[111] Thus the tradition that a man's home is his castle harks back not to English tradition but to classical Athens.

In addition, the citizen was not subject to corporal punishment. That was also a major distinction between the freeman and the slave. The slave, says Demosthenes, was accountable with his body for all offenses. Freemen even in the most unfortunate circumstances could protect their persons since the law in most cases obtained satisfaction from them in the form of money.[112] Status was one of the origins of individual protection against arbitrary punishment.

Though Athenian citizens did enjoy numerous forms of protection against the abuse of the state's authority, there was one area of criminal behavior where the absence of such protection is very striking in comparison with modern liberal standards. As pointed out above, the Athenians displayed a real phobia about treachery and attempts to undermine or overthrow democracy. At the time of the excitement over the trial of the naval commanders at Arginusae one of their attackers claimed that, according to a decree then in force, if anyone wronged the people of Athens, he was to plead his case in fetters before the people.[113] To say the least, this procedure amounted to a partial removal of the presumption of innocence until tried and found guilty.

Indeed, in cases of treason or the overthrow of democracy, one orator claimed that punishment ought to precede the crime whereas in other cases it should follow the crime.[114] The orator in this instance is expressing a wish and not describing actual procedure. His justification is not completely devoid of sense. After a treasonable act has been committed, says Lycurgus, the perpetrators are too powerful to be brought to justice. Nevertheless his proposal, which he put forward seriously in the course of a trial, would have made a flagrant mockery of justice in trials for treason. It is also characteristic that Lycurgus attacks the advocates for the defense as associates in crime and men who should be required to plead their own defense instead of seeking pardon for another.[115] These vehement assertions were of course part of the characteristic rhetorical exaggeration often found in speeches before the law courts. That such exaggeration was characteristic is, on the other hand, the important fact from the standpoint of our inquiry. If that was the atmosphere of the court, the critic of democracy could hardly expect a fair hearing.

We cannot leave the discussion of protection for the individual under Athenian legal procedures without a few words about torture. Free Greeks could not be put to torture, although in times of panic or emergency this did happen. According to the Athenian Constitution, after the murder of Hipparchus in 514 B.C., Aristogeiton under prolonged torture revealed the names of confederates.[116] In the case of slaves it was widely though not universally taken for granted that torture constituted the most reliable way to elicit evidence. The reason seems to have been that a slave who knew anything would frequently belong to one of the parties to the litigation, and therefore would be afraid to say anything contrary to his owner's interests unless put to torture. In one case Demosthenes remarks to the court, "Now you consider torture the most reliable of all tests in both private and public affairs."[117] Though some modern scholars have claimed that no example is known in which a slave actually was tortured, there are three fairly clear cases in which an investigation by the *boule* or the Assembly involved the torture of witnesses.[118] In the case of torture, as with other practices, only male citizens had full legal rights protecting them against abuses of public authority. Slaves, it seems, had few or none, while the position of the metics or resident aliens was closer to that of the citizens. Once again we perceive that freedom and private rights first emerged as a special prerogative of high status.

If we stand back and look at the record over a longer span of time, it appears that the taming of personal revenge was the first achievement of the public in the course of human cultural history. The obstacle in the case of murder was not necessarily the power of the motive for revenge. Quite the opposite is the case in a number of nonliterate societies. In classical Greece when a murder does occur, either nothing happens or there is great reluctance to undertake revenge. After all, that can be a nasty and dangerous task. Even Orestes in Greek mythology found the obligation utterly horrifying. Public intervention is both more impersonal and relatively more certain.

A second point also deserves emphasis. In ancient Athens there grew up under the influence of democratic ideas an impressive set of measures to prevent the arbitrary misuse of authority by public officials and to protect the accused against a miscarriage of justice. Athenian civilization contributed a great deal to the creation of the public and protection against the public.

Private Life in
Theory and Practice

Now that we have analyzed the principles that governed the organization of public life, we are in a position to raise the issues connected with private life. With us the concept of private life denotes an existence apart from and to some extent in opposition to current political and social concerns, a sphere of personal autonomy into which society has no right to intrude as long as the individual refrains from illegal or criminal acts. In Greece, though the distinction between public and private occurred as early as Homer, and the lyric poets often displayed or evoked private and personal emotions (even anti-patriotic ones such as Archilochus abandoning his shield by a bush), private life as a distinct alternative and realistically available choice did not appear before the literature of the fourth century.

When it did appear, the conception of private life was rather more restricted than ours and had to do mainly with the refusal to seek or accept political office. There may be some good historical reasons for the relatively late development of any conception of private life, or more precisely, for its late appearance as an issue for serious intellectual discussion. But it would be wise to recall certain obvious considerations before searching for these reasons.

Private life in the sense of personal autonomy was and remains an option for the educated person with some independent resources. Peasants are likely to have quite a different conception. Aristophanes in one of his antiwar plays, *The Acharnians,* produced in 425 B.C., presents, in the character of Dikaiopolis, a caricature of the ordinary Athenian citizen from a rural background. Even as caricature, however, Dikaiopolis has many plausible traits. He is disgusted with the blather of politicians and the swagger of generals. He wants to be left alone so that he can enjoy the simple pleasures of eating, drinking, and wenching. That is impossible as long as the Peloponnesian War drags on. Similar conceptions of private life, though with more emphasis on being left alone to be able to do a hard day's work, were probably quite widespread among ordinary Athenians. This simple form of apolitical yearning for a private existence occurs of course in many societies. It is not something to be treated with condescension by political thinkers whose answers don't work. Nor for that matter is the yearning a search for a purely private existence since it usually includes a willing participation in local forms of social life based on economic cooperation, kinship, and religion.

This desire to be left in peace was probably strongest among Athenians with ties to the land, since enemy troops often ravaged the land and destroyed crops while refraining from attacking the city itself because that was too risky. But the wish to be free from political obligations and to enjoy life must have existed among the more purely urban population as well. There was probably a good deal of cynicism about politicians, much of it well founded in fact. The speeches of Demosthenes reflect this current. On the other hand, politics for the ordinary Athenian provided an exciting spectacle with participation by the audience. In a time of crisis, such as the overthrow of the Thirty Tyrants, large numbers of ordinary Athenians took up arms and risked their lives in defense of democratic institutions—not as a theoretical abstraction but in defense of their personal security and property.

Even if necessarily based heavily upon inference rather than direct evidence, these observations about the mass of the Athenian population are sufficient to cast doubt on any thesis to the effect that the ideal of a private life was a discovery of the fourth century. For a long time the peasant had wanted to cultivate his farm in peace, the owner of an artisan establishment to manage his affairs in his own way. Nevertheless we can discern something new in the air, a stirring among the prosperous and the educated.

Among these people the routine requirements of citizenship set limits on any search for personal autonomy. Lysias tells of a man who never sought public office, but discharged every duty in the production of dramas, equipped a warship seven times, and made numerous contributions to special levies.[119] Clearly he was a man of substance whom Lysias was trying to portray as a model quiet citizen.

Another instance occurs in the case of a man defending himself against an informer's charge of sacrilege. Sacrilege in this case took the form of allegedly removing a sacred olive tree from his farm, a charge the man vehemently denied. Apparently this kind of accusation could crop up any time and destroy the peace and quiet of a prosperous existence. The opening lines of the defense, written by Lysias for this client, explicitly state the ideal of a quiet life:

> Heretofore, gentlemen of the Council, I thought it possible for a person who so desired to avoid law suits and troubles by leading a quiet life [rest, quiet, leisure, and solitude]; but now I find myself . . . unexpectedly embarrassed with accusations and with nefarious slanders . . . .[120]

As in the previous case, this seeker after peace and quiet claims to have zealously performed all duties and public services, to have fought many battles on land and sea and—perhaps most revealing of all—to have been an orderly person under both the democracy and the oligarchy.[121]

This client of Lysias sounds very much like the good citizen who wants to keep to himself and avoid political trouble, something rather difficult to manage in ancient Athens. For one thing, as pointed out earlier, Athens had some of the characteristics of a small town. A man's life in most respects was a matter of public knowledge. Deception about one's general character was impossible in such a community. At least that is what many Athenians liked to think.[122]

According to an old tradition, Solon had passed a law to the effect that under conditions of civil strife whoever failed to join forces with either party would lose his citizenship. Solon, according to the story, was afraid of the Athenians' indifference and tendency to let things slide.[123] By the time of the Spartan garrison in Athens and the rule of the Thirty Tyrants in 403 B.C., this law appears to have been either forgotten or repealed.[124]

The tradition, however, points to the strong pressure to "put one's body on the line" in domestic political strife during a long period of Athenian history, and equally to the strong desire to escape from this pressure. Hence it comes as a bit of a surprise to find that a man accused after the Athenian defeat at Chaeronea of having been a Macedonian sympathizer could use the argument that he had been "quietly and modestly minding his own business much as any other citizen."[125] Here, as in the other sources cited so far, private life appears as a perfectly respectable option, presumably as long as the individual performed his obligations to the polis. With the end of the polis as a viable independent political unit, private life may have become the only choice. But that part of the story falls outside the scope of this inquiry.

In addition to the sources just mentioned, which throw considerable light on what private life meant in practice, all the major writers of the fourth century—Plato, Aristotle, Xenophon, Demosthenes, and Isocrates—discuss the concept of private life from different points of view. All the discussions raised the question of whether it was possible to lead a worthwhile life without accepting the challenge and responsibilities of political action. The main alternative was a life devoted to intellectual pursuits. That of course meant something quite different in fourth-century Athens from the modern situation after the rise of specialized professions. Xenophon and Demosthenes defended, each in his own way, the traditional conception that life for a citizen of the polis *required* active participation in day-to-day politics, including competition for political office. Isocrates presented the most coherent and fully developed argument for the opposite conception: a life devoted to study and teaching, though focused on political concerns. Plato and Aristotle too argued the value of a life devoted to intellectual pursuits. But as original thinkers of the first rank their conceptions were richer, more complex, and, at any rate in the case of Plato, further removed from the realities of Athenian life.

That of course is not true of Plato's *Apology,* also known in English as *The Defence of Socrates at his Trial.* In this famous work Plato presents Socrates in a way that has made him for Western civilization the archetype of the private social critic who pays with his life for a commitment to the ideals of free inquiry. A similar ideal, it is worth noticing, did develop in Chinese civilization but in the bureaucratic context of the scholar-official as principled adviser to the emperor.[126]

The basis of Socrates' commitment, it is sometimes forgotten, was strictly religious. His response when the oracle at Delphi asserted that there was no one wiser than he, and his belief in a divine spirit that told him what to do in various crises,[127] apparently seemed strange and possibly blasphemous to his Athenian listeners, just as these passages have an odd ring for the modern secular reader. Nevertheless I at least see no good reason for refusing to take Socrates at his word. This kind of intellectual independence may be psychologically unattainable without firm beliefs that transcend individual mortality.

As for the material basis of this intellectual independence, it certainly was not wealth and leisure. Just how Socrates made his living is a matter about which Plato does not choose to enlighten us. His father is said to have been a reasonably prosperous sculptor or stonemason, and Socrates himself served in the army as a hoplite.[128] Perhaps he inherited enough to live on in a frugal manner, though he was often a welcome guest in wealthy houses. His refusal to teach and talk for money is well known. Most of his time seems to have been spent in conversational inquiry. In the *Apology* Plato has him say that for this reason "I have no leisure worth mentioning to attend to the affairs of the state nor my private affairs but I am in vast poverty on account of my service to the god."[129]

Socrates' life was public in the sense that he spent most of his time talking to all who wanted to listen. He explicitly rejected the possibility of turning to a life of peace and quiet, because such conduct would be disobedience to the god. It is especially clear in this passage that he did not expect ordinary Athenian citizens to believe him.[130] Socrates also thought of himself as performing a necessary and indeed irreplaceable public service. This image of himself appears in the famous metaphor of the gadfly and the equally well-known passage that the unexamined life is not worth living.[131]

On the other hand, his life was private in two related aspects. One was his intense and very personal religious commitment to a life of inquiry, a commitment that in time aroused the prejudice and dislike of the Athenian multitude. At least according to Plato, Socrates saw his role as that of the lone hero fighting popular prejudice.[132] In turn, his religious commitment, combined with a shrewd sense of what was possible, led him to reject an active part in Athenian politics and stick to the role of private citizen. The passage where he defends this choice is worth quoting in full:

> Perhaps it may seem strange that I go about and interfere in other people's affairs to give this advice in private but do not venture to come before your assembly and advise the polis. But the reason for this, as you have heard me say at many times and places, is that something divine and spiritual comes to me, the very thing which Meletus ridiculed in his indictment. I have had this from my childhood; it is a sort of voice that comes to me, and when it comes it always holds me

back from what I am thinking of doing, but never urges me forward.
This it is which opposes my engaging in politics. And I think this
opposition is a very good thing; for you may be quite sure, men of
Athens, that if I had undertaken to go into politics, I should have been
put to death long ago and should have done no good to you or to
myself. And do not be angry with me for speaking the truth; the fact is
that no man will save his life who nobly opposes you or any other
populace and prevents many unjust and illegal things from happening in
the polis. A man who really fights for the right, if he is to preserve his
life for even a little while, must be a private citizen, not a public man.[133]

That is one of the most somber judgments of popular democracy in
Western literature.

After this defense of the choice of remaining a private citizen,
Socrates goes on to report and justify his behavior when he was
unavoidably caught up in a political role. After the battle of Arginusae
in 406 B.C., the naval commanders were tried before the Assembly,
amid an atmosphere of great popular indignation, for criminal negligence in failing to rescue many men floating about on the wreckage. Six
of the eight commanders were executed despite their defense that a
storm had made rescue impossible. Though the details of what took
place are obscure, and there may well have been criminal negligence
somewhere, the whole affair smelled of illegality and popular passion
that made it a notorious event in Athenian history.[134] Socrates at the
time of the trial was serving as a member of the *boule,* the only office he
ever held. As presiding officer he refused to put the question to the
vote, despite the threats of the orators to impeach and arrest him and
the shouts of the populace urging them on to do so.[135]

On a later occasion the Thirty Tyrants ordered Socrates to go with
four others to Salamis in order to bring back Leon the Salaminian,
otherwise unidentified, to be put to death. According to Socrates' own
account, the government of the Thirty did not frighten him into doing
anything unjust. Risking execution at its hands, he simply went home.
Meanwhile the other four went on to Salamis and arrested Leon.[136]

Thus both of Socrates' encounters with political responsibility
ended in failure. In both cases, but especially in the second one where
he simply went home, a modern revolutionary might accuse Socrates
of merely making a typically individualist gesture to protect his private
conscience and public reputation. To the person who runs the actual
risks this type of moral judgment, quite apart from its disagreeable
odor of moral superiority, can have no logical standing unless it
adduces plausible arguments about how to act effectively in the specific
circumstances of the time.

In any case, Socrates and Plato between them created a new and
highly influential social role, that of the private citizen as social critic.
They did not work entirely without prior models. Socrates was not the

first speculative thinker in Athens to be charged with impiety. Anaxagoras, the friend of Pericles, had preceded him. But Anaxagoras was a natural philosopher, not a social one. As for Protagoras, modern authorities dismiss the tale of his trial and condemnation as an invention or error of later writers.[137]

In turn Diogenes the Cynic (b. 413 B.C.?) took up and played out the Socratic model in an exaggerated fashion. Most of what we know about him comes from a far from trustworthy source, the life written by Diogenes Laertius, who probably lived in the first half of the third century A.D. His account is hardly more than a collection of anecdotes and sarcastic remarks, suggesting that Diogenes the Cynic was a much more savage critic than Socrates, and one who made a point of flouting Athenian rules of respectability in regard to dress and bodily needs. Yet by treating him as a clown or democratic court jester, the Athenians were able to render him harmless.† The Athenians could not or would not do that to Socrates.

After reading the *Apology* it is quite surprising to come upon Plato's negative attitude toward private life in his major political treatises. There is one rather obvious reason for his hostility toward anything that smacks of privacy or private interest. Plato had very little of Aristotle's interest in the anatomy of existing human societies. He defined his task as the speculative working-out of the best possible form of society as a model with which critically to judge existing social arrangements.

Now, in an ideal society there is by definition no need for a private sphere to which the individual can retreat. If social institutions work perfectly and there is in place an educational system that grinds out new personalities suited to the perfect social order, why should there be any need for privacy? Instead, privacy begins to look like a cover for the evasion of ethical and social obligations. (This is the usual attitude even now among revolutionary perfectionists and many enthusiastic reformers.)

Some such considerations may lie behind the absence of all but the most fleeting references to privacy in *The Republic*. At the beginning of Book VIII, Plato does mention requirements for a polis that is to achieve good government. They include community of wives, children, and education among the wise leaders or Guardians, measures that would suppress the private sphere. Further, the rules should see to it that the soldiers were settled in habitations "that have nothing private for anybody but are common for all." As "athletes of war and guardians," they were to receive from the others their yearly sustenance so that they might "devote their entire attention to the care of

†Diogenes Laertius *Lives of Eminent Philosophers* 6.43 says he was loved by the Athenians.

themselves and the state."[138] It is worth noticing, however, that Plato expected political functions to rotate in a way that would leave plenty of leisure for the study of philosophy.[139]

Despite his evident hostility to privacy, Plato recognized its attraction. In the curious and fantastic myth of souls choosing their next life, with which *The Republic* closes, he has Odysseus, recollecting the toils of his previous life, search at length for the life of a private citizen who minded his own business. With difficulty Odysseus finds such a soul, lying in a corner disregarded by the others.[140]

In *The Laws,* reputedly his last work, Plato does address himself more directly to the issues of privacy. Community, sharing, and what a modern might call the virtues of togetherness win hands down over inclinations toward privacy which, in characteristic utopian fashion, he sees as a threat to the good society. At one point he asserts that the lawgiver should arrange for local religious ceremonies

> . . . so that, when assemblies of each of the sections take place . . . the people may fraternize with one another at the sacrifices and gain knowledge and intimacy, since nothing is of more benefit to the State than this mutual acquaintance; for where men conceal their ways from one another in darkness rather than light, there no man will ever rightly gain either his due honour or office or the justice that is befitting.[141]

Plato does not see any possibility that privacy could serve a constructive social or psychological purpose. Instead it is something to be rooted out. On this point he is quite explicit, though he expresses himself in a way that reveals doubts about the possibility of achieving this objective. Despite its awkwardness and length, this passage deserves extended quotation as a prototype of the communitarian tradition in Western thought:

> That State and polity come first, and those laws are best where there is observed as carefully as possible throughout the whole State the old saying that "friends have all things really in common." As to this condition—whether it anywhere exists now, or ever will exist—in which there is community of wives, children, and all chattels, and all that is called "private" is everywhere and by every means rooted out of our life, and so far as possible it is contrived that things naturally "private" have become communized—eyes, for instance, and ears and hands seem to see, hear, and act in common—and that all men are, so far as possible, unanimous in the praise and blame they bestow, rejoicing and grieving at the same things, and that they honour with all their heart those laws which render the State as unified as possible—no one will ever lay down another definition that is truer or better than these conditions in point of excellence. In such a State, whether gods or sons of gods inhabit it, they dwell pleasantly, living such a life as this.[142]

In Plato's day such a community was for the gods. Centuries later there would be attempts to create it for humans, setting off bloody struggles that continue into our own time.

In Aristotle's *Politics* the issue of private life versus active political participation turns up in such a way as to reveal that it was the subject of lively discussion among his contemporaries. Aristotle often summarizes the range of opinions on a given topic as a background to the presentation of his own views. The essence of what he has to say occurs in *Politics* 7.3, a total of less than three pages, though passing references occur elsewhere.† He begins with the observation that "Some disapprove of holding office in the state, thinking that the life of the free man is different from the life of politics," a novel and striking opinion from the standpoint of our inquiry. "Others think the political life is the best life . . . ."

For Aristotle this issue is intertwined with at least five others that he seems to have regarded as more important. One is the contrast between the role of the free man able to rule and be ruled, which Aristotle prefers, and the role of the dominating leader seeking political mastery by violent means.‡ Another is the basis of obedience, which he justifies in terms of the superior virtue and practical capacities of a leader. A third is the general relation between the individual and the polis. On this score it is significant that Aristotle displays scarcely an inkling of inevitable conflict between the individual and the social order.§ This viewpoint implies close limits on any conception of legitimate privacy, though Aristotle does not draw the conclusion.

Two further themes are the nature of human happiness, which he regards as necessarily requiring some form of human activity, and the legitimacy of speculative thought. On the latter point, it is scarcely astonishing that a very distinguished philosopher should assert the value of life devoted to intellectual pursuits. It is best to quote his own words:

> But the active life is not necessarily active in relation to other men, as some people think, nor are only those processes of thought active that are pursued for the sake of the objects that result from action, but far more those speculations and thoughts that have their end in themselves

---

†Aristotle *Politics* 2.8.6; 2.9.1; and an interesting discussion of the tyrant Jason of Pherae at 3.2.6–7. There Aristotle observes that Jason "did not know how to be a private person." Unlike the free citizens of other Greek cities, Jason could command but could not obey.

‡Most of the preceding section, *Politics* 7.2 is devoted to this theme, which is repeated briefly in 7.3.

§At *Politics* 7.2.2 he asserts that what is desirable for the individual is not part of the business of political study and speculation. At 7.3.6 he takes a different position, concluding "that the same life must be the best both for each human being individually and for city states and mankind collectively."

and are pursued for their own sake; for the end is to do well and therefore is a certain form of action.[143]

Thus it turns out that intellectual pursuits constitute *the* justification for a life apart from direct involvement in politics. As far as I am aware, this is the first statement of a thesis that was to become famous in the history of Western thought. Aristotle's position is distinct from, though not necessarily opposed to, priestly speculation, which is of course much older and would last for centuries beyond his time. But priests are not private persons. For the Aristotelian position to appear, there had to be in existence at least a small group of persons devoting most of their lives to speculative and perhaps also empirical inquiry more or less independent of both religious and political demands. Beginning with the cosmological speculations of the sixth century B.C. and continuing through the sophists, the growth of this type of educated and specialized elite does not seem to have proceeded far enough until about the fourth century B.C. to create a justification for its existence. We cannot be sure of the dates, and there is always the danger of constructing a circular argument. Yet the general thesis that a certain specific type of social differentiation had to precede this form of justification for private life seems indisputable.

Xenophon, as already mentioned, furnishes evidence for the continued existence of a more traditional and somewhat negative attitude toward private life. To be sure, in the *Oeconomicus,* a literary exercise in the form of a treatise on estate management, he presents us with the only existing detailed account of private life, the domestic existence in the fourth century B.C. of a very prosperous Athenian country gentleman. Many of the details, to be discussed in another context, are obviously idealized and rather hard to believe.

But in any case Xenophon did not conceive of this idyllic rural existence as a permanent refuge from public and social obligations. Quite the contrary was the case. At one point he has Socrates make the familiar conservative arguments that husbandry gives the body "the greatest measure of strength and beauty [and leaves] to the mind the greatest amount of spare time for attending to the affairs of one's friends and the city." Husbandry is "held in the highest estimation by our city states, because it seems to turn out the best citizens and most loyal to the community."[144] Later he has the estate owner assert his hope that the city would lack no adornment that his means could supply and that this was one of the main purposes for making the estate yield a surplus.[145] Finally, Xenophon chose to place this ideal estate within easy walking distance from the town.[146] In real life, as we have had many occasions to notice, a prosperous estate owner would ordinarily be expected to assume heavy financial burdens on behalf of the city in both peace and war.

Elsewhere Xenophon, through the mouth of Socrates, rebukes a somewhat self-indulgent young man who denies that he wants to take part in ruling a city. Considering how hard it is to provide for one's own needs, says the young man, he finds it absurd to shoulder the burden of supplying the wants of the community as well. "That anyone should sacrifice a large part of his own wishes and make himself accountable as head of the state for the least failure to carry out all the wishes of the community is surely the height of folly." In Athens of that time there was probably a substantial *jeunesse dorée* making such remarks. The reply that Xenophon attributes to Socrates has some of the air of a hearty football coach advising a confused youngster of our own time. First of all, he retorts, there is no escape into private life because domination on the one hand and slavery on the other hand exist as much there as elsewhere. Nor will it work to avoid life in one community and try to be a stranger in every land, as the young man proposes. No one will have anything to do with him. Hence in the end there is no choice but strenuous effort leading up to good and noble deeds.[147]

In a quite different situation, where Xenophon sketches Socrates encouraging a talented but very shy young man to speak up in the Assembly and seek the role of an active political leader, there is an interesting recurrence of the agonistic theme: one must accept a challenge. According to the dialogue, a man capable of victory and gaining honor in the great games, thus adding to his homeland's fame, who yet refuses to compete would be treated as an effeminate coward. Likewise, if a man were to shrink from the affairs of the polis though able to strengthen it and bring honor to himself, it would be reasonable to regard him as a coward. The exchange continues with a contemptuous reference to the Assembly: "Who are they that make you ashamed?" says Socrates. "The fullers or the cobblers, or the builders, or the smiths, or the farmers, or the merchants, or the traffickers in the market-place who think of nothing but buying cheap and selling dear? For these are the people who make up the Assembly."[148]

From these remarks it is evident that Xenophon, the bluff old soldier, was a believer in public spirit but with little faith in the real Athenian public or its actual institutions. It is also plain that he had no objection to private life as part of a larger existence. What he objected to was a life entirely devoted to private pursuits.† Xenophon's accept-

---

†Xenophon did not always insist on the necessity of seeking public office. He has Socrates claim that by teaching, one fulfills the duty of a citizen and a gentleman. Twitted later by Antiphon for claiming to make politicians of others when he avoided politics himself, Socrates supposedly replied, "How now, Antiphon, should I play a more important part in politics by engaging in them alone or by taking pains to turn out as many competent politicians as possible?" See *Memorabilia* 1.6.13–15. This remark is similar to the position taken by Socrates in Plato, *Apology,* discussed above.

ance of private life, in the sense of looking after one's household and family affairs, distinguishes him sharply from Plato who was thoroughly suspicious of such personal ties.

Demosthenes was the other spokesman on behalf of the overriding importance of public life and public obligations. Unless I have missed something in his voluminous surviving works, which take up seven volumes of the Loeb Classical Library, his speeches and writings do not contain any general discussion of private life. That is understandable in the case of a man who was above all an active politician. From his political role as the man who tried to rouse the Athenians to take effective military action against Philip of Macedon, it is not difficult, on the other hand, to see what his position was bound to be. The complaint that Athenians put their private pleasures ahead of unpleasant political realities recurs as a refrain in many of his speeches.[149] The patriotic spirit that made possible the victories over the Persians has, he claims, given way to ostentatious private display. Good men scorn the acquisition of wealth and the pleasures of life; their whole desire is for virtue and words of praise.[150]

Since the basic themes are both predictable and conventional, there is nothing to be gained by going into them in further detail. Like many a social critic, Demosthenes paints his country's past in romantic hues. After all, the great hero Themistocles had to trick the Athenians into fighting the battle of Salamis and ended his life in the service of the Persian king. Nevertheless Demosthenes' speeches do contain a substantial element of truth. As this discussion has already made plain, fourth-century literature gives many indications of a shift away from public concerns to a greater emphasis on private ones.

The shift is very noticeable in the case of Isocrates. Of all the thinkers whose works have survived he went the furthest toward establishing the model for a private life devoted to serious intellectual pursuits. For many moderns he would be an appealing figure were it not for his querulous vanity. As matters stand, hardly anyone except a classicist would be likely to recognize even his name today. It is also important to recognize that with Isocrates this new note in praise of privacy comes from a double failure, both personal and political. It was personal in the sense that he lacked the voice and confidence necessary to succeed as an orator and therefore turned to teaching and writing. It was also a failure in the sense that during his lifetime the polis as an independent unit subject to continual fratricidal warfare ceased to be a viable political form. Such warfare, it is safe to assert on the basis not only of Greek experience, but also that of the Italian city-states centuries later, was endemic to this social formation. Isocrates recognized this weakness. But in the end his only solution was imperialist expansion at the expense of Persia.

Though we may look askance today at the imperialist solution to social problems, it would be unfair to tax Isocrates with its inadequacy. Nor is it by any means clear that modern thought has so greatly improved on this type of diagnosis and remedy. In practice Marxist solutions to social conflicts have neither reduced cruel domination at home nor introduced the brotherhood of man as a principle of international conduct even among socialist states.

In the first and foremost of his political essays, the *Panegyricus,* Isocrates asserts that under earlier Athenian hegemony private households achieved their highest level of prosperity and the cities became greatest.[151] Irrespective of the truth of this claim, it is significant that he places private gains first, a new note in the celebration of Athenian attainments.

The essay begins with a somewhat plaintive observation about those who have toiled in private for the public good and have trained their own minds so as to be able to help their fellow men: in public estimation they stand lower than prize-winning athletes.† The complaint, however, which could easily arouse sympathetic echoes today, demonstrates that working in private for the public good had by his time become an acceptable if somewhat unusual career.

As the essay proceeds, it creates the image of a man aloof from public life, yet concerned with the major political issues, while political activists dissipated their energies in trivialities.[152] In addition to the writing of political discourses, "toiling in private" for Isocrates meant teaching. Such teaching had a substantial moral component. With considerable pride he accepted responsibility for his followers.[153]

Thus his private life was focused on matters of public concern for which he claimed to feel responsible. Politics still remained the main focus for a private citizen who wanted to devote his life to serious intellectual pursuits. Other secular alternatives such as natural science, the arts, and literature had not yet developed beyond a rudimentary state or were held in low repute. Presumably the priesthood offered another alternative, though so far as I am aware no Greek author discusses the life of a priest.

In the *Antidosis,* which amounts to a defense of his way of life, Isocrates quotes the remarks of a possibly imaginary associate to the effect that he has never brought anyone to trial nor stood trial himself, save in the matter of an exchange of property (this in itself was imaginary, since the *Antidosis* dealt with an imagined situation). Furthermore he has never appeared as counsel or witness for others, nor engaged in any of the other activities that make up the civic life of Athenians. This claim is probably a rhetorical exaggeration. It is hard to believe that every Athenian citizen, or even every well-to-do citizen, was at some point in his life involved in a lawsuit. But Isocrates

---

†*Panegyricus* 1. In the *Antidosis* 151 he contradicts this assessment.

certainly saw his own life as unusual. "And to these peculiarities and idiosyncracies," his purported associate continues, "you add another, namely, that you have held aloof from the public offices and the emoluments that go with them. . . ."[154] A few paragraphs later Isocrates tells his readers that he chose this type of life because he loved peace and tranquillity, and most of all because he saw that men leading such lives were looked up to both in Athens and other parts of the world.†

That may well have been the case. On the other hand, Isocrates' statements have a defensive ring, as if he were trying to justify a new and unfamiliar pattern of life. That the pattern was available to others as a second choice appears in some remarks about his students. Only two or three turned out to be real oratorical champions, the main purpose of rhetorical training, the rest retiring from their studies into private life.[155]

Isocrates provides some insight into the material basis for a life of peace and quiet, though more exact details would be helpful. He was the son of a rich man whose fortunes deteriorated during the Peloponnesian War.[156] At the time he wrote the *Antidosis* he was enrolled among the twelve hundred who paid the war taxes and bore the costs of liturgies; he had discharged the trierarchy three times and performed the other services more generously than the laws required.[157] By Athenian standards, in other words, he was very wealthy. As a boy, he remarked bitterly, wealth seemed secure and admirable. Now a man, he had to be ready to defend himself against being rich as if it were the worst of crimes.[158]

Since teaching and writing were not as a rule especially lucrative occupations, it is likely that some of his wealth was inherited. Gorgias, one of his early teachers, devoted his life, Isocrates reports, to making money. He had no fixed domicile in any city and therefore paid no tax. Gorgias must have been one of the first rootless cosmopolitan intellectuals. Despite the fact that he paid no tax, at his death he left "only a thousand *staters*," a very modest fortune.[159]

Isocrates acknowledged that he received many presents from Nicocles, king of the Salaminians and an admirer. But he claims that all of his resources came from abroad, that is, mainly from foreign students. There is a story that he charged no fees to Athenian students. According to a secondary source, his fees were high: he is said to have charged a thousand drachmas for his course.[160] Since Isocrates had, by his own account, more students than all the others together who

---

†Isocrates *Antidosis* 151. Once more he characterizes this kind of life as more agreeable than that of men who are busy with all sorts of things. Isocrates' love of peace and quiet stands in sharp contrast with that of his near-namesake, Socrates.

occupied themselves with philosophy, he might have made a very comfortable living from his teaching alone. In any case, whether his income was solely from teaching or also included rental income, for example, he was able to maintain himself from his private resources.[161]

None of this would have been possible without a clientele of students eager to learn his skills in the use of the Greek language and to hear his moral teaching. Presumably they were drawn from all over the Greek-speaking world. From this we can infer the emergence of a cosmopolitan intellectual elite alongside and fusing with those based on land, military prowess, and trade.

Another work by Isocrates sheds much light on the culture of this new elite, the main carrier of the ideal of private life. He wrote a moral discourse in the form of ethical and worldly advice to a young gentleman that brings to mind Lord Chesterfield's advice to his son. This is a difficult literary form to interpret for sociological purposes because it is hard to tell what if anything is to be taken seriously. The author is likely to stress a mixture of impossible ethical precepts and cynical advice, neither of which necessarily corresponds to actual behavior. On the other hand, it is possible to discern in such a document themes that actually exist in the culture of the period even if these themes are overemphasized for the sake of literary effect. There are further difficulties in the case of Isocrates' *To Demonicus,* since it happens to be addressed to a well-to-do young man of Cyprus. At the same time, since it was written by an Athenian, it is safe to assume that it indirectly reflects Athenian mores. On balance therefore we may take it as a model for a young Athenian private gentleman of the fourth century B.C. One feature is likely to strike a reader at once: the complete absence of any mention of how to behave when seeking or holding political office. The advice it offers is strictly limited to private behavior as Athenians defined the term. The omission may be due to the fact that the discourse was directed to an inhabitant of Cyprus. But it may also reflect the predilections of Isocrates for a life of peace and quiet.

There are several clues to a new fourth-century conception of what qualities a private gentleman should display.† Upper-class men in Homeric times and well into the classical period were expected to display physical and moral courage as well as polite accomplishments. By the time of Isocrates they were also expected to possess cultivation or "brains" in the slightly snobbish present-day sense of this expression. Brawn, beauty, and property were no longer enough, even when

---

†The Greek term translated here as gentleman is καλὸς κ'αγαθός (kalos kagathos), literally "beautiful and good." In Herodotus, Aristophanes, and Thucydides it was used loosely as a favorable characterization for upper-class males. Later it acquired a positive moral connotation. See Liddell and Scott's *Lexicon* for an interesting collection of citations.

combined with an articulate command of the Greek language. Or so Isocrates thought.† Similar views occur in Plato and Aristotle. But we cannot be sure that professional thinkers had been any more successful in imposing a new conception of proper upbringing in ancient Athens than in modern times. In some circles a cultivated intelligence may become a social handicap, I suspect, in just about any human culture.

Another theme is that of the proper restraint and decorum to be expected of a young gentleman. By itself the theme of self-restraint was a common one in Greek literature. Here, however, the emphasis is on restraint to avoid the risk of exposure and shame. If possible, one should avoid drinking parties altogether. If that is impossible, one should leave politely before getting intoxicated.[162] In older times eating or drinking in a tavern was allegedly something that no one, not even an honest slave, would do.[163] Presumably this was a form of relaxed social contact with social inferiors that a gentleman should avoid. (Half a century ago an English gentleman would not go into a village pub even when thirsty after a vigorous hike.) "Whatever is shameful to do," advises Isocrates, "you must not consider it honourable even to mention."[164] The repression must include even verbal behavior. "Grieve in moderation," he also advises, "and . . . do not expose your heart to others." This is the opposite of the Russian upper-class penchant, so noticeable in the great nineteenth-century novels, for heart-to-heart *(po dyshy)* talks on all emotionally charged topics.

Hence the Athenian private gentleman of the fourth century was expected to be a very reserved and private person. The emotional tone seems light-years away from the world of Aristophanes, which may be party due to a difference in personalities. (Their lives in fact overlapped. Aristophanes was born some time between 457 and 445 B.C. and died about 385 B.C.; Isocrates was born in 436 B.C. and died in 338 B.C.) As might be expected, keeping secrets was regarded as a matter of honor, and friendship was supposed to be a guarded and even wary relationship.[165] Indeed there is more than a touch of deviousness in the relationship. Isocrates advises the young Demonicus if he needs advice from a friend on any matter about which he feels ashamed, to pretend that it was someone else's affair. Then he will get the benefit of his friend's opinion without giving himself away.[166] Isocrates fails to add that this device would fail to arouse suspicion only if the friend were naïve and unsuspecting, in which case the advice would probably be worthless.

Looking back at our limited evidence on Athenian conceptions of

---

†He emphasized the point at *To Demonicus* 33, though part of this long sentence is obscure. *Paideia,* a much discussed term, I have rendered here as cultivation and brains or "brains" alone. A few paragraphs later in *To Demonicus* 40, Isocrates admonishes: "Give careful heed to all that concerns your life, but above all train your own intellect; for the greatest thing in the smallest compass is a sound mind in a human body."

private life brings to mind some sociological and historical generalizations. Many Athenians, including slaves, must have at some time longed for a protected private existence in the sense of freedom from erratic and crushing social burdens due to wars and domestic political upheavals. This theme runs through the comedies of Aristophanes. For prosperous citizens the ideal of a life of peace and quiet devoted to intellectual pursuits had become clearly defined and socially respectable by about the middle of the fourth century B.C. Western culture did not have to wait until the triumph of capitalism for the appearance of this cultural model. The emergence of a reading public that partly replaced oral literary communication in the first half of the fourth century[167] may have been a sufficient facilitating condition. On the other hand, because Athenian society was far less differentiated than that of nineteenth-century England, and in particular lacked more than a most rudimentary set of independent professions, no more than a limited development of this conception of private life was possible in Athens. There were not enough activities open for a private gentleman for this role to receive the major cultural emphasis that it did in Victorian England and Western Europe generally.

The Family, Human Biology, and the Public

For the Athenians the distinction between public and private coincided with the distinction between the realm of politics and the realm of household affairs and domestic life. The public realm, except for some religious rituals, was a male realm; the private realm belonged to both sexes, but was largely subject to female management. The boundary between the two was not impermeable. In any society there is a public interest in sexual behavior, the procreation and rearing of new members of the social order. In what follows I shall discuss the public interest in Athenian family life. From there we shall turn to an examination of domestic social relationships and the rules governing privacy within the family. Only after we understand the structure of domestic life and sexual relationships that enjoy full social approval can we turn our attention profitably to other sexual relationships: concubinage, extramarital affairs, and homosexuality.

Both Aristotle and Plato advocate a degree of political control over family life in hortatory terms that show such control did not exist in the democratic Athens of their day. Aristotle describes the polis as "a partnership of families and of clans in living well."[168] Here, as elsewhere, his language is that of the social engineer who knows how to contrive social arrangements that will yield virtue and contentment. The lawgiver, Aristotle asserts, ought to control sexual unions so as to get the best bodily frames for the children. Women should marry at about the age of eighteen, men at the age of thirty-seven or a little earlier. (Aristotle had some odd ideas about the marital sexual habits of his Athenian compatriots which it will be more appropriate to discuss in another connection.) Deformed children, he argued, were to be exposed. If custom prevented exposure, there must be a limit to procreation. Abortion received his approval so long as it took place before sensation was possible for the fetus. Fornication by either males or females should be an act punishable by the loss of privileges, adapted to the nature of the offense.[169] From his account it seems reasonably plain that none of the practices he endorsed prevailed in Athens. Such a degree of control over private life would have been intolerable to a people who, as Aristotle remarks elsewhere, were democrats in the sense that everyone wanted to live the way he liked.

In *The Laws* Plato took an even stronger position than Aristotle by stating flatly that marriage should benefit the polis. He wanted to impose both a fine and a loss of social esteem on males who had not married by the age of thirty-three.[170] Like Aristotle, Plato held that the purpose of marriage was to produce children of the greatest possible goodness and beauty for the polis.[171] Unlike Aristotle, Plato proposed a system of detailed police controls over marital behavior. There were to be female inspectors with the right to enter the houses of young people in case of disputes. By threats and admonitions the inspectors were to make the young couples desist from sin and folly. Just what sins and follies he had in mind Plato failed to reveal.[172]

By their obviously fanciful nature such proposals furnish strong evidence for the conclusion that the polis did not interfere seriously with the selection of marital partners or the details of conjugal behavior. The philosophers' objections to marital privacy prove that such privacy existed. In real life, then, how were such choices made? And in what circumstances did the polis actually intervene in the affairs of the family?

Romantic attraction does not seem to have played an important role in the selection of a mate, if indeed it played any role at all. That is not because the Greeks, as in sometimes asserted, lacked any conception of romantic passion and its capacity to shatter social regulations. Their language and literature furnish plenty of evidence that they were quite aware of romantic passion. Euripides' tragedy *Hippolytus* is a sensitive and psychologically acute study of Phaedra's illicit attraction to her stepson Hippolytus. On the other hand, Greek literature makes little or no distinction between heterosexual and homosexual attraction.[173] The availability of the homosexual alternative may have helped to erect a barrier to making romantic attraction the basis for choosing a mate. There was another. Xenophon remarks that outside marriage, whose purpose was the creation of legitimate offspring, lust could easily be satisfied.[174] To a considerable extent, it appears, "joyous" sex was regarded as a pleasure to be sought outside marriage.

Instead of depending on the gusts of passion to produce a stable child-rearing union, the Athenians appear to have relied on the insights and social connections of the parents, especially the father, in finding a mate for their marriageable offspring. Considerations based on property and continuity of the family (and its obligations) were very important. Some remarks in the legal literature give the impression that the girl or woman was often no more than a pawn in a game of grown-up politics.[175] That impression is probably an exaggeration since it is unlikely that a lasting union could be established against the chosen spouse's determined opposition.

The polis intervened in at least three aspects of family life. According to a law cited by Demosthenes, the king archon was required to take charge of orphans, pregnant widows, and families about to become extinct.[176] Strong sentiments underlay this legislation, aimed at preventing the breakup or extinction of a lineage. Individuals tried to forestall such extinction by adopting children in order to ensure the continuation of sacrifices and customary rites. If the family was a wealthy one, the polis had an interest in ensuring that a unit capable of bearing the expenses of a trierarchy did not become extinct.[177] The concern was moral more than economic. Legal speeches are full of pleas for special consideration of an individual because that individual belongs to a lineage with a record of distinguished service to the state. The contrary is also true: it was somewhat of a disgrace for a lineage to have failed to have made the contributions in wealth and manpower that, according to its reputation, it could have made.

The other area in which the polis intervened was in cases of adultery.[178] The intervention was limited insofar as the polis left it open to the offended husband to exact revenge if he caught the pair in the act. Still, the role of the polis was to stand foursquare behind the husband's monopolistic rights to his wife's sexual favors. And as we shall see later, the polis intervened to require that children support their parents and give aid to other relatives.

In addition to these forms of intervention there are tantalizing clues to others. Aristotle's *Politics* contains three references to the offices of "Superintendent of Women" and "Superintendent of Children."[179] These officials were to supervise the movements of well-to-do women and children, keeping them within the confines of the family property and mainly out of the streets. The assumption was, I infer, that in aristocratic households servants and slaves could fetch and carry in all food, other supplies, and run errands. Among the poor the situation was clearly different. Having no slaves or servants, as Aristotle puts it, "How is it possible to prevent the wives of the poor from going out of doors?" Such women were exempt from the restrictions (as well as the protection) exercised by the City Controllers.[180]

Turning now to domestic social relationships, we find contrasting descriptions of their emotional tone in Aristotle and Xenophon. Aristotle was somewhat of a misogynist as well as no friend of democracy. The combination was repulsive to him; in the final or radical stage of democracy, he asserts, women become dominant in the home in order that they may carry abroad reports against the men. Lack of discipline appears among the slaves for the same reason. Slaves and women, he continues, do not plot against tyrants, and if they prosper under them, must feel well disposed to both tyrants and democracies because they favor the common people.[181]

Xenophon's account stands in sharp contrast to Aristotle's remarks. In his handbook on the management of a country estate, the *Oeconomicus,* he offers us a series of curious glimpses into upper-class domestic intimacy. Evidently he set down his conception of the ideal relationship between husband and wife, not necessarily one that actually existed. The wife's role was fundamentally that of a business manager in a large commercial undertaking. While the husband's efforts and property yielded income, the wife controlled most of the disbursements.[182]

This rather odd document is cast in the form of a discussion between Socrates and an estate owner. At one point the following exchange takes place: "Is there anyone to whom you commit more affairs of importance than you commit to your wife?" Socrates asks.

"There is not."

"Is there anyone with whom you talk less?"

"There are few or none, I confess," says the estate owner.[183]

To the extent that this interchange is credible, it reflects a situation very far from the modern middle-class ideal of marital companionship and partnership. But the Athenians had a different ideal. In the ideal division of labor (which may in fact not be purely Athenian, as Xenophon was a cosmopolitan with some leanings toward Sparta) the wife took care of all indoor tasks. In this sense she was really in charge of private life. To manage a large household she needed many skills, tact, and intelligence. In the idealized case presented by Xenophon, the husband provided the lion's share of the wife's education in the form of on-the-job training. The husband's pomposity in describing the training is matched by the wife's docility in accepting it, all to the point where the relationship seems scarcely believable.[184]

Nevertheless there are a few light touches. After the husband has delivered to his spouse a little lecture on the superior attractiveness of a fresh unpainted female countenance in contrast to one covered with rouge and eye grease, he observes that all such deceptions are bound to be found out anyway while they are dressing in the morning. This is the fate of overdecorated wives: "They perspire and are lost; a tear convicts them; the bath reveals them as they are."[185]

Putting together the somewhat sour picture of domestic life given by Aristotle and the almost ludicrous image of patriarchal authority painted by Xenophon, we can infer a weakening of this patriarchal authority under the influence of popular democracy, urbanization, and commerce.

In *Politics* Aristotle says that the upbringing of children and women should take place with due regard to the political character of the polis. Women, he remarked, constitute half of the free population and children constitute the next generation. In a similar vein Aeschines refers to the tradition of Solon and Draco's alleged concern with moral education,[186] without, however, giving any information about what the polis actually did. So far as I can make out, the polis as such did not do anything.

Education was private, fee-paying, and not compulsory. The *grammatistes* taught reading, writing, and arithmetic as well as literature. Education in literature consisted in learning by heart the works of poets selected for their apparent value for moral training. Homer was a favorite. The *kitharistes* taught music and the works of lyric poets; the *paidotribes*, gymnastics, games, and deportment.[187] Thus it is plain that the Athenians had an organized procedure for transmitting the essentials of their own culture even if this transmission took place without formal action by a public institution. A great deal of education must have taken place through conversation and example. Advanced education of a sort could be obtained in Athens and other great centers of learning by studying literature and law, or by an apprenticeship in medicine, or by attending lectures by itinerant sophists.

As we turn our attention from the rearing of children to obligations of adults toward their parents we come upon a variety of legal and social sanctions against the mistreatment of these and some other relatives. The frequency and vehemence with which these sanctions crop up in the literature indicate that such mistreatment was by no means a rarity. In court actions for ill-usage of parents, anyone who wanted to might act as a prosecutor without fear of penalty for failure to win the case.[188]

Demosthenes refers to laws that compel the maintenance of parents—apparently a private form of social insurance enforced by the polis—and that ensure that they will be honored by due observance when they die. According to the text of a law he cites, any man arrested after being found guilty of mistreating his parents, or shirking military service, or entering any forbidden place after notice of outlawry, fell under the authority of The Eleven, who were to imprison him and bring him before the Court of the Heliaia.[189] The assimilation of the crime of mistreating parents with other crimes against the polis reveals the character of respectable sentiment in the fourth century.

According to Xenophon, the polis inflicts penalties on the man who is discourteous to his parents, holding that it would be a sin for such a man to offer sacrifices on behalf of the polis and that he is unlikely to do anything else in an honorable and upright fashion. If a man fails to honor his parents' graves, the polis looks into that behavior too when it examines candidates for office.[190]

Isaeus asserts that "the law enjoins us to support our parents, meaning by 'parents' father, mother, grandfather, grandmother," and *their* parents, if still alive.[191] To be descended from hardy stock on both sides must have been rather an economic burden in fourth-century Athens. In another case he asserts that the claims of kinship, the laws, and a sense of shame obliged the claimants to support their grandfather and either marry the granddaughters or else provide dowries and find other husbands for them.[192] One portion of this extensive and rather arduous set of obligations did, however, disappear at a rather early date. Solon relieved sons born out of wedlock of the obligation of supporting their fathers.[193]

Athenian family law contained several provisions for the protection of an heiress. The son of an heiress was required to become the guardian of his mother's estate and provide for his mother's maintenance.[194] If a woman lacked a father or other suitable male relative who could give her in betrothal for a lawful marriage, and was also an heiress, her guardian was required by law to marry her. If she were not an heiress, the man to whom she might entrust herself was to be her guardian.[195] Husbands of heiresses on more than one occasion had to give up their wives when the heiress' father died without having a legitimate brother. In this case the heiress passed into the legal power and hands of the next-of-kin male. In Athenian law, property could be inherited by a woman, but she could not dispose of it as she wished. In our modern sense she did not own it, but could use it until she produced a son who would inherit it. There was also a certain reluctance to letting a woman with a substantial property under her care pass out of one's own lineage.[196]

In legislation concerning inheritance one can discern the same tension between the individual's desire to designate the recipient of his property after death and obligations to the family enforced by the polis. At quite an early date Solon is reported to have taken one of the first steps to increase the testator's freedom of choice. Solon's legislation about wills is reported to have ranked friendship above kinship.[197]

According to a law cited by Demosthenes, however, a man had the right to dispose of his own property through his will only if he lacked male children. The testator also had to be demonstrably capable of independent judgment; that is, his mind should not be impaired by lunacy, old age, drugs, or diseases, nor should he be under the influence of a woman, under constraint, or deprived of his liberty.[198] The Athenians also distinguished between an individual's personal property and that which descended through a family line.[199] If a man died without making a will, the law specified in detail the claims of potential heirs. Males and the sons of males took precedence, though females could of course inherit. No illegitimate child of either sex had the right of succession to either religious rites of civic privileges. The text of the law does not mention their exclusion from the right to inherit property.[200]

One feature of Athenian legislation must have encouraged litigation over wills. According to the law, any Athenian had the right to challenge any inheritance in court. If he established a better claim, he could take possession of the estate.[201] The quarrels promoted by such a law may have undermined family solidarity. At the very least it must have led to much waste of substance in the form of legal expenses.

This law contradicted strong Athenian beliefs that the family was a moral unit. There was something disgraceful about allowing disputes with relatives to become public,[202] though such breaches of privacy were quite common. There was such a thing as family reputation (as there is in our own society if in a much weaker form). It was possible to discuss the whole family and its reputation before a jury court with perfect propriety. Neither the prosecution nor the defense was expected to limit the discussion to specific acts. Vengeance against any member of a family whose leader had injured Athens might be called a duty by the prosecution.[203] In times of severe political struggle many Athenians evidently came to regard a whole family as innocent or guilty.[204] But the notion of family guilt was not limited to such tense circumstances. In the course of a case concerned with local hatreds in a single Attic *deme,* Demosthenes remarked: "With whatsoever wrongs a man may be charged during his lifetime it is right that for these his children should forever be held accountable."[205]

Although the Athenians perceived the family, or more accurately the lineage, as a moral unit, their political ethics did set limits on the individual's loyalty to this unit. At the time of the excitement over the trial of the naval commanders at Arginusae, Xenophon reports that someone urged the trial of a kinsman, saying that it would be base to think more of a kinsman than the general interests of the polis.[206] In a similar fashion Xenophon has Socrates argue that one must not rely on the domestic bond in evaluating a father or brother but on that person's soul, usefulness, and capacity for acting in accord with reason. He also has Socrates express vehement disapproval of any person who cannot help the army, the city, or the people in time of need.[207] As proclaimed sentiments, such judgments were commonplace. For Athenians as well as other Greeks, the polis was the real community. Loyalty to the polis as a whole overrode loyalty to any component unit. The public interest came first, at least in theory.

Within the Athenian household there were clear rules to secure privacy. Almost all of those about which we have any knowledge have sexual overtones in the sense that they serve to protect female members of the household against intrusion by males. We hear of the women's rooms in one house where a man lived with his sister and nieces. Their lives were supposedly so well ordered that they were ashamed to be seen even by the owner's kinsmen. For a male visitor to enter this house in a drunken state, break down the doors, and enter the women's rooms was so monstrous a form of misbehavior that neighbors appeared on the spot and helped to drive the intruder out by force.[208] Such an episode incidentally reveals what could happen about a breach of the peace in the absence of a police force. The community's sense of propriety was evidently sufficient to take care of the situation. From another source we learn that no one would dare to serenade a married woman. Nor did married women accompany their husbands to banquets or think of feasting in the company of strangers, especially chance visitors.[209]

In well-ordered households where young and old lived together it was reputedly customary for the old people to pretend they did not notice the behavior of the young and vice versa. This tacit agreement about social invisibility made it possible, says Demosthenes, to sustain amicable relationships even though the habits of the groups were very different.[210]

Since the house was in general a place of safe retreat, it was believed possible to keep a disreputable marriage secret from friends and family.[211] Analogously, out of regard for the feelings of the wife, it was not customary for a man to bring a prostitute into the house.[212] In reality, however, the house was very far from secure and the privacy it offered anything but impermeable. Slaves could acquire knowledge about a master's habits that put him in their power and enabled them to take vengeance. Even neighbors obtained information about matters a person might try to keep hidden from anyone.[213]

Marital sexuality is the subject of far less discussion than other varieties in the surviving literature. According to Pindar, both gods and men should have the modesty and restraint not to consummate a marriage in the light of day.[214] Aristotle speaks of copulation in winter for the sake of producing children as if it were general practice familiar to everybody.[215] But there is no reason why he should have known. On the other hand, the notion that marital sex took place mainly in wintertime instead of the spring or summer suggests that it was more of a routine affair than a source of ecstatic pleasure. That was undoubtedly true in some cases. Solon is reported to have required the husband of an heiress to approach his spouse three times a month as a mark of esteem that removes many sources of quarrels.[216] But this apparent disinclination could not have been true most of the time. Otherwise the hilarious plot of Lysistrata's sexual strike of wives would have made little sense to an Athenian audience.

Within the family circle the main restriction on sexual satisfaction was the prohibition on incest. Xenophon in a revealing discussion describes the rules as prohibiting sexual intercourse between parents and children. He says nothing about intercourse between brother and sister. In his account the issue of incest emerges in connection with the idea of unwritten laws. Unwritten laws, says one speaker, are those observed uniformly in every country. They cannot be man-made because all men cannot meet together and do not speak the same language. (Once again we encounter the conception of human society as, at least in part, a deliberate, secular, human creation.) Hence unwritten laws seem to be laws made by the gods for men. On the other hand, the prohibition against sexual relations between parents and children does not look like a divine law because some people transgress it. This transgression is mentioned in a perfectly matter-of-fact way without any of the horror that supposedly accompanies the thought of violating the incest taboo. The speaker might just as well be talking about violating a parking regulation. At this point Xenophon has Socrates observe that the fact of transgression does not disprove the divinity of a law. All laws, he remarks, are subject to transgression. But the person who disobeys a divine law cannot escape paying a penalty.[217]

Rather characteristically, Socrates is not content to let the issue rest there. Somehow a divine prohibition does not seem to be enough. He casts about rather clumsily, as many have done since then, to find a secular and biological explanation. He comes up with the theory that children born of such unions are bound to be inferior because both parents cannot be at the age of maximum physical vigor. At that point the conversation changes to another topic. Xenophon's discussion, differing sharply in tone from the awe-inspired treatment by Sophocles, is closer to childlike curiosity. Evidently both attitudes existed in Athenian culture.

There was a long-established tradition of public concern about extramarital sexual relationships, or more precisely their heterosexual forms. Athenian legislation concerning adultery, rape, seduction, and the resort to courtesans (for which there does not seem to have been any serious penalty) was traditionally attributed to Solon.[218] It seems likely that the legislation was actually much older. As pointed out earlier, prostitution was subject to a degree of public control through the system of farming out the taxes on harlots, of whom a list was regularly compiled.[219] According to Athenian law, a man could not be taken as an adulterer if he had a relationship with a woman who sat professionally in a brothel or openly offered herself for sale.[220] Men who gave out their women as mistresses ordinarily stipulated the benefits—that is, the payment—in advance.[221]

Privacy was the norm governing both marital and extramarital intercourse, including homosexual affairs. There has already been occasion to mention Pindar's observation that the consummation of marriage ought not to take place in the light of day. Herodotus refers to the Hindu Indians, who allegedly "have intercourse openly like cattle."[222] In the *Anabasis* Xenophon reports briefly on the Mossynoecians, who wanted to have intercourse openly with the camp followers of the Greeks because that was their particular practice. They were, the Greeks thought, the most uncivilized people encountered and the furthest from Greek customs, doing habitually in public what other people would only do in private.[223] Presumably the Greeks behaved otherwise. Homosexual acts, according to Aeschines, were "carried on in secret, and in lonely places, and in private houses."[224]

There were of course violations of the norm of privacy. One man took a famous courtesan to dinners where there was much drinking. He had intercourse with her openly wherever and whenever he wished, making his privilege a display to onlookers. At one feast many had intercourse with her, including the host's servingmen, when she was drunk and her owner was asleep.[225] Other lively parties were not so gross. Xenophon ends his *Symposium* with a tableau of Ariadne and Dionysus that included much realistic kissing. The guests at the party were all males. As the guests saw that the couple were about to leave for the bridal couch, the unwedded ones swore that they would take wives while the married ones rode off to enjoy their spouses.[226] This description of general erotic arousal betrays no sign of uneasiness, far less shame or guilt. On the other hand, Athenian attitudes toward sexuality were by no means completely free of these feelings.† The Greek "polite" word for genitals was not "private" parts (as in now somewhat old-fashioned English) but a term that can be translated as "things of shame," though it is shame in the sense of "awe, reverence, and fear."‡

Athenian literature expresses a wide range of contrasting attitudes toward homosexuality. Since the topic has been the subject of exhaustive treatment by K. J. Dover, mine will be rather selective. Homosexual seduction by an older male appears to have been a far-from-

---

†Demosthenes *Erotic Essay* 5 suggests that love without shame is somewhat unusual. Though this work may be a forgery, it still provides evidence on Athenian attitudes.
‡See the discussion in Henderson, *Maculate Muse*, 3–5. But it seems to me that the author overdoes the healthy absence of guilt in Greek attitudes, and that guilt appears in the very word for genitals.

unexpected event in early adolescence.† This was merely a stage in growing up. It did not interfere in any observable way with subsequent heterosexual attachments. In the *Phaedrus* and the *Symposium* (notably the speeches by Pausanias and Alcibiades) Plato becomes quite lyrical in his description of the emotional sentiments aroused by this relationship.‡ On the other hand, Plato always expressed some negative judgments toward *any* form of intense physical pleasure, regarding such pleasure as inferior to the joys of the intellect. Frequently he sounds like a precursor of Christianity. Among the Athenians this attitude may have been limited to Plato himself, though it has had a powerful effect on Western culture.

There is no reason to doubt the emotional intensity of first love, whether it be homosexual or heterosexual. In the passage of the *Phaedrus* mentioned above, it is shared by both partners. According to Xenophon, on the other hand, the passive partner in a homosexual relationship did not derive any pleasure from the act.[227] At the same time Xenophon's account does show that strong emotional attachments grew out of homosexual relationships since he tells us that Athens forbade the practice of making such attachments the basis for loyalties.[228]

If the older man was a model whom the younger one could respect as well as love, the general attitude toward an adolescent homosexual love affair appears to have been quite favorable. But there was evidently widespread fear that the affair might turn out badly, leading to some sort of shock of disappointment for the junior partner. Apparently for that reason it was customary for fathers to put tutors in charge of their boys to prevent conversation with their lovers.[229] For the senior partner the code apparently required that the affair *not* be concealed: "It is more honorable to love openly than in secret."[230] Presumably openness was a sign of generally honorable intentions; more specifically, that no money had changed hands and that the older partner would not desert the boy for a more attractive male or female partner.

In the comedies of Aristophanes, which almost certainly reflect popular attitudes more accurately than the writings of Plato, the treatment of homosexuality is quite negative. According to Dover, the characteristic assumption of comedy is that all homosexual submission is mercenary. The ordinary Athenian, he concludes, could pride him-

---

†There is an extended discussion in Plato *Phaedrus*. The final seduction at 255C–D, following which they live happily ever after, may strike the modern reader as deliciously comical. At 256C Plato remarks that what they do is not approved by the whole mind.
‡The strongest praise put in terms of the way homosexual attachments induce a love of beauty that I have come upon occurs in Plato *Symposium* 211B.

self on wasting no time on homosexual love affairs, like idle young men with more money than was good for them.[231] At best, homosexuality in the form of occasional enjoyment of a boy appears in comedy as a harmless vice. In the case of grown men who are fond of other men or who are actually effeminate, homosexuality represents corruption, decadence, shamelessness, wickedness, or perversion.[232] It is hard to distinguish this judgment from that prevailing in the "backbone of the country" today in most modern societies. Yet in the relative acceptance of adolescent homosexuality as the first form of romantic experience, Athenian culture did differ sharply from our own.

There were disreputable as well as socially acceptable forms of homosexual relationships, just as there were disreputable and acceptable heterosexual ones. As already indicated, an acceptable one was a long-term attachment free of any commercial taint, in which the senior partner served as a desirable model for the junior one. To some Athenians this was even an admirable relationship. This senior model was not prominent in heterosexual affairs. Otherwise it is impossible to distinguish between the two. A disreputable affair was one in which either the female or passive homosexual partner sold favors for cash. The more frequent the sales and the change of partners, the more disreputable was the behavior. The purveyor was regarded as far more disreputable than the customer. Selling and procuring were punished by law, but not buying.[233]

Aeschines draws a distinction between the kept man who practices homosexuality for pay and the common male prostitute. The kept man he was almost willing to consider decent, even though such behavior was illegal. Selling one's body to one person after another, on the other hand, aroused contempt and disgust.[234] Later in the same speech he expatiates on the distinction between honorable and dishonorable homosexual love. "To be in love with those who are beautiful and chaste is the experience of a kind-hearted and generous soul; but to hire for money is the act of a man who is wanton and ill-bred."[235]

It was not merely the purchase that was objectionable. It was the manner. Here too one can see the general Greek objection to *hybris*, the arrogant and uncontrolled satisfaction of impulses. Uncontrolled satisfaction in this connection also implies very frequent intercourse. In other words, a discreet and controlled affair was socially acceptable. The use of money to satisfy a wild and indiscriminate passion was not. The first could be wrapped in a cloak of privacy. The second could not.

According to the law, both the responsible adult male who let out a boy for hire as a prostitute and the man who hired him were subject to prosecution and, if convicted in this instance, to identical but unspecified penalties. There was also a law which exacted the heaviest penalties (presumably including death) for any person acting as a pander in the case of a freeborn child or freeborn woman.† Finally, there was a law against committing outrage against *any* man or woman, free or slave. Outrage presumably included rape and, according to Aeschines, also included hiring out.[236]

On the other hand, as pointed out before, there was a regular tax on prostitutes,[237] which demonstrates that prostitution was an accepted and legal practice. If the legislation seems inconsistent, so were the attitudes and the behavior the laws sought to control. The main ethical rule that emerges from this conflicting evidence about sexual behavior would seem to be the Aristotelian "Nothing too much," which might also be translated as "Anything goes—occasionally." There is nothing specifically Greek here. It is the working rule of most human societies.

Not surprisingly, a cuckolded husband often preferred to keep his situation secret. In his prosecution of Timarchus, Aeschines announced to the jury court that for the sake of the offended husbands he would say nothing about Timarchus' licentious treatment of the wives of freemen. Since he goes on to remark that he will leave the task of investigating these matters to members of the jury court, we are entitled to suspect that his overt discretion was a device to arouse prurient suspicion against the accused.[238]

The Athenians had a series of rules and customs governing indecent exposure. Their obvious purpose was to reduce sexual, and primarily homosexual, temptation. There were detailed regulations about the behavior of teachers and their contacts with young boys. As Aeschines notes, the lawgiver distrusted the teachers and was exceedingly suspicious of their being alone with a boy or in the dark with him.‡ Slaves were forbidden by law to take exercise or to anoint themselves in the wrestling schools. Under penalty of fifty lashes a slave was not to become the lover of a free boy or to follow after him.[239]

From the evidence I have seen, it does not appear that homosexual love was ever altogether free of shame. Thus Lysias has one of his clients express shame at having to make public before the court his erotic indiscretion with a boy.[240] Xenophon treats the idea of the old Socrates stripping for exercise before a crowd at his age as merely comic.[241] Theophrastus defines buffoonery—or as we would say the extreme of brutal bad manners—as objectionable and shameful playfulness. He gives as an example the man who will show his genitals to

---

†But note again Isaeus *On the Estate of Pyrrhus* 39, showing that those who gave out their women as mistresses stipulated the benefits in advance. Perhaps giving out one's own women for the regularized status of concubine or mistress did not count as pandering.

‡Aeschines *Against Timarchus* 9–12. The text of the law is given in the last section. But the translator of the Loeb edition of Aeschines says the law was probably composed by an ancient editor.

freeborn women. He does not indicate any special penalty for such behavior.[242]

There were rules against indecorous exposure when addressing the Assembly. The standards seem to have become less demanding with the passage of time. It had once been the custom not to speak with one's arm outside the cloak. Cleon is said to have been the first to violate this rule.[243] According to Aeschines, Timarchus made a spectacle of himself by throwing off his cloak and leaping around like a gymnast half-naked, exposing a body befouled through drunkenness and lewdness. A law was proposed but not passed to curb such behavior.[244] As in the case of Socrates' body, the rule against exposure for older people seems connected with disgust rather than temptation though, as any Freudian will point out, there is a close connection between the two.

There also appear to have been customs requiring the concealment of excretory acts, though I have been unable to pin down their precise nature. In a curious passage on human biology Xenophon observes that the mouth, through which food goes in, is set near the eyes and nostrils. But "since what goes out is unpleasant, the ducts through which it passes are turned away and removed as far as possible from the organs of sense."[245] Athenians used privies for defecation. In *The Peace* by Aristophanes, where Trygaios plans to ride to heaven on a balky monstrous dung beetle, there is a reference to sealing off the dung heaps and privies so that the beast will take off.[246]

While defecation was definitely obscene and used for obscene humor in the comedies, that was not true of urination.[247] According to a distinguished student of the history of privacy in Western culture, "Very few Athenian houses had toilet facilities, and persons simply relieved themselves in a corner, with the waste eventually thrown out into the street."[248] The waste had to be removed to a place far outside the city walls, apparently by public slaves. As Aristotle's *Athenian Constitution* (50.2) indicates, one of the functions of the City Controllers was "to prevent any scavenger from depositing ordure within a mile and a quarter of the wall."

In Olynthus, however, archaeologists have found a block of houses dating from about 430 B.C. with latrines situated in the open court. Drains ran from them into the street or blocked alley which divided the backs of the houses. Plans of third-century houses in Delos show a bathroom equipped with a latrine.[249] The rareness of toilet facilities in Athenian private houses may be due to the fact that, until well into the fourth century, the Greeks put their architectural energies and resources into public buildings.

Though there is not a great deal of information about privacy and sexual behavior among metics and slaves, there is enough to indicate that Athenian society conformed to a pattern of controlled access to females that prevails widely in stratified societies. The main elements of this pattern are the following. First of all, the dominant stratum tries with varying degrees of success to control the breeding behavior of the lower strata, especially slaves. In the second place, males from the dominant stratum have special access to females from the lower strata. At the same time, males from the lower strata have either no access or a highly restricted one to females from the dominant stratum. Finally, the system rewards beauty and brains among a few females in the lower strata with opportunities short of full marriage for joining the highest circles of the ruling elite.

These features can be found in the American south in the days of slavery, under Russian serfdom, in the Chinese empire, in Japan, and in many other societies. They also appear quite plainly in the world's first civilized democracy and have obvious implications for the organization of privacy. In the estate described in Xenophon's *Oeconomicus* the women's quarters were separated by a bolted door from the men's, to prevent the removal of property and keep the servants from breeding without their master's permission. Honest servants, Xenophon adds, generally prove more loyal if they have a family, but rogues in wedlock are more prone to mischief.[250] Evidently Xenophon thought that there were more rogues than honest servants. I doubt very much that the precaution of bolting the door interfered very seriously with the erotic autonomy of Athenian house slaves.

For modern romantic individualists there is something especially disagreeable about this kind of explicit restriction by a dominant caste on the erotic autonomy of the lower strata. Sexual choices appear to many moderns as the most personal and private of choices, the ones where the public has the least right to intervene. But all human societies do exercise and must exercise a variety of controls over the reproductive process. The choice of where to invest libidinal energy depends on the availability of suitable objects for affection. That in turn is determined by demographic, social, and political forces. Our erotic choices are always manipulated by forces beyond our control, and the most visible forces are not necessarily the most offensive and dangerous ones.

Handsome females in Athens as in other societies were valued for their erotic attractiveness as well as for their capacity to furnish labor power. I have not come upon examples of metics who made their way upward through such talents, though such cases must have occurred. *Hetairai* was the Attic euphemism for those women, slave or free, who traded sexual favors for long or short periods outside wedlock. According to one authority, the term applied equally to streetwalkers, the inmates of civic or private brothels, or accomplished and expensive courtesans. Of the latter, the most famous was Aspasia, the mistress of Pericles. The late fifth to the third century B.C. was the great age of the expensive courtesan.†

In the *Memorabilia* Xenophon has Socrates engage in some heavy-handed banter with a most successful courtesan called Theodoté, who describes some of the techniques of her trade. One important technique was to engage an agent to "track and find rich men with an eye for beauty."[251] Evidently romantic attraction was already subject to big-business techniques as early as the fourth century B.C.

Males of course frequently quarreled over the favors of an attractive courtesan. She in turn exploited these disputes to make her way in the world. Some of the arrangements do seem rather odd by contemporary standards. A slave girl might become the common possession of two men to settle a quarrel.[252] At one point in her colorful career the famous courtesan Neaera was assigned by arbitrators to live with two different men on alternate days.[253] In the absence of further information, the reader curious to know how problems of privacy were solved in such situations must resort to speculation. Similar difficulties must have arisen in the case of prostitutes who found it possible to charge higher fees by getting a husband and pretending to live as respectable married women, a device to which Neaera also resorted.[254]

By and large the harlot seems to have been the object of intense hostility and jealousy at the hands of virtuous Athenian female citizens. Or was Demosthenes, in appealing to such presumed emotions, merely projecting male guilt over male privileges of one-sided escape from the bonds of matrimony? A major theme in his extended diatribe is the threatened dilution of the privileges of citizenship and the dissolution of property rights that would occur if poor Athenian girls found it necessary to take to harlotry.[255] If citizenship and property rights were predominantly male concerns, the women also depended on clarity about these matters for the security of their own status. And, finally, plain sexual jealousy, which is a major source of the demand for privacy and private property in the human body, was quite clearly a major emotion in the delicious scandal of Neaera, a scandal that called upon the skills of the greatest master of spoken Greek prose.

Moral Autonomy

Here I shall use the expression "moral autonomy" to denote the individual's capacity to make independent moral choices. For the strict

---

† Oxford Classical Dictionary, s.v. "Hetairai." But see the distinction between *hetaira* and *porne*, the common prostitute, in Dover, *Greek Homosexuality*, 21.

determinist, no such thing as moral autonomy or for that matter free choice in any area of human behavior can possibly exist. Though this position has been taken seriously by religious thinkers and philosophers, there is no need to discuss it here. I have come upon no sign of it in classical Athens. Instead, ordinary educated Athenians by the fourth century B.C. (and no doubt earlier) had worked out quite clear conceptions of individual conscience and moral autonomy.

As might be expected, these conceptions had a strong aristocratic flavor. The basic ideas appear most clearly in the form of negative statements about what a morally decent person ought not to do. The moral objection to the gluttony, lust, and gambling of Timarchus, whom Aeschines successfully prosecuted on a morals charge, was that no wellborn and free man ought to be slave to such passions.[256] Xenophon expresses the same idea in similar language: that man is not free who is ruled by bodily pleasures and is unable to do what is best because of them. Self-control is the opposite of such subjection and a great blessing.[257]

In one of his oratorical flights Demosthenes presents a revealing list of the ethical rejects of contemporary Athenian society: lawbreakers, jailbirds, sons of criminals put to death by the people, citizens disqualified after obtaining office by lot, public debtors, men totally disfranchised, and men who by repute or in fact are utter rascals.[258] This miscellaneous collection looks like a fair specimen of the commonsense view of the public consequences of the failure of individual conscience. As is shown by the inclusion of sons of criminals, the failure might occur in a previous generation. Fourth-century Athenians did not believe in purely individual moral responsibility; there remained in law and the beliefs of ordinary people a considerable element of collective responsibility. But by this time the notion of individual responsibility was quite strong.

In accounts of the brawls of the *jeunesse dorée* and their abusive drunken behavior, Demosthenes describes in vivid detail what we would call indecency and breaking the peace. He expresses special horror at a man of over fifty who not only acted as the leader of these brawls but had failed to bring up his own son properly.[259] In our terms, as well as those of Demosthenes, such a man had failed to equip his son with an adequate conscience or sense of shame. In still another speech Demosthenes echoes the aristocratic conception of conscience when he contrasts shame, as the sanction on a freeman's behavior, with stripes and bodily injury for a slave.[260]

As long as the main enemy of moral automony remains instinctual gratification, moral admonitions do not rise above the level of a primitive boy-scout morality. There was plenty of that in Greek culture, as there probably has to be in any human culture. But there was also a great deal more. In addition to controlling his physical instincts, the person with an independent conscience resisted injustice even at great personal risk. There were three cultural models for such behavior, one of which was taken from real life. There was the *Prometheus* of Aeschylus, the *Antigone* of Sophocles, and Socrates as he appears in Plato's *Apology* and some of the writings of Xenophon. Though all three culture-heroes sought their own destruction rather than betray their own conception of moral obligation, there are important differences among them.

The case of Prometheus is the most ambiguous and complex. According to one modern source, the original Prometheus was an entirely nonmoral divine trickster similar to the Coyote in certain American Indian myths. In this role he stole fire from the gods and gave it to man.[261] The legend reveals an important general truth. "Immorality" in the form of rebellion against established morality appears here as a source of moral independence. In a similar vein a psychiatrist once remarked to me that the child's first successful lie was also the first step toward moral independence. Among some children, diplomats, and others, however, it may also be the only step. Modern romantics often forget that not all forms of moral independence and rebellion are equally valid.

Aeschylus makes us and probably also his Athenian audience identify sympathetically with Prometheus by his negative portrayal of the tyrant Zeus and especially the latter's servile minions, Hephaestus and Kratos. These two are typical authoritarian officials with a vindictive delight in executing cruel commands. Indeed, the negative portrayal of the traditional deities in this play has given rise to an extensive modern literature that includes the suggestion that Aeschylus did not even write the play.[262] But it seems more likely that Aeschylus reflected fairly recent Athenian experience with arbitrary government, drawing on live historical memories. Nor is the *Prometheus* inconsistent with the concerns Aeschylus expressed in the other surviving tragedies. As is well known, he was deeply preoccupied with the destructive cycle of murder and vengeance and their effects on the human conscience. In the *Eumenides* he tried, somewhat unconvincingly, to present a mechanism for reconciling and controlling these destructive forces in the justice of Athena.

To return to the *Prometheus,* the most significant feature from the standpoint of the present inquiry is the strong humanitarian and almost populist theme that runs through the play. The audience is made to sympathize with Prometheus not only because he is the victim of Zeus (who in typical Aeschylean fashion must destroy Prometheus in order to save his own skin), but also because he chooses to benefit humanity at enormous risk to himself.

In a somewhat milder form the same humanitarian and near-populist themes occur in the *Antigone* of Sophocles. Antigone appears as the protagonist of an older and higher morality that enjoys widespread support among the Theban population. That is what makes her potentially dangerous to Creon. He in turn is the spokesman for a new rationalist and secular morality, the morality of public order, partly for its own sake and partly for reasons of state in a military crisis. The mass of the Theban population does not want to see Antigone lose her life. In demanding her punishment, it is the new royal authority that seems cruel and arbitrary.

In the Socrates of Plato's *Apology* this near populism has disappeared. The role of "the masses" is the reverse of that in the *Antigone*. They now clamor for the death of Socrates, presented as a lone hero who has the courage to resist popular injustice. In the character of Socrates, Plato created for Western civilization the archetype of the lone critic who pays with his life for his commitment to the ideals of free inquiry. This was a tremendous intellectual achievement. But, as noted earlier, the basis of Socrates' commitment and the source of his moral autonomy were religious.† His belief in a "divine" spirit that told him what to do in various moral crises apparently seemed strange and possibly blasphemous to his Athenian listeners, just as these passages have an odd ring for the modern secular reader. Nevertheless there is no good reason for refusing to take Socrates at his word. This kind of moral independence may be psychologically unattainable without firm beliefs that transcend individual mortality. All three of the Athenian cultural models for moral autonomy, Prometheus, Antigone, and Socrates possessed a religious basis for their independence.

Thus it remained for Aristotle to attempt the construction of a purely secular basis for autonomous moral judgment. Like Xenophon and Aeschines, Aristotle starts with the prevailing aristocratic conception of independence, that of *arete* which can mean excellence of any kind, including moral virtue, though it generally carries strong overtones of manly qualities. Like Xenophon and Aeschines, he uses a negative case to make his first point. *Arete* is necessary for human society, Aristotle observes near the beginning of his *Politics*. When devoid of *arete,* man is the most unscrupulous and savage of animals, and the worst in terms of sexual indulgence and gluttony.[263] Some form of inner control is therefore necessary. This inner control he posits rather than explains. As he puts the point in one of his ethical treatises, the political man purposely chooses noble actions for their own sake, while the majority of men embrace that mode of life for money and gain.[264]

Though his starting point does not differ from the prevailing

†Plato *Apology* 23B, 28E, 29D, 30E, 31C–32A, 33C, 40B–C, 41D. This is only a partial list of the relevant passages showing Socrates' inner, religious conviction that the pursuit of truth and honesty should govern the behavior of the private individual who is outside of public office (as so vividly appears in 31D–E).

upper-class common sense of his time, Aristotle developed this conception much further. He did this in three ways. First, he defined moral goodness as the capacity for following reason. By this step he made moral goodness at least in part an intellectual quality. Simultaneously he showed that moral decisions involved consciously reasoned choices.

The second step was the presentation of his doctrine of the mean; that is, the assertion that virtue is a middle state between two emotional extremes. For instance, courage stands halfway between rashness and cowardice.[265] Whatever one may think of the doctrine of the mean—it has been called a "knife-edge . . . inserted into the heart of rationalism"[266]—in Aristotle's hands it did serve to make ethical discussion more concrete and orderly by providing a rough-and-ready classification of numerous aspects of ethical behavior. The human conscience began to appear, with its huge variety of real problems.

Aristotle's third contribution arose from his attempt to distinguish between voluntary and involuntary acts. In this way he hoped to make possible a conception of individual moral responsibility. From the standpoint of the issues under discussion, that is his most important contribution.[267]

The key concept in his rather complicated discussion is that of choice based on reflection. The responsible individual is aware that he acts for certain specifiable reasons and that he could act differently. The possibility of acting differently is crucial to the whole conception of an autonomous moral agent. Without this possibility, there is no choice and no behavior that deserves to be considered moral. Choices made under compulsion are not real moral choices.

Aristotle displays an awareness of the difficulties in his own position. There are many sorts and degrees of compulsion. A man who does something to save his parents or children from the hands of a tyrant is far from a completely free moral agent. Eventually Aristotle finds it necessary to pin the label "voluntary" on any act in which there was *some* participation by the agent. It seems to me that this move was unwise. It would have been better to leave the argument open so that the forms and degrees of compulsion might be brought out in each individual case before reaching a judgment about moral responsibility. To what extent, to take a modern example, was the German citizen under Hitler responsible for the atrocities against the Jews? The answer would depend on the position of the particular German in the Nazi social system, the opportunities to resist authority and penalties for resistance, and finally on the individual's own strength of character. Some individuals are capable of the moral autonomy that requires resistance to unjust authority, and others are incapable. There are innumerable degrees of capacity or incapacity between the two extremes, as well as various explanations for such differences. Hence moral judgments very often depend on evidence that is poorly understood or very hard to come by.

Thus discussions of the meaning of moral autonomy can be expected to continue indefinitely. Only a believer in strict and universal determinism can reject them. On the other hand, a belief in some degree of determinism or causal connection among facts is necessary for serious moral argument and a belief in moral autonomy. The difficult point in every case is to discover the range of possible and effective human intervention. It would be absurd to fault Greek speculation for the failure to solve all possible problems in advance. We owe to the Greeks the model of the independent moral agent and general methods for assessing the possibility of realizing this model. That is no small contribution to human culture.

Personal Morality and Public Office

Both Athenian and modern Western beliefs and behavior about the connections between personal morality and the holding of public office display contradictions and inconsistencies. Though it is unlikely that the contradictions are or were soluble, they are at least historically comprehensible. There are differences and similarities between ancient and modern beliefs and practices. To see what is distinctly Athenian, it will be helpful to begin with some brief comments on contemporary traditions and their origins.

In moderately well-educated Western circles there exists the belief that certain aspects of a person's behavior ought to be excluded from any judgment about that person's performance in holding office or playing a political role. This exclusion first came about in connection with religion. Before 1914 German Social Democrats had a saying that religion was purely a *Privatsache,* or nothing more than a person's private business. They did this because they wanted to create a mass party and did not want to antagonize their potential following by stirring up religious sentiments and thus jeopardize what were to them far more important political and economic goals. They were of course under a special handicap due to the connection between Marxism and atheism.

German Social Democratic policy about religion was no more than a logical continuation of ideas about religious tolerance that grew up following the destructive religious conflicts of early modern Europe. The basic idea behind religious tolerance was to agree to disagree in order to make social life possible. Religious beliefs were, so to speak, bracketed in order to make economic and political cooperation possible. It is one of those mistaken ideas that has contributed enormously to the reduction of human misery and the advance of civilization. Nevertheless it is mistaken. An individual's religious beliefs or lack of such beliefs can have a very powerful influence on the way that person uses political power when entrusted therewith.

Much more recently, there has been a similar tendency to bracket sexual preference and the use of alcohol as purely private matters which have nothing to do with a person's performance of a public role either in business or politics. So far, this point of view seems mainly confined to an educated but very influential elite. Newspaper reporters have been inclined to be very discreet about the drinking habits and sexual behavior of high government officials. For the most part, scandals find their way into the major media only in cases of behavior so flamboyant as to render discretion impossible.†

The Athenians did not believe in this kind of bracketing-off of certain aspects of private behavior, at least not overtly, though it seems highly unlikely that every potential scandal was automatically allowed to become public knowledge. Athenian orators appealed to well-established traditions and prejudices in affirming a close connection between private morality and behavior in public office. Aeschines attacked Demosthenes for publicly celebrating the news of the death of Philip of Macedon at a time when he was still in mourning for the death of his own daughter. To us Demosthenes' reaction seems perfectly understandable. But it is most unlikely that it seemed that way to an Athenian audience, or Aeschines would not have used this accusation to discredit him. According to Aeschines, a man who breaks mourning in this fashion is one "who hates his child and is a bad father" and so "could never be a safe guide to the people." The man who is wicked in private relationships, he asserted further, would never be trustworthy in public affairs.[268]

Earlier in his successful prosecution of Timarchus on a morals charge—in itself a good indication of Athenian beliefs about morals and politics—Aeschines used almost exactly the same wording:

> To the lawgiver it did not seem possible that the same man could be wicked in private and trustworthy in public; he believed that the public man who comes to the platform ought to come prepared not merely in words, but before all else, in life.[269]

As mentioned earlier, a citizen who beat his parents, failed to support them, or provide a home for them was not allowed to address the people of Athens. This failure to perform a private obligation was equated with public dereliction, such as failure to complete military service or throwing away one's shield.[270]

In still another passage Aeschines draws on Euripides to urge the

†The contrast between the treatment of Wilbur Mills and rumors about John Kennedy and Henry Kissinger—to mention only a few—is instructive in this connection.

jurors to look at how the man on trial conducts his daily life since that indicates how he will conduct the affairs of state. Euripides also "does not hesitate to express the opinion that a man is like those 'whose company he loves to keep.' "[271] Here the difference between modern and ancient conceptions appears most sharply. Hardly any modern prosecutor in a liberal democratic society would dare to accuse a person of criminal acts explicitly on the basis of domestic behavior and associates. The connection would have to be presented in an indirect fashion if done at all.

Demosthenes detested and despised Aeschines. But he expresses identical opinions about the connection between private life and the responsibilities of public office. In the *De Corona* Demosthenes had to vindicate his anti-Macedonian policy after the policy had resulted in complete failure and the defeat of Athens. The task was hardly an easy one. Near the beginning he observes that he must render account to the jury court "of the whole of my private life as well as of my public transactions."[272] In a later passage he goes so far as to assert that the public conduct of a state, like the private conduct of a man, should always be guided by its most honorable traditions.[273] We shall return to this high-minded rhetorical claim after a look at what the Athenians did, if anything, about the private morality of their public figures as well as some other Athenian ideas about the problem.

Before taking up an official position, Athenian officials underwent a public scrutiny and another one on completion of their term of office. Both scrutinies, however, appear to have been rather formal affairs that did not as a rule pry very deeply into private behavior. The examination prior to taking office was called the *dokimasia*. Its main purpose appears to have been to obtain assurances that the candidate for office met the legal requirements for eligibility. Thus men already chosen, whether by lot or by vote, were formally interrogated to ascertain whether they were thirty years old; whether in the case of certain offices, such as the archonship, they belonged to a particular census class; and whether they were not precluded from one office because they had held it before or were holding another. The only possible source of inquiry into private affairs came from attempts to make sure that the candidate had not been deprived of civil rights, which could occur on moral grounds as well as several others.[274]

On completing a term of office every officer of the polis underwent an examination of accounts called the *euthyna*. It was primarily an accounting of the use of public funds. But it also provided an occasion at which any qualified citizen could present any complaint on a public or private matter against an outgoing magistrate. If the complaint appeared to be a legally valid one, it would go before a jury court.[275] The whole procedure was clearly a protection against illegal appropriation of public funds and the arbitrary abuse of power and not to any degree an investigation of the private behavior of the office holder. Both the *dokimasia* and the *euthyna* could have been used or abused as devices to pry into the private lives of public officials, but I know of no evidence that this happened.

As in other democracies, the Athenians appear to have been subject to occasional fits of vindictive respectability. Demosthenes casually mentions that "all" the Athenians expelled from the city were men of "far" looser morals than the average conjuror—"Callias the hangman and fellows of that stamp, low comedians, men who compose ribald songs to raise a laugh" at their boon companions.[276] If such "low characters" could be expelled from the political community, it is safe to assume that men with similar reputations could not hold office.

There is also the well-known case of Timarchus, mentioned earlier, who was successfully prosecuted by Aeschines for having been a homosexual prostitute and generally disreputable. The real reason for the prosecution was not moral but political. For Aeschines the prosecution was a defensive move against Demosthenes. But the fact that a morals charge succeeded in destroying Timarchus and weakening Demosthenes reveals a great deal about the culture of fourth-century democratic publics.

Aristotle also saw a close connection between private morality and political behavior. But he analyzed the relationship in more general terms. In *Politics* he remarked that since men cause revolutions through their private lives, there ought to be a government agency "to inspect those whose mode of living is unsuited to the constitution— unsuited to democracy in a democracy, to oligarchy in an oligarchy, and similarly for each of the other forms of constitution."[277]

This is a proposal for a universal *Sittenpolizei*. I cannot think of any Greek assertion more odious to modern liberal beliefs about the distinction between the public and private sphere. On the other hand, it is necessary to admit that the distinction cannot be absolute and that Aristotle was aware of the necessity for a shared moral code as the basis for political unity. In the same section he discusses in more detail the educational and moral basis of the polity, ending with a sharp criticism of democracy: "Hence in democracies . . . everybody lives as he likes, 'and unto what end he listeth,' as Euripides says. But this is bad; for to live in conformity with the constitution ought not to be considered slavery but safety."[278]

The Athenian belief that a man's private behavior is relevant in judging his probable political performance does make very good sense. There is a large body of human experience to support it. General reputation based on past behavior remains the basis for selecting people for many jobs and social roles—not just political ones—in modern industrial societies, socialist as well as capitalist. But if general reputation constitutes a reasonable basis for selecting people for political office, that does not mean that it is sufficient for condemning and punishing a criminal. According to the modern liberal view, a person on trial for a criminal offense cannot be condemned on the basis of reputation. It is necessary to demonstrate the performance of the specific illegal acts for which that person is charged. To judge from the surviving forensic speeches, the Athenians did not draw the distinction between reputation and behavior nearly as sharply as do our modern courts.†

In situations where society provides a negative model or tells people how they ought not to behave, there are likely to be at least some signs of a positive model or definition of desired and approved behavior. Lack of control over one's impulses and appetites was a negative trait in many contexts. Conversely a high degree of self-control was a highly valued trait in assessing a man's capacity to hold political office. Plutarch presents Aristides as the model of a personally and politically upright statesman, one who "walked the way of statesmanship by himself, on a private path of his own."[279] Demosthenes restates a similar model of private rectitude, absence of display, commitment to the public interest, and refusal to seek popular acclaim.[280] We may now return to Demosthenes' rhetorical assertion to the effect that the same high moral standards ought to apply to both individual private conduct and the conduct of the state. This was a respectable position in Athenian political thinking. Plato's *Republic* argues the same thesis, though it is important to recall that Plato was discussing an ideal polis, not one that actually existed. Aristotle, too, as indicated earlier, saw individual morality in a more generalized light as an important force to help form ideal political structures.

The notion of an identity or even very close connection between private ethics and political morality was, however, far from dominant in Greek political thinking. The amount of intellectual effort Plato put into his attempted refutation of the right of the stronger is by itself sufficient evidence of the existence of contrary viewpoints. The most powerful challenge came from Thucydides.

Centuries before Machiavelli, Thucydides presented a realist's view of politics, most notably in the Melian Dialogue. There the Athenian envoys treat with icily polite contempt all of the appeals of the Melians to refrain from destroying their independence, appeals based mainly on moral grounds but also on the claim that humanitarian treatment would in the end serve Athenian purposes more effectively. This the Athenians flatly denied on the grounds that gentle treatment of Melos would only encourage disaffection and revolt to surface

†Note in this connection Aeschines' well-known praise of the goddess Pheme (or Common Report) as the basis for public knowledge about private behavior in *Against Timarchus* 127–132.

elsewhere. That observation, on the other hand, is no more than a minor note in Thucydides' realism.

As I understand Thucydides' argument, expressed not only in the Melian Dialogue but intermittently throughout his whole work, the main point is that no real choice exists between an amoral and frequently cruel policy and a humanitarian one. Given human nature, which Thucydides regards as more or less constant, and the inevitability of conflict that flows from political fragmentation, there can be no politics except power politics. As he has the Athenian envoys say, we found these laws in existence and they will continue to exist long after we have ceased to do so.

This is a doctrine of the iron necessity of ruthless behavior in political conflict. Thucydides would, in my judgment, have been on stronger grounds had he put less weight on human nature, which does show considerable variation from culture to culture, and more on inevitably recurring social factors derived from the existence of several independent centers of power. Even as it stands, the doctrine is a powerful one. It makes a mockery of any claim to the effect that private morality can be a sufficient guide for political behavior. The imperatives of private and public morality turn out to be permanently contradictory. Yet there has to be some effort to reconcile the two if society is not to fall into a war of all against all. No generally acceptable resolution of this dilemma has yet been found. Nor does it seem likely that mankind will ever discover one.

This then is the real issue of private versus public morality, far more significant than those arising from religion, sex, alcohol, or even bribery and financial probity. Fortunately civilization can exist without resolving all dilemmas. But at times the failure to solve this problem makes it difficult to distinguish civilization from barbarism—difficult for Thucydides and also for us.†

†Thucydides did not create his view of the conflict between morality and politics from scratch. The figure of Odysseus, already in the *Iliad* the first military intellectual in Western history, provided one possible starting point for a realistic tradition of political analysis. Odysseus always used his head to conserve his own brawn and Greek manpower. That meant frequent resort to deceit. In Sophocles' *Ajax*, Odysseus appears as the realistic solvent of an outmoded warrior ethic. In the *Philoctetes* he is the procurer through deceit of the supreme weapon. But Thucydides goes beyond the poets and philosophers in demonstrating the imperatives that recur to produce amoral behavior. In *The Republic* Plato tries to make the reader believe that a supreme effort of human intelligence will enable virtue to triumph. Thucydides offers no such comfort. His thesis is the exact opposite. The greater the intelligence, the greater will be the insight into the limited and tragic alternatives of power politics. Since Thucydides has a definite moral position, he shows no trace of glee in contemplating the prospects of suffering and destruction.

A tradition of amoral realism denying the relevance of personal virtue for political action appeared also in ancient China and India at about the same stage in the development of social speculation. For texts see J. J. L. Duyvendak, *The Book of Lord Shang* and Johann Jakob Meyer, *Das Altindische Buch vom Welt- und Staatsleben*. Since the issue itself is universal, the cultural response has been broadly similar.

Friendship
and Privacy

The English word friendship denotes a personal and private relationship with, as a rule, little or no erotic component. (In the youth culture, to be sure, the expression "my friend" often indicates a sexual relationship, but these terms are relatively recent and localized.) We distinguish liking from loving, friends from lovers. Though the Greeks certainly knew the difference between these emotional states, their language did not separate them as does ours. The Greek word *philia* covers a range of social and personal relationships, all the way from passionate love through family affection to mild and de-eroticized liking. One can get a useful sense of the range of meanings from the opening portion of Aristotle's discussion of friendship that takes up Books 8 and 9 of the *Nichomachean Ethics*. (Book 7 of the *Eudemian Ethics* is also devoted to friendship.) There Aristotle refers to friendship as a universal human sentiment that appears to form the bond of the polis. He gives as some examples the affection of parent for offspring and children for parents. Later he refers to friendship as part of the relationship of lovers.[281]

With his characteristic passion for definition and classification Aristotle divides friendship into three types, according to the sources of the attraction. The highest and purest kind is a form of mutual respect and affection based on the possession of admirable moral qualities by both parties. Aristotle writes as though this kind of friendship could arise only among mature males. The young are too flighty and the old too cross for such a relationship. It is one that requires a long period of time to develop since both parties must get to know each other thoroughly. Because this kind of friendship, the only true kind, requires so much time and energy, it is impossible to have more than a very small number of friends. In this sense the relationship is exclusive, directed against the outside world, and hence private, though Aristotle does not draw this conclusion.[282]

The two lower forms of friendship in Aristotle's scheme are those based on pleasure and utility. We may take pleasure in the company of a witty man, a pleasure that forms the basis of a friendship. Utility here means the capacity to do favors and render services. By and large, Aristotle expresses a negative and somewhat condescending attitude toward the utilitarian aspects of friendship. On the other hand, what he calls civic friendship is the one most heavily based on utility because it derives from the individual's lack of self-sufficiency. Hence mankind has to create civic unions, that is, the polis. Civic friendship is also another word for the degree of concord or harmony *(omonoia)* prevailing within the state.[283] From Aristotle's point of view, utilitarian friendship serves to widen and extend social bonds. Unlike the pure form of moral friendship, utilitarian friendship would be a force working against privacy.

The utilitarian conception of friendship was probably rather widespread before Aristotle wrote about friendship in general. The utilitarian one is the only one that Xenophon considers in an extended discussion. In his treatise on estate management he refers to friends as more profitable than cattle.[284] In the *Memorabilia* he has Socrates assert that current circumstances afford an opportunity of acquiring good friends very cheaply.[285] Xenophon's attitude toward friendship, at least as expressed in his surviving writings, is thoroughly commercial and cynical. At times a modern reader may think he is reading a rather crude parody of Marxist criticisms of the nature of friendship under late monopoly capitalism. Probably Xenophon did intend to be somewhat satirical. At one point he has Socrates give advice on how to choose and acquire friends. The techniques include a reference to the Siren's spells and sound quite similar to present-day newspaper advice about the problems of daily life.[286]

Perhaps his attitude was uniquely cynical even for his own time and social position. At least it seems on occasion highly exaggerated. For example, Xenophon tries to demonstrate the lack of effort and emotional investment in friendship with the claim that people take better care of a sick servant than a sick friend. If both die, "they are vexed at losing the servant but don't feel that the death of the friend matters in the least."[287]

The utilitarian aspect of friendship, with its stress on the mutually advantageous exchange of services, furnished Aristotle with a general theory of friendship. He was not able, however, to apply the theory consistently. Most of the time he argues that the principles governing the behavior of friends are, in effect, the principles of justice. For Aristotle, justice is a set of rules about the distribution of goods and services, including in this case emotional values such as honor, respect, and affection. Justice may take the form of an equal distribution or of distribution in accord with merit and performance.[288]

At the same time, he shows an awareness of the inadequacy of this explanation. Near the beginning of his discussion of friendship in the *Nicomachean Ethics* he observes that ". . . . if men are friends, there is no need of justice between them; whereas merely to be just is not enough."[289] In the beginning of the corresponding discussion in the *Eudemian Ethics* he refers to friendship as "either the same or nearly the same thing" as justice. Then he proceeds to draw a distinction. "And our private right conduct towards our friends depends only on ourselves, whereas right actions in relation to the rest of men are established by law and do not depend on us."[290]

In these passages Aristotle was, I suggest, working his way toward an interpretation that differs considerably from the one he actually presented. Friendship by this other view is mainly a personal and private relationship. Such relationships, when they are strong, are to a great extent immune to the spirit of calculating benefits received and conferred. In the public realm, on the other hand, where this emotional and personal bond is lacking, principles of calculation that are generally acceptable have to be found and adhered to in the distribution of goods and services for the sake of general contentment and social stability. We will return to the discussion of this theory later.

Plato's conception of friendship is much less intricate than Aristotle's.† It is curious that he has nothing to say about friendship in *The Republic* since this work amounts to a general treatise on human society and human nature. There are, on the other hand, several brief and occasionally penetrating discussions in *The Laws*. He shows an awareness of the ambiguities of the term *philia*. In the course of a discussion of the prospects for a legal prohibition on homosexuality, he remarks that it is necessary to discern the nature of friendship *(philia)*, desire *(epithumia)*, and so-called love *(ta legomena erota)*, if we are to understand them correctly. The utmost confusion and obscurity, he says, come from the fact that the term "friendship" includes liking and passionate love as well as a third emotion compounded of them both.[291]

In an earlier passage Plato asserts that the fundamental purpose of the laws under discussion is "that the citizens should be as happy as possible and in the highest degree united in mutual friendship."[292] Plato's critical targets here are the lawsuits and quarreling that arise over money. The way to prevent them is to prohibit gold and silver and moneymaking by vulgar trading, usury, etc—the usual conservative anticommercial remedies.

Plato's conception of friendship here resembles the modern notion of consensus. But it is more than that: it also harks back to mythical notions of community and primitive harmony. As he says later, the purpose of the rather complicated measures for selecting priests and priestesses was "to secure mutual friendliness, in every rural and urban district, so that all may be as unanimous as possible."[293] This kind of unanimity is essentially totalitarian and inherently opposed to privacy. That, as we have seen before, is the general trend of Plato's thinking. Where all the citizens share the same friendly sentiment toward each other, there is no place for private sentiments and attachments. On this score Plato's position is the opposite of Aristotle's, which recognizes the exclusive quality of close friendship.

Elsewhere, however, Plato displays acute psychological insight.

---

†Most of Plato's *Lysis* is devoted to an abstract and confusing discussion of friendship. Since the participants in the discussion are unable to get anything out of it, the modern student may be permitted to ignore it.

Some degree of longing, he asserts, is necessary to friendship. Unrelieved proximity causes friends to fall away from one another, owing to a surfeit of each other's company.[294] In other words, Plato recognizes the emotionally taxing aspect of intimacy and the necessity for intermittent escape. Human beings need privacy even from those dearest to them. Aristotle, so far as I have been able to discover, fails to see this. The only remark about intimacy that I have come upon in his works treats it merely as a possible prelude to pure friendship.[295]

Greek mythology sheds an indirect light on Greek friendship, complementing that shed by philosophical speculation. The myths report the adventures of several pairs of close friends: Castor and Pollux, Orestes and Pylades, Achilles and Patroclus, Damon and Pythias, and, with a much weaker attachment, Antigone and Ismene. These pairs resemble the hunting and trading partnerships that anthropologists have found in several nonliterate societies. They involve intense though not necessarily permanent loyalties. In the Greek mythical examples there are certain common features. There is a dominant and a subordinate partner as in sexual unions, including homosexual ones. In the second place, the pair acts as a team in a threatening environment, usually a series of dangerous exploits. The emotional tone is that of the pair against the world. Thus the mythology recognizes the exclusive and private character of intense friendship, presenting such loyalty as a defense against the surrounding social order.

Athenian society included social arrangements to promote the pleasures of friendship among males. In the Platonic dialogues we catch many reflections of the Athenian male's delight in friendly and informal intellectual conversation. Sometimes women could take part, though probably not in the more spontaneous gatherings. Aspasia, the mistress of Pericles, is reported to have conversed with Socrates. Plato makes most of the dialogues resemble spontaneous and almost accidental gatherings of men who already knew one another reasonably well. The only requirement for admission to one of these gatherings seems to have been intellectual curiosity. Theophrastus in his brief essay "Loquacity" presents a caricature of the boring intruder who certainly would not have been welcome.[296] In a sense these gatherings were private. The membership was certainly self-selected and far from representative of the Athenian male population, even the moderately well-educated males. As everyone who has read Plato's *Apology* knows, Socrates' conversations eventually aroused enough suspicion of sacrilege to bring about his prosecution and execution.

To judge from the semifictional accounts of Xenophon and Plato, the invitations to the parties could be very spontaneous and casual. On this score they differed sharply from modern dinner parties, which in other ways they resembled. In Xenophon's tale, Callias the host caught sight of Socrates and four companions just before the party was to begin. He informed Socrates that he would rather have them as guests than a series of generals, cavalry commanders, and office seekers. (The occasion of the banquet was the horse races at the greater Pan-Athenaic games.) Socrates and his companions at first demurred, but on seeing Callias' disappointment, agreed to come.[297] The opening of the banquet in Plato's *Symposium* is, if anything, more casual. As Socrates is about to join the party, he runs across a friend, Aristodemus, and takes it upon himself to invite him to join the party. Aristodemus accepts, enters, and is immediately accepted as a guest. Meanwhile Socrates has fallen into deep thought and refuses to join the gathering although he is finally persuaded to do so.[298] (Neither Plato nor Xenophon tells us how the cooks or servers felt about these casual habits.)

Thus banquets provided an opportunity for friends to share food, liquor, talk, and, on many occasions, sex. Depending on the company, they might turn into high-flown intellectual discussions or sexual brawls.[299] It is not surprising that the rather prim Isocrates expected a proper Athenian gentleman to avoid such parties if he could do so without giving offense. Banquets gave males an opportunity to escape from the demands of domesticity, public business, or just plain work.

As in most societies, such opportunities were far more freely available to males than to females. There is very little information about female patterns of friendship and their relationship to privacy. Domestic obligations made it much harder for them to get away from the house and see their friends. When Lysistrata in Aristophanes' comedy tries to collect the women together to organize a sexual strike, one of her friends says to her:

> 'Tis hard, you know, for women to get out.
> One has to mind her husband: one to rouse
> his servant: one to put the child to sleep:
> one has to wash him: one to give him pap.[300]

The more respectable and prosperous a woman was, the greater the obstacles appear to have been to getting away from the house. Poor women presumably went to the market where they could exchange news, gossip, and grievances with their friends. Only the distinguished courtesan could at times mingle in what was essentially an all-male society. Athenian houses, though set close to one another, were structurally oriented toward what went on inside the house. I am unaware of any evidence pointing to the equivalent of housewifely chats over the back fence. Nor is there to my knowledge any indication that women got together on their own in informal social gatherings. For the exchange of confidences, the Athenian housewife seems to have been limited to slaves.†

There were, on the other hand, religious groups about which very little is known, open only to women. The indirect evidence that we have from male dramatists, Aristophanes' *Ecclesiazusae* and Euripides' *Bacchae,* strongly suggests that female religious cults provided at the very least a symbolic release of pent-up hostility against males.

Anyone who has lived long enough to have had a moderately wide experience of friendship in our own culture and to have read about it in the literature of other times and places may well be struck by the curious absence of certain themes in the surviving Greek literature. One such theme is loneliness or the absence of friendship. To my knowledge, there is no extended treatment of this theme in the surviving literature. A few poignant lines of Sappho about abandonment by a lover are the closest that I can recall. In addition there is the figure of Oedipus at the end of his life, abandoned by all except his daughter Antigone. But in his long series of laments there is nothing about loneliness as such or as many modern individuals experience it, not only in old age, but often as a very painful aspect of adolescence.

Another curious gap is the absence of any explicit awareness of friendship as a supplement to or substitute for prescribed affection. This aspect is prominent in our own culture: witness the familiar remark that you can choose your friends but not your relatives. Since it is often extremely painful to be forced by duty to love an inherently unlovable individual, the absence of this theme is especially difficult to explain.

There is of course the possibility that the absence of these themes is due to the accidents governing which writings have survived and which have not. But since so much has survived and Greek literature displays such a variety of themes and literary forms—from the exquisite lyric to the trashy novel—I suspect that the absence of these themes reflects the absence or relative unimportance of certain experiences in Athenian life or, to be more specific, Athenian urban life. Certain historical considerations, which I will now try to set out, also support the view that Greek society and culture did not generate the type of experience or conscious awareness of this experience that would have led to these two literary themes.

There are qualitative differences in the experiences of friendship and loneliness in different cultures and historical epochs. To see them more clearly, let us contrast the situation in early pre-urban civilizations with that prevailing in a modern industrial city. With these two

---

†As noted earlier, Aristotle contrasts the freedom of movement of poor women in the larger towns with the limits imposed by the Superintendent of Women, who watched over upper-class women *(Politics* 6.5.13).

contrasting types before us, it becomes easier to place classical Athens on a historical evolutionary scale and to understand some of the probable effects on personal relationships.

Many simple hunting bands, nonliterate tribal societies, and even a number of stable and isolated peasant communities can with only slight exaggeration be characterized as societies without strangers. In such societies a young person can grow up without coming into contact with anybody unknown to the parents or the young person. Every social encounter takes place with an individual whose place in a network of social relationships is already known or subject to rapid determination. It is the sort of situation that is quite remote from modern American experience and rather hard for most of us to imagine.

The social network has a place for everybody. The place includes a set of prescribed sentiments varying from affection to hostility. In an area where feuds prevail, rapid identification of the correct sentiment is a matter of survival. Where there are no feuds, there are almost always enough quarrels to make it essential to know the socially prescribed sentiments. Though the prescriptions may be vague for some encounters that do not occur on a daily basis, practically every individual a person encounters will fall into one of the categories of affection, respect, dislike, or hatred.

In such a closed social system there is little room for friendship in the sense of freely chosen companionship. The individual has very little choice over his or her close associates at work or at home. (The distinctions between being at work or at home are themselves unlikely to be very clear.) The people with whom one associates most of the time are part of the given facts of existence like the climate and the nature of the soil. In such situations the most that can occur is that the accidents of personality and character put a strain on some prescribed forms of friendship or hostility and intensify others. All brothers may be expected to lend a helping hand in a pinch or show kindness in an emotional crisis, but one brother is cool and evasive while another brother is warmhearted and generous.

Nor is it the case that choice and friendship are totally absent. As pointed out earlier, there are the hunting and trading partnerships that are both voluntary and subject to renewal or abandonment at the will of either party. But there is very little room in such closed systems for close friendships based on congeniality of temperament which serve as a substitute for or escape from obligatory, yet resented affection. And there is practically no occasion for the loneliness of abandonment. Instead the individual is smothered with human company to the point where a modern Westerner wonders why he or she does not suffocate emotionally.

To choose a familiar example, the young bride who must move to her husband's household, leaving her own family behind and become her mother-in-law's servant, faces prescribed obligations of respect and affection with very little prospect of escape. At most, she can count on help from her father or brothers in the case of extreme abuse as defined by the standards of the community. Loneliness can certainly exist in such a community. But, to repeat, it is the loneliness of suffocation at the hands of unfriendly or uncongenial associates, the loneliness of no privacy, and no freely chosen friends. Relief comes only with advancing years and the opportunity to dominate the household in turn. It is not the modern loneliness of abandonment, of dying helplessly by oneself in a cheap rented room in a large city.

In many ways the modern city is the opposite of the small, closed, pre-urban community. To be sure, prescribed sentiments and obligations still exist and take their toll on some personalities just as they provide emotional and social support for others. But the modern city is above all the place for escape from traditional ties of kin and community. The individual who makes more or less of a success of life in the city, even a very minor success, ordinarily acquires some friends who at least relieve the pressure of prescribed sentiments. For men, and increasingly for women, the place of work is usually different from the home, and the alternation between the two permits the pressure of unavoidable human contacts to be felt in different parts of the psyche. In both places and in the increasing periods of leisure there are opportunities to turn strangers into friends.

In the modern city there is enough social space to permit continuous escape from the emotional abrasions created by traditional ties. Indeed one can claim that only in the modern city has friendship, in the sense of a freely chosen emotional relationship replacing the prescribed sentiments of earlier times, been able to develop. At its best such friendship is the finest flower of private existence and indeed one of the finest flowers of civilization itself.

Athenian citizens, I suggest, lived in a world more akin to the closed community of pre-urban societies than that of the large modern city. The primacy of kinship obligations was taken for granted even if such obligations were violated with some frequency as shown by the laws governing obligations to parents and the numerous legal cases about quarrels over women and the inheritance of property. The assumed primacy of kinship and the community may be the reason we hear next to nothing about a conflict between the obligations of kinship and those of friendship. Though the Athenians were aware of conflict between the obligations of kinship and the holding of high office in the polis, there is also little sign of a conflict between the obligations of friendship and loyalty to the polis. It is hard to imagine an Athenian making the disenchanted remark that if he were called upon to choose between betraying his country or a friend, he would hope he would have the moral courage to betray his country.

In such a community the loneliness that comes from never seeing a familiar face must have been a rare experience if it occurred at all. For metics as resident foreigners, however, it may have been a common one. And for the captured Greek slave there must have been such a wrench. But in the surviving literature we do not hear about such experiences, or indeed hardly about any that took place among the lower classes. That is partly explicable in terms of the development of literary techniques and conventions. Centuries were to pass before the creation of the modern realistic and sociological novel. Strangers of course existed. But Plato could still speak about them as holy, in a manner that recalls the primitive community, when he asserts that a man should regard "contracts made with strangers as specially sacred."[301] In classical Athens, it seems, the opportunities and needs for close friendship, for turning strangers into friends, were less than is the case in a modern urban environment. The polis, standing closer to the village community than the modern metropolis, may not have been ready for private tragedies more in keeping with our own time.

PRIVACY, PROPHECY, AND POLITICS IN THE OLD TESTAMENT

Introduction

Rereading the Old Testament after a prolonged immersion in Greek literature can be an odd experience. It is not merely the explicit bloodiness and brutality; after all there is plenty of that in Homer. It is the absence of familiar landmarks and intellectual assumptions and the encounter with a different and considerably older set of beliefs. The distinction between public and private affairs was built into the Greek language as far back as Homer. Though lacking Hebrew and therefore unable to make a comparable linguistic analysis, I was unable to find any text suggesting such a distinction before the period of the monarchy, or roughly a thousand years after the traditional beginning of Hebrew history.† In place of this distinction and in the place of Zeus ruling a motley collection of deities with dubious moral qualities, we find the single terrifying figure of Yahweh, from whom no secrets are hid.

---

†As far as I can tell, in *Nelson's Complete Concordance of the Revised Standard Version Bible,* the English words "private" and "privately" occur only three times in the Old Testament. One text (Deut. 25:11) refers to a woman's efforts to rescue her husband from an opponent in a fight by seizing her man's "private parts," whereupon any onlooker is admonished to observe God's statutes by cutting off her hand without pity. There may be an oblique awareness here of a conflict between personal and public duties, but the relationship is obscure. The other two passages (1 Sam. 18:22 and 2 Sam. 3:37) refer to individuals speaking to other individuals "in private" or "privately" in the sense of "out of the hearing of others." According to the same *Concordance,* the English word "public" occurs also only three times. In Leviticus 5:01 we read the phrase "a public adjuration to testify." The other two references (2 Sam. 21:12 and Isa. 59:14) are to "public squares" in towns or cities.

According to this evidence, the ancient Hebrews at some point came to distinguish public from private in about the same way we do when we tell a child not to do something in public, or when we speak of a private conversation. Thus the distinction was by no

According to Biblical tradition, Yahweh created human life and continued to supervise it with the help of his human agents thereafter. The very notion of an area of social and individual life marked off as private and immune to divine interference would be an impossible absurdity from this standpoint. Many fourth-century Athenians also of course believed that the gods could interfere in any aspect of human life they chose, but the Athenians conducted a large part of their daily affairs as though such interference was unlikely to happen. For the ancient Hebrews divine intervention appears to have been devoutly hoped for, as well as greatly feared, nearly all the time. Despite the near absence of an area of personal autonomy, belief in Yahweh made it possible for some outstanding individuals, especially the prophets, to become highly articulate critics of their own social order and its moral climate.

The belief in Yahweh seems to have acquired its main forms by the time of Moses and the flight from Egypt, which modern scholarship places around 1250 B.C.[1] That is already over six centuries into the history of the ancient Hebrews, of which it will be useful to give a very brief sketch at this point. According to Biblical tradition, the story begins with Abraham and the age of the patriarchs. Abraham may have left the Sumerian city of Ur to take up a seminomadic life around 1900 B.C. Especially for this early period the chronology is very uncertain. The age of the patriarchs ended with the period of bondage in Egypt, whose beginning date appears to be unknown. It ended, as just mentioned, some time around the middle of the thirteenth century B.C. with the exodus from Egypt and the sojourn in the desert.

Soon after 1200 B.C. began the invasion of Canaan and the occupation by the Hebrews of the hill country of Palestine. It is only at this point that we find incipient political institutions, which culminated in the creation of David's kingdom, from about 1012 B.C. to about 972 B.C. His son and successor, Solomon, ruled from about 972 B.C. to about 932 B.C., a reign that marked the apogee of Hebrew secular power. After that came the split of 922 B.C. that produced the Kingdom of Israel in the North with its capital at Samaria and the Kingdom of Judah in the South with Jerusalem as its capital.

Two centuries later, that is, in 722 B.C., the Assyrians conquered Israel, and in 587 B.C. Nebuchadnezzar conquered Judah, bringing the history of the ancient Hebrews to a close shortly before Athenian civilization reached its zenith. The exiles from Israel lost their identity,

---

means absent from Hebrew culture but its context, development, and meaning were very different from those found in fourth-century Athens, as later discussion will show. In any case, there are limits to what linguistic evidence can demonstrate. In their behavior people may reveal distinctions missing from their speech. Since behavior is what counts, extensive inquiry into the working of institutions is necessary to answer the questions raised by this inquiry.

merging into the general population. That is the origin of the conception of the ten lost tribes of Israel. The exiles from Judah met a different fate. As part of a reform movement in Judah before 587 B.C., the sacred scriptures were organized into the books of the Old Testament in a form close to the one we know today. Hence the fall of Judah resulted in the creation of a religious community without a geographical home, the fate of Judaism for most of its subsequent history.[2]

Thus the history of the ancient Hebrews falls into four distinct periods: (1) the age of the patriarchs, (2) the Egyptian bondage, (3) the conquest of Canaan and the period of the rule by judges, and (4) the monarchy. Between about 1900 and 1000 B.C. the ancient Hebrews evolved from a seminomadic tribal social organization into a centralized bureaucratic monarchy. Religious conceptions and conceptions of public and private underwent corresponding changes. Unfortunately the Bible, which is a late editing of earlier traditions, does not permit more than a very rough reconstruction of this historical development, because there is rarely any way to be sure that a given text describes ideas and practices at a specific point in time. The text may accurately reproduce much older practices or it may take later habits and dignify them with an ancient origin. The most one can assert with confidence is that ideas and practices found in the Bible form part of a canonized tradition. That is sufficient for the purposes of this inquiry, because this tradition has played such an important role in Western culture.

The Character
of Yahweh

By the time of Moses the God of the ancient Hebrews had become not only a terrifying deity but an exclusive one. The first commandment as brought down by Moses from Mount Sinai tells the people of Israel "You shall have no other gods before me."† This had not always been the case. There is evidence that the patriarchs worshiped other gods in addition to the one that came to be known as Yahweh.[3] The transition to a single deity must have involved severe disagreements, about which we know nothing, though we do know about the struggles to maintain the belief in the single God once his exclusive character had been decreed. The very wording of the first commandment takes the existence of other gods for granted. It merely denies their legitimacy as objects for Hebrew worship.

The main effort to establish the exclusive worship of Yahweh took

---

†Exod. 20:3. All citations to the Bible are to the Revised Standard Version unless otherwise noted. Though it reads oddly to one brought up on the King James Version, the Revised Standard Version is presumably more accurate.

place in the course of the conquest and settlement of Canaan. Joshua told the leaders and people of Israel: "Put away the gods which your fathers served beyond the River and in Egypt and serve the Lord."† At another point the Hebrews were commanded to stone to death any man or woman who served other gods, worshiped the sun or the moon or any of the host of heaven.[4] Further, in another admonition: "whoever sacrifices to any god, save to the Lord only, shall be utterly destroyed."[5] In the course of repeating the prohibition on graven images Moses asserted, "For the Lord your God is a devouring fire, a jealous God."[6]

Yahweh was not only exclusive and intolerant; as a warrior God he also delighted in the destruction of Israel's enemies and on occasion was correspondingly punitive toward Hebrew sinners. The destruction of the Canaanites and other inhabitants of Palestine was a religious obligation. "When the Lord your God gives them over to you and you defeat them; then you must utterly destroy them; you shall make no covenant with them and show no mercy to them." This destructive attitude reflected a fear of the attractiveness of the Canaanites and the threat that Israel would lose its identity by intermarriage, as appears in the next sentences: "You shall not make marriages with them. . . .For they would turn away your sons from following me, to serve other gods; then the anger of the Lord would be kindled against you, and he would destroy you quickly."[7] And later: "In the cities of these peoples that the Lord your God gives you for an inheritance you shall save alive nothing that breathes. . . ."[8] If the Hebrews did not obey the voice of the Lord, he "will take delight in bringing ruin upon you and destroying you."[9]

It is evident that the ancient Hebrews attributed to Yahweh a vindictive pleasure in the destruction of their enemies that they themselves felt. Generally the impulse to destroy comes from Yahweh. But in some passages it comes from the Hebrews themselves. "And Israel vowed a vow to the Lord and said, 'If thou wilt indeed give this people into my hand, then I will utterly destroy their cities.' And the Lord hearkened to the voice of Israel, and gave over the Canaanites; and they utterly destroyed them and their cities."[10]

The most famous episode when Yahweh's wrath turned against his own people is that of the Golden Calf. When Moses was absent on Mount Sinai, the people turned in discontent to Aaron, the first high priest. Aaron told the people to bring him their golden ornaments, which he made into a calf for the people to worship. In anger Yahweh

---

†Josh. 24:14. In the text I have used as synonyms the words "Yahweh," "God," and "the Lord." According to the Preface of the Revised Standard Version (vi–vii) the words "God" and "the Lord" have generally been used in the Bible to render the four consonants "Yhwh" God or the Divine Name, regarded as too sacred to be pronounced.

told Moses he would destroy the people for their corruption. Significantly, Moses managed to prevail on Yahweh not to do this by pointing out what the Egyptians would be able to say about God's act in leading the Hebrews out of Egypt only to destroy them, and by recalling his promises to Abraham, Isaac, and the people of Israel. On some rare occasions it was possible to negotiate with Yahweh. But severe punishment there had to be. When Moses returned to the camp, he called out, and the sons of Levi—that is, the priests—came to his side. Moses said to them:

> Thus says the Lord God of Israel, "Put every man his sword on his
> side, and go to and fro from gate to gate throughout the camp, and slay
> every man his brother, and every man his companion, and every man
> his neighbor." And the sons of Levi did according to the word of
> Moses; and there fell of the people that day about three thousand men.

Later Yahweh also sent a plague upon the people on account of the calf.[11]

As the episode of the Golden Calf shows, the vindictive and cruel streak in the Hebrew image of their deity was by no means limited to the period of the conquest of Canaan, even if it was most intense then. The God who told Abraham to sacrifice his only son Isaac[12] was cut from the same cloth. That was near the beginning of ancient Hebrew history. Near its end the prophet Jeremiah was to say, "Cursed is he who does the work of the Lord with slackness and cursed is he who keeps back his sword from bloodshed."[13]

In other words, there was to be no standing apart from the contest between vice and virtue, a frame of mind inimical to any conception of privacy or private life. The notion of a punitive deity acting through a variety of human agents dominates Hebrew religion. By providing an explanation for misfortune and suffering that is beyond the reach of factual evidence, this belief may have helped that unhappy people to bear tragic suffering and oppression and hence to survive.

Yahweh was a god from whom the human heart could hide no secrets. The heart is deceitful above all things, wrote Jeremiah. But the Lord searches the mind and tries the heart in order to give to every man according to his doings.[14] Secrecy from God was equated with wickedness. "You felt secure in your wickedness, you said 'No one sees me.' . . . But," continues Isaiah, "evil shall come upon you for which you cannot atone . . . and ruin shall come on you suddenly, of which you know nothing."[15] In another passage the prophet asserts that there is no privacy from God, for it serves evil purposes. "Woe to those who hide deep from the Lord their counsel, whose deeds are in the dark, and who say 'Who sees us? Who knows us?' "[16]

Though there were no secrets from Yahweh, as the above passages show, there were people who tried to keep secrets from God. Certain passages describe efforts to ferret out and destroy such subversive individuals in ways that foreshadow the work of police agents in twentieth-century totalitarian regimes.

> If you hear in one of your cities . . . that certain base fellows have gone out among you . . . saying "Let us go and serve other gods, . . . then you shall inquire and make search and ask diligently; and behold, if it be true and certain that such an abominable thing has been done among you, you shall surely put the inhabitants of that city to the sword, destroying it utterly, all who are in it and its cattle with the edge of the sword. You shall gather all its spoil into the midst of its open square, and burn the city and all its spoil with fire, as a whole burnt offering to the Lord your God; it shall be a heap forever, it shall not be built again.[17]

As in modern totalitarian states, family members or close friends who learned of someone secretly enticing a person to serve other gods were ordered not to pity or protect such an individual. Instead they were to kill him: "Your hand shall be first against him to put him to death, and afterwards the hand of all the people."[18] It is impossible to imagine anything further from the relatively tolerant spirit of pagan antiquity or most primitive religions. The ancient Hebrews, according to this evidence, were the inventors of religious persecution.

Ecclesiastes, perhaps the least Hebrew text in the Bible, strikes a different note. The book of Ecclesiastes advocates a retreat from life and an avoidance of struggle while warning that even in solitude there is no end of toil. There is a mood of escapist hedonism with a touch of cynicism. "Enjoy life with the wife whom you love" is part of this book's advice, because the world after death is mere emptiness, "with no work or thought or knowledge or wisdom. . . ."[19] But the book ends on the same note as the great prophets: "For God will bring every deed into judgment, with every secret thing, whether good or evil."[20]

The imagination of the ancient Hebrews created in Yahweh not only an intolerant and vindictive deity but one who also would use deception against his own chosen people. At times this deception appears as a test of loyalty and devotion, about which Yahweh could never be absolutely certain. There has already been occasion to mention Abraham and the near sacrifice of Isaac, showing that according to tradition this suspicion was an ancient trait of deity. In his last words to Moses, God says that he expects disobedience from his people and threatens vengeance upon them.[21] The most remarkable passage of this type that I have come upon occurs in Ezekiel, where God is made to say, "Moreover I gave them statutes that were not good and ordinances by which they could not have life; and I defiled them through their very gifts in making them offer by fire all their first-born, that I might horrify them; I did it that they might know I am the

Lord.''[22] Still another text presents a long list of curses that God will inflict on the ancient Hebrews if they fail to obey his voice or execute his commandments. Near the end, the text asserts, ''And as the Lord took delight in doing you good and multiplying you, so the Lord will take delight in bringing ruin upon you and destroying you.''[23] In these passages cruelty and deception do not appear as momentary outbursts of anger from an otherwise benevolent father figure. Instead they are a regular policy. One can only conclude that there was a powerful current of sheer hatred in God's attitude toward the Hebrews and vice versa.

No conception of a deity is likely to be altogether consistent. If Yahweh often appears hateful, he also appears at times benevolent. Complaints to and against God could sometimes get results. When the people complained in the wilderness that there was no sweet water, the Lord arranged to provide some. He also promised to keep the people of Israel free from the diseases that afflicted their recent masters, the Egyptians. When the people again murmured that in Egypt they ate their fill, while in the wilderness all were about to die of hunger, God provided them with bread from heaven in the form of manna.[24] Much later, at the time of the Temple under the monarchy, the deity still appears accessible to all the people. Solomon's prayer in dedication of the Temple asked God to respond to whatever prayer or supplication was made by any man or by all the people, ''each knowing his own affliction and his own sorrow.''[25]

From very early times too, Hebrew religion displayed an ethical content that was absent from Greek religion. There is nothing like the Ten Commandments in classical polytheism. The Ten Commandments include prohibitions on murder, theft, and adultery, which are found in a large number of human cultures, but they also include injunctions to honor parents, refrain from bearing false witness against a neighbor. The Tenth Commandment is especially significant in requiring not only moral behavior but a moral attitude in that it forbids one to covet a neighbor's house, wife, manservant, maidservant, ox, ass, or any other possession. It suggests a regime of strictly private property.

At the same time, throughout the Old Testament Yahweh appears as a defender of the needy, the weak, and the poor. Orphans and widows, that is, persons afflicted by misfortunes over which they have no control, are the prototype of those deserving special protection. Justice was on the side of the unfortunate and downtrodden.[26] Any critical response to misfortune was therefore likely to take the form of a religious appeal to ''make the system work.'' There was little or no possibility for a private ethical rejection of the social and religious order as such—except by the wicked, who often prospered, to the horror of the faithful and virtuous.

There are ethical notions also in the recurring theme of a covenant between the Lord and his people. In a covenant God offers protection in return for obedience and other specified forms of good behavior. As I have argued in *Injustice*, this is the general form of social contract that explicitly or implicitly underlies all forms of legitimate authority. God's arrangements with Adam and Eve have the form of a covenant though the term does not occur. In return for refraining from eating of the tree of knowledge, God will enable them to be fruitful and multiply, fill the earth and subdue it, taking dominion over every living thing that moves upon the earth.[27]

The promise of an opportunity to be fruitful and multiply recurs frequently. That is exactly what a small semi-nomadic group living in an insecure environment would want. Increase of flocks and crops and increase of human beings provided the best guarantee of security against hunger and depredation by animals and other human beings. In making a covenant, God was believed to take on an obligation. Thus God promised Noah in the form of a covenant that there would never again be a flood to destroy all flesh.[28]

The covenant also served to define the members of the Hebrew community. In God's covenant with Abraham circumcision was adopted as a sign for males of membership in the community. Uncircumcised males were to be cut off from the people because such a man had broken the Lord's covenant.[29] Since the covenant was the source of moral commands, group identity, and of rights to territory, for the Hebrews it was part of the process of creating a "public" to which all the Hebrews belonged.

According to one version of the covenant of Sinai, presented by the Lord to Moses three months after the departure from Egypt, God told Moses to inform the people of Israel, "Now therefore, if you will obey my voice and keep my covenant, you shall be my own possession among all peoples; for all the earth is mine, and you shall be to me a kingdom of priests and a holy nation."[30] At this point, according to the Biblical tradition, the Hebrews finally received the essence of their identity as a holy people chosen by the Lord.

As the occasion for the proclamation of the Ten Commandments the covenant of Mount Sinai deserves its prominence as one of the most important events in the canonical version of ancient Hebrew history.† But the covenant of Sinai, and in fact the whole relationship between Yahweh and Moses after the flight from Egypt, are at least equally important as providing a license to plunder. In return for good behavior the Lord promised the Hebrews land to take and cities to destroy. As emphasized above, the moral obligation to destroy the

---

†A full account of what was expected in the way of obedience and the penalties for disobedience to God's commands and ordinances may be found in Leviticus 26. The Ten Commandments occur in Exod. 20:3–17 and Deut. 5:7–21.

enemies of Israel was a central feature of the whole bargain. As events turned out, the Hebrews either failed to carry out a policy of total destruction or worshipped other gods, thereby incurring the wrath of the Lord.[31]

A society organized for war with a religious and moral commitment to exterminate the enemy is unlikely to have much social space for private behavior, especially the kind of private behavior that comes to terms with the religious practices of the target peoples. But as the repeated complaints about lapses into idolatry make plain, such pacts with the enemy did occur, and on a fairly wide scale. We can only conclude that the intensity and unity of Hebrew religious faith was more of a hope than a reality, perhaps a priestly ideal rather than a folk belief.

The ancient Hebrews were above all a religious community. The religion of Yahweh as enforced and explicated by the priests—and later the prophets—was the source of the Hebrew sense of belonging to a distinct group. Religion was their public authority. It was public in the sense of constituting a system of shared ritual and doctrine, and as the external source of morality and social obligation. As such, it confronted the individual in all the decisions of daily life. It was also a public from whom no secrets were hid and which left little or no autonomous area for private existence.

Despite some ethical concerns and attributes, the deity created by the tortured Hebrew imagination was exclusive, intolerant, cruel, and deceptive. Religion intensified rather than relieved the emotional burdens pressing on the Hebrew people. Why, then, did they do this to themselves?

A look back over the history of this gifted people suggests some answers. The society of the early patriarchs does not appear to have had any social unit larger than the extended family.[32] The care of flocks and crops did not generate any wider units of social cooperation. The social effects of this type of economy were to create a society of small independent units.†

In this fragmented and probably marginal existence the Hebrews ran a serious risk of conquest and absorption, or destruction and extinction at the hands of other peoples. As Theodor Mommsen remarked somewhere about the ancient world as a whole, for a people to survive it had to have the character of the hammer or the anvil. The belief in Yahweh made the Hebrews resemble both. That is not to claim that the Hebrews created their religion in order to survive, but merely that

†Vaux argues that the patriarchs were neither nomads nor settled folk. They had sheep and goats, which needed some water and confined their owners to the edge of the desert. Occasionally they picked up some cattle, which tended to limit their movements. Then they might acquire lands and begin to cultivate them. See his *Histoire ancienne*, I. 220–222. The description suggests a precarious existence.

matters worked out that way. Especially after the exodus from Egypt the religion of Yahweh was very well suited to provide cohesion for a set of moderately greedy herders and cultivators forced to stake out a new territory. Their sense of being the objects of a special providence resembled the mentality of conquering settlers at many points in subsequent human history.

In Egypt the Hebrews had no "public" of their own; it was a foreign imposition. As a simple nomadic society they had not yet created public institutions. In the religion of Yahweh and its priestly servants they created for the first time their own public as well as key aspects of their own identity. Under these historical circumstances it is hardly surprising that the cultural result was a novel religion, and that the religion displayed a powerful strain of paternal terrorism.

The Growth of Public Authority

During the patriarchal period of seminomadic life on the edges of the desert there is no sign of any organized authority over the Hebrew tribes as a whole. Except for the deity there was no public symbol or authority. It is not even clear whether the individual tribes had a chief.[33] But social relationships were anything but anarchic. Within the family, patriarchal authority was great, at least according to the received tradition. The father was master of his wife. He possessed full authority even over married sons who lived with him, including the right of life and death.[34]

In the absence of any system of authority above the tribe, the law of blood vengeance and group solidarity in crime and punishment governed individual behavior.[35] Thus the tribe constituted the public for any given male. The solidarity of the tribe was preserved to a great extent by an institution known as the *go'él*. If misfortune or imminent loss threatened the lot, life, or property of an Israelite, this custom obliged a closely related male to act as redeemer, defender, or protector to ensure that the person or property not be lost. The role of *go'él* followed certain kinship lines, passing from paternal uncle to his son and then to other relatives. It was the obligation of the *go'él* to exact blood vengeance.[36]

During the period of Egyptian bondage the supreme secular authority was of course the pharaoh. Biblical tradition ascribes the creation of a new system of authority to Jethro, the father-in-law of Moses, shortly after the departure from Egypt. Jethro supposedly told Moses that he could not continue to judge all disputes among the people of Israel without wearing himself out. Instead Moses should represent the people before God, bringing their cases to God and teaching the people the statutes and decisions. Thereby Moses should make the people know the way in which they must walk and what they must do. Therefore Moses should choose able God-fearing men who hated bribes, and put them over the people as rulers of thousands, hundreds, fifties, and tens. Great matters they should bring to Moses for decision, but small matters they should decide themselves, to make matters easier for Moses.[37]

Social relationships had become more complex, mainly, it seems, due to an increase in the number of people. This text treats the role of the holder of authority as one of settling disputes. It reports nothing about deciding what activities individuals should perform or how they should carry them out. Presumably, routine activities like food-getting should continue to be governed by custom and habit, while the strategy of migration and contest with other societies should be managed by a charismatic leader like Moses. In any case, a single system of public authority had begun to take shape under the pressure of novel circumstances.

Upon the death of Moses, authority passed into the hands of Joshua. On the occasion of his accession, according to the Biblical tradition, the people promised to obey him as they had obeyed Moses. "Whoever rebels against your commandment," they announced, "and disobeys your words, whatever you command him, shall be put to death. Only be strong and of good courage."[38]

During most of the period of the conquest and settlement of Canaan, however, the Hebrews appear to have been governed by a series of "judges" in a manner roughly similar to the one Jethro suggested to Moses. Their rule followed the lex talionis widespread in early social systems: "Your eye shall not pity, it shall be life for life, eye for eye, tooth for tooth, hand for hand, foot for foot."[39] How the judges actually obtained their position we do not know: supposedly the Lord raised them up and thus saved the people from the power of those who plundered them.[40] Society must have been somewhat chaotic. "In those days there was no king in Israel; every man did what was right in his own eyes."[41]

Under these circumstances it is not surprising that in the course of time there appeared a movement on behalf of a king. It appears to have started among the elders of Israel toward the end of Samuel's tenure of the office of judge. Samuel reacted negatively to the plea "Give us a king to govern us," and warned of the heavy burdens that a monarch would impose upon the people. But the people rejected his advice. They insisted on having a king over them that they might be like other nations, with a king to go out before them and fight their battles. At this point, it is said, the Lord told Samuel to give them a king.[42]

Samuel then called together the people. Lots were cast which came up with Saul, whom the people accepted as king. "Then Samuel told the people the rights and duties of kingship, and he wrote them in a book and laid it up before the Lord."[43] The book constituted a charter of royal rights and duties. Significantly the Bible fails to give any indication of what this charter contained. Yet the fact that a charter existed signifies the first appearance of a distinction between public authority and private rights. For this distinction to appear in the context of Hebrew experience, secular authority had first to take on royal trappings.

From the beginning there was a conception of limits on this authority. Two famous episodes from the time of the monarchy reveal the working of these limits in practice. Both have to do with unjust behavior by the king in the form of violations of the commandment against coveting one's neighbor's wife or his possessions. In both a human agent has to confront the monarch with his sinful and unjust behavior, after which the monarch suffers divine punishment.

The first episode has to do with King David and Bathsheba, the wife of Uriah the Hittite. David, while walking upon the roof of his house, saw her bathing. She was very beautiful. David sent messengers, took her, and lay with her. She conceived. Thereupon King David arranged to have her husband killed while fighting the enemy by putting him in the forefront of the hardest fighting and ordering his associates to draw back. The stratagem succeeded. After she had finished mourning for her husband, David brought her to his house and married her. At this juncture Nathan the prophet intervened, we are told, at the instigation of the Lord, who was displeased at David's behavior. Nathan told David a touching story about a poor man who loved his one little ewe lamb like a daughter but was forced to sacrifice it when a rich man received a traveler but was unwilling to take one of his own flock to prepare for the traveler. David responded to the tale with a burst of anger at the rich man's crude injustice. Then Nathan said to David "You are the man . . . you have smitten Uriah the Hittite with the sword and have taken his wife to be your wife. . . ."

Through the mouth of Nathan, God threatened David with the prospect that his neighbor would lie with David's wives in the light of the sun, and that David's child by Bathsheba would die. This child did die shortly afterward, though she bore him a second son, who became King Solomon. Later, Absalom in the course of his conspiracy went in to the concubines of his father King David "in the sight of all Israel."[44] If we are to believe this moral tale, a Hebrew monarch was expected to refrain from infringing on the marital rights of his male subjects. Since the king had numerous concubines, one might expect the risk of this particular sin to be minimal. But passionate attraction could overwhelm all other considerations.

The second episode concerns landed property instead of a coveted woman. It took place much later, under King Ahab and his queen

Jezebel. Next to the palace of Ahab there was a vineyard belonging to a man called Naboth. Ahab wanted this vineyard to make into a vegetable garden, and offered to give Naboth a better vineyard or cash in return.† But Naboth refused, saying, "The Lord forbid that I should give you the inheritance of my fathers." On being refused, King Ahab became so vexed and sullen he would eat no food. When Jezebel, his queen, learned the reason for his refusal to eat, she said to him, "Do you now govern Israel? Arise, and eat bread, and let your heart be cheerful; I will give you the vineyard of Naboth. . . ." Jezebel then wrote, using the king's seal, to the elders and nobles, arranging to have Naboth stoned to death on a false charge of having cursed God and the king. As soon as Ahab learned of Naboth's death, he took possession of the vineyard.

Then the word of the Lord came to Elijah the Tishbite, ordering him to confront the king and say to him, "Thus says the Lord, 'Have you killed and also taken possession?' " Evidently the Hebrews believed that divine intervention was necessary to start the machinery of justice moving against so powerful a figure as the king. But the king is described as expecting something of the sort, for he greeted Elijah by saying "Have you found me, O my enemy?" Elijah threatened the king and Jezebel with utter destruction. At this point in the story, it turns out that Ahab had also acted abominably in going after idols, which presumably added to the divine rage of which Elijah the Tishbite was the mouthpiece.

At this crucial point, however, Ahab succeeded in partially evading the consequences of his evil behavior. When he heard Elijah, he rent his clothes, put sackcloth upon his flesh, fasted, and went about dejectedly. These traditional forms of self-abasement were enough to mollify in part the anger of the deity. The Lord then came to Elijah the Tishbite, saying, "Have you seen how Ahab has humbled himself before me? Because he has humbled himself before me, I will not bring the evil in his days, but in his son's days I will bring the evil upon his house."[45] Thus injustice was avenged, but the main impact of vengeance fell upon the next generation. Eventually, when Ahab was killed in battle, dogs licked his blood, and harlots washed themselves in it as Elijah had once threatened.[46] But he had to die some time, and the connection with his earlier misdeeds seems to be a chronicler's afterthought.

Looking back over the record, we can see that as Hebrew society grew larger and more complex, a distinct and primarily secular authority put in an appearance in the form of the monarchy. Simultaneously

---

†On the king's traditional respect for the property of a subject, see 1 Chron. 21:18–27, where King David insists on paying for a site on which to build an altar for the Lord, although the owner wanted to make a free gift of the site.

there appeared restraints on the monarchy in the form of private or individual rights. The monarch was not to use his power against a subject purely for his own personal advantage. In this situation the king was subject to the same ethical restraints as any other adult male member of the community. These restraints, embodied in the Tenth Commandment, long antedated the monarchy.

In these cases we can see plainly how traditional religion supported the rights of the ordinary individual against arbitrary actions by the king. This was a significant achievement in the cause of privacy. To be sure, divine intervention in the form of prophecy was necessary to put the restraints into effect. Belief in Yahweh was the source of the prophet's moral courage. Secular authority was in the end still subject to religious authority. Though we must retain reservations about the overall effectiveness of this religious protection of private rights, the tradition that such rights existed remains significant.

Monarchy and Prophecy

By the time of King Solomon (ruled about 970 to 932 B.C.) Israel had developed a powerful and complex public sector. There was a body of royal officials overseeing a system of taxation and forced labor. A professional army had come into existence. There was also an organized priesthood.[47]

A body of law, known as the Torah, had also grown up. The word "Torah" means both the Pentateuch, or first five books of the Bible, and the body of rules that govern the relationships of men with God and among themselves.[48] Thus, according to the ancient Hebrew conception, the social and legal order included God. The king had no legislative power.[49] In other words, only God could make laws. Unlike the Greeks, the Hebrews reveal no sign of the idea of human society as something human beings create and change on their own.

Heads of families or clans sat at the city gate, where all the affairs of the community were discussed, to settle disputes and legal cases. There were also professional judges, appointed, it appears, by the king. Some cases went on to superior authority.[50] Priests too took part in rendering justice. There are indications that their role increased with the passage of time.[51]

The practice of blood vengeance executed by the *go'él* never disappeared. The law continued to recognize it, but tried to limit its abuses by distinguishing voluntary from involuntary homicide and by establishing places of refuge where an involuntary killer could find asylum.[52] Thus public institutions did not completely supersede private arrangements for the control of aggression within the community.

In any case the ancient Hebrews did not make a distinction between public and private realms of conduct even though in practice they recognized, as we have seen, private rights that set limits on royal power. The absence of a clearly recognized distinction between public and private realms of behavior was in large measure due to the persistence of a religious conception of law and society. There could be no secrets from God, and the most intimate affairs of what we would call private life were subject to religious norms and public intervention.

For example, if parents were plagued by a stubborn and disobedient son, they were expected to bring him before the elders at the city gate, saying "This our son is stubborn and rebellious, he will not obey our voice; he is a glutton and a drunkard." Then all the men of the city were to stone the youngster to death, thereby purging the evil from their midst and setting an example for all Israel to hear.[53] How often this actually happened, if at all, we cannot know. But the text demonstrates the existence of a highly punitive attitude, based on the fear of a generalized social threat, with characteristic overtones of pollution.

The extensive public apparatus created by the time of Solomon may well have produced benefits in the form of magnificence and internal peace. But it also put a new burden on the people and was capable of abuse. We have already had occasion to notice isolated but important acts of protest sparked by the prophet Nathan against King David and Elijah the Tishbite against King Ahab. These protests did not take the form of a generalized specification of individual or private rights against public authorities. There was no need for that. Instead these prophets could reach back for traditional standards of justice with which to condemn royal behavior. Now we shall examine the record of two of the greatest Hebrew prophets, Isaiah and Jeremiah, to ascertain the objects of their wrath and their implicit and explicit standards of condemnation.

Isaiah preached and prophesied during the latter part of the eighth century B.C., when the kingdom of Judah was clinging to a precarious independence amid the struggles of the great powers Egypt and Assyria. Lacking direct political responsibility, Isaiah could preach that social justice rather than the cult or military strength should be Judah's real concern. Hence Judah should not rely on novel military technologies such as the horse and chariot nor on Egypt's promised aid. At the same time Judah ought not to rebel against Assyria. The Assyrian emperor was seen by Isaiah as a mere tool in the hands of the God of Israel, a tool who would be destroyed in his turn after having unconsciously fulfilled his function.[54]

Set down in a powerful verbal imagery that reveals a huge reservoir of aggression, the theme of total destruction as a necessary prelude to total happiness runs through the book of Isaiah. Though some passages speak of a saving remnant as the source of the future world,[55] others portray a destruction that will spare no one:

> Behold, the Lord will lay waste
>> the earth and make it desolate,
> and he will twist its surface and
>> scatter its inhabitants.
> And it shall be, as with the people,
>> so with the priest;
>> as with the slave, so with his master;
>> as with the maid, so with her mistress;
>> as with the buyer, so with the seller;
>> as with the lender, so with the borrower;
>> as with the creditor, so with the debtor.
> The earth shall be utterly laid waste
>> and utterly despoiled;
>> for the Lord has spoken this word.[56]

The paradise to come is also a total one that reverses all prior experience:

> The wolf shall dwell with the lamb,
>> and the leopard shall lie down
>> with the kid,
> and the calf and the lion and the
>> fatling together,
>> and a little child shall lead them.[57]

In due course this image of destruction, redemption, and paradise was to take on a secular form and reappear in Marxism. In Isaiah the reason for destruction is failure to obey the Lord.[58]

The specific targets of the prophet's anger are wealth, display, unrighteousness, liquor, and fornication. Traditional sources of human pleasure, or more specifically the primary male pleasures, appear as growing out of evil roots.

> I will punish the world for its evil,
>> and the wicked for their iniquity;
> I will put an end to the pride of the
>> arrogant,
>> and lay low the haughtiness of
>> the ruthless.[59]

So spoke the Lord, according to Isaiah. In another passage there is a vindictive anti-urban motif.

> "May the descendants of evildoers
>> nevermore be named!
> Prepare slaughter for his sons
>> because of the guilt of their
>> fathers,
> lest they rise and possess the earth,
>> and fill the face of the world with
>> cities."[60]

The Lord's sympathies are with the unfortunate.

> "Is not this the fast that I choose:
>   to loose the bonds of wickedness,
>   to undo the thongs of the yoke,
> to let the oppressed go free,
>   and to break every yoke?"[61]

In another passage he speaks of justice:

> For I the Lord love justice,
>   I hate robbery and wrong;
> I will faithfully give them their
>   recompense,
>   and I will make an everlasting
>   covenant with them.[62]

The abuse of liquor is a recurring theme, tied in with arrogance and injustice:

> Woe to those who rise early in the
>   morning,
>   that they may run after strong drink,
> who tarry late into the evening
>   till wine inflames them!
> They have lyre and harp,
>   timbrel and flute and wine at
>   their feasts;
> but they do not regard the deeds of
>   the Lord,
>   or see the work of his hands.[63]

And eloquently repeating the curses, Isaiah cries:

> Woe to those who are wise in their own eyes,
>   and shrewd in their own sight!
> Woe to those who are heroes at drinking wine,
>   and valiant men in mixing strong drink,
> who acquit the guilty for a bribe,
>   and deprive the innocent of his right![64]

The condemnation of sexual attractiveness is equally vivid.

> The Lord said:
> Because the daughters of Zion are haughty
>   and walk with outstretched necks,
>   glancing wantonly with their eyes,
> mincing along as they go,
>   tinkling with their feet;
> the Lord will smite with a scab
>   the heads of the daughters of Zion,
>   and the Lord will lay bare their
>   secret parts.[65]

Except for intermittent statements about unjust treatment of the poor and downtrodden, there is little to be found in Isaiah that has to do with what we would call private rights against the social order. The reason is not far to seek. Isaiah has little interest in correcting the abuses of the prevailing order, much as he hates them. Instead his imagery focuses on the total destruction of that order and its replacement with one that transcends all previous human experience. In that sense he deserves to be known as the first thoroughly revolutionary thinker in Western culture.

As already mentioned, much of his spirit remains alive to this day among modern secular revolutionaries. There is the same passionate hatred of hierarchy, arrogance, injustice, and sensual pleasure, and the same belief in a total transformation of social relationships and emotions. I suspect that this attitude reflects an anarchist streak that runs through human nature. More specifically, it comes down to a refusal to recognize any need for command-obedience relationships and organized inequality as the price human beings have to pay for living in large complex social units or, even more simply, as the price for civilization. Since not all inequality is socially necessary and since authority readily lends itself to abuse, there are likely to be grounds for this anarchist leaven as long as civilization continues.

Jeremiah too is of course a prophet of impending doom, so much so that his name has passed into the languages of those who read the Bible. To me his imagery seems less powerful than that of Isaiah. But he is much more clearly the lone prophet and moral critic whom the authorities try to silence and who risks life and limb to make public his message.

Much of the hostility to Jeremiah derived only quite indirectly from his moral criticism. He was what moderns would call an agent for Nebuchadnezzar, King of Babylonia, who was to destroy Jerusalem in 568 B.C.[66] Like Isaiah, Jeremiah preached from the vantage point of no political responsibility. Toward Babylonia he advocated a policy of no resistance. He did this not out of any admiration for Nebuchadnezzar, whose eventual destruction he also predicted,† but because he saw Babylon as the agent for the Lord's punishment of the Hebrews.

On one occasion Jeremiah made his prediction of the taking of Jerusalem before the princes, saying that those who went over to the enemy would save their lives. Quite understandably the princes asked that he be put to death ". . . for he is weakening the hands of the soldiers . . . and the hands of all the people, by speaking such words to them." The authorities cast him into an empty cistern, from which he was later rescued.[67]

---

†Jer. 25:12; 50–51. From 46 to 51 there is a miscellaneous collection of prophesies predicting the destruction not only of Israel but her neighbors and rivals. Jeremiah was as much a believer as Isaiah in total destruction as the prelude to happiness on earth.

That was only one of several narrow escapes. From the beginning Jeremiah saw himself as the lone prophet utterly dependent on the Lord's guidance and support.

> I did not sit in the company of merrymakers,
>   nor did I rejoice;
> I sat alone, because thy hand was upon me,
>   for thou hadst filled me with indignation.[68]

On one occasion the priest and chief officer heard Jeremiah prophesying and beat him and put him in stocks. Jeremiah felt himself to be a laughingstock and object of universal mockery.[69] Later when he spoke before priests, prophets, and people, all laid hold of him and threatened him with death. But he managed to convince at least some that he spoke in God's name and was spared.[70] Later King Zedekiah of Judah imprisoned him.[71]

Under another king, Jeremiah's prophesies, taken down by his scribe Baruch, were read aloud to the court. As three or four columns were read, the king cut them off with a penknife and threw them into the fire. Then the king commanded his officers to seize Baruch and Jeremiah. But, according to the account, the Lord hid them.[72] Later while in another place Jeremiah was beaten and imprisoned.[73] Despite these vicissitudes he seems to have survived the capture of Jerusalem, when his captors offered him the opportunity to go to Babylon and be well taken care of or to reside elsewhere. He chose not to go to Babylon but to dwell "among the people left in the land."[74] The date and manner of his death are unknown.

The targets of Jeremiah's prophesies and preachings are the usual ones of ill-gotten wealth—prophets seem unable to see any other kind—injustice, good food and drink, attractive women, and, perhaps most of all, idolatry. The ritual of sacrifices, it is worth noticing, is not acceptable to God in the absence of moral behavior.[75] Jeremiah's wrath is indiscriminate:

> Therefore I am full of the wrath of the Lord;
>   I am weary of holding it in.
> "Pour it out upon the children in the street,
>   and upon the gatherings of young men, also;
> both husband and wife shall be taken,
>   the old folk and the very aged."[76]

In one passage Jeremiah raises the famous question "Why does the way of the wicked prosper?" For an answer he merely asserts that God plants the wicked and they take root, surely one of the least satisfactory answers in the history of human thought. The best Jeremiah can do is ask God to pull them out like sheep for the slaughter.[77] Jeremiah's criticism of wealth is uncompromising. Wealth is the consequence of treachery.[78] Everybody from the least to the greatest "is greedy for unjust gain.''[79] The person who gets riches "not by right" is "like the partridge that gathers a brood which she did not hatch."[80] Elsewhere he chants:

> Woe to him who builds his house by unrighteousness,
>   and his upper rooms by injustice;
> who makes his neighbor serve him for nothing,
>   and does not give him his wages;
> who says, "I will build myself a great house
>   with spacious upper rooms,"
> and cuts out windows for it,
>   paneling it with cedar,
>   and painting it with vermilion.[81]

Thus wealth always appears as the product of dishonesty or oppression. Its use is for ostentatious display. Yet despite his criticism of the rich, there is no sign that Jeremiah became an accepted spokesman for the poor. In at least one passage he himself criticized the poor for having no sense and being ignorant of God's way and the law. They too have "made their faces harder than rock" and "refused to repent."[82] Like the priests and the other prophets, the people called for his death when they heard him speaking.[83]

Thus he was truly the lone prophet, essentially dependent on divine support. There are signs that the society he addressed had become atomized by political danger and changes in the distribution of wealth:

> Let every one beware of his neighbor,
>   and put no trust in any brother;
> for every brother is a supplanter,
>   and every neighbor goes about as
>   a slanderer.
> Every one deceives his neighbor,
>   and no one speaks the truth . . . .[84]

Even if Jeremiah was exaggerating the degree of mutual distrust, it would have been very difficult for anyone who believed this to have served as the leader of any organized opposition.

It would be a serious mistake, however, to regard new wealth and new forms of exploitation as the direct causes of prophetic wrath. These economic factors may well have done a great deal to create the situation that made prophecy possible. But they were not perceived as the cause of evil. Like Isaiah, Jeremiah diagnosed the evils of his day as due to the people forsaking the Lord their God, indeed rebelling against him.[85] "Do you not see what they are doing in the cities of Judah and in the streets of Jerusalem?" asks Jeremiah in a typical passage. "The children gather wood, the fathers kindle fire, and the women knead dough, to make cakes for the queen of heaven; and they pour out drink offerings to other gods, to provoke me to anger."[86] The remedy is included in the diagnosis. After God's anger has fulfilled itself in destruction, there will be reconciliation in the form of a new covenant, and once more joy and prosperity will come to the land of Israel.[87] In its Marxist secular reincarnation the new world would emerge out of destruction as the classless society.

Thus the conception of Yahweh as an exclusive and intolerant deity lay at the root of the prophetic impulse. A God who tolerated no deviance among his people was the source of prophetic individualism, a form of deviance from collective practice that had enormous consequences for Western history.

Sin and the Individual

Up to this point we have for the most part been looking at Hebrew society from the top down by examining the conception of the deity, the growth of a sphere of public activities, and the prophetic responses to this transformation. Now it will be necessary to shift our perspective in order to determine what concrete duties membership in ancient Hebrew society entailed for the ordinary individual. In other words, what were the rules by which Hebrews tried to live and where did these rules come from?

Certain general characteristics of these rules emerge from a comparison with the obligations of membership in the Athenian polis. It will be useful to comment briefly on some of these as a preliminary background to a more detailed analysis. Among the Hebrews all social and moral legislation came directly from God. For the Athenians too there was a divine component in their legislation. But the Hebrews had no conception of moral and social legislation arising from the people's own discussions and decisions when gathered together in assembly. The Hebrews had a powerful conception of sin but no conception of secular democratic politics. Secular politics was the affair of the king by the time the Hebrews came to have one, and even then it was subject to judgment by religious and ethical standards.

Another striking characteristic from a comparative standpoint is the relatively weak development of obligations to society among the Hebrews. Taxes and corvées emerged at a late point under the monarchy. There were rather loose military obligations all along, although these diminished with the growth of a professional and partly mercenary army under the monarchy.[88] Hebrew social duties were not obligations to the social order but rules about what it was that individuals, for the most part adult males, must and must not do to and for each other while living in the same society. They included restraints on aggression and mistreatment of the weak and unfortunate, as well as rules governing sexuality, to be discussed separately in more detail. In addition there were rules about the practice of the cult and regulations about food, cleanliness, and some aspects of personal appearance that reflected ideas about the holy and the profane, the pure and the impure.

At no point in Hebrew history do we find any well-developed set of activities that require the cooperation of all or most adults or even just adult males. They were not members of a hunting band like the Mbuti. Stock-raising and peasant farming were family undertakings with the help of a few slaves or hired laborers. In the absence of cooperative activities that could create social solidarity, the sense of community, if there was to be one, had to come from other sources.

At the behest of their religious leaders the Hebrews did make a tremendous effort to create and sustain the idea of a separate community. Many of their social rules and cult practices have the maintenance of a distinct Israelite identity as their stated purpose. This sense of being a special people chosen by God was important to them as a subject people under the Egyptians and as conquering settlers in Canaan. Though we know much less about the situation in patriarchal times, it is not hard to see that a sense of familial and tribal identification provided the individual with the only form of social protection available.

The absence of social duties in the narrow sense of specified obligations to the society as a whole is obvious in the most famous codification of morality in the Old Testament, the Ten Commandments. Instead, the first five commandments specify the character and obligations of the cult. They include the prohibition of the worship of other gods, graven images, taking the Lord's name in vain, and the obligation to observe the sabbath. The remaining five are rules governing the behavior of individuals toward each other. After enjoining respect for parents, come the prohibitions on murder, adultery, theft, false witness against a neighbor, and, finally, coveting a neighbor's wife and property.[89]

The Tenth Commandment about proper attitudes toward a neighbor's wife and property is the most interesting from the standpoint of our inquiry. Unlike the preceding commandments on murder, adultery, theft, and false witness, which deal with overt and concrete behavior, the Tenth Commandment enjoins a specific emotional attitude. Even the Sixth Commandment "Honor your father and your mother. . . ." does not go that far. One can honor one's parents by meeting specific economic and ceremonial obligations to them even if one bitterly resents the obligations. Though that is not the way one ought to feel, and unfilial attitudes were almost certainly subject to reproach, it is still the behavior that counts. But, to repeat, the Tenth Commandment prohibits a potentially dangerous attitude. It says nothing about behavior. In fact there is no need to, since the earlier prohibitions on murder, adultery, theft, and false witness cover the behavioral consequences quite effectively. For these reasons the Tenth Commandment is really superfluous. Since attitudes are notoriously difficult to ascertain and even harder to enforce, there are strong grounds for wondering why the Tenth Commandment is there at all.

Presumably it is there as an extra safeguard against what appeared to be an especially threatening and socially divisive temptation. Women and property have, after all, been major sources of conflict throughout human history. Homer made such conflicts the central point of the *Iliad*. Yet the fact that Greek culture produced the *Iliad* and Hebrew culture the Tenth Commandment reveals central emphases in both cultures. The Tenth Commandment attempts to control the emotional tone in a set of personal relationships that would have been labeled private in fourth-century Athens as they would be in our time. Private and intimate social relationships were the object of tremendous society-wide concern among the ancient Hebrews, and they created for themselves a terrifying God to embody and express this concern.

The Ten Commandments were evidently part of a far-reaching moral revolution associated with the names of Moses and Yahweh. In connection with the handing down of new statutes and ordinances, the Bible attributes to Moses a speech to the Hebrews in which he says, "You shall not do according to all that we are doing here this day, every man doing what is right in his own eyes. . . ."[90]

Among various segments of the Hebrew population there must have been powerful resistance to this revolution. There has already been occasion to mention evidence for an undercurrent of bitter hostility to God and his workings. The blaming of deviant behavior on foreign sources, especially on the Canaanites, and the religious injunction to exterminate such sources of moral infection take on new meaning as we become aware of this hostility. To blame others was in part a safe way for Hebrews to deflect this hostility. A major source of the hostility may have been the attempt to impose new and intrusive religious rules on the conduct of daily life. The Tenth Commandment is only one example of this effort, though a very important one. Furthermore the Ten Commandments by themselves yield only a limited and distorted picture of ancient Hebrew religion and ethics.

A long passage in Leviticus, all of Book 19, adds considerably to our information because it constitutes a brief yet reasonably complete statement of just about all the explicit rules of conduct governing the life of the ancient Hebrews. Its most remarkable feature, at least on first reading, is the range of human activities covered and what seems to a modern reader their different degrees of importance. They vary from belief about the deity and the most serious ethical issues raised in the Ten Commandments (largely repeated here in a slightly different form) to rules about planting fruit trees and against trimming the beard.[91]

Turning to the text itself, one notices that it comes down to a series of injunctions to do this and not to do that. By my rough count the thirty-seven verses add up to thirty-five commands, though one could find more than thirty-five or fewer depending on one's interpretation. Most of them are orders not to do something, as is the case with most social rules. Just to give the flavor I will mention one series of prohibitions that happen to follow each other: prohibitions on reaping a field to its border at harvest time, on stealing, on false witness, on mistreating neighbors, on cursing deaf people and putting a stumbling block before the blind.[92]

Despite this confusing mixture of large and small, the series of injunctions does fall into a pattern easy enough for a modern reader to understand if one asks the simple question: what are people supposed to do? There are the injunctions to respect parents and the aged that have already appeared. There are prohibitions on injustice and aggression, terms that will of course need further explication. There are a series of rules about kindness to the poor, oppressed, and unfortunate. There are also some rules about sexual behavior.

Let us begin with a closer look at the prohibition on injustice: "You shall do no injustice in judgment; you shall not be partial to the poor or defer to the great, but in righteousness shall you judge your neighbor."[93] The message is terse if not altogether unambiguous. The part that strikes us, and was certainly important to the ancient Hebrews, is the simple sentence "You shall not be partial to the poor or defer to the great." It is almost impossible to make the same point in other words without sounding like a bad sociologist. But the risk is unavoidable. There are situations, we might say, in which one must treat people exactly alike despite differences in wealth and status. It is worth noticing that this simple statement is about injustice, not justice. Finally it is a statement about simple homely affairs such as dealing with neighbors.†

To what sort of situations in everyday life did this injunction apply? Where did the ancient Hebrews get such an idea? It is impossible to give firm answers to these important questions. Since the date of this text from Leviticus is highly uncertain, like most others in the Old Testament, one cannot use the text to locate ideas and behavior at a specific point in time the way scholars can use most texts about Athenian society. But if we treat the statement as applying to a society halfway between nomadism and settled agriculture and with a very

---

†That also happens to be true of what is perhaps the most famous story in the Bible about justice, not injustice: the tale of the judgment of Solomon. The central figure in that episode is a mother who runs the risk of seeing her baby killed, an intensely tragic experience of private life in any society. See 1 Kings 3:16–28.

loose political organization, some inferences become possible. I suggest that we see in this striking sentence a reflection of age-old notions of fairness and fair exchange. When a powerful neighbor in a simple society borrows a tool, he ought to return it, *no matter who he is*.

Even the rule of an eye for an eye and a tooth for a tooth, or more technically the lex talionis, which we have already encountered in Hebrew society, is a rule about fair exchanges. But the rule of an eye for an eye and a tooth for a tooth often has different applications to different people. In some societies to knock out a rich man's eye is a far more serious offense than to knock out a poor man's. The simple rule of impartial justice found in Leviticus 19:15 specifically denies that aspect. For us that is its most interesting feature. The ordinary private individual seems to be getting some very special rights, even though neither the word "private" nor anything close to it appears.

This situation obviously has something to do with righteousness, a term that also occurs frequently in the Bible. The fullest definition of righteousness that I have come upon is from another part of the Bible. It presents mainly a rather miscellaneous list of things people ought not to do, and for which the penalty is death. Here God himself appears as the authority for the death penalty. The main part of the passage that in defining righteousness says something about behavior reads as follows:

> If a man is righteous and does what is lawful and right—if he does not eat upon the mountains or lift up his eyes to the idols of the house of Israel, does not defile his neighbor's wife or approach a woman in her time of impurity, does not oppress anyone, but restores to the debtor his pledge, commits no robbery, gives his bread to the hungry and covers the naked with a garment, does not lend at interest or take any increase, withholds his hand from iniquity . . . he is righteous.[94]

Not surprisingly righteousness involved the same concern about idolatry and the neighbor's wife that appears in the Ten Commandments. It also includes a taboo on sexual intercourse during menstruation. It includes rules about property, especially borrowing and lending. There are also some major positive injunctions, such as giving bread to the hungry and covering the naked with a garment. All the injunctions apply to adult males and adult males only. There is nothing terribly surprising about that since among the ancient Hebrews as in most societies, adult males were the ones who could do the most dangerous things, dangerous to themselves and to others.

Righteousness, in these texts, turns out to mean doing just about anything that is ethically approved. God is right there with the death penalty for disobedience. Nobody can escape, no matter who he is. The idea that no one can escape is of course characteristic and terrifyingly important. But it also conveys the hope that wealth, power, and prestige will not matter. Here again we see signs of the ordinary man getting rights against the prevailing social order. But the word rights does not occur.

If the rich man breaks social rules, supposedly he will face horrible punishment. It is a comforting thought. It also implies that the more rules there are, the better are the chances that somebody one detests—not necessarily just a rich man—will get caught. That may well be one reason the ancient Hebrews made so many rules and such complicated ones.

That is about all one can do in an attempt to see what the ancient Hebrews meant by such terms as justice, injustice, and righteousness. They pointed to concrete behavior, just as many of us would. In this attempt we have come upon signs of a high level of aggression in Hebrew society. If that is the case, it will be worthwhile to turn back once more to the capsule version of social rules in Leviticus 19 in search of further evidence. What barriers against aggression did these people try to erect? Who got mad at whom and why? Do we find rules protecting the potential victim of explosions of anger?

The absence of any specific treatment of murder in this capsule version of morality is at first glance somewhat striking. But that is of no great consequence since the prohibition on murder is well known. What the ancient Hebrews did about it is not an easy question to answer and one I shall set aside, since Roland de Vaux has already presented a careful analysis of the available evidence.[95] For the sake of exposition I will also omit sexual aggression in order to discuss sexual matters later.

There is a prohibition on stealing, certainly an aggressive act. By itself a prohibition on stealing merely reveals that the Hebrews had property worth stealing and fighting about, which is not the case in some of the societies anthropologists have studied. But this prohibition is tied in with a prohibition on lying, false dealing, and what we might call perjury: swearing falsely by God's name and thereby profaning it.[96]

Immediately thereafter follows another prohibition on stealing that is much more concrete. (From the text it seems that God thought the injunction could bear repetition.) The text as a whole deals with aggression and is worth quoting:

> You shall not oppress your neighbor or rob him. The wages of a hired servant shall not remain with you all night until the morning. You shall not curse the deaf or put a stumbling block before the blind, but you shall fear your God: I am the Lord.[97]

Here a whole series of potential victims of aggression receive whatever protection the injunction offers. They are of course neighbors, hired servants, and those afflicted by the physical handicaps of deafness and blindness. Deliberate torture of the deaf and blind may have occurred then. It happens in our society and nauseates us. In a different way and in a religious context it must have nauseated the ancient Hebrews also.

The next statement, about aggression, a few verses later, also gives information about potential victims. It begins with the sentence "You shall not hate your brother in your heart, but you shall reason with your neighbor, lest you bear sin because of him."[98] The abrupt transition from brother to neighbor probably means nothing in this context. In near-tribal societies neighbors may be called brothers, though the concrete obligations to each are likely to differ. The significant point for our purposes is that personal quarrels—which are not petty for the persons involved—should be settled through sensible discussions and not lead to violence. We have seen the importance of this idea among the Athenians, how it formed the basic ideal of discussion in their Assembly, as well as its many failures and short-comings. The institutional development of this idea among the ancient Hebrews was, as we know, very different. But they too had the ideal, or perhaps we should say the norm. To violate it was a sin.

The next verse is also quite specific about possible victims of anger. It suggests that the notion of reasoning about conflicts instead of fighting them out to the bitter end may reflect the experience of vengeance organized in the form of the blood feud. In any case the verse also indicates rather desperate efforts to hold the Hebrew community together, whatever that much abused word "community" may mean in this murky situation. Here is the famous verse: "You shall not take vengeance or bear any grudge against the sons of your own people, but you shall love your neighbor as yourself: I am the Lord."[99] Neither the historian nor the sociologist can say that the terrors of Yahweh were "necessary" to hold the ancient Hebrew community together, to overcome divisive tendencies, some perhaps stemming from the blood feud, and embark on the conquest of Canaan. But it is clear that some very important ancient Hebrew leaders had very similar ideas. Their conception of necessity centered around sin, or *any* form of ethically disapproved behavior.

I will not discuss here in any detail vivid injunctions to respect the aged and individual strangers.[100] That is not because these issues are irrelevant. The stranger as a lone individual in a strange society, for instance, was subject to religious protection in Athenian society as he was among the Hebrews. He was not to be the victim of capricious rage in either society. Hence such individuals did have in both societies some limited social protection against rough treatment, an essential aspect of privacy. Yet since these ideas and practices were not a prominent aspect of the social scene until international commerce began to take hold on a worldwide scale centuries later, we may press on with the issues at hand.

Let us turn then to the final injunction in this capsule code. It is against cheating in the marketplace. The main part of the text reads: "You shall do no wrong in judgment, in measures of length or weight or quantity." The next sentence is an elaboration on what the existing measures were.[101] The injunction recalls Athenian efforts to control the workings of the market. But those required a complicated administrative apparatus with a strong secular flavor. This injunction has no sanctions behind it except God. In the first place this is rather good evidence that markets existed and were important to the workings of the social order. For the most part they were, before the monarchy, mainly local markets near or in well-settled areas.

One should be very cautious about saying how much of a strain they imposed on this society. But there was enough strain to make cheating with false weights and measures an issue.† The injunction prohibits these practices and tells the people to use "just" weights and measures, naming two of them. Very likely these changed their meaning over time and were themselves the source of quarrels. I do not propose to pursue this lead, however, because the evidence also supports another point closer to our immediate concerns.

Being cheated in the market place obviously makes a person angry. It can happen to rich and poor, male and female, young and old. But in a simple material sense it hurts the poor more than it does the rich. Economists have correctly emphasized this point for a very long time. To be cheated out of one's last few pennies can be a disaster for the poor. For the well-to-do it is at most a maddening annoyance. The main victims of cheating in the marketplace, certainly one form of aggression, were liable to be the poor. It is therefore legitimate to regard this injunction as part of what today would be called a social welfare policy. The unfortunate deserved care and compassion.

This interpretation sheds a useful new light on many of the other injunctions in this capsule code. For instance, the one about reaping and taking care of fields and vineyards is quite clearly a simple form of welfare policy. The landowner was not supposed to strip the land bare at harvest time. According to these ethical rules he was expected to leave gleanings or bits of the crop "for the poor and the sojourner."[102] The injunction against mistreatment of the deaf and blind, mentioned a few moments ago, is a compassionate social rule. So is the injunction against oppressing one's neighbor and holding back the wages of a hired servant. The same is true of the rule against hating one's brother.[103]

There is no need to go much further. Clearly there was in this

---

†It was evidently the practice of some people to carry in their bags two sets of weights, a large and a small, and to keep in their house two kinds of measures, a large and a small. Presumably the big ones were used for purchases and the small ones for sales. Deuteronomy 25:13 prohibits such practices.

society a powerful attempt to take care of the poor and the unfortunate. The frequency of references to "homey" details is in my judgment convincing evidence that these injunctions were not mere talk. Evasion there certainly must have been. But it would be absurd to dismiss altogether this evidence of an organized and coherent effort. The poor, the sick, the old, the widow, and the orphan are after all recurring figures in the Old Testament as a whole. By any standard I can see, this is quite extraordinary.

If there was an obligation to take care of the poor and the unfortunate, on whom did the obligation rest? In ancient Athens the obligation rested on the polis. Here we see nothing of the sort. The obligation rested squarely on the individual. Every injunction is a divine order *to an individual* to behave in a specific way. There is no hint here of folk sanctions on behavior, though as a social scientist I believe *some* existed, probably in this case rather weak. Whoever wrote this document did not think they were even worth mentioning. Terrorist divine sanctions—and a powerful sense of compassion— would have to take the place of folk sanctions.

If the obligation of compassion rested on the individual rather than on some specifiable social unit, how did individuals feel about the obligation? Were there any limits to the obligation? From the standpoint of privacy, that is of course a crucial question. Again looking back at fourth-century Athens, we have had occasion to notice how many social obligations stopped quite literally at the front door of a citizen's house. That was true of the demands of the polis and in day-to-day relations with neighbors. So far as one can tell, theory and practice ran in roughly the same direction. Do we encounter a comparable situation among the ancient Hebrews in the premonarchical period?

The answer to this question must, I think, be a resounding no. Here is how the prophet Isaiah, admittedly a later source, defines compassion: "Is it not to share your bread with the hungry, and bring the homeless poor into your house; when you see the naked, to cover him, and not to hide yourself from your own flesh?"[104]

With all due allowance for poetic and prophetic exaggeration this passage asserts the obligation to bring the poor and unfortunate right into one's own home, to feed them, and to share one's clothes with them. (Nakedness and hiding are matters to discuss more fully later.) Taken at all seriously, this is an obligation that almost certainly would have outraged a well-to-do fourth century Athenian male just as it would shock most present day well-to-do American house owners, male and female.

Did such an obligation really exist in Hebrew society before the period of the monarchy? One cannot be positive. Like all prophets, Isaiah created a past that was partly imaginary, partly true. There could be an echo here of older social rules about generous treatment of strangers and poor relations. The concreteness of the imagery suggests such an interpretation. It is not difficult to imagine a situation in which taking the poor and unfortunate into one's own dwelling and sharing food with them was the normal and expected thing to do. It is also quite easy to see that in this type of situation poor and unfortunate individuals would fall under a special form of religious protection. Such practices fit quite well with seminomadic life, or even just a great deal of moving about and fighting.

It is also highly likely, as the anthropological materials have shown in other contexts, that rules of hospitality and/or charity would be abused from time to time. When that happens, people get mad. Then it is necessary to strengthen the sanction or, in this particular case, give Yahweh more power. Without being able to suggest a specific point in time, I strongly suspect that this theme entered ancient Hebrew culture at an early stage. The important point for our purpose is the evidence that it was a religious obligation that, in theory at least, overrode feelings about one's personal possessions. Such an obligation must have created severe anxieties and moral anguish. It still does. So do other moral obligations in the ancient Hebrew moral code.

Religious Purity and Intimate Affairs

In analyzing ancient Hebrew social obligations we have often noticed how difficult it was to discern any specific social unit to which the obligations were due. In the main texts, such as the Ten Commandments and Leviticus 19, we just do not see anything like a tribe or a polis. But we can see families and individuals. Why is this the case? The explanation, I shall argue, is both very simple and absolutely crucial for understanding privacy in this society.

The authors of these and other social rules had little or no reason to distinguish between obligations to a specific social unit and obligations among individuals or households. They were putting forth ethical demands that supposedly applied to everybody. "Everybody" in this case clearly meant all good Hebrews. Those who were not good were sinners, of which there are plenty in the Old Testament. Furthermore, these ethical demands covered most if not all aspects of human behavior. This strongly ethical and ritual viewpoint did not and in fact could not draw a distinction between social and personal or public and private realms of behavior.

The ancient Hebrews did not develop a distinction between public and private affairs the way the Athenians distinguished between the affairs of the polis and the affairs of the household. The ethical and ritual outlook associated with Moses and the worship of Yahweh appears to have pushed Hebrew culture onto another developmental path. The Hebrews did create an elaborate public sector under the monarchy. But their main effort was to make the monarchy as ethical as possible according to traditional conceptions. This was the thrust behind prophecy. After the time of Moses the original religious spirit may have lost some of its *élan* and become ossified. Nevertheless it remained highly influential in the affairs of daily life.

And from the standpoint of these pristine beliefs every detail of personal conduct becomes an ethical issue requiring ethical rules with a strong religious sanction. For the true believer the distinction between ethics and ritual likewise vanishes, as ritual acquires powerful ethical meanings. As we shall see shortly, household activities, especially eating and sexual behavior, required the observance of religious rules and were subject to community-wide sanctions. The Athenians too knew the distinction between sacred and profane, pure and polluted. But their rules did not require continuous supervision of what went on in the household.

Before examining the intimate aspects of ancient Hebrew society, I want to explore briefly what there was in Hebrew culture that calls to mind a concept of privacy. The closest the Hebrews came to the notion of private was in connection wih certain qualities of the deity and the purity of objects connected with the cult. According to Deuteronomy 29:29 "The secret things belong to the Lord our God, but the things that are revealed belong to us. . . ." God alone, it appears, had privacy. His right to privacy manifested itself most clearly at Mount Sinai, when Moses said to God "The people cannot come up to Mount Sinai for thou thyself didst charge us, saying 'Set bounds about the mountain and consecrate it.' " Aaron could accompany Moses into God's presence. But the priests and the people were not permitted to break through and come up to the Lord.[105] On numerous occasions too the Old Testament reports that God spoke of the children of Israel as his personal and, as we might say, private possession.

Religious taboos likewise limited access to the main tangible objects of the cult, the ark and the tabernacle. The Lord charged Moses to tell Aaron, his brother, not to come at all times "into the holy place within the veil, before the mercy seat which is upon the ark, lest he die; for I will appear in the cloud upon the mercy seat."[106] The general populace was required to separate from their uncleanness lest they die in their uncleanness by defiling the tabernacle in their midst. Uncleanness in this context had the specific meaning of impurity coming from bodily discharges.[107] The ark was the major cult object of the ancient Hebrews. Endowed with magical powers, it traveled with them in their campaigns to subdue Canaan. It helped to separate the waters in the crossing of the Jordan and to bring down the walls of

Jericho. Once captured by the Philistines, it wrought destruction in their ranks until returned to the children of Israel. Finally it came to rest at Shiloh.

Now we may turn to the more intimate and personal aspects of ancient Hebrew life, so far as it is possible to reconstruct them from the Old Testament. Here our concern will be with such simple everyday matters as going into or out of houses or onto another person's land, and what enters and leaves the human body. Both forms of entering and leaving may or may not be highly charged emotional issues, depending on individual circumstances and the prevailing social order. The reader may recall the Siriono Indians with their extremely casual attitudes toward sex and defecation, as well as toward entering and leaving the band's collective dwelling. On the other hand, the frequency of hunger pangs generated such highly charged attitudes toward the limited supply of game that women were suspected of hiding meat in their vaginas. Ancient Hebrew attitudes toward all these matters were anything but casual. To understand them it is necessary to begin with a brief glance at the structure of the family.

For that purpose I will draw primarily but not exclusively on the careful work of Vaux, adding a few points especially relevant to privacy and individual rights. In the oldest documents the form of the family appears as strongly patriarchal and, one might add, definitely patrilineal. Genealogies are always given in the paternal line. The father is master of the wife and has full authority up to the right of life and death over married sons if they live with him.[108]

On the other hand, in legislation as early as that attributed to Moses, we can discern the grant of specific rights to the wife even if these rights were theoretically subject to the husband's veto. According to this legislation, the wife had the right to assume obligations through vows, oaths, or pledges. If the husband heard of these obligations, he had to express his disapproval on the same day in order to exercise his veto. Then the Lord would release her from her vows and forgive her. Otherwise the obligation would be valid. The same situation prevailed for a young unmarried woman still under the authority of her father. If the husband delayed in nullifying the wife's vows after he had heard of them, he became responsible for his wife's iniquity. There was no comparable rule limiting the delayed action of a father.[109]

As noted earlier, the *go'él* and the right of protection constituted an interesting set of arrangements. If an Israelite had to sell himself into slavery because of debt, he could expect to be repurchased by the *go'él*. To exact blood vengeance was also at one time the obligation of the *go'él*. A certain order of kin relationships determined who was to be the *go'él* in any given situation.[110]

With the transition to a more sedentary life the authority of the head of the family declined. As might be anticipated, some aspects of his authority passed to what we can recognize as public authorities. Thus the father could no longer put his son to death even in the case of a crime against the parents. Instead elders of the town rendered judgment.[111]

Though the monogamous ideal appears in the book of Genesis, polygyny existed under the rule of the judges and the monarchy.[112] In all likelihood only the prosperous could afford polygyny. The Ten Commandments, as we have already noticed, treat the wife as a form of property. There are three references in the Old Testament to a bride price that might take the form of labor.[113] Ordinarily upon marriage a woman left her relatives to live with her husband, though exceptions are mentioned for which there appears to be no clear explanation.[114] The age of marriage seems to have been relatively young by contemporary standards: sixteen and younger for males. The parents played a decisive role in the choice of a mate. The girl was not consulted and often not the young man. But evidently some room was left for the inclinations of the young. Girls were not confined and had opportunities to meet young males, a situation that created opportunities for seduction. When that happened, the accepted procedure appears to have been payment of the bride price and marriage.[115]

One piece of legislation about marriage is especially important for our purposes because it reveals the existence of a conflict between private and public obligations even though the terms private and public do not occur. It is also significant that the law resolves the conflict in favor of private obligations. Here is the text: "When a man is newly married, he shall not go out with the army or be charged with any business; he shall be free at home one year, to be happy with his wife whom he has taken."[116]

The Ten Commandments condemn adultery, which was perceived as a crime punished by God. The penalty for adultery with a married woman was death by stoning for both partners. Though marital fidelity was recommended to the husband, his infidelity was subject to punishment only if he injured the rights of another male by taking as his sexual partner a married woman. The wife faced a more restricted situation. The husband could forgive her but could also repudiate her.[117]

Magical methods were at one time available for testing and punishing a wife suspected of infidelity. A priest wrote curses into a book which he then washed off into what was known as the water of bitterness. The suspected wife then drank this water. If she were guilty, the water of bitterness was expected to cause great pain, make her body swell and her thigh fall away, after which she became an execration among the people. If the woman had not defiled herself, she should be allowed to go free and conceive children.[118] The text does not report any guilty wives who managed to drink the water of bitterness without these dire results. On the basis of what is known about the effectiveness of taboos and curses in nonliterate societies such evasion seems highly improbable.

One structural feature deserves emphasis though I shall not attempt to document it in detail. Since we are looking for the basic cell in ancient Hebrew social structure, we should keep in mind the household rather than the family. The household often included both strangers or sojourners, as they are sometimes called, and slaves. Both groups we shall encounter later in the course of more detailed discussion. Though it is highly unlikely that all households contained these two types of individuals, it is reasonably clear that the ideal patriarchal household was expected to have them.

Slaves performed both household tasks and helped with the flocks and work in field and vineyard. A Hebrew "brother" or a Hebrew woman could be sold as a slave, though the law stipulated that they were to be freed after six years of service.† Just what the role of the stranger was is much harder to determine. Possibly they were wandering traders, though I have not noticed any text describing what the strangers or sojourners actually did. But we do know that they were protected by law and religious injunction, in a manner roughly similar to foreigners in Athens.

From this schematic summary it is plain that much of life's ordinary routine took place within a social context dominated by adult males. They appear as the ones who made the real choices. I think this image requires some qualifications. In addition to fecund and devoted wives, the Old Testament contains too many accounts of powerful women who were a threat to male dominance to accept this picture of male authority at face value. Eve herself as well as Delilah and Jezebel come to mind as some examples. In the second place it seems highly likely that many intimate groupings arose outside the family and perhaps even in competition with the family. Close associations among males are so common as to scarcely require documentation, though the career of King David is especially rich in examples.[119] Indications of a flourishing feminine subculture of friendships and cliques are much harder to come by.

The Book of Ruth is a moving tale of women helping women. Since it mainly concerns a widow and her daughters-in-law, it only constitutes evidence for intimate relationships within the family circle. It also shows, however, that women unaccompanied by males could wander about freely in an attempt to better their fortunes, an attempt that succeeded in this case. In the light of the relatively light restrictions on women's activities, restrictions very much lighter than those in fourth-century Athens, it seems highly likely that a flourishing

---

†Deut. 15:12. Many slaves, perhaps most, seem to have been foreigners. For a detailed discussion of slavery see Vaux, *Institutions,* I, 125–140.

feminine subculture did exist, at least after the conquest of Canaan. That it did not leave strong traces in the text of the Old Testament is hardly surprising, since the text as we have it was almost certainly written by men for a predominantly adult male audience.

Households probably lived first in tents and then subsequently in houses, to which I will limit the discussion here since there is not enough trustworthy detail about the earlier period. We have already come upon a sharp contrast between fourth-century Athenian and ancient Hebrew ethical attitudes toward the family dwelling in Isaiah's injunction to bring the poor into one's house and share with them one's food and clothing. Let us now look more closely at this situation.

Early legislation mentions houses in walled cities and houses in villages without walls. Village houses were parts of units of family property that included fields for cultivation. The whole formed a patrimony that in theory should not be sold or alienated, though in practice this happened often enough to generate rules about the re-demption of family property subsequent to its sale.[120] In turn the Tenth Commandment theoretically protected the wife, servants, animals, and tools necessary for operating the family property against the covetous eyes of a neighbor.[121] All this suggests a society with the small peasant proprietor (but often with a substantial flock or herd) as the moral tone setter by the time the Hebrews had conquered or destroyed their rivals in Canaan.

Hebrew religion placed ethical brakes on the grasping selfishness that often characterizes the small proprietor. Rules about going onto another person's property allowed people to help themselves to grapes and grain as they did so, but within carefully specified and easily recognized limits. Perhaps we should call it a law of limited trespass, promulgated of course by Yahweh.

> When you go into your neighbor's vineyard, you may eat your fill of grapes, as many as you wish, but you shall not put any in your vessel.
> When you go into your neighbor's standing grain, you may pluck the ears with your hand, but you shall not put a sickle to your neighbor's standing grain.[122]

Trespass by wandering animals was, on the other hand, a more serious offense, probably because animals could do really serious damage. If a man deliberately allowed his animals to graze over a field or vineyard, or just let them loose so that they happened to feed in another man's property, he was required to make restitution from the best in his own field and vineyard.[123] If widely practiced, the limited rule against human trespass must have substantially curtailed rights of private use and enjoyment of one's own property.

The same spirit of religiously enforced generosity appears in the story of Nabal, Abigail his wife, and David. Nabal is described as very rich, churlish, and ill-behaved. Abigail, on the other hand, was of good understanding and beautiful. On one occasion Nabal, suspecting that David was part of a band of runaway servants, refused a request from him for food for himself and his men, saying, "Shall I take my bread and my water and my meat that I have killed for my shearers, and give it to men who come from I do not know where?" Learning of the refusal, Abigail decided to treat the men generously with food and drink, partly out of fear that David's men might do violence to the house on account of Nabal's ill nature. Some ten days later, according to the story, the Lord smote Nabal and he died. Shortly afterward Abigail became David's wife.[124] The obvious moral of this tale is that a rich man ought not to regard the obligation of hospitality as an intrusion on his privacy.

Yet there was a sense in which the house was supposed to be a place of secure retreat. This attitude appears in the story of the slaying of Ishbosheth, son of Saul. Those who committed the murder thought they were doing David a favor by taking vengeance on the offspring of Saul, now dead, who had once sought David's life. But David was outraged, and especially outraged by the circumstances of the murder: ". . . when wicked men have slain a righteous man in his own house upon his bed, shall I not now require his blood at your hand, and destroy you from the earth?" David carried out his threat at once.[125]

Within the house, and perhaps even within a tent, there must have been strict rules of privacy since the Hebrews had divinely ordained rules about nakedness. These will come up for discussion in connection with sexuality.

Now that we have examined some of the rules about entering and leaving houses, we may turn to what enters and leaves the human body, beginning with food. Both food and sex presented to the ancient Hebrews highly charged emotional issues. They called into play ideas about purity and pollution, the holy and the profane, sin and virtue.

In very many human societies the act of eating serves as an occasion for drawing social boundaries. That was certainly true of the ancient Hebrews. In the Old Testament the emphasis is on the taking and selection of food as a way to define and demonstrate membership in the Hebrew community. The best-known example is the rite of the Passover. It arose in Egypt. Through Moses Yahweh commanded the Hebrews to eat unleavened bread for seven days, beginning on the fourteenth day of the first month in the evening. Anyone who ate what is leavened was to be "cut off from the congregation of Israel, whether he is a sojourner or a native."[126]

The original occasion that this rite commemorates also required among other things that the Hebrews mark their doorposts and lintels with sacrificial lamb's blood to distinguish them from the Egyptians, marked out for divine destruction.[127] Thus the whole ritual was suffused with ideas of group preservation amid threatening crisis and extreme danger, a major recurring theme in ancient Hebrew and later Jewish history. At the same time the ritual of the Passover remained what we would call a private act carried out in the intimacy of the household. Once again I must point out the absence of any terms for private in the texts describing this ritual.

The inclusion of the sojourner in this exclusive ritual presents interesting problems that I am unable to solve satisfactorily. A later passage states explicitly that no foreigner, sojourner, or hired servant may eat of the Passover. But every slave bought for money might eat of it after undergoing circumcision. Likewise strangers were allowed to keep the Passover, provided all males had been circumcised. No uncircumcised person was to eat of the Passover. "There shall be one law for the native and for the stranger who sojourns among you," the passage concludes.[128] Still another text merely asserts that strangers can keep the Passover and that there shall be one statute for the sojourner and the native, without mentioning the requirement of circumcision.[129]

The rule against oppressing strangers is worth noticing once more in this context. Hebrews were expected to "know the heart of a stranger," that is, empathize with a stranger, since they themselves had been strangers in Egypt.[130] Yet it is plain that in some sense strangers presented a threat to their exclusive sense of identity, manifested through food taboos and the special treatment of the male sexual organ in circumcision.

The food taboos themselves formed part of a ritual of group identification as a people chosen by God. The list in Deuteronomy 14 begins with a prohibition on the practices of scarification and cutting one's hair for the dead, practices similar to many found in nonliterate societies. Before listing what Hebrews may and may not eat, the text continues: "For you are a people holy to the Lord your God, and the Lord has chosen you to be a people for his own possession, out of all the peoples that are on the face of the earth."[131]

This is very close to the concept that the Hebrews were God's private property to do with as he pleased. It is a sentiment that recurs widely throughout the Old Testament. Along with the assumption of divine interest in and control over the affairs of daily life, this identification as God's "private" people helps to account for the apparent absence of any notion of a private realm of behavior. Another reason is the relatively late development of independent political institutions in the form of the monarchy, which, as the criticisms of the prophets demonstrate, never gained complete legitimacy. Thus in theory, at any rate, an ancient Hebrew could never eat without being reminded of his very special and religiously determined character. The very complexity of the taboos would guarantee this result for anyone who took them seriously.[132]

It is hard to believe that a group of scattered tribes engaged in what we would now call a guerilla war and struggling to establish themselves in new and strange surroundings would or could have followed these dietary prescriptions and prohibitions in full detail. But that may not be decisive. As Douglas has pointed out, the key idea that permeates these and other prohibitions, including sexual ones, is the idea of holiness with overtones of purity.[133] By its very nature holiness is unattainable for most ordinary mortals. It requires the concept of sin and an abundance of sinners. Hence difficult or impossible dietary rules might be very useful in keeping alive the sense of holiness and the special identity based thereon.

In the course of a reasonably assiduous search I have come upon only one reference to excretion in the Old Testament. Since it seems to be unique, I reproduce the full text despite its length. It is in the form of a command that is part of the Mosaic corpus of legislation:

> You shall have a place outside the camp and you shall go out to it, and you shall have a stick with your weapons; and when you sit down outside, you shall dig a hole with it, and turn back and cover up your excrement. Because the Lord your God walks in the midst of your camp, to save you and to give up your enemies before you, therefore your camp must be holy, that he may not see anything indecent among you, and turn away from you.[134]

The law applies to the situation that existed in an armed camp, one that prevailed for a long time during the conquest of Canaan. It reveals nothing about practices in more settled times or in towns. It tells us nothing about possible segregation by sex or whether defecation occurred alone or in company. Nor does it say a single word about urination. Perhaps, as was the case among the Fulani, according to Riesman, urination was not subject to any social sanction. Hence the text is in one sense singularly unrevealing.

Nevertheless the reasons given that purport to explain and justify this ancient Hebrew rule provide welcome confirmation and elaboration of points already suggested. For these people the important distinction was not between public and private but between holiness and defilement. If one insists on some distinction, however vague, between public and private, or collective and individual concerns, it is God who plays the role of the public in this intellectual and moral system. But there is no need to insist. The important point is that God supposedly walks in the midst of the camp. That is, of course, comforting in a time of chronic danger. Evidently the Hebrews felt they needed all the divine assistance they could get. Lest God turn away and cease his assistance, the camp had to be kept holy. Therefore feces had to be deposited outside the camp and buried where God in the normal course of events would not be expected to notice them or step in them.

Official Attitudes
Toward Sexuality

Conceptions of sin, pollution, and defilement likewise suffused ancient Hebrew ideas about sexuality and the erotic relationship. According to God's commands, sexual behavior was definitely not a private matter subject to the free choice of the individual, as it is according to a powerful though hardly dominant current of contemporary Western opinion. Instead the individual's sexual behavior was for the ancient Hebrew religious authorities a matter of the highest concern to the community as a whole. These authorities used the most drastic threats and powerful sanctions they could imagine to channel the sexual impulse within socially acceptable limits. As might be expected in a patriarchal society, the main concern was with male sexuality though from time to time the texts do indicate limits on female sexuality as well. Since the society was patriarchal, it is a fair inference, occasionally supported by the actual wording of a prohibition, that the prohibitions had considerable support in Hebrew communities.

Despite the vehemence of these prohibitions, the ancient Hebrew religious authorities, so far as I can sense their underlying assumptions, were not really Puritanical about sexuality. There is no indication in the Old Testament of a generalized fear of sexuality as such, nor an overall condemnation of sexuality as sinful or "dirty." That current of opinion appears to be mainly Christian, though it occurs in other "high" cultures—most notably Hinduism—as well.

For the ancient Hebrew authorities sexuality within the marital relationship was expected to be satisfying and presumably most enjoyable. According to the Old Testament, by the time of King Solomon the marital relationship could include, in the case of so exalted a figure, seven hundred wives and three hundred concubines.[135] This degree of erotic self-indulgence for aristocratic males, which some circles in our own culture have tried to make available to everybody including females, was a relatively late development in Hebrew culture. As we have seen, there was in the prophets a vehemently articulate reaction against the hedonism of the dominant classes.

The punitive character of the older legislation appears most dramatically in (1) rules governing the virginity of the wife and (2) the list of sexual offenses subject to the death penalty. The rules about virginity read as though they were the codification of actual practice. If a man spurned his new wife on the false ground that she turned out not to be a virgin, the parents of the bride were to take the tokens of her virginity to the elders at the city gate and spread the garments before them. Then the elders of the city were to whip the man and fine him one hundred shekels of silver, which were given to the bride's father because the bridegroom had "brought an evil name upon a virgin of Israel." The slander in other words affected the whole community. Then the bridegroom was compelled to accept the woman as his wife for the rest of his life.

If, on the other hand, the new husband's accusation seemed to be true because "the tokens of virginity were not found in the young woman"—there is no mention of the biological possibility of virginity without "tokens"—the young woman was to be taken to the door of her father's house. There the men of the city were to "stone her to death with stones, because she has wrought folly in Israel by playing the harlot in her father's house; so you shall purge the evil from the midst of you."[136] Thus the young woman's presumed sexual misbehavior appeared to the ancient authorities as a grave insult to her father and a form of pollution from which the community must purge itself.

Since many writers have explained the concern with virginity and wifely fidelity as a reflection of concern with legitimate descent and property rights, it is worthwhile to point out that there is no sign of such concerns in this quite detailed text. Instead, the concerns are about family honor and the honor of Israel. To me at least, these concerns look like a straightforward projection of male sexual jealousy and desire to monopolize the sexual favors of the female. The text as such provides no clue to the extent to which females might or might not share such feelings.

The list of sexual offenses subject to the penalty of death at the hands of men presumably reports those forms of sexual behavior that Mosaic law regarded as the most serious violations of morality.[137] In the well-known passage in Leviticus 20, verses 10 through 16 call for the death penalty for specific acts ranging from adultery through varieties of incest and perversion. In the outline below one can readily see the nature of the crime and reasons given for the punishment. Variations in the form of how death was to occur throw further light on this set of punitive limits on sexuality.

Definition of crime	*Justification of death penalty*	*Form of death penalty*
1) Man commits adultery with wife of his neighbor.	None given in this text. But this was a major preoccupation of Hebrews. See Ten Commandments.	Both put to death. Form not specified.
2) Man lies with father's wife.	He has uncovered father's nakedness. Blood is upon them.	Both put to death. Form not specified.
3) Man lies with his daughter-in-law.	They have committed incest. Blood is upon them.	Both put to death. Form not specified.

Definition of crime	*Justification of death penalty*	*Form of death penalty*
4) Man lies with a male as with a woman.	Both have committed an abomination. Blood is upon them.	Both put to death. Form not specified.
5) Man takes a wife and her mother.	It is wickedness.	All to be burned with fire so that there may be no wickedness.
6) Man lies with a beast.	None given.	Man and beast to be killed.
7) Woman approaches a beast and lies with it.	Blood is upon them.	Woman and beast to be killed.

Obviously the above list includes a whole series of potential sexual targets that would be likely to occur in the intimate setting of a series of patriarchal households with flocks to tend. There is a curious concern with cross-generational intimacies (father's wife, daughter-in-law, wife and her mother) that is strange to us but plausible in that context. But it is only in other passages in the Old Testament that we find references to certain forms of intimacy that are even more probable: father and daughter, brother and sister. (We shall examine other evidence about incest shortly.) The absence of any penalty for sexual relations among females when death was the penalty for male homosexuality is equally striking. That this sexual deviation was permitted is highly unlikely. It is more likely that the mere possibility of sexual activities among females was so shocking to ancient Hebrew male sensibilities that they did not dare mention it even in the form of a prohibition. But we do not know and very likely never will.

Turning now to the ancient Hebrew definition of incest, we do find a prohibition on intercourse between a man and his sister in a list of sexual acts by males subject to a ritual curse by all the men of Israel.†
The curse applies to a daughter of one's father or of one's mother, that is, a half sister, and presumably also to full sisters, although this is not explicit. The rule about half sisters is understandable enough in a polygamous society.

A tale much later in the Old Testament, however, strongly suggests that the monarch had the power to lift this prohibition in individual cases if he chose to do so. It is the moving tale of Tamar, who

†Deuteronomy 27:22. Brother-sister incest in Leviticus 20:17 in the Revised Standard Version carries the penalty of being "cut off," presumably from Hebrew society as I read it, although the Hebrew term *karet* or death by God for deliberately committed sins is to Hebrew scholars ambiguous, at times interpreted as "extirpation" or as "premature death," with the means unspecified. See *Encyclopaedia Judaica* (Jerusalem, 1972), X, s.v. *karet*, 787–789.

became the victim of her half brother Amnon's passion. Both were children of King David. At the moment when Amnon tried to seduce Tamar, she objected:

> No, my brother, do not force me; for such a thing is not done in Israel; do not do this wanton folly. As for me, where could I carry my shame? And as for you, you would be as one of the wanton fools in Israel. Now therefore, I pray you, speak to the king; for he will not withhold me from you.[138]

Another possible interpretation of the episode is that the patriarchal father had the right to lift this prohibition on his own son and half sister if he saw fit to do so. Violation of the rule evidently did not entail a penalty beyond some form of shaming and social ostracism. In this particular episode Amnon raped Tamar, after which his passion turned to hatred and rejection. Eventually Absalom, Tamar's brother, murdered Amnon in revenge for his treatment of Tamar. Thus the story as a whole is a tale of male passion breaking the dike of social prohibitions. The woman appears as a tragic but essentially passive victim.

The only discussion of father-daughter incest that I have been able to find in the Old Testament is the clearly legendary tale of Lot and his daughters that serves to explain the origin of the Moabites and the Ammonites (in no way connected with Amnon), peoples with whom the ancient Hebrews had frequent conflicts.[139] The vivid detail about how each daughter seduced her aged father, first making him drunk with wine, in order to beget progeny suggests that this form of incest was not unfamiliar in ancient Hebrew experience.† Not a word of condemnation occurs in this brief but vivid account of incestuous seduction. Hence the text does not in any way prove that the ancient Hebrews objected to father-daughter incest.‡ But one cannot use this piece of evidence to prove much of anything about actual behavior because the incestuous origins of human groupings is a widespread motif in folklore.

Nevertheless, the absence of any explicit and outright condemnation of father-daughter incest in the Old Testament is quite striking. Two explanations come to mind. One might argue that in a society where the father had so much authority the practice was so widespread as to defy explicit prohibition. Since Hebrew religion did prohibit adultery, which was probably rather more common (though it would

---

†A contemporary student of incest in modern American society reports that "father-daughter incest is the most frequently reported form of sexual abuse within the family and has great potential for long-lasting harm to the child. The sexual contact usually begins when the child is between six and twelve, and it typicaly consists of fondling and masturbation. Thereafter it often continues for many years and may proceed to intercourse." See *The Harvard Medical School Health Letter* 6, no. 5, 3.

‡The otherwise useful article on sex in the *Interpreter's Dictionary of the Bible, Supplementary Volume,* is clearly mistaken on this score.

also produce far more serious rows), this explanation does not seem very convincing. I shall suggest another, one that may have already ocurred to an alert reader.

There is a certain pattern to many of the prohibitions on sexuality in ancient Hebrew society. They tend to prohibit *not* the most dangerous or attractive sexual object, but the one next to it. Thus in this case there is no death penalty for father-daughter incest. But there is one for coitus with a daughter-in-law. In the case of brother-sister incest the text, at least in English, is not absolutely clear, and the stress is on prohibiting incest with a man's half sisters. Similarly there is a death penalty for coitus with the wife of one's father, who is not necessarily one's mother in a polygynous society. Male homosexuality is forbidden but not sexual relationships between females. Thus for all their punitive rigor, these ancient prohibitions on the most intimate of all human relationships display a certain prudish hesitation. That may be the most significant psychological finding of all in this portion of our inquiry.

One source of this punitive attitude is traceable to the strenuous effort to create and sustain a distinctive moral and religious identity amid a welter of warring peoples during the conquest and settlement of Canaan. A closely related cultural theme is the ancient Hebrew horror of ritual impurity. At times this dread took the form of prohibitions on mixtures. Thus one of the injunctions in Leviticus reads: "You shall not let your cattle breed with a different kind; you shall not sow your field with two kinds of seed; nor shall there come upon you a garment of cloth made of two kinds of stuff."[140]

Another passage reflects the same attitude in the familiar form of sexual ethnocentrism. First comes one of the frequent lists of sexual prohibitions that need no repetition here. It ends, however, on a slightly different note. Women are forbidden to have intercourse with a beast because it is a "perversion." In discussing these passages Douglas has pointed out that "perversion" is an incorrect translation. The rare Hebrew word, she reports, actually means mixing or confusion.[141] Following the list of sexual prohibitions comes the divine admonition: "Do not defile yourselves by any of these things, for by all these the nations I am casting out before you defiled themselves; and the land became defiled so that I punished its iniquity, and the land vomited out its inhabitants."[142]

Except for their vehemence and divine origin there is nothing very unusual in these sentiments. It is a commonplace of human experience to regard other peoples' sexual practices as both disgusting and dangerously attractive, and therefore to embroider them with prurient imagination. Herodotus and Xenophon displayed traces of this sentiment, while in modern times the tendency to regard homosexuality as the vice of other nations has been quite widespread. Yet the Hebrew case is different. There we come upon an effort to enforce a set of punitive regulations and make them part of a religiously sanctioned national consciousness. Though the Old Testament never says so explicitly, sexual deviations were "public" matters in any sense of word.

A whole range of bodily secretions, which I do not propose to discuss in detail, was also matter of general concern because these secretions were regarded as "unclean" and required acts of ritual purification. Some secretions, such as those connected with menstruation, nocturnal emissions, sexual intercourse itself, and childbirth, had to do with sexual functions. Others seem to reflect disease.[143] The term "unclean" seems nearly identical with our expression "dirty" in regard to bodily secretions, except for the fact that among modern educated people sanitary notions have completely replaced ritual and religious conceptions. With us too such excretions are so far as possible concealed except when it is necessary to reveal them for medical reasons. Among the ancient Hebrews, on the other hand, purification rituals meant that nearly everybody in the community would be likely to learn what had happened. There may of course have been considerable evasion, just as we don't bother about sanitary precautions all the time. But there is no information on that aspect of these rules.

Though the vast majority of rules about sexual behavior took the form of prohibitions on males, there was one positive injunction on males that deserves brief discussion at this point. If a man's married brother died without leaving offspring, it was the man's obligation to have intercourse with his dead brother's wife in order to produce descendants for the dead brother. The first mention of the rule[144] merely describes the case of Onan, who refused to fulfill the obligation and spilled his semen on the ground. For this act, the origin of the term "onanism," the Lord is said to have slain Onan. In this early account there is no mention of an obligation to marry the deceased brother's wife. That obligation does occur in a piece of divinely inspired legislation that contains picturesque details, suggesting once more that this law codified existing practice.

The law applied to brothers who lived together, thereby presupposing the intimacy of the household. According to the law, the surviving brother could refuse to take his sister-in-law as a wife though the refusal was subject to strong sanctions. The woman so refused was to go to the elders at the city gate and announce her brother-in-law's refusal. The elders at the gate were then to try to persuade the surviving brother to carry out his obligation. If he still refused, there was to be a ceremony in which the offended woman pulled the sandal off the foot of her recalcitrant brother-in-law and spat in his face, all in the presence of the elders. As she did so, she was to say, "So shall it be done to the man who does not build up his brother's house." Thereafter the surviving brother's house, evidently in the sense of lineage, was to be known throughout Israel by a special name that meant "The house of him that had his sandal pulled off."[145]

This law or custom exemplifies in a very concrete fashion the functional attitude toward sexuality as a socially necessary activity to generate legitimate descendants. But it is important to remember that this was an official attitude and not necessarily the one prevailing among the population at large. Even this text reveals the possibility of individual attempts to evade strong social pressures.

At this point we may turn to the rather limited efforts to control aggressive and exploitative aspects of male sexuality. If a man seduced or raped a virgin, divine legislation required that he pay a bride price to the woman's father and take her to wife. Furthermore in the case of rape the man had to keep her as a wife for the rest of his life.[146] There were different rules governing the seduction of a betrothed virgin in the city and the rape of a betrothed virgin in the countryside. The penalty for seduction in the city was to stone both partners to death at the city gate because the woman had not cried out for help and the man had violated his neighbor's wife. In the case of rape in the countryside, on the other hand, only the man was to be put to death. The law treated this offense as similar to murdering a neighbor because the woman (presumably) cried for help and there was no one to rescue her.[147] The assumption that someone would rescue the unfortunate woman in both town and countryside if she did call for help provides an interesting clue to the attitudes prevailing in the ancient Hebrew community.

A man's right to sell his daughter as a slave appears to have been taken for granted. Such a slave did have certain rights, however. If she did not please her new master, he was to let her be redeemed and could not sell her to a foreign people, "since he had dealt faithlessly with her." If the new master designated her for his son, he was to treat her as a daughter. If the new master kept her for his own use and later took another wife, he was not allowed to diminish the food, clothing, or marital rights of his original slave spouse. Should the owner fail to do these three things, he was required to let the woman go without payment of money.[148] It is not clear who was expected to pay money in other cases of releasing a female slave or what the release amounted to. Nor is it clear how the other regulations safeguarding her limited rights could be enforced. Hence, despite its detail, this piece of legislation appears more ethical than effective.

Another divine law seems easier to enforce. It covers the situation where a man has intercourse with a slave betrothed to another man and not yet ransomed or given her freedom. Presumably the man to whom the slave had been betrothed was free. In this situation the death penalty for adultery did not apply since the woman was not free. Instead an inquiry was to be held and the seducer (or rapist?) was to bring a ram as a guilt offering to the door of the tent of the meeting, which appears to have been a place of general assembly for the Hebrew community. Then the priest was to make atonement for the guilty man with the ram as a guilt offering to God, who would then forgive the sin.[149] In other words, a female slave, even if betrothed to another male, was a semilegitimate sexual object. If the seducer could obtain a ram and go through a specified procedure before the community, there would be no more trouble. We may infer that seduction (or rape?) of an unbetrothed female slave caused even less trouble. To my knowledge no Old Testament text speaks to this situation.

A few comments on the role of the harlot will round out this image of male dominance. In the Old Testament there is a punitive preoccupation with the harlot that we do not find in the surviving records of Athenian culture. She seems to have been an early and ubiquitous figure in ancient Hebrew society. An early divine injunction tells the Hebrew male not to profane his daughter by making her a harlot "lest the land fall into harlotry and become full of wickedness."[150] By playing the harlot the daughter of a priest profaned her father: she was to be burned with fire.[151] "To play the harlot" is a common term in the Old Testament. It means to present or succumb to a variety of temptations, not necessarily just sexual ones. Thus the term carries strong overtones of polluting intimacy. Despite this generally negative image, there is evidence that temple prostitutes existed at least for a brief time.[152] There are also occasional brief sketches of revelry with harlots that bring out their erotic attractions in vivid detail, presumably for the purpose of pious edification.

From the standpoint of a concern with privacy, the theme of erotic passion bursting through the dikes of social convention acquires special importance. From time to time I have come upon the thesis that this theme does not become prominent in our culture until the time of the troubadors nor reach its full flowering before the realistic novel *Anna Karenina*. Such notions strike me as containing a strong dose of historical provincialism, though they may be correct about the development of psychological insight into individual concerns. Certainly the Old Testament contains many concrete examples of the dangers from forbidden forms of erotic passion. That is hardly surprising in the light of the strict taboos that the religious authorities tried to inculcate, mainly, so far as we can tell, in connection with the establishment of the worship of Yahweh and the conquest of Canaan. We may close this part of the discussion by recalling some of the major stories.

As the tale of Joseph and Potiphar's wife shows, the ancient Hebrews were familiar with seduction by a woman, and the disruption it might cause.[153] Since the tale purports to show Egyptian duplicity, however, rather than Hebrew customs, it will be best to leave it aside. Other stories that we have already discussed are those of King David and Bathsheba, the wife of Uriah the Hittite; and the sad account of the rape of Tamar by her half brother.

The legend of Samson and Delilah,[154] which we have not discussed so far, is an especially interesting study of the erotic relationship. Samson was a Hebrew hero with legendary strength; Delilah a Philistine agent, with whom he fell in love. Hence the story is a tale of the erotic relationship versus the obligations of religion and the desire for self-preservation. Delilah tried three times to pry out of Samson the secret of his strength. Three times Samson lied to her and each time Delilah reproached him for not really loving her. The fourth time he gave away the secret of his hair as the source of his strength, an admission which led to his capture and blinding by the Philistines. But in the end Samson won suicidal revenge by pulling down the temple upon himself and all the people in it.

Even in this legend, as in the other cases mentioned, the main actors are clearly recognizable and very human individuals. They are neither stock heroes nor stock villains. They face what we would call personal and private issues that the artistic talent of the unknown authors raises to the level of universal human problems. The presentation is more realistic and individual, I will venture to suggest, than in the tragedies of Sophocles, though not some of Euripides (for example, *Medea*).

In the Song of Solomon—the one piece of love poetry that somehow found its way into the Old Testament rather to the embarrassment of later Christian authors—the reverse is the case.† Even in the wooden language of the Bible in the *Revised Standard Version* the poetry can appeal to a modern reader. There are lovely if occasionally exaggerated and "Oriental" descriptions of the physical attractions of unnamed human males and females and equally lovely descriptions of physical settings for an erotic relationship. In Hebrew society at this time, we learn with interest, it was acceptable for the woman to play a very active role in searching for a lover.[155] There is a hint of brother-sister incest in one set of verses and a moving tribute to the overwhelming power of erotic passion in another.[156]

Yet despite these graphic details there is no hint of the insight into individual feelings that we find in the lyrics of Sappho or Catullus. No one appears as a recognizable human being. On the basis of the other sources just discussed, as well as the poetry of the Psalms, it seems plain that the Hebrews could have written poems in the manner of a Sappho or a Catullus. Perhaps they did elsewhere. But within the religious and artistic framework of the Old Testament, this treatment of the erotic relationship could not find a place.

---

†According to *The New Columbia Encyclopaedia*, s.v. "Song of Solomon. . .," 2563, modern scholarship dates this text around the third century B.C. though it is traditionally ascribed to King Solomon and accepted as an allegory of God's love for Israel.

Ancient Hebrew culture possessed a complicated cluster of rules and ideas about the exposure of the human body. All of them are rather obviously associated with the punitive official attitude toward sexuality. In the light of that attitude it is scarcely surprising that we find no trace of the idealization of the human body that slowly developed in the Greek treatment of the nude. The Old Testament has a great deal to say about nakedness, nothing about the nude.†

But there was an idealization of a different kind. In the Garden of Eden rules about covering the body did not exist at first. That was part of the suspension of all irksome restraints on everyday life in Paradise. When God created a woman, ". . . the man and his wife were both naked and were not ashamed."[157] But after Adam and Eve had tasted the fruit of the forbidden tree, their eyes were opened; "they knew that they were naked; and they sewed fig leaves together and made themselves aprons." Immediately afterward they heard the sound of God walking in the garden in the cool of the day. Evidently embarrassed, ashamed, and guilty all at once, they tried to hide themselves among the trees of the garden.[158]

As everyone knows, it was no use hiding. God drove Adam and Eve from Paradise. But before doing so, God made clothes for the pair.[159] Thus for the Hebrews, clothes and shame came from God, along with work, guilt, conflict, and social obligations (which appear for the first time in the story of Cain and Abel),[160] or all the unpleasant features of daily life. But Paradise was to linger on as an image of a world where clothes and social obligations did not exist. By the last quarter of the twentieth century it had become the staple of advertisements for vacation resorts.

Mosaic legislation contains a long list of prohibitions on uncovering the nakedness of near kin.[161] Since the rules parallel those against incest, there is no need to reproduce them here. But some brief comments are in order. First, the rules tell us something about restrictions on personal contacts within a household. The rules as such are much stricter than the practice prevailing in many a contemporary American middle-class household. In the second place, these rules are close to our theories about privacy. In effect they assert that the nakedness of another person is private property and belongs only to the person who has the right to look with sexually curious eyes. Hence the prohibitions are extended to menstruating women and the frequently tabooed neighbor's wife.[162] As part of its set of prohibitions on mixing things, early legislation also forbids women to wear men's clothes and vice versa.[163]

In the writings of the prophets the theme of aggressive exposure as a punishment for sin occurs from time to time. Those to be uncovered

---

†For the distinction, which may be limited to English, see Kenneth Clark, *The Nude,* chap. I, "The Naked and the Nude."

are well-dressed and decorated persons of high status. In two of the three instances that I noticed, women are specified, which suggests that aggressive exposure is a wrathful reaction to erotic exposure. Ezekiel writes of uncovering transgressions "so that in all your doings your sins appear." The passage continues with invective against a prince of Israel who will have to remove a turban and crown, a rather limited degree of exposure of a distinct loss of status.[164] Isaiah's outburst against sexual attractiveness is much more vivid, as we saw earlier.[165] Jeremiah, threatening woe to Jerusalem on account of its abominations and lewd harlotries, has God himself assert "I myself will lift up your skirts over your face, and your shame will be seen."[166]

Thus, taken as a whole, the official religious attitude was that the naked human body should be a private spectacle available only to the person enjoying marital rights, and that by extension there was something wicked in the public display of sexual attractiveness. Though the terms "private" and "public" do not occur in the texts, the terms describe very accurately the rules and attitudes just discussed.

The Theme of Loneliness

At the close of the discussion of Athenian society I drew attention to the near absence of the theme of loneliness or unhappy privacy in Greek literature. The ancient Hebrew tradition differs sharply on this score. Loneliness is a quite prominent theme in the Old Testament. Two poignant lines from the Book of Proverbs convey this sentiment in a way that transcends the centuries: "The heart knows its own bitterness, and no stranger shares its joy."[167] Differences between Athenian religious and ethical systems and those of the ancient Hebrews go a long way toward explaining this distinction.

In the Old Testament there is the recurring image of the lonely individual surrounded by wickedness, who must put his trust in God in order to survive. It occurs, for example, in Psalms 119 in the lines that begin "I hate double-minded men, but I love thy law."[168] Many of the Psalms (for example, 141–150) repeat this theme of necessary reliance on the Lord and the frailties of secular human help. This was also a collective image for Israel as a whole. The isolated and chosen people, the private possession of God, would win out against wickedness with God's help. Though this faith was put to severe tests, there was always something positive about this image of loneliness. Especially in the prophets this religious faith formed the basis for courage in opposing the moral values of secular authorities and the rest of the social order. As a cultural legacy it contributed as much as Greek democratic ideals to the development of Western conceptions of individual worth and individual rights.

The Old Testament also provides intermittent glimpses of a strictly secular aspect of loneliness that comes from the abrasive aspects of sustained intimacy. "Let your foot be seldom in your neighbor's house, lest he become weary of you and hate you."[169] Jeremiah expresses a similar sentiment in much stronger language in a passage already quoted:

> Let everyone beware of his neighbor,
>   and put no trust in any brother;
> for every brother is a supplanter,
>   and every neighbor goes about as a
>   slanderer.[170]

In the case of this prophet such advice and sentiments were part of an exhortation to the virtuous to set themselves apart from the rest of the population. Nevertheless the advice provides insight into personal relationships under the stress of intermittent surges of renewed virtue. The conflicts between friendship and kinship come to light in another text:

> Your friend, and your father's friend,
>   do not forsake;
> and do not go to your brother's house
>   in the day of your calamity.
> Better is a neighbor who is near
>   than a brother who is far away.[171]

That this text contradicts earlier ones about relationships with neighbors need not arouse our concern since this aspect of human relationships is itself contradictory. Intimacy and dependence, as we have seen earlier, can often generate hostility and a struggle for independence. Like friendship, loneliness has its price as well as its attraction. The Athenians must have known this as well as the Hebrews. But the frictions of daily life did not find expression in a literature concerned mainly with heroic struggles as readily as it did among the Hebrews where religion regulated so much of daily life. And among the Hebrews it did so in a way that made loneliness a more prominent aspect of human experience.

Individual Defenses Against Society Among Ancient Greeks and Hebrews

At this point in our inquiry significant differences between Athenian and ancient Hebrew responses to organized injustice emerge into view. These differences have to do with the nature of social pressures in the two societies as well as the individual's reaction to them.

So far as we can tell, the original state of Athenian society before the onset of democratic and popular movements, or about 700 B.C., was one in which the aristocracy held a firm monopoly of political power. Hence the excluded classes tried with considerable success over a period of some three centuries to cope with injustice by breaking this monopoly and acquiring full membership in the political community. By gaining control over political or public affairs they became able to change the laws to suit their own interests. The rest of their effort went into attempts to protect the individual against miscarriages of justice.

Before the establishment of the monarchy the situation among the ancient Hebrews could hardly have been more different. They were a religious community rather than a political one. With but the most rudimentary political institutions under the patriarchs, and no independent ones during the era of Egyptian bondage, we find no sign of any group excluded from political power. Religious exclusiveness there certainly was, but it served to keep foreign religious influences, sin, and pollution at bay. In this situation the most private acts and social relationships, including especially sexual ones, became matters of community-wide or public concern.

After the establishment of the monarchy the role of social critic and defender against injustice became partly institutionalized in prophecy. It was the prophets who called the king to account by showing that the same ethical standards applied to all Hebrews, including the king. Thus belief in Yahweh served as the source for prophetic individualism, which was also a reaction against the hedonism and display of the dominant classes under the monarchy. The conceptions of injustice and righteousness provided moral grounds for criticizing exploitative and grasping behavior among the well-to-do. The concepts of righteousness and injustice defined certain forms of behavior as ethically unacceptable no matter who engaged in them. Likewise, and here in sharp contrast with Athenian individualism, the Hebrew ideals of compassion, which meant opening one's home to the unfortunate and sharing one's possessions with them, offered at least some protection to the less favored numbers of the Hebrew community.

Thus in very different ways both ancient Athens and ancient Hebrew society worked out ways to protect weaker individuals against the harsher consequences of the prevailing social order. At the risk of some oversimplification, we might call the Athenian method the political one and the ancient Hebrew method the moral one. These two cultural grooves have guided efforts to cope with injustice in Western history ever since that time. Now we may turn to an examination of the different ways in which this same set of problems presented itself and the different solutions found in a major civilization almost entirely outside the realm of Western influences, that of ancient China.

ANCIENT CHINESE CONCEPTIONS OF PUBLIC AND PRIVATE

CHAPTER 4

Preliminary Remarks

To take the reader on a foray into ancient China, a civilization independent of Western influence and tradition, I have chosen a period rich in philosophical speculation that happens to be nearly contemporaneous with a similar flowering of philosophy in ancient Greece. To historians of China the period is known as the age of the "hundred philosophers," from about 551 B.C. to 233 B.C. It overlaps what is known as the period of the Warring States, 403 B.C. to 221 B.C., an era of anarchy and bloody wars, though with numerous signs of economic growth. It was also a time when Chinese thinkers were trying to decide what kind of a society they wanted and what kind was possible. In ancient Greece, we may recall, Socrates, Plato, and Aristotle wrestled with very similar problems at a time of roughly similar social disorder. But Greek political and social speculation came at the end of the age of the city-state, whereas Chinese political speculation preceded and, to a considerable extent, anticipated the creation of imperial institutions.

The expression "a hundred philosophers" is of course no more than a Chinese way of saying there were a great many. Some ten names have survived. Of these we shall examine in English translation the texts of six philosophers that include the three major intellectual traditions of the period—Confucianism, Taoism, and Legalism.

The first and oldest text is by Confucius, whose traditonal dates are 551–479 B.C., though there does not seem to be any compelling reason to accept the tradition.† His *Analects,* the only document that

---

†See the discussion in Arthur Waley, trans., *The Analects of Confucius,* 78–79. Chinese ideas about the importance of dates differ sharply from those now prevailing in the West.

modern scholars regard as presenting mainly Confucius' ideas, advocates rule by an elite, open to merit and suffused with a moral attitude toward politics. Mencius defended and amplified Confucius' ideas at a time when they were the object of serious challenge. His life, according to at least one tradition, fell entirely within the fourth century B.C.[1] The text that goes by his name presents a rather optimistic view of human nature.

The third exposition of Confucian doctrine is by Hsün Tzu (Master Hsün), who was born about 312 B.C., when Mencius was well along in years. The date of Hsün Tzu's death is unknown, though he might possibly have lived long enough to witness the unification of China under the first emperor of the Ch'in in 221 B.C. Often critical of Mencius, Hsün Tzu held that human nature was inherently evil but could be controlled sufficiently by a mixture of social education and individual willpower to yield a morally satisfactory social order.[2]

In its formative period Confucianism faced three major competitors. One was in the concepts of Mo Tzu (470–391 B.C.?), born shortly after the death of Confucius and who died shortly before the birth of Mencius (that is, between 479 and 372 B.C.). His main interest to us derives from his strong sympathy with the common people. Another distinctive trait was his advocacy of universal love.[3] He is the one philosopher in the group who failed to found a permanent school. By Han times (100 B.C.–220 A.D.) his work had all but dropped out of sight.[4]

The other two competing sets of ideas were Taoism and a theory of moral realism that has come down to us under the somewhat misleading label of Legalism. The principal classic in the Taoist tradition is the *Lao Tzu*, once thought to be by an older contemporary of Confucius. A recent translator, however, whose text I have used, doubts that there ever was a Lao Tzu and regards the work bearing his name as an anthology complied by a series of editors in the fourth to third centuries B.C.[5] Another classic of Taoism is known as the *Chuang Tzu*. Though it contains very little on privacy and its social context, its implicit and explicit assumptions cast a useful light on habits of mind that prevailed in some educated circles in the latter part of the fourth century B.C.[6]

In sharp contrast to the Taoist classics, the writings of Han Fei Tzu (280?–233 B.C.), a leading spokesman of the Legalist school, shed abundant light on the actual working of political and social institutions in the period just before the unification of China under the Ch'in emperor. As a moral realist, Han Fei Tzu displays a strong interest in understanding how and why human beings behave the way they do, though he has an equal interest in promoting what he believed to be the cure for the evils of his age. The essence of this cure was the adoption by the ruler of an explicit code of punishments and rewards, from which comes the label Legalist. Bureaucrats selected by the ruler were to replace feudal officials in enforcing the new code.[7] Another Legalist text, *The Book of Lord Shang*,[8] contains relatively little material that sheds additional light on issues of privacy in ancient China.

Some Western writers draw a sharp contrast between the disenchanted moral realism and emphasis on rules and punishments characteristic of the Legalist school and the stress on moral education so prominent in the Confucian tradition. The distinction is certainly there, though rather less prominent than the secondary accounts might lead one to think. Han Fei Tzu was a student of Hsün Tzu, whose variant of Confucian doctrine was also morally disenchanted. For all their variety and mutual criticism, the Chinese authors examined here reveal to a curious and sympathetic outsider the stamp of a shared culture distinct from our own or any so far examined in this inquiry.

Since the principal sources are the purported writings of philosophers, generally in the form of texts compiled well after the author's death, this chapter contains more intellectual history than those on ancient Athens and the ancient Hebrews. Nevertheless because the Chinese thinkers were primarily moral philosophers and social critics, their writings reveal a great deal about the actual state of affairs in pre-imperial China. Therefore I have tried so far as possible to place their doctrines in the context of the social situation in which they arose.

Early Distinctions Between Public and Private

By the third century B.C. and probably much earlier, Chinese thinkers had developed a sharp distinction between the concepts of public and private. Since Han Fei Tzu and his followers advocated a strong state, it is not surprising to find a heavy emphasis on this topic. Nor is it surprising to find the patina of high antiquity gracing this distinction, since Chinese thinkers generally claim great age for any practice or institution that they advocate. In ancient times [wrote Han Fei Tzu]

> when Ts'ang Chieh [a mythical culture hero] created the system of writing,† he used the character for "private" to express the idea of self-centeredness, and combined the elements for "private" and "opposed to" to form the character for "public." The fact that public and private are mutually opposed was already well understood at the time of Ts'ang Chieh. To regard the two as being identical in interest is a disaster which comes from lack of consideration.[9]

---

†In the outline of traditional Chinese history at the beginning of Watson's *Han Fei Tzu* we see that the invention of writing (as well as fishing and trapping) was also attributed to Fu Hsi, mythical sage-emperor.

As the acerbic last sentence shows, there must have been some thinkers taken seriously in Han Fei Tzu's day who failed to use the distinction between public and private affairs. A passage in an early chronicle-commentary, however, refers to the distinction in a way that shows it had been familiar for some time.†

A few pages later Han Fei Tzu remarks that some rulers listen to wild theories that bring destruction to the state and ruin to themselves because they do not distinguish clearly between public and private interests.[10] His vehemence suggests that he was having an uphill struggle in making his point. Several other passages show clearly that royal power was far from firmly established in the kingdoms that made up Chinese society at this time. Early in his discussion he speaks hopefully about putting an end to private scheming and making men uphold the public law.[11] In another passage he declares that the ruler "must not allow officials to use their funds to build up their own soldiery." In a similar vein he must never pardon the offense of men who have taken up arms in a private quarrel.[12] Elsewhere Han Fei Tzu expresses strong disapproval of the bands of knights who sell their services in private vendettas.[13]

One of the great steps on the road to a distinction between private and public realms of behavior is the ending of private justice in the blood feud and the development of a public system for settling disputes among members of the society. Private justice and the blood feud were vivid memories in the time of Mencius.[14] Han Fei Tzu speaks about fierce feuds of private swordsmen as familiar events.[15] It seems that during the period of the Warring States only an exceptionally strong ruler was able to stamp out the blood feud. Under an enlightened ruler, evil and malicious men will find no opening to carry out their private schemes.[16] The same viewpoint appears in a number of other passages.[17]

The general conception of the social order that emerges from the writings of Han Fei Tzu is one of a relatively weak royal power struggling to establish its prerogatives over its own officials and an unruly population. The royal power is all that Han Fei Tzu can see as the embodiment of the public interest. The conflict between royal power and the rest of the population is for him permanent and inevitable. As he observes at one point, " . . . laws and policies are actually inimical to the private interests of the officials and the common people."[18] There is not the slightest hint that the mass of ordinary people in the state might somehow embody the public interest. It is plain from his discussion that the population as a whole would be better

---

†Couvreur, S. J., trans., *Tch'ouen ts'iou et Tso tchouan,* III, 65. This is a French translation of the *Spring and Autumn Annals* and the *Tso Commentary.* Private is rendered here as *particulier* in contrasting a private anniversary with *les affaires publiques.*

off under the social order imposed by a strong monarch than under the violent disorder characteristic of a weak one. In this sense Han Fei Tzu resembles Hobbes.

In the context of Chinese thinking about morals and politics Han Fei Tzu was a deviant figure. Generations of Chinese scholars have professed shock at his cynicism and moral realism. But there has never been a time when he was unread.[19] Though Confucianism became the professed doctrine of the Chinese empire, in its actual workings there remained a strong current of the traditions expressed by Han Fei Tzu. If he said things that somehow needed saying, let us examine the traditions with which he competed.

Confucius, who stands at the beginning of recorded Chinese thought about human society, distinguished between affairs of state and private business as well as between private and public life.[20] For Confucius, public denoted the affairs of government while private referred to family life.[21] There is a difference here from Han Fei Tzu. Unless I have overlooked some passage, Han Fei Tzu never has anything positive to say about private behavior. For him it is always potentially subversive. That is not at all the case with Confucius. In a famous passage to be discussed again later in connection with the family, the *Analects* asserts that the private obligation of a son to care for his father overrides the public obligation to obey the law against theft.[22] In a rather more characteristic vein he speaks of private virtues as supporting a desirable form of government.[23]

As we shall see, the moral basis of good government receives strong emphasis in the writings of Mencius. So far as I could discover, on the other hand, the *Mencius* makes no explicit contrast between private and public affairs. This contrast is explicit in at least one passage in the *Analects*.[24] Confucius may also mention private conduct without saying anything about public life.[25] There is also one mention of a private audience at court[26] and some brief remarks about the proper attitude toward public business: one should ponder over it untiringly at home and execute it loyally at the appropriate time.[27]

One intriguing passage that has nothing to do with politics as such suggests that cultivated Chinese strongly disliked unwarranted intrusions into what they regarded as their private space. Confucius uses a revealing phrase about privacy when he says that a timid man who is pretending to be fierce is like a man who is so "dishonest as to sneak into places where one has no right to be, by boring a hole or climbing through a gap."[28] A man of substantial means might have a shoulder-high wall around his property, over which it was easy to peep and see the good points of the house. But a really high official might have a wall many times a man's height so that no one not let in by the gate could realize the beauty and wealth of the palace.[29]

The scattered remarks about public and private affairs in the

Analects show that while Confucius was certainly familiar with the distinction, it did not for him raise issues as salient as they became for Han Fei Tzu. Confucius thought mainly about the prospects of a moral overhaul of the social order by officials who accepted the advice of wandering scholars like himself. That was even more the case with Mencius. By the time of Hsün Tzu, the last great spokesman for Confucianism in the pre-imperial epoch, the relationship between public and private affairs had become for Confucians a secondary issue.

In Hsün Tzu's writings, as selected by Burton Watson, I could find only a few brief references to the problems of privacy. Some explicitly contrast private with public life. For instance, we learn without much surprise that a gentleman should "suppress personal desire in favor of public right," allowing "law to prevail over personal feeling."[30] Under an energetic king, "the common people will . . . clearly understand that if they do evil in secret, they will suffer punishment in public." If the translation is accurate, it shows that the Chinese had the expression "in public," a conception that differs from the word "public" as a shorthand expression for the state or its government. In an ideal state artisans would not dare "to manufacture sculptured or ornamented decorations privately at home."[31] Evidently they were expected to devote all their efforts to satisfying the court and aristocratic patrons. "When ritual principles are not obeyed, family affairs and outside affairs are not properly separated, and men and women mingle wantonly. . . ."[32] This brief observation reflects the author's concern with social order, a major concern shared by all the social philosophers. Hsün Tzu saw in ritual a social device that permitted the expression of powerful emotions without damage to the social fabric. Finally we come across the characteristic Confucian observation that a man who could not understand the duties of a father or a son in family life would be unable to comprehend the correct relationship between ruler and subject in public life.[33]

Though these scattered remarks shed revealing light on the workings of Chinese society in pre-imperial times, all of them are incidental observations showing that the relations between private and public spheres of behavior were not a central concern to the Confucianists. Hsün Tzu was much less interested in a moral overhaul than Confucius or Mencius. Instead he tried to work out social devices such as ritual—and also music in which Confucius too displayed an interest—that would correct and control antisocial tendencies that Hsün Tzu believed were inherent in human nature.

If we turn back now to the Taoist tradition as expressed in the *Lao Tzu* and the *Chuang Tzu,* the first reaction is likely to be that this tradition has nothing to say about the issue of privacy. I could find nothing specific about private or public matters in the first seven chapters of the *Chuang Tzu,* which, according to Burton Watson, constitute the heart of the book, are probably the earliest in date, and contain all the important ideas.[34] In the *Lao Tzu,* I could find only one far-from-revealing observation to the effect that the sage was able to accomplish his private ends because he is without thought of self.[35]

On reflection this impression dissipates and turns into its opposite: quite possibly the Taoist corpus deserves to be read as a critical reaction to all the other philosophies that were attempts to make human beings into loyal subjects of the state. From the Taoist point of view all such moralistic efforts are in the end simply futile. Instead, the Taoist classics impart an ethic of "non-contention" and no meddling, in which weakness stands impregnable before strength and the soft virtues win out over the harsh ones. To the extent that Taoism advocates anything at all, it is survival in a utopia of reduced consumption.[36]

Hence the Taoist texts as a whole can be taken as a plea on behalf of privacy, in the sense that it is better to let human beings seek their own solutions to life's problems than it is to bully them into being loyal subjects of the state. To be sure, there is a very noticeable antisocial current in the Taoist tradition: inaction is better than action and uselessness better than usefulness.[37] These antistatist elements and even the antisocial ones help to explain the steady attraction of Taoism down through the centuries of the empire's existence, as well as its limits as a doctrine of opposition. Taoism made an excellent foil for Confucianism and pleasant relief from its endless platitudes. It is hardly a wonder that literate Chinese wanted to keep both traditions alive.

On the basis of this sketch it is plain that during this period of intellectual ferment there was no single predominant tradition in China about public and private realms of behavior. Instead there were at least three competing perceptions of this relationship. For the moral realists, or Legalists as they are generally known, there was a permanent conflict between public and private interests. Furthermore, private interests connoted asocial and subversive pressures that had to be watched with suspicion and kept under control.

The Confucian tradition was quite different; problems posed by chronic social disorder were to be solved through a moral overhaul of the governing strata. There is an individualist streak in Confucian doctrine, especially as presented by Hsün Tzu. The moral overhaul will come about through a large number of individual efforts, a process that can be set in motion by a scattering of individual examples. The result will be a perfect harmony between the private and public spheres of conduct. The virtuous ruler will promote virtuous—that is, in effect docile—behavior in clan and family groupings. This docile and morally exemplary behavior will in turn promote virtues among the rulers.

Only one ruler is needed to start the process off, because ordinary people will flock to such a ruler from all parts of China to escape the harsh conditions of evil rule. The family under these conditions becomes a microcosm of public authority.[38] Distinctions remained between the authority of a ruler and that of a father, as we shall see in due course. Yet the parallels are what count.

Finally Taoism, as just pointed out, amounted to a rejection of the social virtues, or at least the social pretensions of both Legalist and Confucian theorists. Taoism was a negative and escapist doctrine which set a high value on private freedom. In effect, this was a freedom to do nothing, a conception that must have had a strong appeal in an age of forced loyalties and brutal fighting.

Obligations to the Ruler and on the Ruler

For the mass of the population, the peasants, there were three obvious obligations to the ruler. One was military service. The second was compulsory labor service or corvée duties carried out on some public undertaking such as the Great Wall. The third obligation took the form of taxes.†

In return the ruler was expected to supply physical security against bandits and depredations by foreign troops; justice; and economic plenty. The ruler was also expected to supply enough food, by the indirect method of keeping taxes and corvée duties down to the point where the peasants could grow enough to meet their own needs comfortably. In addition there seems to have been a notion that good crops and good weather went together with good government and bad weather with bad government. Traces of this notion still exist at the present time.

The *Analects* of Confucius has little to say about the mutual obligations of ruler and ruled, possibly because Confucius, very much to his chagrin, never obtained an important post. What he does have to say is rather general. His most concrete statement is the following:

> The master said, A country of a thousand war chariots [roughly a medium-sized state] cannot be administered unless the ruler attends strictly to business, punctually observes his promises, is economical in expenditure, shows affection towards his subjects in general, and uses the labour of the peasantry only at the proper times of year.[39]

---

†A rough notion of the size of the burden comes from the remark in an old chronicle-commentary about a badly governed state. There the labor of the people was divided into three parts, two of which went to public service, leaving only a third with which to obtain food and clothing. The source also mentions the existence of a public granary, which, however, had fallen prey to rot and insects. See Couvreur, *Tch'ouen ts'iou*, III, 56–57.

Though this set of remarks does express the benevolent paternalism of Confucian doctrine, it is still rather vague. In another well-known passage, Confucius urges his followers to drum out one of the group who had increased the revenues of an already prosperous family.[40] Other passages embroider this theme of paternalism without adding anything of substance.[41]

It is to the *Mencius* that one must turn to discover the concrete social message of early Confucian doctrine. The *Mencius* expresses a romantic and backward-looking conservatism in critical response to current trends. But it does contain quite specific admonitions.

For the sake of emphasis, it is worthwhile pointing out once more the historical and intellectual context of the message. The age of competing philosophical schools was also an age of bloody competition among the small independent states that constituted China in the pre-imperial period. Some of the states were ruled by kings or, as we might say today, kinglets. Other states did not claim even that much. Their rulers called themselves dukes and marquises. In many areas ambitious ministers or prominent families usurped royal power. Yet behind all this turmoil there lurked the tradition of a time when China had been united under a benevolent emperor. In fact, the tradition included three dynasties, each with a virtuous founder and a degenerate ruler at the end. Thus the theory of a dynastic cycle, which has profoundly influenced Western interpretations of China, has been a prominent theme in Chinese culture for quite a long time.

Just how long it is impossible to state with any certainty. China's early history was in early imperial times subject to Confucian editing for edifying and didactic purposes. An old tradition claims that Confucius himself did a great deal of the editing. Be that as it may, the theory of the dynastic cycle was already part of the general intellectual equipment of the philosophers under discussion. It set the terms of the discussion in the following way. Since there had been a period of peace and order under imperial auspices, the problem became one of finding out how to restore this situation. Chinese political philosophy is profoundly conservative in that it seeks to restore a largely mythical past. The hope was that a new virtuous and benevolent emperor might arise out of the prevailing competition. The theory is not quite as naïve as it sounds because it stressed the need to gain and hold popular support if a ruler were to take over the empire and found a new dynasty. The Legalists, in contrast, emphasized the creation of a bureaucracy to be guided by a clear set of rules with explicit rewards and sanctions as the necessary framework for the new empire to come. They were not quite advocates of a policy of blood and iron to create the new empire, but they were close to it.

The events of subsequent history yielded an ambiguous form of support for both theories. By a policy of conquest that certainly looked like one of blood and iron, the rulers of the state of Ch'in did manage to unify the country by 221 B.C., but their terrorist rule lasted for only fourteen years. It became a byword for everything an imperial government ought to avoid, especially the burning of the Confucian classics and the persecution of scholar-officials. Stability of a sort set in in 202 B.C. under what became known as the Former Han dynasty, which lasted until 9 A.D. The way the Ch'in won power justified the critics of Confucianism. The way they lost power justified the Confucians.

With this general background in mind, let us examine what the *Mencius* has to say about corvée and taxes. Near the very beginning of the *Mencius* there is a brief and highly idealized account of the construction of terraces and a pond for a king with the labor of the people. It is enough to demonstrate that the corvée existed. Supposedly the people did not object to the royal terraces and pond because they were able to share in its enjoyment.[42]

Two other passages shed light on taxation policies. One of them has Mencius assert, "If tillers help in the public fields but pay no tax on the land, then farmers throughout the Empire will be pleased to till the lands in your realm."[43] A later passage gives more detail. The fields were divided up and boundaries established in a way that looks like a game of ticktacktoe, that is, with nine equal squares, one of which is in the center. Under this system, known as the well-field system, the tax on the land was supposed to be one part in nine. In other words, the central field was public land whose produce should go to the king.[44]

The same passage mentions another form of the land tax known as the *kung* method. Under this system the payment due was calculated on the average yield over a number of years. In good years yielding a surplus crop of rice, the peasants did not pay an extra tax, but in bad years the peasants still had to pay the full quota, which, according to Mencius, led to resentments because the people toiled incessantly throughout the year without being able to feed old and young family members.

Thus the *kung* method was deemed harsher than the well-field system, the only one with public land cultivated by the people. Mencius claims the *kung* method was older than the well-field system. It seems more likely that the *kung* method of a simple land tax was replacing the well-field system of public and private lands because a tax is easier to collect than it is to enforce common labor obligations. But we cannot be certain. There is also the possibility that the well-field system was no more than a product of Mencius' romantic imagination. Be that as it may, Mencius clearly regarded heavy taxation—that is, a tax rate of more than one part in nine—as outright theft.[45] He was neither the first nor the last romantic conservative to side with the people.

Mencius' conception of the obligations on the ruler were those of a generous paternalism. From Mencius' comments it is also plain that few if any rulers lived up to such obligations. Except in an emergency like a famine, Mencius does not argue that the ruler ought to support the unfortunate out of his own resources. Rather it is up to the ruler to keep down his own demands and promote by his policies the conditions for prosperity. Mencius often has quite concrete suggestions. Speaking to a king he supposedly said:

> If you do not interfere with the busy seasons in the fields [by imposing a corvée], then there will be more grain than the people can eat; if you do not allow nets with too fine a mesh to be used in large ponds, then there will be more fish and turtles than they can eat; if hatchets and axes are permitted in the forests on the hills only in the proper seasons, then there will be more timber than they can use.[46]

Mencius continues with advice that mulberries be planted in every homestead with five *mu*† of land so that people over fifty could wear silk. If chickens, pigs, and dogs (a source of meat down to the present day) did not miss their breeding season, people over seventy could eat meat. Characteristically Mencius' index of prosperity is derived from the surplus available for taking care of older people. With enough food, people will meet obligations to the elderly. But the social duties proper to sons and younger brothers have to be taught in the village schools. Mencius ends these detailed recommendations with sharp critical comments on the actual state of affairs.

> When people die, you simply say, "It is none of my doing. It is the fault of the harvest." In what way is that different from killing a man by running him through while saying all the time, "It is none of my doing. It is the fault of the weapon." Stop putting the blame on the harvest and the people of the whole Empire will come to you.[47]

Elsewhere Mencius is willing to endorse a display of royal magnificence including chariots and horses with banners and musical performances with drums, bells, pipes, and flutes as long as the people could share this enjoyment. In a similar vein Mencius opposes restrictions on hunting for deer, pheasants, and hares in the royal park.[48]

For Mencius it was the obligation of the king to make sure that no one in the realm suffered from hunger. As we have just noticed, the king could not evade this obligation by appealing to "objective" circumstances such as a bad harvest. Royal responsibility extended to the conduct of royal officials.[49] The ideal government is one that tolerated no suffering. The ideal is consistent with Mencius' stress on the importance of benevolence in relations between superiors and inferiors.[50] "In governing the Empire," said Mencius, "the sage tries to

---

†One *mu* is a little less than 200 square meters.

make food as plentiful as water. When that happens, how can there be any amongst his people who are not benevolent?" One way to achieve this was to put the fields of the people in order and lighten taxes in order to make the people affluent.[51] Thus Confucian theory, as it emerged from the hands of Mencius, had a materialistic explanation of ethics.

In his idealized view of paternalist government, Mencius retained an important place for the hereditary aristocracy. The emperor was expected to make tours of inspection among the feudal lords, and the feudal lords were to pay homage to the emperor with a report on duties. If the emperor found that in the territory of a feudal lord the land was opened up, the fields well-cultivated, the old cared for, the good and wise honored, and men of distinction in positions of authority, then the emperor should reward the feudal lord with more land. If the opposite turned out to be the case, the emperor should issue a reprimand. Mencius has nothing to say about the effectiveness of a reprimand.[52]

Mencius recognized that an enlightened ruler might have to promote men of low position over the heads of those with exalted rank and distant relatives over near ones.[53] Like Confucius, Mencius placed merit above kinship in the selection of royal officials. Yet Mencius seems reluctant about doing so, adding that such a decision was not to be taken lightly. On this crucial issue it seems to me that Mencius constitutes a step backward from the Confucian position.

In Hsün Tzu, the paternalist ethic of Mencius undergoes a not very subtle transformation. In Mencius, the ruler's obligation to make sure that there was no material suffering in the realm appears as either a value in its own right or as characteristic of a harmonious universe. In Hsün Tzu, the obligation is demoted to a rule of prudence. The ruler should look after the welfare of the people in order to save his own skin. "If the common people are frightened of the government," says Hsün Tzu, "then the gentleman cannot occupy his post in safety." And: "The ruler is the boat and the common people are the water," he says, quoting an ancient text. "It is the water that bears the boat up and the water that capsizes it." Developing this train of thought further, Hsün Tzu posits the existence of three great obligations on the ruler:

> . . . if the gentleman desires safety, the best thing for him to do is to govern fairly and to love the people. If he desires glory, the best thing is to honor ritual and treat men of breeding with respect. If he desires to win fame and merit, the best thing is to promote the worthy and employ men of ability.[54]

In this formulation the welfare of the people becomes only one of the obligations on the ruler. From the ruler's standpoint this was the least attractive or rewarding of the three main obligations.

On the other hand, Hsün Tzu stops well short of treating the common people as a mere pawn in the game of power politics. Rewards and punishments, force and deception, says Hsün Tzu, in a jibe at the Legalists, may be the way to deal with hired laborers or tradesmen, a remark that throws an interesting light on the etiquette of class relationships in ancient China. But they are no way, Hsün Tzu continues, to unify the population of a great state or bring glory to the nation. Instead one should lead the people through the edifying sound of virtue, love them, and give them a place in the government by honoring the worthy and employing the able. This Confucian platitude is as far as any ancient Chinese thinker was willing to go in the direction of popular government. The people could rule only if they became proper members of the dominant class.

Hsün Tzu continues with some remarks close to Mencius about lightening the burden on the common people. The result, he claimed, would be to establish uniform customs among the people, a sort of moral consensus. If some of the people depart from this moral consensus and refuse to obey their superiors, "the common people will as one man turn upon them with hatred, and regard them with loathing, like an evil force that must be exorcised."[55] Hsün Tzu's theory is a Marxist theory of class consciousness in reverse. This view was congenial to Hsün Tzu because he believed that inequality, including social inequality, was ordained by Heaven and earth as part of the natural order of the universe.[56]

Turning now to the Taoist *Lao Tzu,* which raises inaction to the level of a principle, it is not surprising that its author or authors have very little to say about obligations to or on a ruler. To the extent that the *Lao Tzu* has any political message, it is that the less a ruler does, the better off his people will be. The following lines attributed to the sage are characteristic.

> I take no action and the people are
>   transformed of themselves;
> I prefer stillness and the people are
>   rectified of themselves;
> I am not meddlesome and the people
>   prosper of themselves;
> I am free from desire and the people
>   of themselves become simple like the
>   uncarved block.[57]

An evaluation of different kinds of rulers has a similar theme:

> The best of all rulers is but a shadowy
>   presence to his subjects.
> Next comes the ruler they love and praise;
> Next comes one they fear;
> Next comes one with whom they take liberties.[58]

The first line gives these verses their distinctly Taoist flavor. The rest could have come from a Confucian brush. There are a few more verses stating similar themes.[59] But by and large in its advocacy of "the virtue of non-contention," this is an antipolitical document. So is the *Chuang Tzu,* better discussed at a later point.

The writings of Han Fei Tzu fall at the opposite end of the spectrum from the *Lao Tzu*. Han Fei Tzu sees a political implication in just about every act of ruler and subject. His thought is of course cast in the form of advice to a ruler. "The height of good government," he says in a sentence expressing the theme of the whole book, "is to allow subordinates no means of taking advantage of you."[60] Eternal vigilance is the price not of liberty but stability, in the sense of retaining control of government. For instance, the ruler must retain control over orders to disburse emergency funds or open up the granaries for the benefit of the people. There is a risk that a high minister may dole out grain to the common people in order to win popular support.[61] These strictures by Han Fei Tzu point to the ruler's obligation to provide food in times of severe shortage. Indeed, this appears to have been just about the most important of the government's obligations.

In connection with obligations to the government, Han Fei Tzu warns the ruler against imposing too much compulsory labor service. The reasons are sociologically revealing. A people with grievances, he says, will generate local power groups that exempt individuals from labor service. These local power groups threaten the authority of the center. A contented people, on the other hand, will not generate local power groups or undue authority on the lower levels. For this reason, as already pointed out, the right to dispense favors to the population must reside in the sovereign.[62]

The same reasoning applies to all high levels of the government. Han Fei Tzu continually warns against the schemes and plots of high ministers. Suspicious of any form of entrenched privilege, he disapproves of grants of land and rich rewards for ministers.[63] At another point he repeats the advice to a ruler to confiscate all titles and stipends of enfeoffed lords after the third generation.[64] Since the hereditary aristocracy was losing out to the central power of specific states at the close of the pre-imperial period, it is evident that Han Fei Tzu's recommendations were based on existing trends.

In the state of an enlightened ruler there would be no books. Law would supply the only instruction. There would be no sermons on former kings. Officials would serve as the only teachers. Finally there would be no fierce feuds of private swordsmen, or in other words, no vendettas.[65] Unlike other political philosophers, Han Fei Tzu rejected established custom as a criterion for political decisions. Instead he sought effectiveness. Likewise an enlightened ruler must be willing to oppose the will of the people.[66] But ideally a minister ought to be able to oppose a monarch in argument without incurring blame.[67] On this issue Han Fei Tzu is surprisingly close to the Confucian position with its emphasis on the right of remonstrance, a topic to be discussed shortly in more detail. In his judgment, the ruler could not count on the people doing good, but must prevent them from doing what was bad. The people, he asserted, have the minds of little children.[68]

These passages show that Han Fei Tzu put little stock in the government's obligations to the underlying population. Instead he focuses his attention on how the ruler can maintain his autonomy. An intelligent ruler does not enrich powerful families or ennoble his ministers. Nor does he allow cities to become too large.[69] Regarding both wealth and poverty as the consequence of innate moral qualities, a viewpoint that makes sense only in a society with considerable social mobility, Han Fei Tzu objected to giving land to the poor or taxing the rich.[70] All in all, he appears as a spokesman for a strong central authority in a time of social upheaval.

The Right of Remonstrance

The right of remonstrance is interesting as the principal check on royal authority. It developed early in the Chinese tradition, the main idea long antedating Confucianism. It appears in a cynical form in the *Book of Odes* thus:

> God [the ruler] is very bright
> Don't go too close to him!
> Were I to reprove him,
> Afterwards I should be slaughtered
> by him.[71]

This early version has the merit of making plain the risk of putting the right to the test. The *Analects* does not have a great deal to say about this right—or obligation—possibly because Confucius never acquired high office. The great minister, Confucius is reported to have said, is one "who will only serve his prince while he can do so without infringement of the Way [that is, without violating moral principles], and as soon as this is impossible, resigns."[72] This is a counsel of perfection. In a later passage Confucius asks, "How can he be said to be truly loyal, who refrains from admonishing the object of his loyalty?" Here remonstrance appears as an obligation rather than as a right. These two brief mentions in the *Analects* reaffirmed what was evidently an older tradition and kept it alive.

It was Mencius who applied and amplified the ideal, if the account of his acts is accurate. Mencius linked the right of remonstrance to the

monarch's obligation to promote the material well-being of his subjects. To one monarch Mencius said, ". . . when men drop dead from
starvation by the wayside, you fail to realize it is time for distribution."[73] To another king he said that any ruler who was not fond of
killing his subjects in war would have the people "turn to him like
water flowing downwards with a tremendous force."[74]

Mencius is not at all like a Hebrew prophet who threatened
destruction for a ruler who violated morality. Instead Mencius promises rulers the empire for good behavior if they will change their ways.
The ruler should extend his bounty to the people instead of seeking to
unify the country by military means. To use military methods was like
looking for fish by climbing a tree.[75] On this point it is easier to
sympathize with Mencius' moral ideals than to admire his political
acumen. When unity came to China, it came through the bloody
conquests of the despotic state of Ch'in.

Mencius expressed a strong belief in his own mission. Heaven, it
seemed, did not as yet wish to bring peace to the empire. "If it did, who
is there in the present time other than myself? Why should I be
unhappy?"[76] By rectifying the prince, he believed, it was possible to
put the state on a firm basis.[77] Nevertheless on other occasions Mencius recognized the obstacles present if a ruler was unwilling to correct
his evil heart. "Today when a subject whose advice has been rejected
to the detriment of the people has occasion to leave, the prince puts
him in chains." Moreover the prince seizes his land the day he leaves,
instead of waiting for the customary period to elapse after a man is
dismissed in disgrace.[78] Mencius also recognized circumstances that
justified the voluntary departure of a counselor from the realm: the
ruler's putting to death of an innocent gentleman or of innocent
people.[79] In some cases advice was futile because the ruler was beyond
advice. In that situation the only courses were silence and then, if
possible, departure.[80]

The opportunist scholar-adviser who merely promised to extend a
ruler's territories and fill his coffers was for Mencius an object of
contempt. Such a ruler, he asserted, could not hold the empire for the
duration of a morning, even if it were given to him.[81] On this score one
has to credit Mencius with acute political insight. He believed that
popular support based on prosperity was necessary for political stability. The Ch'in were able to unify the empire by despotic means, but
were unable to consolidate their conquest. Instead they were over-
thrown in a popular uprising. In general, later dynasties depended on
popular support or at least popular acquiescence for their stability.

Mencius had very clear notions about the conditions under which
a scholar-official should accept or relinquish office. Fundamentally
they amount to (1) treatment with the greatest respect and all proper
rites and (2) attention to his advice; that is, it should be put into

practice. If his advice was not put into practice, he could stay as long as the courtesies were meticulously observed—but no longer. Mencius also foresaw the possibility of a scholar-official's starving in the household of a prince who ignored his advice. But in such a case the prince was supposed to be so overcome with remorse at the failure to heed the advice and so fearful of shame lest the official die while in his domain that he would take steps to ward off starvation.[82]

Though all this seems rather farfetched, it does indicate that the official was completely in the hands of the monarch. This appears to be the fundamental weakness in the right of remonstrance: the individual who remonstrated had no power with which to back up his criticism. He seems to have been an easily replaceable cog in a machine. (In contrast, in medieval England, the upper classes made sure that they had control of taxes when they wanted to remonstrate with their monarch.)

The *Chuang Tzu* presents the sharpest possible contrast, and sometimes a welcome one, with the high seriousness of the *Mencius*. It is a fundamentally antipolitical fantasy. In one passage the author presents a list of legendary or semilegendary persons who tried to reform others or who guarded their own integrity—only to dismiss these models of accepted virtue. They "slaved in the service of other men but could not find joy in any joy of their own."[83]

Later the author rejects the whole idea of a ruler devising and upholding moral standards, the basic theme of Confucian teaching. All this becomes part of a charming tale about how to rule the world, a tale that ends with the advice "to follow along with things the way they are, and make no room for personal views."[84] It is hard to imagine anything further from the strenuously offered advice of a Mencius. Yet the *Chuang Tzu,* if not a remonstrance, was clearly a form of social criticism. The remonstrance assumes shared moral premises while this form of criticism rejects the premises.

With Mo Tzu we return briefly to the sober and sobering realities perceived by a critic of Confucian doctrine. According to Mo Tzu, the Son of Heaven proclaimed this principle as the basis of his rule over the people of the world:

> Upon hearing of good or evil, one shall report it to his superior. What the superior considers right all shall consider right; what the superior considers wrong all shall consider wrong. If the superior commits any fault, his subordinates shall remonstrate with him; if his subordinates do good, the superior shall recommend them.[85]

How it is possible for the superior to have perfect judgment and still commit faults Mo Tzu does not explain. Insofar as Mo Tzu takes seriously the claim of official infallibility, his position is much more conservative than that of his Confucian rivals. Mo Tzu criticized them for holding that officials should keep silent unless directly questioned. A superior man, asserted Mo Tzu, should warn his lord of impending danger, especially if he is the only one who knows of that danger. If those whom a superior man serves have any fault, the superior man will admonish them.[86] This time the *Mo Tzu* explicitly acknowledges the possibility of error on the part of high authorities. Consistency was not a major virtue of early Chinese philosophy.

It is somewhat surprising to find any mention of the right of remonstrance in the *Han Fei Tzu,* a work advocating a highly centralized state. Most of the book discusses the devices bureaucrats use to deceive their sovereign. Yet among the Ten Faults to which sovereigns may succumb is failure to learn from the remonstrances of ministers.[87] Later the author amplifies this point by reminding the reader of a Duke Huan, who though able at first to march his armies at will across the empire was assassinated by his ministers and became the laughing-stock of the world. All this happened because the duke failed to heed the advice of a loyal minister.[88]

In the *Han Fei Tzu* the brief discussion of the right of remonstrance is not linked to any policies benefiting the people. As in the *Mo Tzu,* it is instead based on a purely prudential consideration of the monarch's power: since the king's judgment is not infallible, it is in the king's own interest to take the advice of a loyal and intelligent minister. A modern reader may wonder how a headstrong ruler could be made to recognize good advice, far less to heed it. To these simple questions the texts provide no answer.

Though the episode falls outside the chronological scope of this inquiry, I want to review briefly one instance in which political discussion in ancient China broke out of the bounds of formal remonstrance to take on the form of wide-ranging debate of the major issues facing the Chinese government. This is the case of the famous Debates on Salt and Iron that took place in 81 B.C.

Emperor Wu (r. 140-87 B.C.) of the Han dynasty (successor to the short lived Ch'in dynasty) was a powerful and strong-willed ruler who expanded the borders of the empire, built roads and canals, and undertook many expensive projects to strengthen the nation and impress China's neighbors with its power and glory. To finance these costly measures he resorted to typical Legalist measures, including the establishment of government monopolies in the salt and iron industries. In 81 B.C., shortly after his death, a debate was held at court between the Legalist-minded officials in charge of these monopolies and a group of Confucian literati opposed to them. The Confucians had been selected to voice the complaints of the common people against these measures, which, surprisingly enough, the Confucians did in a very lively fashion.

Both the Legalist and the Confucian views received vigorous and thorough expression. Neither side showed any inclination to compromise. As far as the formal debate goes, the result was inconclusive. But what is significant from our viewpoint is how circumstances impelled the Confucians to turn toward sympathy with the common people, a sympathy that, so far as I am aware, Confucian doctrine under the empire never completely lost. It remained part of the moral code by which emperors were judged. Burton Watson gives a vivid excerpt from one of the Confucian speeches that is unfortunately too long for quotation here. A few sentences, however, may convey the flavor:

> Those who live in high halls and spreading mansions, broad chambers and deep rooms, know nothing of the discomfort of one-room huts and narrow hovels, of roofs that leak and floors that sweat. . . . Those who sit in the place of authority and lean on their writing desks, examine criminal charges brought before them and scribble their decisions, know nothing of the terror of cangues and bonds, the pain of whips and rods.[89]

Perceptions of the Common People

We may turn now to the different images of the common people that these social philosophers expressed. Our specific interest will be in beliefs about the common people's capacity to rule, explanations and justifications for any alleged incapacity to rule, and the possibilities for individuals or groups to overcome the shortcomings supposedly inherent in their social position and rise above it. Looking behind the screen of such prejudices, it is often possible to discern a great deal about the actual workings of any society.

Confucius expressed quite bluntly his low opinion of the intellectual capacities of the common people. They can be made to follow the Way, he asserted. But they cannot be made to understand it.[90] Since the Way in the *Analects* generally means the Way of the ancients insofar as it could be reconstructed from stories about the founders of the Chou dynasty,[91] it is hardly surprising that ordinary people knew nothing and cared less about such an antiquarian model of social conduct.

To the Confucians this attitude may have been a bit discouraging at times, though there are good reasons for concluding that popular attitudes didn't matter much, so long as they were not overtly subversive. Confucius and his followers were not trying to stir up a popular movement. That was not how to rescue society from its disorders. If the common people didn't understand much about the early ways of the Chou dynasty, such ignorance meant that Confucian intellectuals had that much more of a monopoly on ways to save the state. In the passage just cited, Confucius is telling his followers that if the people behave themselves, that is all one can expect.

For Confucius the right to speak up about political issues was strictly a matter of rank anyway. "He who holds no rank in a state does not discuss its policies."† There is another curious passage which holds that "when the Way prevails under Heaven commoners do not discuss public affairs."‡

In this passage Confucius is lamenting the decay of authority in his own times. His general message appears to be that when things go well, there is no reason to talk about politics; when people become excited about politics, the situation has already gotten so far out of hand that nothing can be done. There is no hint in Confucius or the other Chinese philosophers examined here of a possible democratic solution to political tension and political disorder. The notion of the people taking over the government and running it the way Athenians ran their government in the fourth century B.C. was utterly foreign to both the Confucians and their competitors. The Confucians did not have to argue against a radical egalitarianism that rejected both the division of labor and any inequalities in the distribution of goods and services.[92]

The justification for excluding the common people from positions of authority came down to the fact that ordinary people lacked the qualities of a gentleman. These qualities were a mixture of moral principles emphasizing consideration for others and self-control. Etiquette for the Chinese was not just a matter of surface politeness, but was suffused with moral principles. Etiquette was a part of ritual which in turn served to control emotional impulse for the sake of social order.§ Moderation, Confucius asserted, was to be found only rarely among the common people.[93]

Gentlemen set their hearts upon moral force, whereas the commoners set theirs upon the soil. Gentlemen think only of punishments. Commoners think only of exemptions.[94] The lowest class of the common people were, in his view, those who toiled painfully without ever managing to learn.[95] At no point does Confucius raise the question of how grinding toil might prevent human beings from acquiring the moral qualities and cultivated tastes he advocated and admired. But he did recognize that a high-spirited individual who suffered from poverty would not remain law-abiding for long.[96]

Evidently the cultural differences between social classes, and

---

†*Analects* VIII, 14. This may not be so much an expression of contempt for the common people as a jibe at the chatterings of unemployed wandering scholars who competed with Confucius.

‡*Analects* XVI, 2. Waley in a footnote adds that here "commoners" means people not belonging to the imperial family.

§This aspect was developed and made explicit in the *Hsün Tzu;* see "A Discussion of Rites," section 19, pp. 1, 94. But it is implicit in the *Mencius* and the *Analects.* For an example from the latter, see XIII, 4, where the elitist element is also prominent.

between men and women, created obstacles to social intercourse. At one point Confucius was led to observe that "Women and people of low birth are very hard to deal with. If you are friendly with them, they get out of hand, and if you keep your distance, they resent it."[97]

If the Confucian conception of the gentleman served to create and sustain social inequalities based on social polish and intellectual cultivation, it also served to undermine others. The notion of social status based on morality and intellectual merit stood in sharp contrast to older aristocratic conceptions of high status derived solely from blood and kinship. The triumph of the Confucian meritocracy distinguished the Chinese upper classes from other preindustrial ones. The conflict between the two systems was acute during the pre-imperial phase of Chinese history, and the victory of their version of a meritocracy did not become clear until the empire was established on a firm footing.

Confucius himself emphasized strongly the element of merit. Belief in the general intellectual incapacity of the common people did not preclude the possibility of talented and energetic individuals from among the common people acquiring the personal and intellectual qualities necessary for a gentleman and positions of authority. On this point Confucius was explicit. He was willing to ponder a query raised by a simple peasant and thrash the matter out with all its pros and cons to the bitter end.[98] Though Confucius accepted only eager and bright students—from the very poorest upwards, beginning with the man who could bring no better present than a bundle of dried flesh—no one ever came to him without receiving instruction.[99]

The Confucian system's ability to recruit talent, or at least one specific form of humanistic talent, very likely contributed to the very long life of this particular form of social inequality. Only the papacy, which has also offered careers open to talent, has endured for an equally long time. A touch of equality contributes greatly to the preservation of systematic inequality.

In comparison with Confucius, Mencius sounds a new note by stressing the importance of popular support for the emperor. In judging some of Mencius' statements, it is wise to recall that he was talking about an ideal situation, not the actual state of Chinese society. The empire was still beyond the historical horizon. In one passage he is reported to have said:

> The people are of supreme importance; the altars to the gods of earth and grain come next [according to the translator's note, these altars were symbols of the independence of the state]; last comes the ruler. That is why he who gains the confidence of the multitudinous people will be Emperor. . . .[100]

In another passage Mencius claims that acceptance by the people was a necessary aspect of an emperor's legitimacy.[101] A common man could come to possess the empire. To do so, however, he must have not only the virtue of one of the early legendary rulers but also the recommendation of an emperor. Mencius goes on to explain that this is the reason why Confucius never possessed the empire.[102] Lose the hearts of the people and you will lose the empire. "Win the people and you will win the Empire."[103]

In his stress on the importance of popular support Mencius comes close to proposing a democratic theory of the Chinese empire. But he stops well short of this position and remains like Confucius within the framework of a strictly paternalist theory. The people should support the emperor if he deserves their support but without taking any part in the government. "To talk about lofty matters when one is in a low position is a crime."[104] Elsewhere Mencius notes that if people with no official position are uninhibited in the expression of their views, this is a sign of disorder and social decay. To safeguard the Way of former sages he wanted to "banish excessive views," that is, those of competing philosophers.[105] Mencius had even less use for freedom of speech than Confucius.

Though the early Chinese philosophers are unanimous in holding that the common people should be excluded from politics, in an older historical commentary, the *Tso chuan,* there are traces of a different practice:

> The people of Cheng were in the habit of discussing the administration of the state when they gathered at leisure in the village schools. Jan Ming said to Tzu-ch'an, the head of the government, "How would it do to abolish the village schools?"
> "Why do that?" said Tzu-ch'an. "In the morning and evening when the people have finished their work and are at leisure, they gather to discuss the good and bad points of my administration. The points they approve of I encourage, and those they criticize I correct."[106]

We have here an expression of the ideal of constitutional monarchy if not of democracy. One can only speculate on the reasons why this seed never took hold and grew in Chinese soil, as it did under different conditions in ancient Greece. One possible factor may be differences in the organization of warfare. Athenian hoplites were expected to supply their own arms. That was one source of their independent spirit. Another was the knowledge that they as the citizen body were essential to the defense of the state. I have come upon no sign of similar arrangements in China. Independent men at arms were a threat to the state. The main trend, especially apparent in the state of Ch'in, was for the state to supply, organize, and discipline troops.

Mencius' arguments for keeping ordinary people out of the political arena were basically similar to those of Confucius: by and large, ordinary peopole lacked the moral and intellectual qualities necessary to share in authority. According to Mencius, "The multitude can be said never to understand what they practise, to notice what they repeatedly do, or to be aware of the path they follow all their lives."[107] Once the common people "have a full belly and warm clothes on their back they degenerate to the level of animals if they are allowed to lead idle lives, without education and discipline." Therefore they have to be taught the nature of human relationships.

For Mencius, as for many Chinese before and after him, these relationships were: "love between father and son, duty between ruler and subject, distinction between husband and wife, precedence of the old over the young, and faith between friends."[108] These relationships, about which it will be necessary to say more later, made up the content of Chinese morality. Elsewhere Mencius asserted that the difference between man and the brutes was slight. The common man lost this distinguishing feature. But the gentleman retained it.[109]

More than the other writers whose views have come down to us, Mencius stressed the paternalist conception of the ruler's relationship with the common people. "A good ruler is always respectful and thrifty, courteous and humble, and takes from the people no more than is prescribed."[110] In this whole ethic, however, and in the institutions that supported it, we cannot detect ideas or practices that would serve effectively to protect the individual subject or mark him off as an individual with specific rights against royal authority or the social order. What limits there were on arbitrary royal action depended on the monarch's moral character and personal inclinations, a frail safeguard indeed. In this basic sense there is little or no privacy as a guaranteed right. On the other hand, for the educated classes, ritual and etiquette served to protect the individual from unwanted intrusion through elaborate rules of access.

Between them, Confucius and Mencius said nearly everything about the common people that the Confucian school wanted to say. Hsün Tzu merely repeats the same themes about the necessity for popular support and the incompetence of the people for taking political responsibility, with less detail though adding some piquant touches. His most striking remarks concern ancestor worship, whose forms, he claims, depended on the status of the living individual. Thus he who rules the world, that is, the emperor, sacrifices to seven generations while the ruler of a territory supporting only three chariots sacrifices to two generations. Finally, "He who eats by the labor of his hands is not permitted to set up an ancestral temple."[111] If this regulation corresponded to actual practice, the vast majority of the population were debarred from this form of ancestor worship. Though Hsün Tzu does not say so, presumably they could still worship before the ancestral tablets in the family dwelling.

Like Confucius and Mencius, Hsün Tzu was also a believer in the acquisition of high status through moral merit. A man whose forebears were commoners should be promoted to the post of prime minister or high court official if he has acquired learning, is upright in conduct, and can adhere to ritual principles.[112] By the third century B.C., it appears, the ideal of a career open to talents had taken firm hold. The talents, it is worth stressing, were not merely technical ones or signs of administrative ability, though skills in handling people must have counted for a great deal. Indeed, to say that careers were "open to talent" somewhat misrepresents the Chinese situation, where the stress was on ritual, etiquette (or ritual in practice), and on the moral qualities of probity and generosity in the treatment of social inferiors.

Unlike Mencius and Confucius, Hsün Tzu had quite a bit to say about military affairs. It was in this connection that he stressed the importance of popular support. The essential point in military undertakings, he claimed, was to be good at winning the support of the people. Plots and stratagems would be effective only in situations where the ruler lacked popular support. In carrying out punitive expeditions, the king's army does not, the *Hsün Tzu* asserted, punish the common people. Instead it punishes those that lead the common people astray. But if part of the common people fought on the side of the enemy, they too became enemies.†

More generally Hsün Tzu considered the loyalty of the people to the ruler as an aspect of social and political health. When courtiers abandoned the principles of loyal service and pursued selfish aims, he asserted, their behavior was a sure sign of dynastic decay. It was also a time when the common people hated selfish courtiers, spoke ill of them, and refused to obey their commands.[113] This necessarily bald summary makes Hsün Tzu sound more sociological than he really was. Dynastic decay was for him, as well as other Chinese thinkers, fundamentally a moral problem. This was especially true of the Confucian tradition, though the concern with morality is quite prominent too in the competing traditions.

As we turn to the Taoist tradition, it is necessary to be especially wary. In their different ways both modern Western scholars and indigenous Chinese scholars from early imperial times onward have tried to read political meanings into these early texts, making them the charter of acceptable popular and educated opposition to the regime.

---

†*Hsün Tsu,* "Debating Military Affairs," section 15, pp. 56–57, 67. Warfare in ancient China differed sharply from the forms found in classical Greece or among Hebrews of the Old Testament, where there were frequent contests between two or more independent political units that might or might not share a common culture. From the beginning it appears that the tradition of Chinese unity was strong enough to make possible only two kinds of warfare: one, against barbarians; the other, a form of civil war within the civilized world, i.e., China. Civil wars were usually referred to as "punitive expeditions," giving the moral advantage to the established regime. That seems to have been the case even during the period of the Warring States, when many wars were rapacious acts of plunder undertaken by one fragment of China against another fragment. Since most wars were civil wars, it was possible for Chinese thinkers to develop a streak of pacifism and treat war as a disturbance of the civilized world.

There is certainly some basis for this judgment. In the period with which we are concerned, the *Lao Tzu* may well have been, as Burton Watson suggests, a "reply to the busy do-goodism of the Confucians and the Mo-ists."[114] Such a reply, on the other hand, need not preclude, and in the case of the *Lao Tzu* certainly did not preclude, a highly ambiguous attitude toward the capacities of ordinary people to manage their own affairs or take part in larger ones. At this point it is also worth noticing that educated Chinese in the late Warring States period had as elastic a conception of who "the people" actually were as do polemical writers in the West from the eighteenth century onward. "The people" sometimes refers to other educated people like the writer and at other times to the general population in town and country. In the *Lao Tzu* the broader meaning is quite common.

One remarkable passage reveals clearly the fundamentally ambiguous attitude of the *Lao Tzu* toward ordinary people. The opening lines read, "The sage has no mind of his own. He takes as his own the mind of the poeple."[115] If the translation is at all accurate, the text certainly asserts that in some sense the educated man ought to be a spokesman for popular demands, an idea that is not completely alien to Confucianism at a somewhat later date. A few lines later we are offered exactly the opposite idea: "The sage in his attempt to distract the mind of the empire seeks urgently to muddle it. The people all have something to occupy their eyes and ears [the text has been emended at this point by the translator] and the sage treats them all like children."[116] Here a sage's patronizing attitude toward the mass of the population comes to the surface in about as blunt a form as possible.

The attitude of superiority takes a different form in these lines from another, longer chapter. Once again a sage is speaking.

> My mind is that of a fool—how blank!
> Vulgar people are clear.
> I alone am drowsy.
> Vulgar people are alert.
> I alone am muddled.
> . . . .
> The multitude all have a purpose.
> I alone am foolish and uncouth.
> I alone am different from others
> And value being fed by the mother.[117]

To me it seems probable that this passage too is another jab at the endlessly edifying efforts of competing philosophers. But there is more to it than that. Here and elsewhere in the early Taoist writings, there is a strain of mystic elitism, a praise of confusion for its own sake as a way to distinguish one's ineffable thoughts from those of the common herd. It is a form of literary preciousness common enough in Western culture from classical times down to the present.

Once more in the whirling contrasts and contradictions that are an

essential feature of this early mystical tradition, we come upon the
observation that "The reason why the people are difficult to govern is
that they are too clever."[118] Here it is important to note the context in a
chapter too long for full quotation here. It amounts to an attack on the
wandering scholars—rhetoricians or sophists they would have been
called in Greece of the fourth century B.C. According to this text, the
wandering scholars from early times onward, by deceiving the people,
made them too clever to govern. Therefore cleverness is bad for the
state and getting rid of it will be a boon for the state.

In the language of our own time this was a revolutionary proposal
even for the fragmented China of the Warring States period. Here we
can see plainly the popular or even populist element in early Taoism.
But what is to take the place of the clever chattering of the wandering
scholars or intellectuals? After all, we have here not a modern text or
even one from ancient Greece where we might expect a secular
political proposal. The answer here is "Mysterious virtue . . . profound and far-reaching" that will somehow result in "complete conformity."[119]

As every student of ancient China knows, an attempt to silence
the chattering intellectuals and impose "complete conformity" did
take place in 213 B.C. in the notorious burning of the books under
China's self-styled First Emperor and founder of the short-lived Ch'in
dynasty. In this hostility toward Confucian book-learning we can see
the rapprochement between Taoism and Legalism. Most of the burned
books seem to have been Confucian texts, some of which survived to
become the charter of Confucian doctrine under later emperors. I
suspect that this conflagration, if it actually took place, was far from
being the least popular act of the First Emperor.

To return to the *Lao Tzu,* this collection contains many expressions of outright sympathy for the plight of the people. The repeated
theme that weakness overcomes strength, submissiveness overcomes
hardness,[120] displays a natural affinity with the underdog. One chapter
contains specific advice, presumably to a ruler, not to press down on
the people's means of livelihood. "It is because you do not press down
on them that they will not weary of the burden."[121] Finally, at least one
chapter is explicitly critical of existing authority:

> The people are hungry:
> It is because those in authority
>   eat up too much in taxes
> That the people are hungry.
> The people are difficult to govern:
> It is because those in authority are
>   too fond of action
> That the people are difficult to govern.
> The people treat death lightly;

> It is because the people set too
> > much store by life [one character omitted]
> That they treat death lightly.
> It is just because one has no use for
> > life that one is
> Wiser than the man who values life.[122]

As it stands in this translation, the poem ends on a mystical note. But its message is plain enough. The people are in such despair that life is not worth living. We can leave to others the task of determining who were the authorities against whom this bitter attack was directed. Very likely this question can no longer receive an adequate answer. For our purposes the answer scarcely matters. This poem, and others like it that are much more ancient,[123] demonstrate that explicit and severe criticism of authority in the name of the people existed in ancient China. It took a very different form from that in Athens of the fourth century B.C. and was expressed through very different channels. The most significant difference appears to be that in China the most severe criticism still took the form of advice to a ruler from a member of the educated classes. So far as I am aware, the fragmentary record available to us contains no direct expression of popular anger. But its existence, at least to me, appears plain beyond all doubt.

As mentioned earlier, the other major Taoist text is the *Chuang Tzu,* said to have been written by a philosopher called Chuang Chou, who was active in the last half of the fourth century B.C. That would make him a contemporary of Mencius.[124] It is the only ancient prose work that does not deal with politics and statecraft. Burton Watson has asserted that "Freedom is the central theme of the work—not political, social or economic freedom, but spiritual freedom, freedom of the mind,"[125] a judgment that seems to me absolutely correct.

From the standpoint of our present concerns, the question immediately arises: freedom for whom? A close reading of the seven "inner chapters," or the core of the work,[126] suggests to me that the intended audience was the wandering scholar and unsuccessful or unemployed official. Still we cannot dismiss this delightful work as reflecting no more than the complaints of early Chinese intellectuals. That would be a most cavalier judgment. In the first place, as Confucius' willingness to talk with ordinary peasants suggests, the barrier between scholar and the common folk may have been more permeable at this time than it became under the bureaucratic empire. There is an even stronger reason for examining it here: the whole tone of the work makes it an appeal to the powerless and the unsuccessful, no matter what sort of position they held in Chinese society.

Humor is often the weapon of the powerless, and the *Chuang Tzu* is full of humor, mainly in the form of fantasy. Even a modern Western reader may sense that the author had a great deal of fun writing this book and mocking just about everything that was supposed to be respectable, or more accurately, everything that other thinkers were trying to make respectable in an age of political and moral chaos. The other side of this humor is the difficulty a modern reader faces in trying to decide how seriously to take any specific passage. Yet there are certain themes that shed light on our concerns.

One is the notion of individual moral autonomy, which emerges in at least two passages. The first one appears to be a jab at the Confucians.

> If a man follows the mind given him and makes it his teacher, then who can be without a teacher? Why must you comprehend the process of change and form your mind on that basis before you can have a teacher? Even an idiot has his teacher. But to fail to abide by this mind and still insist upon your rights and wrongs—this is like saying that you set off for Yüeh today and got there yesterday. This is to claim that what doesn't exist exists.[127]

The message here seems reasonably clear. If one claims to have a mind of one's own, one can't abdicate this claim to a teacher and then talk about the injustices one has suffered. Some conception of private moral judgment appears to be making its way to the surface here.

In the second passage it surfaces briefly again only to be overwhelmed by the familiar advice to stay out of trouble. The passage, too long for quotation here, concerns a scholar who was appointed tutor to a notorious crown prince who was forced to flee from his state because he plotted to kill his mother. The *Chuang Tzu* uses this episode for a page and a half of miscellaneous advice about how to respond to the moral and political dilemmas inherent in such a situation.

Supposedly the scholar-tutor asked a minister of this state what he could do with such a man. "A very good question," replied the minister. "Be careful, be on your guard, and make sure that you yourself are in the right! In your actions it is best to follow along with him, and in your mind it is best to harmonize with him. However, these two courses involve certain dangers." As might be expected, the rest of the passage is a colorful elaboration on failure or success in dealing with the dangers. It mentions the old tale of the "praying mantis that waved its arms angrily in front of an approaching carriage, unaware that they were incapable of stopping it" and continues with another, more realistic story about tiger trainers, to wind up with another semiparable about horse training.[128] The implicit burden of this pyrotechnical discussion is that a man of character would do well to stay out of such an impossible situation.

Elsewhere in the *Chuang Tzu* this advice is explicit, to the point of rejecting all social obligations. Indeed the burden of the chapter in which the following passage occurs is a rejection of all forms of commitment and social duty. This is a sufficiently strong theme in all of the "core chapters" to justify looking upon the *Chuang Tzu* as a text on moral nihilism. But again the humor leads to doubts about this or any other label. At one point the author has some sly fun by putting his own code for successful behavior into the mouth of Confucius, who is supposedly giving advice on how to carry out a diplomatic mission. Confucius in this transformation ends up stating in a nutshell the essence of the *Chuang Tzu*'s advice to harried humans:

> Just go along with things and let your mind move freely. Resign
> yourself to what cannot be avoided and nourish what is in you—this is
> best..What more do you have to do to fulfill your mission? Nothing is
> as good as following orders (obeying fate)—that's how difficult it is!†

There is here a conception of privacy in the sense of personal integrity. But this integrity can only be achieved through surrender, a view characteristic of many forms of mysticism.

On occasion the *Chuang Tzu*'s advice takes the form of prudence in a confusing world. "If you do good, stay away from fame. If you do evil, stay away from punishments. Follow the middle, go by what is constant, and you can stay in one piece. . . ."[129] If not quite a picaresque individualism, this viewpoint must have been refreshingly unedifying. Elsewhere the author has one character remark, "The way I see it, the rules of benevolence and righteousness and the paths of right and wrong are all hopelessly snarled and jumbled. How could I know anything about such discriminations?" If taken seriously, such a skeptical remark amounts to moral nihilism. The intent does appear serious, since a few sentences later comes a description of the Perfect Man, who knows nothing of such distinctions. (Nietzsche comes to mind in reading this passage.) The Perfect Man is a godlike figure. Fire, cold, lightning, and howling gales cannot frighten him. He rides the clouds and mist, straddling the sun and moon. "Even life and death have no effect on him, much less the rules of profit and loss!"[130]

This powerful imagery displays a contempt for the prevailing chatter about social virtues‡ and a yearning to escape the burdens of daily life. From the examples cited it is, I hope, plain enough that the *Chuang Tzu* reflects mainly the trials and tribulations of men with some education. Women are not noticeable. We can do no more than guess what these sentiments may have meant to contemporary Chinese peasants and artisans, if they knew about them. Hardly any of them could have afforded the luxury of totally rejecting social obligations

---

†*Chuang Tzu*, chap. 4, "In the World of Men," p. 61. As Burton Watson explains, "following orders," and "obeying fate" are the same characters in Chinese, and both meanings are almost certainly intended.

‡Note also the sarcastic remark "Fame is something to beat people down with, and wisdom is a device for wrangling" in *Chuang Tzu*, chap. 4, "In the World of Men," p. 55.

and conventional morality. On the other hand, there may well have been considerable resentment not only against some obligations to those in authority but also against the talk of philosophers. On balance, it seems likely that the hostilities expressed in the *Chuang Tzu* did have some resonance among the common people.

The philosopher who took the strongest stand on behalf of the common people was Mo Tzu, whose *floruit* his translator, Watson, places in the last half of the fifth century B.C. He may also be the dullest writer in any language who has defended the common man. Though his school was for a time a formidable competitor with the Confucianists, it was soon forgotten.† In his stern hostility to the display and pleasures of the upper classes Mo Tzu seems un-Chinese and brings to mind the attitudes of English radicals who opposed the monarchy. Yet by giving us a glimpse of attitudes that failed to establish an independent tradition though very influential in their time, the *Mo Tzu* acquires a special interest for the social historian.

According to the *Mo Tzu*, "There are three things the people worry about: that when they are hungry they will have no food, when they are cold they will have no clothing, and when they are weary they will have no rest."[131] It is hard to imagine a more simple and direct statement. It is part of a general attack on the festivals of the wealthy. These he describes in vivid detail with "the sound of the great bells and rolling drums, the zithers and pipes . . . the sight of carvings and ornaments . . . the taste of the fried and boiled meats . . . lofty towers, broad pavilions and secluded halls. . . ." But from the standpoint of the welfare of the world these things bring no benefit to the common people. "Now if the rulers and ministers want musical instruments to use in their government activities, they cannot extract them from the sea water, like salt, or dig them out of the ground, like ore. Inevitably, therefore, they must lay heavy taxes upon the common people. . . ."[132]

All this is probably true. In the *Mencius*, which attacks Mo Tzu from time to time, one can find occasional expressions of similar sympathy for the burdens of the people. But they are not as polemical. The *Mencius* is more likely to urge a ruler to share his luxuries with the common people in a show of paternalist benevolence. The *Mo Tzu* is more "radical" in seeking the outright abolition of luxury.

The *Mo Tzu* is also a strong advocate of careers open to talent. The text asserts that this was actually the policy of the sage-kings, claiming like the Confucians, the mantle of antiquity to justify their own political demands. According to the *Mo Tzu*, the sage-kings would

---

†In his *Early Chinese Literature,* 154–155, Watson attributes the failure of his school to the flat style of the collected texts, some of which are probably by later hands. In the introduction to selected texts he takes a gentler position, pointing out that the main ideas were compatible with traditional Confucian doctrine and could be absorbed by the Confucian school. See Watson, *Mo Tzu,* 13–14.

even promote a low-born person if he had ability. "Thus no official was necessarily assured of an exalted position for life, nor was any member of the common people necessarily condemned to remain forever humble."[133] Not content with the sanction of the sage-kings, the *Mo Tzu* also calls upon the sanction of Heaven. It is the most explicitly religious of the surviving philosophical texts. "For Heaven too shows no discrimination between rich and poor, eminent and humble, near and far, the closely and the distantly related."[134] It is the will of Heaven that "those who possess wealth will share it with others." And: "Heaven loves the people generously."[135]

The best-known doctrine in the *Mo Tzu* is that of universal love. Here the author tries to distinguish between universality and partiality. By the latter he apparently means loyalty and affection for a limited and specific group, such as the members of one's own state or family combined with hostility toward those belonging to other such groups. Partiality is, he argues, the cause of all the great harms in the world. He is aware that most people will regard the doctrine of universal love as highly laudable and equally impractical.[136] As usual, he claims that it was the actual practice of the sage-kings of antiquity.[137] The people do not appear as a special object of universal love, perhaps because that would destroy the quality of universality. While the exposition of this doctrine has the ring of sincerity and high purpose, it is strangely cold and lacking in passion. Though the text antedates the Sermon on the Mount by several centuries, today it reads like a parody of the Christian ideal.

Some inconsistencies in the *Mo Tzu* shed light on popular beliefs in the fifth century B.C. The text expresses vigorous opposition to fatalism, which it claims was widespread among the people and undermined their capacity for moral effort and willingness to work.[138] On the other hand, the author tried to encourage the belief in ghosts and spirits. He sought to impress upon the people the "fact that the ghosts and spirits reward the worthy and punish the evil," and to make this belief a cornerstone of state policy.[139] Perhaps the opposition to fatalism and the advocacy of a belief in ghosts are not altogether inconsistent because, in the mind of a Mo Tzu, both can serve to encourage an individual's sense of moral responsibility and willingness to make a moral effort. Be that as it may, the striking point in the discussion of ghosts is the tone that shows it would be an uphill struggle to establish this belief. This tone in turn indicates that a literal belief in ghosts and spirits—probably connected with ancestor worship—had already begun to weaken, even among the uneducated at this early date.†

†Evidently it had not died out completely since, at one point in this discussion (p. 99), he somewhat reluctantly discards popular belief in ghosts as unfit "proof" of their existence for a "superior gentleman," preferring evidence from the alleged behavior of the sage-kings.

The *Mo Tzu,* as we have seen, expresses strong sympathy for the plight of the common people and some sharp criticism of the luxurious life of the dominant classes. In the name of ancient tradition it also attacks current practices of bureaucratic promotion on the basis of wealth and kinship. Merit, which in this case means moral merit, is to be the sole quality that justified authority. Even a farmer or an artisan might display the merit that justified high official position.[140] If anything, the *Mo Tzu* stresses the importance of moral merit and open recruitment rather more heavily than the surviving Confucian spokesmen of this period. At the same time the *Mo Tzu* reaffirms the ideal hierarchy and repudiates with especial vehemence any notion of popular participation in politics. Honoring the worthy is the foundation of government and social order. But "when the stupid and humble rule over the eminent and the wise, there will be chaos."[141] If his ideas have come down to us without serious distortion, it is clear that Mo Tzu was an elitist in a form that was to become familiar under the empire. For all his dour simplicity, he was a moral and intellectual snob.

At the same time the very vehemence of his statements suggests the possibility that there may have been in the air tiny wisps if not a current of democratic egalitarianism that failed to leave other traces in the historical record. It is, I think, the target of this passage, especially at the end:

> Subordinates do not decide what is right for their superiors; it is the superiors who decide what is right for their subordinates. Therefore the common people devote their strength to carrying out their tasks, but they cannot decide for themselves what is right. There are gentlemen to do that for them.[142]

Righteousness, according to another passage on the Will of Heaven, "does not originate with the stupid and humble, but with the eminent and wise." A few sentences later we learn that righteousness in fact originates with Heaven because "Heaven is pure eminence and pure wisdom."[143] In other words, the Chinese meritocracy in its ideal form was taken to be built into the structure of the universe. On this point the Mo-ists appear to have been even more explicit than the Confucians.

We may close this part of the discussion with some very brief comments on the *Han Fei Tzu.* In this text I found very few explicit references to the common people. Since the Legalists were mainly interested in the doings of monarchs and ministers, this exiguous result is not altogether surprising. But the first passage is an interesting one because it reveals the deliberate manipulation of public opinion by high ministers. Among the eight villainies that can undermine royal power, the *Han Fei Tzu* lists two that have to do with public opinion and which show that it was a force to be reckoned with in the ancient Chinese state. The fifth villainy is called "Making use of the people."

Ministers often distribute funds in order to gratify the people, and hand out small favors in order to win the hearts of the commoners, until eventually everyone in both court and countryside is praising them alone. Thus they come to overshadow their ruler and are able to do as they please.[144]

Presumably no minister would seek to bribe public opinion in this fashion unless he thought it was worth having. The seventh villainy is called "Making use of authority and might."

Rulers sometimes believe that the officials and common people are capable of wielding authority and might, and hence whatever the officials and the common people approve of, they approve of too; and whatever the officials and common people condemn, they condemn also.[145]

This passage is even more interesting than the preceding because it likewise indicates the existence of a democratic current of thought, which we could discern behind the vehement rejection of such ideas in the *Mo Tzu*. But if we are to believe the *Han Fei Tzu*, the main consequence of these ideas was anarchy. Ministers gathered armed bands of retainers, proclaiming that whoever worked in their interest would profit, while others would die. In this fashion high officials intimidated the lesser officials and the common people, merely promoting their own interests.

Though Han Fei Tzu is a biased witness, there is plenty of other evidence for the existence of armed bands that may very well have had popular support. His evidence does show that public opinion existed, that it differed from the intellectual currents among the dominant classes, and that its support could make a significant political difference. Nevertheless there is no indication, or at least none known to me, that public opinion ever developed beyond inchoate sentiments to create distinct political institutions. We hear of no corporate bodies in the towns. Unlike the situation in medieval Europe, Chinese artisans were dependent on the palace. Free artisans were unknown.[146] Thus there was little or no possibility for political action by guilds.

According to the most detailed secondary source I have been able to find, the peasants did have their own social organization: the village community, but by the time of the classical Chinese philosophers, it had lost many of its egalitarian and collective traits, if indeed it had ever possessed them. (I suspect that the attribution of these traits to the village may reflect the myths of Engels and Chinese tradition more than ancient social reality.) Be that as it may, we are told that an assembly of the households in the village elected a council of elders who served as the main authority in the community. The council of elders organized the work of members of the village and was responsible for village security. It also had the task of distributing the tax burden among the various households and collecting the tax as well.[147]

The mention of elections is intriguing in that it suggests that the seeds of a democratic development may not have been altogether absent in ancient China. Rather more important, however, were the tasks these elected village officials were expected to perform. Apparently they were supposed to make the frequently crushing tax burden seem palatable and fair to the peasants. There was not much room for them to become spokesmen for the peasants against orders from above.

Intimate Relationships

Though most of the available information about personal and private relationships, such as those involved in courtship, the family, and friendship, takes the form of a statement of norms rather than descriptions of actual behavior, the frequent repetition and justification of norms provide insight into actual behavior. The Confucian norm was a patriarchal family, where the bride came to live in the husband's household and respect for parents was the predominant virtue. As I shall argue below, the Confucian stress on harmony and obedience was probably a response to the tension and conflicts built into this particular structure of intimate relationships. In this area of life as in others, Confucian writings give the impression of a somewhat desperate effort to impose ethical ideals on a refractory and turbulent reality. There is very little direct evidence on the role of women, and even less on the structure of the family outside the dominant classes. Hence my discussion will have to be limited to the situation among the upper classes. Fortunately there is enough information about them to shed valuable light on the varieties of human experience.

In Confucian writings women appear for the most part as docile objects of male desires and concerns. On this score at least there was no serious challenge from other philosophers. But this had not always been so. The *Book of Odes* or *Songs,* the first anthology of Chinese poetry, presents quite a different picture. This collection was probably compiled around 600 B.C., though many of the songs are several centuries older.[148] Hence it bears somewhat the same relation to the Chinese philosophical texts as Homer does to the orators and philosophers of fourth-century Athens.

Curiously enough, there is the same contrast in the status of women between the earlier and later texts in both cultures. The women in Homer, especially in the *Odyssey,* are free and active agents, much as they are in the *Book of Odes,* though the literary forms are different. Does this similarity mean that the status of women deteriorated in a manner similar to what apparently happened in Greece? That is a distinct possibility. But there is also the possibility that the situation we find in the *Book of Odes* continued to prevail in practice later while disappearing from our view behind the screen of Confucian rhetoric. Perhaps both causes were at work. In any case, it is worthwhile taking a brief look at the *Book of Odes* to see some of the historical substratum—and perhaps eternal human nature—on which the Confucian doctrines acted.

Several songs show that women had plenty of choice among males and were expected to show a certain amount of flirtatious initiative. Here is one simple refrain:

> If you tenderly love me
> Gird your loins and wade across the Chen [a river]
> But if you do not love me—
> There are plenty of other men,
> Of madcaps maddest, oh![149]

In another song or poem a lovesick woman sings:

> Thick grows the cocklebur;
> But even a shallow basket I did not fill.
> Sighing for the man I love
> I laid it down on the road.[150]

In still another, a woman complains to her swain that he is slow to court her.[151]

Such poems, which have some of the characteristics of folk songs, reflect courting practices that could turn up in most, though perhaps not all, human cultures. That is one reason for suspecting that in practice women retained a good deal of initiative despite the spread of Confucian doctrine.

In some situations the male was expected to show a very high degree of initiative. Evidently in some areas it was the custom for the rural lover to visit his lady at night. "She expected him to show his courage and resourcefulness by climbing walls and forcing doors so silently that the dog did not bark nor the parents wake."[152] In early times such behavior appears to have been a half-condoned and half-condemned invasion of the parents' privacy. There are signs of a changed attitude by the time of Mencius, though it is also possible that he was just being stuffy. After observing that all parents want their children to find spouses, Mencius points out that there are proper and improper roads to marriage. He scolds:

> But those who bore holes in the wall to peep at one another and climb over it to meet illicitly, waiting for neither the command of parents nor the good offices of a go-between, are despised by parents and fellow countrymen alike.[153]

Arthur Waley summarizes the details of the marriage ceremony as they are found in the *Book of Songs*. The main features appear to have remained constant for a very long time. They include fetching the bride from her parents' home by the groom or his representative, expressions by the bride of agitation and sorrow at this transfer of residence and loyalties, a feast or ceremony of unification at the groom's house, and rites to ensure pregnancy.[154] The essence of the ceremony in China as elsewhere throughout most of the world was the public affirmation and legitimation of a new social union with clearly specified obligations.

According to Confucian doctrine, the official consideration in the choice of a wife was the welfare of the husband's family. The *Analects* advises:

> Marry one who has not betrayed her own kin,
> And you may safely present her to your Ancestors.[155]

The *Mencius* asserts that "there are times when a man takes a wife for the sake of his parents,"[156] a statement that implies the existence of occasions when the parents' needs were not the main consideration. Presumably the future of the lineage would count most heavily. Character counted for much in the selection of both a wife and a husband. The *Analects* mentions the case of a father who chose for his daughter's husband a man who had been imprisoned. Because he had been imprisoned through no fault of his own, he was "not an unfit person to choose as a husband."[157] Very likely this was an unusual case of character overriding misfortune. Yet it is very much in line with the Confucian emphasis on the importance of moral merit in the selection of individuals for higher social status.

There is abundant information about sexual mores though it is limited to the upper classes. In early Chou times the monarch supposedly possessed a queen, three consorts, nine wives of the second rank, twenty-seven wives of the third rank, and eighty-one concubines. Certain ladies of the court specialized in the regulation and supervision of the monarch's sexual relations with his wives, an arrangement that sheds an interesting light on the absence of (or limits to) privacy at the apex of the social order. These women saw to it that the king received the wives on good days in the calendar and according to the periodicity established by the Rites for each rank. They kept an exact account of each sexual union, putting it down in writing with special brushes for writing in red. According to the general rule, women from the lower ranks had sexual intercourse before women from the higher ranks and more frequently.[158] Though I did not come upon any references to these specialized ladies in accounts of later periods, the emphasis on the conjugal rights of concubines and secondary wives remains characteristic of aristocratic sexual mores. The physiological aspects, which are somewhat puzzling, we shall come to shortly.

During the latter half of the Chou dynasty, 770–222 B.C., Chinese women were already subject to the "three dependencies": before marriage dependence on her father, after marriage on her husband, and, if she survived him, on her eldest son. In practice at this time, married women enjoyed a remarkable freedom of movement. If they wanted to, they found plenty of ways to carry on illicit affairs inside and outside the household. Only young girls lived in strict seclusion without initiative or freedom of action. Grown-up women could see the friends and guests of the husband and even take part in conversations so long as they remained hidden behind a screen. This practice enabled them on occasion to exercise great political influence. Some princes even permitted their wives to take part in the hunt and in drinking festivals. With this *de facto* freedom in a polygynous household, it is not surprising that many sons had sexual relations with one or more of their father's wives[159]—a form of behavior that the reader may remember was subject to savage punishment among the ancient Hebrews.

More detailed information about sexual behavior comes from manuals about sex that are somewhat later in date though Robert van Gulik believes that they reflect ideas current in Chou times.[160] According to these and other sources, the sexual act served two purposes. First of all, it should make the woman conceive, give birth to a son, and continue the family. In this way the male played the role assigned him in the order of the universe and carried out a sacred duty to his ancestors. Only living descendants could through their sacrifices assure the welfare of the dead. In the second place, the sexual act was supposed to reinforce the vitality of the male by absorbing the *yin* or essence of the female. Meanwhile the woman derived a physical benefit in feeling her dormant nature or *yin* become stirred up.

To return to the male, his essence or *yang* was supposed to be at its peak at the moment of ejaculation if he were to have healthy male offspring. In order to bring his *yang* to its peak, the male should have frequent sexual relations with different women without emitting semen. In this way he would augment his *yang* with the help of their *yin*. The male should learn to prolong intercourse as long as possible without orgasm. The more his penis stayed inside the woman, the more *yin* he would absorb.

What this technique amounted to, in other words, was *coitus reservatus*. It was a way by which the head of a family could satisfy the sexual needs of his wives and concubines, supposedly without damage to his health or sexual power.[161] The general idea was that retention of semen by the male would strengthen the brain and the body generally, a belief also found in Hindu culture. Though the writer is no medical authority, this belief sounds very doubtful. Prolonged retention of semen can produce engorgement of the prostate. Instead, the whole complex of rationalizations about sex looks like a form of conspicuous consumption. Most peasants probably could not afford even one concubine.

As might be expected on the basis of these ideas, onanism was strictly forbidden for males. Among women, however, masturbation and Lesbian attachments were not subject to any sanctions,[162] a sign that for women sexual satisfaction was unlikely within the polygynous household despite rules guaranteeing access to the husband. Literary sources take a surprisingly neutral stance toward male homosexuality, condemning it only when pursued for profit or when it led to criminal or cruel behavior on the part of one of the partners.[163] Perhaps homosexuality, like the resort to prostitutes, which was also tolerated, was a response to boredom produced by the restrictions on ejaculation. Van Gulik reports that one purpose of the manuals on sex was to overcome this kind of boredom.[164] To return to the theme of privacy, the sexual act was sacred like other ritual practices such as prayers and worship of the ancestors. Therefore one should not engage in it or talk about it before strangers.[165]

The Chinese social philosophers of the period we have been studying did not discuss sexual matters except tangentially. The Confucian tradition is noticeably reticent or prudish. In the *Analects* Confucius acknowledges somewhat ruefully, "I have never yet seen anyone whose desire to build up his moral power was as strong as sexual desire."[166] Sensual enjoyment in general was identified with rebellion and disorder.[167] Mo Tzu's opposition to sensuality was even stronger than the Confucians'. He alleged that a sense of decorum in relations with the opposite sex prevailed under the ancient sage-kings, implying that this was no longer the case in his own day.[168]

What little information we have comes from a few remarks in the cynical *Han Fei Tzu* on royal behavior. "The ruler," he asserted, "is easily beguiled by lovely women and charming boys, by all those who can fawn and play at love." They know all the tricks that make sure their requests will be heeded. There is also a brief mention of erotic ties between a ruler and his male favorite in ancient times.[169] Such behavior is hardly unusual. It existed in European court circles in the seventeenth century and no doubt in many other times and places. One of the solaces of royalty is the relaxation of sexual restrictions and one of its disadvantages the absence of privacy for such pleasures. For a king the sexual act becomes a political act.

We may now turn to the family and the tensions inherent in the Chinese variant of the patriarchal form. The *Hsün Tzu* provides a useful if limited introduction to these tensions as it comments on "the unlovely nature" of man's emotions. Men neglect their parents after acquiring a wife and children and neglect their duty to friends after satisfying their cravings and desires. Likewise, though we shall not discuss this aspect here, as soon as a man "has won a high position and a good stipend, he ceases to serve his sovereign with a loyal heart."[170]

Loyalty to one's parents, friends, and sovereign appears to have been the main virtue, which thereby specified three principal human relationships. As the detailed discussion that follows will show, there were many more relationships, even when that with the sovereign is set aside. It will be useful to list them in order to bring out the possible sources of dissension.

1) The husband's ties to his parents versus the ties to his wife
2) The wife's ties to her own family versus those to her husband
3) The wife's ties to her husband versus those to her in-laws
4) The husband's brothers and other kin versus the wife's brothers and other kin
5) The wife versus concubines
6) In royal households and probably others, the wife's authority, which increased with age, versus the husband's authority, which might decline with age
7) The father versus the sons and vice versa
8) Rivalries among and between brothers and sisters

Believing that all extended families, whatever their formal structure, have a tendency to fall under the sway of dominant elderly females as the economic and political power of the oldest male declines, I would hesitate to label the ancient Chinese family as especially prone to conflict except for the heavy emphasis on the duties of children to parents. To this aspect we shall come shortly.

Let us begin with the relationships between husband, wife, and concubines. The *Han Fei Tzu* has some acute if cynical observations on this set of relationships at the level of the ruler in both large and small states. The text asserts the strong probability that the consort, his concubines, and the son designated as heir to the throne will wish for his early death. (It is worth noticing that the monarch designated which of his sons would be his heir, a practice that must have reduced the chances of an incompetent successor.)

The reasons alleged for the consort's macabre wish is that a wife is not bound to her husband by any ties of blood. If he loves her, well and good. If not, there is estrangement.

> A man at fifty has not yet lost interest in sex, and yet at thirty a woman's beauty is faded. If a woman whose beauty has already faded waits upon a man still occupied by thoughts of sex, then she will be spurned . . . and her son will stand little chance of succeeding to the throne. This is why consorts and concubines long for the early death of the ruler.†

There were for the consort definite advantages to be expected from the ruler's death.

†*Han Fei Tzu,* "Precautions Within the Palace," section 17, p. 85. The concubine might be less anxious for the sovereign's death, however, if she was a favorite, because her position depended on the sovereign's affection.

If the consort can become queen dowager and her son ascend the
throne, then any law she issues will be carried out, any prohibition she
decrees will be heeded. She may enjoy the delights of sex as often as
she ever did while her late lord was alive and may rule a state of ten
thousand chariots in any way she pleases without fear of suspicion.
This is why we have secret poisonings, stranglings, and knifings.[171]

Under these circumstances a woman could reach the pinnacle of
power.

Frequently the concubine was the source of vicious court intrigues. Watson has translated the story of one that he regards as
typical from the *Chan-kuo ts'e,* or *Intrigues of the Warring States.* A
king received a beautiful girl from another king and was delighted with
her. The king's consort, aware of the royal infatuation, treated the girl
with special affection. When she felt sure that the king would not
suspect her of jealousy, she told the new girl that though the king was
much taken with her beauty, he did not seem to care for her nose.
"When you go to see him," she added, "I suggest that you always keep
your nose covered." Shortly afterward the king became curious about
this behavior of the concubine and asked his consort to explain it.
After a show of reluctance, his consort replied, "It would seem that
she does not like the way you smell."

"What insolence," exclaimed the king. "Let her nose be cut off at
once!" he ordered. "See that there is no delay in carrying out the
command."[172]

Under some circumstances the wife and the concubine might join
forces against the husband. Mencius offers a few glimpses of this
situation in families lower down the social scale. One wife became
suspicious about her husband's stories of wealthy friends when he
came home full of food and drink. One day she followed him throughout the city and discovered he got his food and drink in the cemetery
by begging from people who were offering sacrifices to the dead.
Returning home, she "said to the concubine, 'A husband is someone
on whom one's whole future depends, and ours turns out like this.'
Together they reviled their husband and wept in the courtyard. Meanwhile the husband, unaware of all this, came swaggering in to show off
to his womenfolk." Mencius closes this little tale with a cynical
observation rather unusual for him: "In the eyes of the gentleman, few
of all those who seek wealth and position fail to give their wives and
concubines cause for shame."[173] The story also indicates that married
men were accustomed to have a private life with other men and apart
from their domestic life, though the women of the household sometimes penetrated this private male existence.

The wife was by no means always the docile cipher presupposed
by some older characterizations of the patriarchal family. It was not at
all unusual for a high official to take his wife's political advice seri-

ously.[174] Wives competed enough with their husbands for authority within the family to create difficult situations that were familiar to intelligent observers. "When one house has two venerables," says the *Han Fei Tzu,* "its affairs will never prosper. When husband and wife both give orders, the children are at a loss to know which one to obey."[175]

Before turning to the relationship between parents and children, it will be appropriate to say a few words about ancestor worship, a prolongation of this relationship. Despite the importance of ancestral cults, the philosophers have little to say about them. Perhaps ancestor worship was taken for granted as a practice generally free of controversy. The *Analects* has Confucius reject a cynical rhymed couplet to the effect that it is better to have a full belly than waste food on ancestors who cannot enjoy it.[176] The existence of the couplet shows that resistance to sacrifice for the ancestors was probably widespread. But he who failed to sacrifice put himself in the wrong with Heaven. There was a positive secular function as well. The sacrifice to the ghosts and spirits was an occasion for "gathering together a pleasant group and making friends with the people of the community."[177] Thus the ceremony reduced the isolation of the family and made it part of the larger community.

As is well known, Confucian doctrine laid heavy obligations on the children, and especially male children, toward their parents. Under no circumstances should children disobey their parents. Taking care that they had enough to eat was insufficient. "Even dogs and horses are cared for to that extent." There should also be feelings of respect.[178] A man could remonstrate gently with his parents. But if he failed to change their opinion, he should resume an attitude of deference. One could feel discouraged but not resentful.[179]

Mencius advocated the same set of attitudes.[180] But he went further than Confucius by making filial respect into a political virtue. "If only everyone loved his parents," he wrote, "and treated his elders with deference, the Empire would be at peace."[181] Filial virtues, he asserted elsewhere, should be extended to the whole empire.[182]

A heavy emphasis on a specific virtue is generally a sign that in practice the exercise of this virtue runs into difficulties. Two considerations help to account for the Confucian emphasis on obligations to parents. Strengthening family ties (and respect for the older generation in general) must have seemed an obvious way to combat the symptoms of social decay that disturbed all thinkers of this period. There was, however, probably a more specific reason in the structure of the patriarchal family. As we know from other remarks in the philosophers, after a son had acquired a wife and children, his affection for his parents was liable to cool. Part of the reason was probably economic. On the one hand, the son was likely to want to manage his share of the family property in his own way by setting up an independent household. On the other hand, there were advantages of scale in maintaining the patrimony intact. Such tensions were likely to be reflected in family sentiments.

The relationship of a son with his parents, and especially with his father, was, according to Confucian doctrine, the most important of human relationships. While the parents are alive, Confucius is reported to have said, a good son does not wander far afield. If he does go away, he goes only where he said he would be going.[183] Within the family the relationship between father and son is the most important, according to Mencius. Outside the family it is the relationship between prince and subject. "The former exemplifies love, the latter respect."[184]

Resorting to a characteristically complex set of categories, Mencius classifies the traits of the undutiful son under five headings. They are (1) neglect of one's parents through laziness, (2) indulgence in games and fondness for drink, (3) miserliness and partiality toward one's wife, (4) indulgence in sensual pleasures to the shame of one's parents, and (5) a quarrelsome, savage disposition that threatens the parents' safety.[185] This looks like a reasonably complete catalogue of negative traits in the private behavior of a male.

Both Confucius and Mencius spoke out on behalf of certain restrictions on the emotional relationship between father and son. The Analects reports a stern and rather chilly relationship between Confucius and his own son, as we see in Confucius' admonitions to the youth to get on with his studies, admonitions the son carries out dutifully.† Mencius adds that a father may not teach his own sons because the teacher is bound to resort to correction and liable to lose his temper, as a result of which father and son will hurt one another.[186] He also draws a distinction between the goodness that friends demand from each other and the love between father and son.[187] The distinction is not altogether clear to me, though it may refer to the generally human and forgiving attitude implied by goodness‡ as opposed to the more specific sentiments of paternal affection. Be that as it may, I doubt that the somewhat distant attitude implied by Confucian doctrine prevailed very widely among the general population, especially among peasants.

According to the Analects, the private tie between father and son should override the public obligation to obey the law. When a high official from another country told Confucius about a man who bore witness against his father for stealing a sheep, Confucius supposedly replied that in his own country the father would screen the son and the son the father.[188] This is a strange position for a moralist in search of social order. As might be anticipated, the Legalist Han Fei Tzu took

†Analects XVI, 13. Waley adds in a footnote based on the Li Chi that there was "a definite ritual severance between father and son," including a prohibition on carrying the son in his arms.
‡See the discussions of jên by Waley in the Introduction, Analects, 27–29.

the opposite position, though in his version of the tale the magistrate put the son to death for his villainy toward his own father. But Han Fei Tzu concludes the story with this observation: "Thus we see that a man who is an honest subject of his sovereign may be an infamous son to his father."[189]

In ancient China, in addition to the family, there were two other groups of relatives—kin and clan—to whom there were certain obligations. Olga Lang describes these three groups as concentric circles, with the family as the most intimate and the clan the most external.[190] The kin were those for whom one wore mourning. Rules for mourning were set forth in the ancient *Book of Ritual and Ceremonies (I Li)*, which remained authoritative under the empire. Within the kin there were three groups, paternal and some maternal relatives, and relatives of the wife. Within these, there were complicated gradations affecting the rules for mourning. Not all maternal relatives, for example, received this honor. In early times it became the custom to address individuals not by name but by social category: for example, "Second younger brother, how are you?" This practice persisted into quite recent times, presumably reflecting and reinforcing the status system within the kinship group.[191]

The clan was a patrilineal group. Men throughout their lives, and women until marriage, belonged to their father's clan. Theoretically everyone with the same surname might share a common ancestor and belong to the same clan. But the main effect was that persons with the same surname refrained from intermarriage. In early times the clan may have been the main unit of economic cooperation. Under the Chou dynasty, however, it is claimed that the clan began to divide into families, and village communities began to appear, composed of neighbors who were not clansmen. Some clans retained landed property that was used to support services for ancestor worship as well as educational and charitable purposes for clan members.[192]

Family, kin, and clan evidently constituted a complex social network of mutual obligations that sustained, more or less, the conventional morality of the day. According to Confucius, a gentleman in dealing with his kin was expected to set an example of generosity for the common people to follow.[193] He neglects to tell us what happened when the common people lacked the material resources for generous behavior. On general grounds we may be fairly sure that the well-to-do had an inclination to avoid the obligations of kinship and the poor an inclination to enforce them. There were other sources of friction too, such as that between relatives by blood and relatives by marriage, the latter always newcomers. A passage in the *Book of Odes* notes that "brothers and kinsmen by marriage ought not to keep their distance."[194] The remark is a good indication that they were often wary of one another. Supposedly kinsmen were persons on whom one could rely.

That is one reason for the conflict between kinship and moral merit in the selection of government officials. Presumably the ruler felt that he could rely more heavily on the loyalty of a kinsman than on a stranger, no matter how able. Such hopes, however, may have been disappointed in the cutthroat intrigues of the time. Except for the Taoists, who were skeptical of all remedies for the evils of the day, all the philosophers came down strongly on the side of moral merit and against what moderns call nepotism.

Since many well-to-do households, and perhaps a number of peasant ones as well, contained a large number of individuals of different age, sex, and status, it is unlikely that the home could serve very well as a private retreat where one could let down one's social guard and relax. A late tale about Mencius, from the first century B.C., gives some of the flavor of a large household.

After Mencius was married, one day as he was about to enter his private chamber, he found his wife scantily clad. Displeased, he left the room without entering. His wife became angry and asked Mencius' mother to let her depart for home, saying, among other things, "I have heard that ceremony between husband and wife does not extend to the private chamber." Then Mencius' mother called him in and scolded him. "According to the *Rites*," she said:

> On entering the gate of a house
> Ask which members of the family are still alive.
> This is in order to pay one's respects.
> On ascending the hall,
> Raise your voice.
> This is in order to give warning.
> On entering the door of a room
> Lower your eyes.
> This is for fear of seeing others at fault.

After this lesson in etiquette Mencius apologized and kept his wife.[195]

There was of course some difference between being at home and appearing in public. When at home, according to Confucius, the gentleman did not use ritual attitudes.[196] In other words, there was some relaxation of etiquette, though we do not know the details. But an older source, a poem in the form of an old man's advice to his son, warns:

> Never for an instant be dissolute.
> You are seen in your own house;
> You do not escape even in the
> curtained alcove.[197]

Some forms of behavior regarded as dissolute, however, did occur. Another poem refers obscurely to lewd and shameful acts that had to be kept secret.[198] Both poems refer to extremes of behavior that would be subject to sanctions in most households in most cultures. Thus, according to the *Mo Tzu,* if a man at home committed some offense against the head of the family, he might run away and hide at a neighbor's house. Then, however, parents, brothers, and friends would all join in admonishing him. They would say, "When you are living at home, how can it be right for you to offend the head of the family?"[199]

If we can take this example seriously, it suggests a surprisingly free and easy relationship with neighbors, in a society dominated by strict etiquette. Perhaps this was the case. The *Analects* reports a story about a man who begged some vinegar (a valued condiment) from the people next door and then gave it to someone as if it were his own gift.[200]

Relationships among male friends were subject to a strict code of etiquette. According to Confucius, gentlemen never competed without strictly observing rules of politeness. Thus, even in an archery match they had to bow and make way for one another on appearing at or leaving the scene of the match.[201] Men of different social status might have friendly relations with one another. Even an emperor could, according to tradition, make friends with a common man. But etiquette required that the differences in status remain apparent. "For an inferior to show deference to a superior is known as 'honouring the honoured'; for a superior to show deference to an inferior is known as 'honouring the good and wise.' These two derive, in fact, from the same principle."[202]

It was humiliating then, as it still is today in many cultures, to be addressed in the second person singular.[203] Presumably this term was reserved for close intimates, children, servants, and some inferiors. The use of personal names was also taboo, though not the use of surnames. The explanation was that personal names were not shared while surnames were.[204] Though the evidence is scanty, it seems that educated Chinese erected a variety of barriers to intimacy. Conceivably these practices were related to the uncertainties of status, into which one ought not to pry too closely.

Loyalty and being true to one's word were, according to Confucius, essential but difficult aspects of friendship.[205] The temptations of gossip were to be avoided.[206] In somewhat priggish tones Confucius asserts (according to a late saying in the *Analects)* that there are three sorts of profitable and unprofitable friendships:

> Friendship with the upright, with the true-to-death
>   and with those who have heard much is profitable.
> Friendship with the obsequious, friendship with
>   those who are good at accommodating their principles, friendship
>   with those who are clever at talk is harmful.[207]

Not for him the joys of lively conversation unless it is also instructive. Having to conceal his indignation and keep on friendly terms with people against whom he felt indignant represented conduct Confucius claimed to be beneath him.[208] There is more than a touch of moral snobbishness in all this.

Feasts and parties were evidently a favorite way for males to relax among friends. One poem in the *Book of Odes* describes vividly such a party. It starts off with orderly, elaborate ceremonies, but later degenerates into a chaotic crowd of tipsy, cavorting guests whose unruly behavior embarrasses those who have been able to hold their wine properly.[209] Hsün Tzu gives a more detailed description of a community drinking party and the ceremonial behavior observed. Ceremony made plain distinctions of age and rank and put a brake on unlimited imbibing. If everything worked out properly, it was possible for all to share in harmonious pleasure without wild behavior, to drink and feast without disorder. To achieve moderation, drinking parties "should begin only after all morning duties have been completed, and should end before the time of evening duties." (The nature of these duties is not specified.)[210]

The etiquette of drinking reflects the characteristic Confucian theme of moderation and self-control, the essence of gentlemanly behavior in ancient China. In a world of collapsing social standards and savage conflict, the gentleman was to save his self-respect through self-control and self-cultivation. That was the private side. The public side was to promote a higher level of public morality in the hope that some powerful leader would see the light and inaugurate a reign of virtue. To my limited knowledge, this never happened.

In the preceding section I pointed out that the paternalist conception of government in ancient China did not include any institutions that protected ordinary people from arbitrary abuses of authority. On the other hand, I suggested that rules of etiquette served a broadly similar function by protecting at least educated people from unwanted intrusions. In closing this section on intimate relationships, it will be appropriate to look more closely at the rules of etiquette governing access to persons of similar and different status. There appear to have been a great many such rules, only a few of which our philosophers chose to discuss. Waley tells us that the domain of Chinese ritual, of obligatory acts and abstentions, was enormous. It contained some three hundred rules of major ritual and three thousand minor ones, all of which a gentleman was expected to know.[211] Presumably most of these had to do with how one could and could not approach another person and the content of good manners after establishing contact.

The ritual for approaching a teacher included purification by washing in water from a new well, making a burnt offering, and ten days of abstinence and fasting.[212] Since Confucius was willing to take all comers, even poor peasants, as students, we may doubt that this ritual applied in all cases. Yet Confucius was by no means free of intellectual snobbery. He is reported to have said that with men who have risen above the middling sort one could talk of even higher things, but it was useless to talk at all with men below the middling sort about things that were above them.[213] The conversation itself with a gentleman had a definite etiquette. One should not speak before being called upon, but should reply when spoken to. And one should not speak without first noting the expression on the face of one's interlocutor.[214]

Complicated rules governed the access of inferiors to superiors as well as vice versa. In ancient times, Mencius claimed, one did not try to see a feudal lord unless one held office under him. When a counselor made a gift to a gentleman, the gentleman had to go to the counselor's home to offer thanks if he had not been at home to receive the gift. One man waited until Confucius was out before presenting him with a steamed piglet. Then Confucius waited until the donor was out before going to offer his thanks. Evidently the ceremony of a visit of thanks was widely felt to be a burden. A disciple of Confucius remarked, "It is more fatiguing to shrug one's shoulders and smile ingratiatingly than to work on a vegetable plot in the summer."[215]

There were correct and incorrect ways for a ruler to summon subordinates: a gamekeeper was to be summoned with a leather cap, a commoner with a bent flag, a gentleman with a flag with bells, and a counselor with a pennon (that is, a streamer attached to the head of a lance). Once upon a time a duke summoned his gamekeeper with a pennon. The gamekeeper refused to answer a summons to which he was not entitled. Though the duke was angry enough to want to put the gamekeeper to death, Confucius deemed the gamekeeper's behavior praiseworthy. We are not told what the duke actually did to him.[216]

There was also a set of rules governing the material support of a gentleman-scholar by a prince. For the prince to send regular gifts of meat was insulting. That was the way the prince treated his horses and hounds. To make a gentleman "bob up and down rendering thanks" was, according to the Confucian view, hardly the right way to treat a gentleman. (Some princes may have thought otherwise.) Instead, gifts were to be made at the outset in the name of the prince. The recipient was to accept them after knocking his head twice on the ground. Afterward it was the granary keeper who should present grain and the cook who should present meat. But these gifts were no longer made in the name of the prince.[217] This procedure presumably preserved the recipient's dignity.

This etiquette served to make clear a hierarchical social order in which every individual had a distinct place. As Hsün Tzu put it, "Eminent and humble have their respective stations, elder and younger their degrees, and rich and poor, important and unimportant, their different places in society."[218] Toward each rank the members of other ranks were expected to display the behavior characteristic of a benevolently paternalist social order. Though the expectations were often violated, they must have provided some limited protection for the social space that was characteristic of each status.

In closing, it is worth pointing out that the scholar's status shows some resemblances to that of the free professions in nineteenth-century capitalist society. The difference of course rests in the fact that in ancient China the scholar was expected to obtain a government post. But we know that Confucius and many others did not obtain such a post. Such scholars had to be content to lead what we would call a private life. They consoled themselves with a belief that knowledge and moral merit were valuable without official posts and recognition. Something like a free market for intellectual skills existed in the possibility of moving from one court to another in search of a post.[219] That must have put a premium on ideas that promised quick political results. The Confucian emphasis on private and public morality was almost certainly a defensive reaction against opportunistic temptations. Scholars who did not get a post must in some cases have lived from the resources of their own property. At least we hear of their losing such property when forced to leave a state.[220] If we can assume that only a minority could obtain posts in the government, the majority must have cultivated their intellects in a manner similar to that of the amateur country gentleman in nineteenth-century England. Both the Chinese and English variants of the gentleman had a classical education that formed their outlook of comfortable superiority to the surrounding world.

SOME IMPLICATIONS AND INQUIRIES

In many ways this book has been for me an exercise in deprovincialization, an effort to find out if other peoples think and feel at all the same way about privacy as we do. The book begins with soundings into several nonliterate societies, partly as an attempt to ascertain the full range of ideas and practices connected with privacy, partly in order to escape as far as possible from the conceptual presuppositions of our own society. There follow more detailed studies of ancient Athens and of the ancient Hebrews, two of our most influential cultural ancestors. Next comes the example of ancient China, again an attempt to step outside the framework of Western cultural traditions, but this time through the analysis of a highly civilized society. In all three "civilized" societies, as well as in the case of nonliterate societies, I have tried to discern how contemporaries felt and acted about privacy and private rights, where such ideas existed, and have deliberately neglected the influence these cultural models may have had on later ages down to our own day.

At this point it is appropriate to ask what these investigations have revealed about the factors that promote or inhibit the growth of rights against intrusion, an expression that includes both personal aspects of privacy and private rights against holders of authority. Before going on, it may be worth drawing attention to the main enemies of privacy in our own time. They are only too easy to identify. One is Community. The other is Political Mobilization, either in a humane cause or a repressive and destructive one. (In modern history humane causes have only too often turned into destructive ones.) Political Mobilization and Community may amount to the same thing: an attempt to

267

produce among individuals a total emotional and intellectual commitment to a cause. The individual gives up his identity and autonomy to the cause. Anyone who does not, so to speak, lay his or her soul openly and willingly on the altar of the cause automatically becomes an object of suspicion.

Political Mobilization is an aspect of economic and social conflict. Community need not be. There can be tightly knit communities, such as villages, urban neighborhoods, or occupational groups such as trade-union locals, where any form of hidden or private behavior arouses the suspicion of deviant behavior that threatens the collective morality and solidarity of the community. Gossip serves as the main sanction of group solidarity. Mrs. Grundy is the traditional voice of Community but hardly that of Political Mobilization, whose spokesman is the Great Leader.

Turning now to the sources of privacy, as we look over the book as a whole, it may be useful to begin with some simple psychological mechanisms. The desire for privacy, in the sense of protection or escape from other human beings, emerges when an individual becomes subject to social obligations that that individual cannot meet or does not want to meet. On the other hand, this desire for privacy can evaporate if the person develops a feeling of dependence on the people who are the source of the onerous obligations. Briggs, in her account of her first days among the Utku Eskimo, reported this series of feelings. But they are hardly confined to so recondite a situation. The same abandonment of the self to dependence on a larger group is a widespread feature of twentieth-century totalitarian movements. The promise of earthly salvation, where all one's needs will be met and painful perplexities disappear, eliminates the need for privacy and private life, to the point where people become ashamed of such a desire.

In simple nonliterate societies the search for privacy, where it exists, amounts to a withdrawal or escape from other people or, in some cases, a more or less tolerated evasion of a diffuse public opinion about proper behavior. There are no private rights against public authorities or a public sector, because the public sector hardly exists. The limited authority of the adult over the child is the only external authority with which the individual has to cope, although the hardships of a sparse supply of food and of the natural environment may set close limits on individual choice.

The near absence of a public draws attention to the fact that privacy is an evolutionary product of social development. A proper understanding of privacy requires a deeper study of this process of social evolution, which of course continues today, with new forces entering the arena and others leaving it. Later in this chapter there will be an opportunity to look at some of the forces that have created specifically Western theories and practices about privacy. Here I want to recall some of the general sources of public authority.

Systems of economic cooperation in pursuit of widely shared objectives, such as the now familiar Mbuti Pygmies' method of net-hunting, create and sustain awareness of a collective interest or public, transcending that of any particular individual or household. Economic cooperation may or may not require a system of authority, depending on circumstances. But the settlement and suppression of conflicts does require and generate public authority. "The public" can arise out of cooperative behavior while "public authority" is more likely to emerge out of conflict.

At an early stage of human history the feud made an important contribution to the development of public authority by imposing a collective obligation for vengeance. Later of course the feud turned into an obstacle to the creation of larger units of public authority. From very early times the settlement of quarrels and more serious conflicts has been a major task of public authorities. In our own time we often think of "keeping order" as their main task. Almost always it is a specific kind of order, based on religious and ethical ideas. Hence settling and preventing disputes generally appear as forms of rendering justice. In defining justice and injustice and conceptions of the ethical human being, religious beliefs have made very significant contributions to the theory and practice of public authority. Economic cooperation and conflict resolution with religious support and sanction thus turn out to be two major sources of the emergence of a public sphere.

A third source is child-rearing. Since child-rearing can exist in societies almost unmarked by economic cooperation or the resolution of conflicts by the group, it is probably the oldest and most primitive source of an awareness of other human beings as a vague collective identity with moral rules and hence at least the germ of a conception of a public sphere. Through nurturant affection and discipline the heavily dependent infant and young child become aware of other people and how to behave with relation to such others. The sphere of "others" may widen.

In societies above the level of simple hunting bands this awareness of others often becomes refined into an awareness of the complicated slots of a kinship system. Such knowledge may include the forms of behavior expected from persons in each slot, as well as the varieties of appropriate attitudes and behavior toward such individuals. Thus awareness of kinship rules is an awareness of other people and of rules of "public" and even of "private" behavior. Yet it would be stretching common usage too far to speak of an awareness of *the* public through kinship. That is because kinship is too fragmented. In more complex societies—China is a good example—kinship ties can come into sharp conflict with obligations to public authority. Only when kinship ties have been to a great extent replaced by obligations to a more inclusive unit, a process that is often violent, protracted, and incomplete, are we likely to find a clear awareness of public authority and a public sphere of action.

Where privacy exists in nonliterate societies, it is no pure blessing. The cooperative relationships, on which affectionate and friendly sentiments depend, break down intermittently in the face of insoluble problems, such as, in a hunting tribe, the scarcity of game. Thus intimacy can generate friction, hostility, and the desire to escape the fetters of intimacy to life in the larger community. Several nonliterate societies display a rhythmic alternation between life in a private context and life in a public one. In our own society the same rhythm takes place in the course of a day. For men, going to the office or the plant in the morning can have the aspect of an escape from domesticity. At the end of the day the return home may be an escape from the tensions and worries of the job. There is at least some relief in changing the psychological bunions on which life's varied pressures pinch.

Though there is a substantial amount of information to be extracted from Greek literature about privacy in personal relationships and private rights against the state in fourth-century Athens, the origin and development of these ideas and practices have largely disappeared from the historical record. Here therefore I will limit myself to two brief points. In the first place, the taming of the blood feud by public authority was probably one of the great achievements of Greek civilization. One can discern traces of the titanic struggle behind this transformation in the *Eumenides* of Aeschylus, a glorification of Athenian justice. We may suspect that the creation of the specifically Athenian form of public authority, ideally a form of internal peace and order based on justice instead of oppression, was a prerequisite for the creation of private rights against the state and the degree of personal autonomy shown in rules of personal privacy.†

Certain other factors were in all likelihood also important. Athens was to a great extent a land of individualist peasant cultivators and individualist artisans and traders. That must have favored a democratic line of development. Athens was also a slaveholding society. But in slaveholding societies the free elite often develops egalitarian and libertarian ideals within its own ranks, perhaps partly in order to distinguish itself more sharply from the slaves, usually deemed incapable of freedom. Finally, many poorer citizens of Athens had an honored if arduous position as oarsmen in the city's fleet of galleys.

---

†For male citizens in Athens there appears to have been considerable autonomy. They could choose their work, friends, and sexual partners if they kept up appearances. Yet it is worth recalling that both Plato and Aristotle argued for much greater restriction on the private sphere, especially in connection with child-rearing.

Kept busy in this needed work, they were incorporated into the social order instead of forming an available mass for social turbulence. This situation, we may infer, reduced the fears of the ruling families and made them more willing to share authority with ordinary or poor citizens.

Examining Athenian society by itself may not reveal the very important relationship between political structures and individual rights. Political democracy, it is worth emphasizing, seems to provide the most favorable background, perhaps indeed an indispensable one, for the development of private rights against the arbitrary abuse of authority by the state. Hardly a startling thesis, it remains an important one, especially for leaders today who are anxious to sacrifice democracy for the sake of grander social goals. Abstractly it is easy to see why democracy might be favorable to privacy. Only where the people have power are they in a position to erect effective barriers against the misuse of power, the capricious intrusion into what they conceive as their own affairs. But that is hardly the whole story. In times of despair large segments of the population are liable to turn against democracy because it seems unable to give them a decent life. Waves of popular hostility to those who are openly critical of conventional morality are also all too common. Socrates is merely the most famous victim.

On more general grounds we can observe that without democracy private rights are either stunted or absent. Powerful rulers avoid granting rights against the misuse of their authority because such rights are both a limitation on, and a threat to, a ruler's dominance. In comparison with fourth-century Athens we saw that private rights were very weak in the two very different theocratic systems discussed earlier in this book: among the ancient Hebrews and among the Chinese of ancient recorded history. My impression is that this relationship holds quite widely. But let us look again at these two cases to see in what ways they resembled and differed from fourth-century Athens.

The main source of information about the ancient Hebrews is, of course, the Old Testament with all of its obvious biases. If a Hebrew Thucydides had been possible, our conception of that society might be quite a different one. Be that as it may, in the available evidence the most significant feature for us is the set of contradictory attitudes, attributed to Yahweh, toward privacy. There is a strong current of hostility to privacy from very early times onward. Yahweh appears as an omnipotent God and an all-seeing deity from whom there is no standing apart.

In the early semi-nomadic phase with very weak political authority Yahweh served as a substitute for a public by providing an authoritative source for shared moral judgments and thereby a sense of Hebrew identity. After the escape from Egypt the Hebrews organized themselves for war, with a religious commitment to exterminate the original inhabitants of Palestine, hardly a situation to encourage any standing apart from the community. But could not the very ferocity of Yahweh's orders be a sign that a good many Hebrews did stand apart from the proclaimed objectives of God's chosen people?

After the conquest of Palestine the intertwining of ethics, politics, and religion ruled nearly all aspects of daily life from food to sex, serving as an obstacle to the emergence of a clear distinction between public and private realms of behavior. With such rules there could be no place to escape from social obligations, no place where individuals could relax and do what they might choose to do.

On the other hand, the belief in Yahweh supported a series of individual rights against the arbitrary abuse of secular authority. Justice in the Hebrew conception is independent of social status and thus contrasts sharply with earlier and later forms in which punishment depended explicitly on social status. The egalitarian version of justice seems to have put in an appearance at a rather early point in Hebrew history. To the extent that it was put into practice, it must have favored the plain man by giving him the same rights as the rich and powerful. Under the monarchy the same spirit appears. The monarch was not to abuse his position by taking the wife or the property of an ordinary person. Likewise the prophets based their moral criticism of the monarchy on traditional religious tenets. Finally, in considering the forms of protection available to the common man we must recall the religious obligations of charity and compassion so heavily stressed in the Old Testament.

Thus evidence from the Old Testament seems to support two conclusions. First it demonstrates once again but in an ancient setting the incompatibility between a religious (and secular) authority that claims to control all aspects of life and the emergence of a protected private sphere. Every act by an individual acquires public significance. But even a highly authoritarian religion can under certain conditions encourage private rights—mainly against secular authorities—if it contains a suitable ethical component that leaves religious beliefs intact. Thus it is incorrect to regard a democratic polity as the only possible origin of private rights against public authority, even if such a polity provides the most favorable conditions for their development.

The Chinese case points to a roughly similar conclusion but drawn from a more secular context. Early Chinese thinkers, unlike the Old Testament Hebrews, were very much aware of the distinction between public and private realms of behavior. But recognition of this distinction did not generate any ideas about the protection of the Chinese individual as such. Confucian writings imply that this protection would come about through the moral behavior of the sovereign, which would in turn ensure the loyal and moral behavior of the subjects. This conception of reciprocal benevolent morality and loyalty was not pure verbiage. In later times strong emperors took a keen interest in the economic welfare of the peasants for prudential reasons and did what little they could to protect them from rapacious officials and local landlords. Peasant rebellions, in other words, secured in practice some de facto rights to the peasantry.

The right of remonstrance is very much in keeping with Confucian thinking. This is not really a right but an obligation resting upon the highest imperial advisers to give good moral and political advice. (Confucian scholars were reluctant to admit that there might be a difference between good moral and good political advice.) The emperor's obligation to heed such advice seems to have been mainly theoretical. Nevertheless in theory the emperor was expected to listen carefully to such advice, no matter how distasteful or painful it might be. One can perceive in the right of remonstrance the germs of a system of loyal opposition within a bureaucratic, instead of a parliamentary, context. If other conditions had been present, it is not inconceivable that the right of remonstrance could have grown into the right to criticize and replace political leaders, a right familiar to Western democracies. Nothing of the sort happened. Instead the right of remonstrance became a sentimental solace for displaced officials.

From early times onward, family ties with high-placed individuals might afford protection against punitive acts by government officials. This protective shield, however, probably existed only among the well-to-do. There is a famous story attributed to Confucius (discussed earlier), in which the sage supposedly asserts that the tie between father and son overrides the obligation of either to obey the law. It is a strange story to hear from the intellectual founder of a system of rank based not on blood and ancestry but on moral and intellectual merit. Nevertheless the tale reflects the importance of family ties, as well as the Confucian belief that the tie between father and son was the moral and political foundation of the state. If this bond dissolved, no imperial laws could hold the state together, even with energetic efforts at stringent enforcement.

Formally, then, Chinese society provided practically no protection for ordinary individuals against the abuses of public authority. Once more we see that an authoritarian regime with claims to a universal moral commitment provides an unfavorable environment for the growth of private rights. Yet again we see that this is not quite the whole story. Just as there were probably more abuses by central and local authorities than have found their way into the Chinese historical record, so also there were probably more informal means to protect oneself against arbitrary interference by authorities. With the possible exception of the short-lived Ch'in dynasty, no imperial regime tried to do very much about the life of ordinary people. If the Chinese polity was authoritarian, its rule did not extend downward very far.

In addition to the workings of the family system in China, we can perceive two other defenses of the individual against the government. One was bribery, a useful adjunct to oral persuasion, but a weapon available presumably for the most part only to the prosperous. The second and probably the most important weapon was distance from the seats of authority. China was huge and in the days before railroads, airplanes, and telephones it took an enormous amount of time for information to reach the central government and for it to react. The thinly spread network of district magistrates could not see and do everything and did not try to. Action might mean trouble and a possible blot on one's record for keeping the peace. Given the absence of vigorous administration or, perhaps better, its impossibility, the mass of the population must have been able to live pretty much as it chose to. It was the local community in town and country that set bounds to this autonomy. Custom and religion made these limits narrow, as they do in just about all human societies.

To summarize very briefly, the evidence shows that even authoritarian regimes with universal moral claims on the population are capable of developing some institutions that protect ordinary subjects from some abuses of power. But there are close limits on how far such trends can go. Democratic polities provide a more favorable setting for such trends and for personal autonomy as well. But in a democracy there are also limits and obstacles. For various reasons, such as war and economic despair, large sections of the population may turn to atavistic forms of loyalty, with suspicion of ideas and thinkers that seem the least bit unconventional. They take up Community with a vengeance and in its name suppress all forms of dissidence. Out of fear or secret sympathy (or both), sections of the elite may abet or even lead such popular movements. All in all, the wonder is not that privacy and private rights have been attacked or suppressed but that they have managed to grow at all.

Now that we have reviewed what the evidence in this study has to tell us about the forces and situations favoring and opposing the development of privacy and private rights, I would like to explore other related themes. Some are elaborations of topics already discussed. Others include an attempt to bring out some of the major historical sources of Western theory and practice concerning private rights against authority.

Privacy cannot be the dominant value in any society. Man has to live in society, and social concerns have to take precedence. In both ancient Greece and ancient China the words for private and public

existed, with the words for private conveying some hint of the antisocial in their meaning. Among the ancient Hebrews prior to the monarchy, we find no distinctions between public and private. Yahweh seems
to have played the role of the public. Thus all three civilizations
displayed a feeling for the priority of social concerns, but this priority
does not mean that *all* social concerns always take precedence. The
great civilizing achievement in the concept of privacy has been its
questioning of social concerns. That was mainly an achievement of
Western civilization.

At the same time, it is important to recognize that there can be
such a thing as a pathology of privacy. One of its more vivid manifestations occurs from time to time in American big cities. Individuals have
been known to watch through parted window curtains as a mugger
stalked and then murdered his victim. Despite the victim's cries for
help the witnesses would not even call the police for fear of getting
involved. Far less dramatic but far more widespread are the cases of
individuals who know but deliberately flout local ordinances against
breaking bottles in the street or against permitting or encouraging one's
dog to defecate on someone else's property. Though symptomatic,
these two examples present relatively minor hazards. A far more
important hazard comes from the corporations that dump poisons
indiscriminately around the countryside. It is a nice question whether
our society suffers more from the pathology of privacy or from threats
to privacy. But it is not a question I can try to answer here.

One might also object that such behavior is merely selfish and that
there is nothing to be gained by talking about the pathology of privacy.
Disliking neologisms as often being a form of pseudoscience, I have
considerable sympathy with this position. But the word "pathology"
has the advantage of drawing attention to the antisocial aspect of such
acts. Antisocial behavior of some sort probably occurs in all societies.
The widespread evasion of rules about distributing food in nonliterate
societies comes to mind in this connection. One can speak of pathology
instead of mere evasion only when it is possible to identify and assess
the social interest that is being damaged. To succor and conceal the
potential victims of a repressive dictatorship is an antisocial act from
the dictator's point of view. From the standpoint of a commitment to
human freedom, it is a constructive act.

If social concerns take precedence, one might ask if any human
societies without privacy exist. At first glance the Siriono Indians in
Bolivia, among whom all physiological activities can and do occur in
the presence of other people, suggest a positive answer to this question. But a closer examination qualifies the answer by giving evidence
of at least a desire for privacy. There are frequent grumblings about the
noise and disturbances that are due to shared living quarters. Lovers
seek assignations in secluded areas away from the camp. Finally, it

does not seem unreasonable to suspect that the obligation to go hunting for a day may be to some degree welcome as an escape from a nagging wife complaining about perpetual shortages of meat.

Since the Siriono constitute an extreme case, it seems safe to posit at least a desire for privacy as a panhuman trait. But as common experience shows, it is a desire that can be easily controlled or extinguished. The case of the Siriono along with other very simple societies also suggests that privacy is minimal where technology and social organization are minimal.

What is completely missing in very simple societies—that is, societies without chiefs or any political organization—is privacy in the sense of rights protecting the individual against public authority. There is no organized public authority against which it would be necessary to create such rights, though in some very simple societies there does exist a moderately well-articulated sense of public welfare. Instead of rights against public authority, one may find rights against other individuals. Where they exist, they may take the form of tacitly accepted social circuit breakers allowing an individual to escape from unwanted company, or rules governing the etiquette of access to other persons.

It is not necessary to discuss at any length the bearing of privacy on human physiological acts of excretion and secretion, including copulation. The data assembled in this book strongly suggest that people prefer privacy for these acts when they can get it, but they can also manage quite easily without these forms of privacy. Urination is often an exception and treated as a matter of no consequence. The availability of privacy depends in turn on the possible uses of space as influenced by physical and technological factors. The Hopi Indians had very little space and the Mbuti Pygmies had a great deal. The inhabitants of a modern Western city have little space, but they have plumbing.

The interesting question is whether there is any connection at all between physiological privacy and privacy in the sense of private rights against intrusive or unjust acts by public authorities. Hoping to shed light on this question when this investigation began, I gradually came to the conclusion that for this purpose the available information had rather limited value. A careful and detailed analysis of Victorian England, *if* the evidence is available, would be much more appropriate to establish the connection between physiological and political aspects of privacy because Victorian England appears to have been quite unusual on both scores. Such a study would require a separate book. I strongly suspect that connections do exist and will set down a few observations here as possible leads for further investigation.

It has been fashionable for some time to deride Victorian prudishness and the shortcomings of liberal society in the nineteenth century as well as the twentieth. But nineteenth-century liberal society—which in England became democratic only toward the end of the century—provided the strongest protection for the individual achieved up to that time in human history. Together with the creation of capitalist industry, this achievement required enormous control over instinctual impulses. A great deal of this control was self-imposed, though in the case of the working classes certainly not all of it. The positive result was a respect for the individual human being that may have at least part of its origin in Christianity. This respect came to include the belief that the individual should be left alone and in peace to meet routine physical needs, that sex should be used for legitimate procreation and not be the source of exploitative fun for males. Certainly there were elements of over-control and hypocrisy in the Victorian ethic. Yet it is reasonably plain that, in comparison with other ages, political freedom and privacy were maximized, along with instinctual control.

Let us look at this combination more closely and yet from a more general standpoint that concentrates on privacy. Stripping a person naked or watching that person defecate is likely to include an element of aggression on the part of the observer and an element of humiliation on the part of the observed. That, I suspect, is true of most civilized societies. Even among nonliterates who go about nearly naked there can be embarrassment if the penis-sheath slips out of place accidentally. To be sure, there are situations where the humiliation is held in check, as in a hospital or even in a crowded middle-class household. Nevertheless such observation catches a person in a relatively defenseless position. It can be an infringement on the respect felt to be due to another human being simply because that person is a respected member of one's own society. (Lower-status persons generally have less privacy, though they are often ingenious at preventing intrusive inspection by members of the dominant stratum.) Respect for a person as an accepted member of one's own society can develop into respect because a person is a human being. Without respect for human dignity and forbearance before human frailty, there can be no privacy in the sense of either seclusion or protection against authority.

We may now turn to the erotic relationship. It displays great variability in both emotional tone and the range of socially permitted partners. The emotional tone ranges from the rather casual feelings reported from the Siriono to the intensities of romantic love found predominantly in Western civilization. Less intense forms of romantic attachment occur very widely, as we had occasion to notice in the Chinese *Book of Odes*. The objects may include persons of the same sex, as in ancient Athens, where homosexuality was widely tolerated as an ordinary aspect of growing up. We are told that the corresponding relationship among females was deeply shocking to Athenians. This attitude may not have existed everywhere in Greece. So far as I have noticed there is no sign of social disapproval in Sappho's own poetry.

Though ancient Athens provides an obvious exception, the erotic relationship among young people has often been a prelude to marriage. In many societies there is a period of tolerated sexual experimentation prior to marriage. Through marriage and the prospect of marriage a social component enters the erotic relationship. The relationship can never be completely private because other people are concerned about the outcome. Older family members are likely to discourage some partners and encourage others on the basis of their suitability as spouses. On the other hand, the private or individual aspect rarely if ever gives way completely to wider social concerns. Even in arranged marriages, the potential partners frequently have in practice something like the right to veto a prospective partner who seems utterly uncongenial.

In all three of the early civilizations examined here, male domination was firmly established. It extended from political affairs through economic decisions to religious matters, though in Athens the women had some religious rites of their own. In the household, male domination included a guarantee of the husband's monopoly rights over the sexual favors of the wife (though in practice this domination seems insecure in Chou China), together with an explicit formulation of the double standard. Male domination was the context of both private and public life. Yet in all three civilizations there are instances of women who exercised a great deal of authority and influence without, however, altering the basic pattern. Male domination has existed in India and Japan as well. Thus it is well-nigh universal in societies with a written language. It has also lasted a very long time, coming under challenge only in relatively recent times.

The double standard, however, does not give the male access to a married woman of equal social status. Thus the most intense and private form of romantic love is forbidden love for a woman who belongs to someone else. The Tristan legend and *Anna Karenina* are classic Western treatments of this theme. By private choice, such a couple stands against the world. There is an intensity of emotion in such a situation that is not possible for adolescent love, except perhaps where both sets of parents strongly oppose the match. This intensity of blocked emotion seems to be a Western phenomenon. (I do not, however, know Asian literatures well enough to make a firm statement.) An investigation of how other civilized societies treat this situation in real life and in literature would add much to our understanding of the erotic relationship.

In any case, recent advances in contraceptive techniques and the accompanying revolution in sexual mores have greatly undermined the possibility of intense private emotions from forbidden love. As my friend Herbert Marcuse was fond of remarking, nowadays Anna Karenina would simply be told to go see her psychoanalyst. The existence of the psychoanalyst is, on the other hand, an indication of residual guilt and the survival of traditional morality.

It is unlikely that this traditional morality will ever completely disappear or that the choice of a sexual partner can ever become a purely private matter that is nobody else's business. Where there is even a prospect of children, there is a social interest in who will take care of them and how they will do it. But prospective children are far from the only consideration. Any social group, large or small, develops an interest in the behavior of its members. Death deprives the group of a member and changes its character. So does the appearance of violent antagonism between two members. The same is again true when two members develop a strong attraction to one another. That is true without any sexual component. In all cases, the members of the group intervene or try to intervene to protect the integrity of the group, efforts that are by no means always successful. Erotic relationships, and even close friendships, are therefore likely to arouse a degree of public or social curiosity and, at the very least, talk expressing approval or disapproval. Disapproval is perhaps more common because any new and strong personal attachment changes the daily habits of a group member and thereby threatens disruption of the group, whether it be a clique at the place of work or a loose set of neighbors and acquaintances.

The retreat into a private sphere, where it is available, is a retreat into an intimate circle where there is less compulsion to maintain the emotional controls characteristic of public existence. But with the passage of time, intimacy exacts its own costs. Minor personal peculiarities get on people's nerves with prolonged close contact. There is a sociological factor too. A small group of people has to have something to do, such as hunting, if it is to maintain emotional stability. Cooperation in a common task is the source of favorable sentiments about other people. But cooperation does not always work. Not every decision about hunting can turn out well. With failure comes recrimination, strain on the group, and a desire to escape from this set of intimate relationships.

We tend to think of the domestic circle as the classic place of intimate retreat. Quite often that is the case. Briggs gave us a vivid picture of the igloo as a place of intimate retreat among the Utku Eskimo. Among the Jívaro in Ecuador, home is a place of retreat from the risk of assassination. There are, however, societies that also provide escapes from domesticity. Among the West African Fulani, the periodic migrations of the cattle provide relief from all everyday social pressures, including domestic ones. In both nineteenth-century England and ancient China, upper-class males could escape from domesticity to the company of other males. In some nonliterate societies women have roughly similar escapes in going out to gather food or tend the gardens and fields. In literate societies their opportunities may be fewer. Well-to-do women in ancient Athens do not seem to have had any way of escaping from oppressive intimacy. But the Athenian situation is unusual, and our image of it may be distorted by the accident of what sources have survived.

In a number of nonliterate societies, socially sanctioned forms of privacy can flourish in the absence or near absence of public institutions. Among the Mehinaku Indians, for example, privacy flourishes in that shadowy area of human behavior that is tolerated but not really approved. Their rules of nonintrusion have to do with extramarital adventures and forms of theft that are widely known, yet about which it is unwise to confront the perpetrator directly. But it is the growth of public institutions and obligations, and especially their varying character, that determines the forms of what is private by confronting the individual with new demands and situations.

It seems highly likely that all civilized societies display some awareness of the conflict between public and private interests. Among the societies discussed in this book the awareness is strongest in classical Athens and weakest among the ancient Hebrews, the two major contributors to Western culture. In the light of this fact, it will be worthwhile to identify in a preliminary and tentative fashion the major social and cultural trends that in Western society have subsequently shaped the theory and practice of privacy and private rights against public authority.

Roman society does not appear to have made any significant addition to the Athenian legacy. If we were to find any such legacy, it would be in Roman law. Perhaps a case can be made for the spirit of rationality and the emphasis on procedural regularity as sources of protection for the individual citizen against arbitrary authority. In practice, however, they do not seem to have kept emperors from doing what they wanted. In any case, there is no strong reason to expect safeguards for the individual in Roman law. In its final codified form of late imperial times this legal system was clearly imposed on the population from the top down. Its central maxim was: "What pleases the prince has the force of law." No maxim could be more clearly opposed to private rights than this one.

In sharp contrast to the Roman era, the Middle Ages were fertile in contributions to the theory and practice of private rights against the holders of authority. I will mention only two, the right of resistance to an unjust king and the feudal practice of grants of immunity.

The right of resistance to an unjust king appeared first among the Germanic and Nordic peoples outside the area of Roman influence. In practice, it meant that the people rejected the king, refused further obedience, and elected another. There was no formal or "legal" process of judging the king, though reasons for rejecting him were given. Every subject, any section of the people, or the people as a whole could object to the king, abandon him, and turn to a new ruler. We are told that the Germanic peoples resorted often to the right of resistance during the period of migrations that followed the collapse of Rome. Later, the right of resistance became an integral part of the Germanic medieval conception of the state.[1]

The Germanic right of resistance took effect, so to speak, from the bottom upward. Later, the Catholic Church, working from contradictory traditions in the New Testament, created a similar tradition to be applied from the top down. The central idea came to be that the unjust king ceased before God to be a ruler. Unlike the early Germanic right of resistance, the ecclesiastical version required a regular legal procedure against the monarch.[2] Germanic and ecclesiastical notions could sometimes flow together. But my impression is that the ecclesiastical one was not particularly effective because it came into play mainly to suit the secular interests of the Church in its continuing contest with royal power. Except during the ninth century, the ecclesiastical theory found little application between the fourth and the eleventh centuries. In the eleventh century the famous Pope Gregory VII (Hildebrand) used it against Henry IV.[3] But Gregory VII's claim to be able to depose emperors and kings and absolve their subjects from allegiance did not take effect despite his well-known symbolic victory at Canossa (1077). Henry was able to continue the fight and in 1081 even attacked Rome and drove Gregory VII into exile, where he died.[4]

The original Germanic notion of the right of resistance may have had more influence on behavior than the ecclesiastical conception. The continual flaring up of local authorities in outbreaks of anger against the king during the tenth and eleventh centuries brought to the surface popular notions about taking justice into one's own hands whenever the king had offended the people's sense of justice.[5] Every medieval king had to take care that he did not offend some traditional right that would stir up armed opposition. Just before the Magna Carta (1215), King John of England had provoked his barons to organize themselves into an "Army of God." After Frankish times, attempts to dethrone a king were actually less common in Germany than in the rest of Western Europe.[6]

Looking back over the record set out in such a masterly fashion by Fritz Kern, I get the impression that the right of resistance may have declined in importance as society partly stabilized itself under feudalism. If that is correct, the main importance of the idea from the standpoint of our inquiry would be cultural and intellectual rather than institutional; that is, the right of resistance in early times helped to make acceptable similar ideas in modern times. These range from the right of revolution to that of limited monarchy.[7]

Another contribution that derived directly from feudalism was the concept of immunity. This had two major forms. One was the transfer of public authority to persons or groups with the consequence of creating a distinct area of local self-government, as in a fief or a manor.[8] Under an immunity the household and possessions of an individual or collectivity became exempt from the fiscal, military, and judicial powers normally exercised by the holder of a public office that had authority over the territory. "The lord's obligation to leave the vassal undisturbed in possession and governance of the fief became the most significant counterpart to the vassal's obligation to aid and counsel his lord, and to extend and mediate his powers at the local level."[9] With the development of the later *Ständestaat* (or state based on corporate estates such as the clergy, the military, and the residual third estate) the differentiated rights of each estate were often designated as "liberties," a conception taken from the older notion of immunity.[10]

The other major form of immunity concerned the grant of special powers to the towns, which became increasingly influential in the later Middle Ages. Through the grant of immunity, the city became a special legal and administrative area separated from the remaining body of the subjects. The model for this arrangement appears to have been the grant of immunity to ecclesiastical bodies.[11] According to Henri Pirenne, the territory of a town was as privileged as its inhabitants. It was a sanctuary, an "immunity" which protected the man who took refuge there from exterior authority, as if he had sought sanctuary in a church. But the policy of the bourgeoisie was entirely selfish. Each town was generally opposed to every other town, and the countryside existed only to be exploited. The bourgeoisie was interested only in exploiting its own privileges. Its exclusive spirit at that time, he asserts, was quite contrary to the spirit of modern democracy.[12]

Both forms of immunity reflect decentralization and even social fragmentation. In an age of limited resources and very poor transportation, higher authorities probably had no other way of maintaining a modicum of control than to grant an immunity. Pirenne's remarks about the bourgeoisie suggest a situation where a pathology of privacy had developed. Be that as it may, the legacy of the Middle Ages was that individuals and collectivities had definite rights against superior authority.

In China there is, so far as I am aware, nothing that resembles the Western theory and practice of immunity. On the other hand, the Chinese concept of the Mandate of Heaven resembles the Western right of resistance insofar as it raises the possibility of the ruler's loss of legitimacy. In Indian or Japanese political traditions, I can think of nothing that remotely resembles the right of resistance. Though the issue requires closer investigation than is possible here, I will hazard the generalization that the tradition of rights against authority, if not quite unique to the West, developed much further here.

Before going on to more recent times, it is necessary to say a few words about Christianity. The Catholic Church as such does not seem to have made any contributions to privacy and private rights beyond its frequent claims to ecclesiastical immunity. Instead, the practice of oral confession aroused widespread fear, anxiety, and resentment as an intrusion into private affairs.[13] On the other hand, Christianity itself from early times onward included a tradition of private contact with the deity unmediated by any ecclesiastical and bureaucratic mechanism. This tradition, an idealized recollection of primitive Christianity, was a continuing source of trouble to the Catholic Church until it finally burst forth in the Reformation. As is well known, the main Reformation leaders, Luther and Calvin, continued to preach obedience to secular authority, or perhaps one should say, the secular authority of their choice. Nevertheless the Reformation brought about a new emphasis on personal faith and individual conscience that has made a contribution to conceptions of individual moral autonomy in the modern world.

Royal absolutism in Europe, reaching its apogee in the seventeenth century, managed to bring the particularist and divisive tendencies of the Middle Ages under some sort of control. Since peace and order are generally favorable to the flowering of private interests, one might expect some improvement. But it is hardly noticeable. The main reason appears to be that although there was order within the state, compared with earlier times there was precious little peace. The new monarchies were constantly fighting one another. It remained for the triumph of commerce and industry, that is, a less parochial bourgeoisie, to generate major new contributions to the theory and practice of private rights.

These contributions did not become clearly visible until the nineteenth century. One was the notion that the ordinary human individual rather than a group or estate was the basic unit of human society. All such individuals allegedly had rights that were not to be abridged except by due process of law. Economic factors played a role in the development of these ideas. Property was quite widely distributed during the early phase of the industrial revolution, especially in England and the United States. With a reasonably secure base in his own property, the ambitious small entrepreneur was in a position to stand up and defend real or alleged threats to his livelihood or person.

Furthermore, it was only with the economic and political triumph of the bourgeoisie that private property became really private. In medieval society the peasant's opportunity to work his land was severely limited by collective usages. Planting times and harvest times were collective decisions in order to permit the cattle to roam over the fields when they were not in active use to grow crops. The emergence of peasants with separate plots instead of strips intermingled with those of other peasants was a slow and at times painful process. A similar situation prevailed among artisans. The individual craftsman was subject to detailed controls established by his guild. He had a more or less guaranteed market for his product but could not actively seek out new customers.

Economic individualism triumphed over these "fetters on production." The consequence was that private property came to mean the right to do as one wanted with one's own. (Some social restrictions must have remained, such as prohibition on arson.) One can also detect a change in the character of work itself from a predominantly social activity to a predominantly private one. It was plain to medieval peasants and artisans that they were working for someone else. For the early industrial worker the customer must have been a remote and shadowy figure. The worker was mainly aware of the wages as the basis of his own livelihood. Though one should not underestimate the early capitalist's belief that he was performing a socially useful function, it is plain that profit or private gain was decisive. Adam Smith's invisible hand was now necessary to convert private selfishness into public benefit.

In practice, equal treatment before the law has often been a mockery. Nevertheless the ideal has been effective and valuable. We appreciate it all the more when it disappears under a police state of either the right or left variety. The rulers of such states put their particular conception of the social order ahead of individual rights, which they treat as either an antiquated liberal prejudice or as downright antisocial.

In the earlier days of liberal capitalism, exactly the opposite view prevailed. Under the doctrine of laissez faire, the state's interference with the life of the individual was supposed to be reduced to a minimum. In other words, there would be little or no abuse by arbitrary authority because such authority would almost disappear. As Franz Neumann has pointed out, however, even at its minimal point in practice the state was always as strong as it had to be in order to protect property at home and some conception of the national interest abroad.[14] The main thing that did happen under the early capitalist state was the growth of private business, whose contribution to privacy was indirect. Yet with all these qualifications, the new bourgeois state with its parliamentary government was in terms of private rights a vast improvement on rule by a tax-hungry and bellicose monarch who tried to regulate just about everything that came to his attention.

Possibly the most important trend to appear under liberal bourgeois auspices was the rise of the professions. As the comparison with classical Athens makes clear, the rise of the professions opened up on a wide scale and for the first time real prospects of a private life, that is, one devoted to intellectual pursuits instead of business or government service. The expansion of law and medicine played an important part. But the novel element came from the natural sciences, which of course transformed medicine. Scholarship flourished too as part of an awakening secular curiosity about mankind, its institutions, and its history. Early in the period, Goethe had remarked that talent develops only in peace and quiet. During the nineteenth century there was enough peace and quiet for many to find out if they really had talent. Here too was the opportunity to use privacy in a socially constructive fashion and on a large scale.

Until near the end of the nineteenth century, the benefits of privacy and opportunities for privacy flowed almost entirely to the propertied and employing classes. Thus there could arise the notion that the concern for privacy is merely a piece of bourgeois ideology. Nevertheless the fact that the employing classes acquired privacy does not mean that the rest of the population did not want it. One can see this clearly in the yearning for a pretty little private house that turns up among German factory workers shortly before the outbreak of the First World War and among American auto workers after the Second World War.[15]

Toward the end of the nineteenth century, industrial workers began to use with increasing success collective means to protect the individual against the threats and hazards specific to their position in the new industrial society. In the course of time a substantial proportion of them in Europe and the United States obtained de facto property rights in the job and insurance against economic misfortune in the form of unemployment payments and old-age pensions. By these measures they won a modicum of protection against the main threats to personal integrity that affect people in their social position.

The achievements, however, fell far short of private security through public means. In the first place, the welfare state either cannot or will not bring unemployment under control. Now, even if unemployment payments came close to original wages—which is hardly everywhere the case, especially when unemployment is prolonged and severe—there are a severe loss of status and self-respect and a great deal of insecurity that go with losing a job. This is a blow to the worker's identity and private space. Nor are the workers the only sector to feel it. So does a notable portion of middle management. Conceivably unemployment is a necessary price for economic and technological adaptive growth. If so, the price in personal tragedy is heavy indeed.

In the second place, as everyone who reads a newspaper knows, the benefits of the welfare state, especially those flowing to the least prosperous sections of American society, are under heavy attack from the administration currently in power in Washington. The idea behind this attack, which is not confined to the United States, is that social expenditures have become a burden on the economy. (Military expenditures appear, on the other hand, welcome and necessary.) At the present writing in 1983, it is difficult to tell just how far this attack on the very limited forms of welfare state will go. But if current trends continue and accelerate, the end result could be an Americanized and updated version of the garrison state. In this extreme case, privacy and private life would become vestigial.

The technological threat to privacy from electronic surveillance and similar devices will probably increase. Since the literature on this threat to privacy is abundant and increasing daily, there is no point in attempting a serious discussion here. One observation, however, may be worth making from a historical and sociological view of such matters. As in the case of firearms and liquor, the spread of intrusive electronic devices depends on a demand for such devices that enjoys very considerable though far from universal social acceptance. The demand is more dangerous than the gadget. In turn, the demand has its own social causes, such as realistic and unrealistic fears about national security and domestic crime. If terrorism ever put in an appearance in the United States comparable to what has existed for some years in Italy, the use of electronic surveillance would probably soar. So, unavoidably, would other threats to privacy—without necessarily producing changes in basic economic and political institutions.

Whenever anyone points to repressive trends or possibilities in liberal capitalism, there is a tendency to infer that socialism is by its very nature free of such possibilities. I remain highly skeptical of such claims insofar as privacy, human freedom, and the protection of human dignity are concerned. It is often asserted that socialism has eliminated the main scourge of capitalism, unemployment. That is true of the Soviet Union, though at tremendous human cost. The case of China is much more ambiguous. One highly sympathetic study of Chinese urban workers reports that between 1949, the year of the Communist seizure of power, and 1960, male unemployment may have run from about one-eighth to nearly one-fifth of the labor force for every year except four, when big campaigns were in effect. A major reason for the unemployment was peasant discontent with collective farms, which sent people flooding into towns and cities in search of industrial jobs.[16]

An authoritative, recent study puts forth the more optimistic conclusion that the only sizable group of urban unemployed are the young men and women who have abandoned rural assignments without permission. Estimates of their number range from several hundred thousand to several million out of the twelve million transferred to the countryside from 1966 to the mid-seventies. With an urban labor force of close to one hundred million, even the higher figure would represent a relatively low rate of unemployment.[17] Since many of the factors at work in the earlier period are still present, there are grounds for treating the more optimistic conclusion with considerable reserve. The paucity of dependable statistics bedevils the whole issue and renders impossible any flat judgment. But bad statistics here as elsewhere are a sign of a situation that a government does not publicize. It is clear, however, that concealed unemployment in the countryside or a superfluity of agricultural labor is a serious problem in China today. In 1981 Chinese economists pointed out that "30 percent of the agricultural labour force is superfluous," and that in certain poor areas (such as Anhui province) the excess number of laborers is far greater.[18]

The other repressive features of socialism in practice, the secret police, the concentration camps, the controls over the arts and intellectual life, the huge bureaucracy that alternately appears overcentralized or out of control, are too well known to require comment. The central problems are: Why do such things exist and what are the prospects that they will disappear? The reasons for the existence of the totalitarian features of socialism boil down to the attempt to impose a new and for the most part unpopular social system at great speed in a world of international rivalries intensifying the need for speed. That will have to do as an adequate first approximation to the truth because it is important to get on to the second question about their disappearance. The argument has been made that as soon as a socialist country has achieved industrialization by admittedly brutal methods, its repressive characteristics will wither away.

Though there have been some trends in this direction in the Soviet Union since Stalin's death, there remain strong grounds for skepticism about how far they will go. Once a repressive apparatus is in place, it develops a vested interest in and capacity for its own perpetuation. Only a stronger segment of the bureaucracy or conquest from outside can disassemble such an apparatus.

There is a more general and stronger reason for skepticism that comes from the very nature of socialism. Every modern industrial society has to have ways to coordinate the activities of its various economic units. For instance, there has to be a way to make sure that steel reaches the automobile factories and leather, the shoe factories. In a modern society there are only two ways of assuring this coordination: bureaucratic command and the price mechanism of the market. Socialism relies essentially on bureaucratic command. It is the only device that can be used to pursue ethical and political goals that run counter to the cues given by market prices. The stronger the latter cues, the greater must be the counterforce exercised by bureaucratic methods such as direct allocations of materials, rationing, and price controls. Socialism's huge and frequently oppressive bureaucracy is therefore a response to an imperative built into the socialist system, one that, to my way of thinking, renders highly improbable any form of decentralized, nonbureaucratic, or democratic socialism.

Modern capitalism too has developed its own bureaucratic machinery to counter the unwanted effects of a market left to its own devices. And both socialist and capitalist systems need bureaucracies to run their big industrial units. It is about as plain as anything can be that big bureaucracies are here to stay and that attempts to restore privacy and individual autonomy by dismantling bureaucracies as such are doomed to failure. This does not mean that specific bureaucratic injustices and inefficiencies should be allowed to pass. Fortunately there seems to be plenty of energy available to combat bureaucratic injustice under both socialism and capitalism. Likewise, there is ironic amusement to be had in the remarkable human capacity to evade bureaucracy and create a protected niche for private existence. Though this capacity is most noticeable in the Soviet Union, it probably exists everywhere.

If there is any permanent solution for the oppressive aspects of bureaucracy, it may lie in the capacity of bureaucracy and machines to reduce sharply the need for repetitious and toilsome human labor. Eventually such changes might make possible a more creative and enjoyable private life in the hours away from work. For such changes to occur, there would have to be profound changes in the cultural climate and probably also in social organization. I am not at all sure that they are possible. How many people would want or could manage a great increase in leisure? If challenging and interesting work became the only kind available, what proportion of the population would be competent to perform it? Though these and related issues deserve serious thought, this book is not the place to explore them.

NOTES

Chapter 1: ANTHROPOLOGICAL PERSPECTIVES

1. *Never in Anger,* 1.
2. Briggs, *Never in Anger,* 15–16.
3. Briggs, *Never in Anger,* 17–19.
4. Briggs, *Never in Anger,* 26; see pp. 26–27 for her account of the first six days.
5. Briggs, *Never in Anger,* 27–28.
6. Briggs, *Never in Anger,* 241, 249, 272.
7. Briggs, *Never in Anger,* 107–108.
8. Briggs, *Never in Anger,* 38–39.
9. Briggs, *Never in Anger,* 42.
10. Briggs, *Never in Anger,* 20–21.
11. Briggs, *Never in Anger,* 67, 209–210, 213, 220.
12. Briggs, *Never in Anger,* 193, 195.
13. Briggs, *Never in Anger,* 211–213.
14. Briggs, *Never in Anger,* 181–185, 199.
15. Briggs, *Never in Anger,* 48.
16. Briggs, *Never in Anger,* 149; see also 93.
17. Briggs, *Never in Anger,* 84n., 120.
18. Briggs, *Never in Anger,* 57–58.
19. Briggs, *Never in Anger,* 76–77.
20. Briggs, *Never in Anger,* 254–255.
21. Briggs, *Never in Anger,* 137–139, 174–175.
22. Briggs, *Never in Anger,* 88, 165, 178–179.
23. See Asen Balikci, *The Netsilik Eskimo,* 189–193.

24. Briggs, *Never in Anger,* 141–145.
25. Allan R. Holmberg, *Nomads of the Long Bow,* xii, xx, 13.
25a. Holmberg, *Nomads,* 17, 22, 26, 34, 38–39, 73.
26. Holmberg, *Nomads,* 51–53, 56–57, 58–59.
27. Holmberg, *Nomads,* 63, 67, 71–72, 83.
28. Holmberg, *Nomads,* 81.
29. Holmberg, *Nomads,* 79–80.
30. Holmberg, *Nomads,* 87–88, 150.
31. Holmberg, *Nomads,* 102.
32. Holmberg, *Nomads,* 154–155.
33. Holmberg, *Nomads,* 155–156.
34. Holmberg, *Nomads,* 152–153.
35. Holmberg, *Nomads,* 98–100.
36. Holmberg, *Nomads,* 260.
37. Holmberg, *Nomads,* 153.
38. Holmberg, *Nomads,* 251.
39. Colin M. Turnbull, *Wayward Servants,* 16–17, 128.
40. Turnbull, *Wayward Servants,* 120.
41. Turnbull, *Wayward Servants,* 157.
42. Turnbull, *Wayward Servants,* 160, 278.
43. For an example see Turnbull, *Wayward Servants,* 108, 198.
44. Turnbull, *Wayward Servants,* 155, 178–179.
45. Turnbull, *Wayward Servants,* 120.
46. Turnbull, *Wayward Servants,* 158.
47. Turnbull, *Wayward Servants,* 100, 283.
48. Turnbull, *Wayward Servants,* 106.
49. Turnbull, *Wayward Servants,* 100–109.
50. Turnbull, *Wayward Servants,* 186.
51. Turnbull, *Wayward Servants,* 181, 180; see also 294–296.
52. Turnbull, *Wayward Servants,* 216–217, n. 10.
53. Turnbull, *Wayward Servants,* 278–279.
54. Turnbull, *Wayward Servants,* 279–281, 297–298, 114, 143–145, 190. On the *molimo* see also Turnbull, *The Forest People,* chap. 8.
55. Turnbull, *Wayward Servants,* 158, 197–199.
56. Turnbull, *Wayward Servants,* 123.
57. Turnbull, *Wayward Servants,* 27, 109, 115–116, 270.
58. Turnbull, *Wayward Servants,* 118.
59. Turnbull, *Wayward Servants,* 127.
60. Turnbull, *Wayward Servants,* 183, 248, 257, n. 7.
61. Turnbull, *Wayward Servants,* 106.
62. Turnbull, *Wayward Servants,* 206–207.
63. Michael J. Harner, *The Jívaro,* 56–58.
64. Harner, *Jívaro,* 48.
65. Harner, *Jívaro,* 170–182.
66. On kinship see Harner, *Jívaro,* 98–101, 103.
67. Harner, *Jívaro,* 170–171.
68. Harner, *Jívaro,* 135.
69. Harner, *Jívaro,* 136, 141.
70. Harner, *Jívaro,* 143–144.

71. Harner, *Jívaro*, 145.
72. Harner, *Jívaro*, 114–115.
73. Harner, *Jívaro*, 36.
74. Harner, *Jívaro*, 38.
75. Stirling, *Jívaro Indians*, 6.
76. Stirling, *Jívaro Indians*, 11.
77. Stirling, *Jívaro Indians*, 46.
78. Holmberg, *Nomads*, 238–239.
79. Mary Douglas, *Purity and Danger*, 6.
80. See E. Adamson Hoebel, *The Cheyennes*, 6–11, for an account of this impressive ceremony. The quotation occurs on p. 8.
81. Douglas, *Purity and Danger*, 132.
82. Laura Thompson and Alice Joseph, *The Hopi Way*, 130, 47, 120–123.
83. Thompson and Joseph, *Hopi Way*, 36–37.
84. Thompson and Joseph, *Hopi Way*, 41.
85. Cf. Sally F. Moore, *Law as Process*, 45–48, 89–91.
86. Holmberg, *Nomads*, 153.
87. For public opinion and its effectiveness note Robert Redfield, "Primitive Law," in Paul Bohannan, editor, *Law and Warfare*, 3–24.
88. Lucy Mair, *Primitive Government*, 82–83.
89. Westermarck, Edward A., *The Origin and the Development of the Moral Ideas*, I, 479–480.
90. Westermarck, *Moral Ideas*, I, 489.
91. R. F. Barton, *The Kalingas*, 148–149.
92. Barton, *The Kalingas*, 218.
93. Barton, *The Kalingas*, 237.
94. Barton, *The Kalingas*, 170, 173–174.
95. C. H. Berndt, summary of communication on "Interdependence and Conflict in the Eastern Central Highlands of New Guinea" by Ronald M. Berndt, Royal Anthropological Institute, *Proceedings*, nos. 116–117, p. 105. See also for more detail Ronald M. Berndt, *Excess and Restraint*, 236–250. See also p. 230 for information suggesting an incipient concept of treason.
96. For a very instructive brief general treatment see L. T. Hobhouse, *Morals in Evolution*, chap. III. The first edition appeared in Edinburgh, 1906.
97. See Joseph R. Strayer, *On the Medieval Origins of the Modern State*, 10–11, 35–36.
98. Maybury-Lewis, *Akwē-Shavante Society*, 67–74, esp. 68–69.
99. Turnbull, *Forest People*, 126–129, esp. 127, 129; also *Wayward Servants*, 113–114, 152 with less detail but a helpful discussion of the family.
100. Holmberg, *Nomads*, 203, 205.
101. Holmberg, *Nomads*, 205–206.
102. Holmberg, *Nomads*, 201.
103. Holmberg, *Nomads*, 209–210.
104. For an old general survey, see Arnold van Gennep, *The Rites of Passage*.
105. See Ronald M. Berndt, *Excess and Restraint*.
106. Berndt, *Excess and Restraint*, 100.
107. Berndt, *Excess and Restraint*, 96.

108. Paul Riesman, *Freedom in Fulani Social Life*, 71–73, 127–129.
109. Riesman, *Fulani*, 122.
110. Joel S. Savishinsky, *The Trail of the Hare*, 4, 26, 34.
111. Savishinsky, *Trail of the Hare*, 59, 61, 68–69.
112. Savishinsky, *Trail of the Hare*, 96, 112–114.
113. Savishinsky, *Trail of the Hare*, 115–118.
114. Savishinsky, *Trail of the Hare*, 118–119.
115. Savishinsky, *Trail of the Hare*, 120.
116. Savishinsky, *Trail of the Hare*, 78–80.
117. Savishinsky, *Trail of the Hare*, 122.
118. Savishinsky, *Trail of the Hare*, 120, 122–126.
119. Riesman, *Fulani*, 117.
120. Riesman, *Fulani*, 120–121.
121. Riesman, *Fulani*, 121.
122. Riesman, *Fulani*, 158–160.
123. Riesman, *Fulani*, 253–255.
124. Maybury-Lewis, *Shavante*, Introduction, 71.
125. Riesman, *Fulani*, 77–78.
126. For a discussion of variations within the general pattern of slavery in the U.S., see Eugene Genovese, *Roll Jordan Roll*.
127. Gluckman, *Custom and Conflict in Africa*, 78. See also 59, 62–63, 69–70, 74 for the role of the lineage, patrilineal, and matrilineal systems.
128. For a brief but illuminating discussion of an apparent exception among the Nayar castes of Malabar in India see Gluckman, *Custom and Conflict in Africa*, 68–69.
129. Napoleon A. Chagnon, *Yanomamö: The Fierce People*, 92.
130. Chagnon, *Yanomamö*, 25.
131. Chagnon, *Yanomamö*, 82–83.
132. Harner, *Jívaro*, 52–55, 81, 107, on wives; 84–93, 103–105, on childrearing.
133. Berndt, *Excess and Restraint*, 69–73, 114–115, 151, 160–161, 282–284.
134. Morgan, *League of the Iroquois*, 324, 327–328.
135. Anthony F. C. Wallace, *The Death and Rebirth of the Seneca*, 28–30.
136. Hoebel, *The Cheyennes*, 24–27, 59, 64.
137. Thompson and Joseph, *Hopi Way*, 73.
138. Briggs, *Never in Anger*, 79–80.
139. Briggs, *Never in Anger*, 85.
140. Briggs, *Never in Anger*, 106.
141. Briggs, *Never in Anger*, 107–108.
142. Turnbull, *Wayward Servants*, 123–124.
143. On the women's role see Turnbull, *Wayward Servants*, 120, 151, 157, 167–168, 271.
144. Arthur E. Hippler in a review of Ronald P. Rohner, *They Love Me, They Love Me Not* in *The Journal of Psychological Anthropology*, 1, no. 1, 139.
145. Savishinsky, *Trail of the Hare*, 96–97.
146. For some illuminating observations see Thompson and Joseph, *Hopi Way*, 110–112.
147. Lawrence Stone, *The Family, Sex and Marriage*, 77, 159.
148. Holmberg, *Nomads*, 98–99.

149. Holmberg, *Nomads,* 198–199.
150. Harner, *Jívaro,* 87.
151. Riesman, *Fulani,* 126, 128–129.
152. Riesman, *Fulani,* 227.
153. Riesman, *Fulani,* 228–229.
154. Riesman, *Fulani,* 251.
156. For a list of persons before whom one should not eat, see *Fulani,* 128.
157. Mischa Titiev, *Old Oraibi,* 205.
158. Malinowski, *Sexual Life,* 309–311.
159. The term comes from C. B. Macpherson, *The Political Theory of Possessive Individualism.*
160. Savishinsky, *Trail of the Hare,* 203.
161. Holmberg, *Nomads,* 165.
162. Holmberg, *Nomads,* 163–165; quotation from p. 165.
163. See Turnbull, *Wayward Servants,* 254, and Malinowski, *Sexual Life,* 326, respectively for Mbuti and Trobrianders.
164. Riesman, *Fulani,* 87–88.
165. Riesman, *Fulani,* 111.
166. Riesman, *Fulani,* 84.
167. Riesman, *Fulani,* 168.
168. Beaglehole and Beaglehole, "Hopi of the Second Mesa," 62.
169. Titiev, *Old Oraibi,* 30.
170. David F. Aberle, "The Psychosocial Analysis of the Hopi Life History" in Robert Hunt, ed., *Personalities and Culture,* 103.
171. Titiev, *Old Oraibi,* 205.
172. Titiev, *Old Oraibi,* 205.
173. *Sexual Life,* 274–275.
174. Malinowski, *Sexual Life,* 322. For an even earlier criticism with abundant evidence from sources then available, see Westermarck, *History of Human Marriage,* I, 302–336; III, 86–94.
175. For a Marxist variant of this exaggeration of the virtue of *Gemeinschaft,* see the Introduction to Robert Sayre, *Solitude in Society.*
176. Lorna Marshall, "Sharing, Talking, and Giving: Relief of Social Tensions among the !Kung," in Lee and DeVore, eds., *Kalahari Hunter-Gatherers,* 350–351.
177. See Thomas P. Bernstein, "Leadership and Mobilization in the Collectivization of Agriculture in China and Russia"; and Bao Ruo-Wang (Jean Pasqualini) and Rudolph Chelminski, *Prisoner of Mao.*
178. Turnbull, *Forest People,* 127–128; *Wayward Servants,* 116–117.
179. Maybury-Lewis, *Shavante,* 86–87, 92.
180. Gregor, *Mehinaku,* 99.
181. Gregor, *Mehinaku,* 101–102.
182. Gregor, *Mehinaku,* 123–125.
183. Gregor, *Mehinaku,* 102.

Chapter 2: PUBLIC AND PRIVATE IN CLASSICAL ATHENS

1. Xenophon *Memorabilia* 3.12.1.
2. See Liddell and Scott, *Greek-English Lexicon*, s.v. *koinos* and *xunos* for an even wider set of meanings.
3. Jeffrey Henderson, *The Maculate Muse*, 33, citing Aristophanes *Frogs* 358.
4. See Aeschines *Against Ctesiphon* 203, 205; Lysias *In Defence of Mantitheus* 11; Demosthenes *De Corona* 268.
5. Thucydides *History of the Peloponnesian War* 7.77. 4–7.
6. A.H.M. Jones, *Athenian Democracy*, 10. The requirement of citizenship on both sides was added by a law passed in 451 B.C. and reenacted in 403 B.C.
7. For the procedures see Aristotle *Athenian Constitution* 42, 1; also Isaeus *On the Estate of Ciron* 19–20 and *On Behalf of Euphiletus*, Loeb Classical Library edition, Introductory notes pp. 429–441 and subsequent text; Demosthenes *Euxitheus Against Eubulides, An Appeal* 54.
8. Demosthenes *Against Neaera* 89–93.
9. Andocides *On His Return* 23.
10. Jones, *Athenian Democracy*, 10–11.
11. M. I. Finley, "Was Greek Civilization Based on Slavery?" in M. I. Finley, editor, *Slavery in Classical Antiquity*, 147–152 provides a useful general perspective.
12. Demosthenes *Against Aristogeiton* 1.51.
13. *Oxford Classical Dictionary* (2nd ed., 1970), s.v. "Population." The 1970 edition is the only one cited in this book.
14. M. I. Finley, *Slavery*, 150–151. He regards the higher figure as far more probable.
15. Demosthenes *Third Philippic* 3; cf. *Against Theocrines* 68 for the grant of freedom of speech to aliens.
16. Aristotle *Athenian Constitution* 7.2–4.
17. *Oxford Classical Dictionary*, s.v. "Eisphora," "Metics."
18. *Oxford Classical Dictionary*, s.v. "Population."
19. *Oxford Classical Dictionary* s.v. "Trierarchy."
20. Demosthenes *Against Meidias* 155.
21. Demosthenes *Against Phaenippus* 21–23.
22. Lysias *On the Property of Aristophanes: Against the Treasury* 21–22.
23. Demosthenes *Against Timotheus* 14–18; see also Introduction to this piece, Loeb Classical Library edition, V, 373–374.
24. Demosthenes *On the Trierarchic Crown* 7–9, 11–12.
25. Demosthenes *Against Polycles* 7.
26. Demosthenes *Against Polycles* 34–36.
27. For a useful brief general treatment of the naval administration see Georg Busolt and Heinrich Swoboda, *Griechische Staatskunde*, 1196–1210.
28. Isaeus *On the Estate of Apollodorus* 36–42.
29. Cf. *Oxford Classical Dictionary*, s.v. "Mercenaries (Greek and Hellenistic)."

30. *Oxford Classical Dictionary,* s.v. "Liturgy," "Choregia."
31. Aristotle *Athenian Constitution* 61.3.
32. *Against Meidias* 33–34, 104.
33. *Against Meidias* 175–180, 201.
34. Demosthenes *Against Meidias* 10–12.
35. See *Oxford Classical Dictionary,* s.v. "Antidosis." See also Ludovic Beauchet, *Histoire du Droit Privé de la République Athenienne,* III, Le droit de propriété, 731–732, where the author expresses strong doubt that properties actually exchanged hands.
36. Andreas Michael Andreades, *A History of Greek Public Finance,* I, 126–127.
37. Andreades, *Greek Public Finance,* I, 334.
38. Andreades, *Greek Public Finance,* I, 284, 278, 280, 274, 276.
39. *Oxford Classical Dictionary,* s.v. "Laurium," "Poletai."
40. Andreades, *Greek Public Finance,* I, 297–299.
41. Andreades, *Greek Public Finance,* I, 314.
42. Andreades, *Greek Public Finance,* I, 316. See 310–312 for the other facts cited in this summary account.
43. Andreades, *Greek Public Finance,* I, 334–335.
44. Andreades, *Greek Public Finance,* I, 328, 335.
45. Andreades, *Greek Public Finance,* I, 337–338.
46. *Against Leptines* 15–16.
47. Lysias *On the Confiscation of the Property of the Brother of Nicias,* 14–15; see also Introduction to this speech in Loeb Classical Library edition, 398–399.
48. *Oxford Classical Dictionary,* s.v. "Sykophantai," 1026, "Dike (2)," 344.
49. Lysias *Against the Corn Dealers* and *On the Refusal of a Pension to the Invalid* provides case materials on both policies.
50. Demosthenes *Against Phormio* 37; further details and what purports to be the text of the law in *Against Lacritus* 50–51.
51. Aristotle *Athenian Constitution* 51.3.
52. Lysias *Against the Corn Dealers* 16.
53. Lysias *On the Refusal of a Pension to the Invalid* is a defense against such a challenge. The information cited above comes from the Introduction to this piece in Loeb Classical Library edition, 516.
54. Except where otherwise noted I have put together the following account from the *Oxford Classical Dictionary,* s.v. "Ekklesia," "Boule," "Prytaneis," "Proedroi." These articles give considerable additional information not included in my summary.
55. Aristotle *Athenian Constitution* 43.6.
56. Demosthenes *Against Timocrates* 18. For the Heroes see Aristotle *Athenian Constitution* 53.4.
57. Demosthenes *De Falsa Legatione* 70 with explanatory note in Loeb Classical Library edition.
58. Aristotle *Athenian Constitution* 16.10.
59. Andocides *On the Mysteries* 95–96.
60. Demosthenes *On the Chersonese* 64.
61. Demosthenes *Third Olynthiac* 32.
62. Demosthenes *For the Liberty of the Rhodians* 1.

63. Demosthenes *Funeral Speech* 26.
64. Demosthenes *Exordia* 36.
65. *Exordia* 29. See also 34.
66. Richard Hofstadter, *The Idea of a Party System*.
67. J. Walter Jones, *The Law and Legal Theory of the Greeks*, 77–80, esp. 78.
68. Frederick C. Teiwes, *Politics and Purges in China*.
69. Sophocles *Antigone* 353.
70. Xenophon *Memorabilia* 4.4.13.
71. Demosthenes *Against Aristogeiton* 1.16.
72. Demosthenes *Against Timocrates* 192.
73. Aristotle *Politics* 4.4.2–7. The sentence quoted occurs in the final section.
74. Hyperides *Funeral Speech* 25.
75. Demosthenes *For the Liberty of the Rhodians* 29.
76. J. W. Jones, *Law and Legal Theory*, 90–92.
77. Xenophon *Memorabilia* 1.2.62 and *Socrates' Defence to the Jury* 25–26.
78. Aeschines *Against Ctesiphon* 252. There is no explanation of the different treatment in these two cases.
79. Demosthenes *Against Leptines* 100, 135.
80. Andocides *On the Mysteries* 20.
81. Andocides *On the Mysteries* 33.
82. Dinarchus *Against Demosthenes* 23.
83. Aristotle *Athenian Constitution* 40.2–3.
84. Antiphon *Third Tetralogy* 1.3–6; Lysias *Against Andocides* 53.
85. Antiphon *First Tetralogy* 1.10.
86. Antiphon *On the Murder of Herodes* 11.
87. Antiphon *First Tetralogy* 3.11.
88. Antiphon *On the Murder of Herodes* 48.
89. Douglas M. MacDowell, *The Law in Classical Athens*, 111.
90. MacDowell, *Law in Classical Athens*, 116–117, also 27–28.
91. MacDowell, *Law in Classical Athens*, 119–120.
92. Hyperides *In Defence of Lycophron* 6–7.
93. Demosthenes *Against Aristocrates* 53, 55.
94. Demosthenes *Against Aristocrates* 61.
95. Lysias *On the Murder of Eratosthenes* 32–34.
96. Lysias *On the Murder of Eratosthenes* 47.
97. MacDowell, *Law in Classical Athens*, 61 ff.
98. Aristotle *Athenian Constitution* 9.
99. MacDowell, *Law in Classical Athens*, 54–57, 61–62; on *hybris*, 129.
100. Aristotle *Athenian Constitution* 52.1.
101. MacDowell, *Law in Classical Athens*, 83; *Oxford Classical Dictionary*, s.v. "Archers."
102. Isocrates *Antidosis* 22.
103. Demosthenes *Against Aristocrates* 25.
104. Demosthenes *Against Leptines* 147.
105. Demosthenes *Against Eubulides* 4.
106. Demosthenes *Against Aristocrates* 28, 31–33.
107. Hyperides *In Defence of Euxenippus* 11.
108. Aristotle *Athenian Constitution* 4.4.

109. Aristotle *Athenian Constitution* 45.2.
110. Demosthenes *Against Timocrates* 197.
111. Demosthenes *Against Androtion* 52.
112. Demosthenes *Against Androtion* 55; cf. Aristotle *Politics* 5.8.13 for the indignity of corporal punishment.
113. Xenophon *Hellenica* 1.7.20.
114. Lycurgus *Against Leocrates* 126.
115. Lycurgus *Against Leocrates* 135.
116. J. W. Jones, *Law and Legal Theory,* 141; Aristotle *Athenian Constitution* 18.4.
117. Demosthenes *Against Onetor* 1.37.
118. MacDowell, *Law in Classical Athens,* 245–246.
119. Lysias *On the Property of Aristophanes* 57.
120. Lysias *Before the Areopagus: Defence in the Matter of the Olive Stump* 1.
121. Lysias *Olive Stump* 31, 41.
122. Cf. Hyperides *In Defence of Lycophron* 14.
123. Aristotle *Athenian Constitution* 8.5; Plutarch *Solon* 20.1.
124. Lysias *Against Philon* 27 and introductory comments in Loeb Classical Library edition 634–635.
125. Hyperides *In Defence of Euxenippus* 21.
126. For an excellent case study, see Howard J. Wechsler, *Mirror to the Son of Heaven.*
127. Plato *Apology* 20E–22C, 23B, 28E, 30E, 31C–E, 33C, 40B–C, 41D. This is not a complete list of such passages.
128. *Oxford Classical Dictionary,* s.v. "Socrates."
129. *Apology* 23B.
130. *Apology* 37E–38A.
131. *Apology* 30E and 38A. A more exact rendering of the latter passage would be "no life for a man."
132. *Apology* 28A.
133. Plato *Apology* 31D–32A.
134. Cf. J. Bury and Russel Meiggs, *A History of Greece,* 315.
135. *Apology* 32B–C; Xenophon *Memorabilia* 4.4.2.
136. *Apology* 32C–D.
137. *Oxford Classical Dictionary,* s.v. "Protagoras"; for an older study, see Eudore Derenne, *Les Procès d'Impiété intentés aux philosophes à Athenes au Vme et au IVme siècles avant J.-C.*
138. Plato *Republic* 8.543A–C.
139. Plato *Republic* 8.540A–B.
140. Plato *Republic* 10.620C.
141. Plato *Laws* 5.738D–E.
142. Plato *Laws* 5.739B–E.
143. *Politics* 7.3.5.
144. Xenophon *Oeconomicus* 6.9–10.
145. Xenophon *Oeconomicus* 11.9, 13.
146. Xenophon *Oeconomicus* 11.14–15.
147. Xenophon *Memorabilia* 2.1.8–20.

148. Xenophon *Memorabilia* 3;7.1–7.
149. For a characteristic example see *I. Olynthiac* 15: ". . . we consult our own pleasure in everything."
150. This appears in *Funeral Speech* 2, an occasion on which such sentiments were expected.
151. *Panegyricus* 103–104.
152. *Panegyricus* 171. The Loeb Classical Library text carries a footnote listing several further references to such aloofness.
153. Isocrates *Antidosis* 104–106.
154. Isocrates *Antidosis* 144–145.
155. Isocrates *Antidosis* 201.
156. *Oxford Classical Dictionary,* s.v. "Isocrates."
157. Isocrates *Antidosis* 145.
158. Isocrates *Antidosis* 159–160.
159. Isocrates *Antidosis* 155–156.
160. Introduction to Loeb Classical Library, *Isocrates,* Vol. I, xxviii, note b, citing Blass, *Die Attische Beredsamkeit,* II, 22.
161. Isocrates *Antidosis* 39–41, 152.
162. Isocrates *To Demonicus* 32.
163. Isocrates *Areopagiticus* 49.
164. Isocrates *To Demonicus* 15.
165. Isocrates *To Demonicus* 22–26.
166. Isocrates *To Demonicus* 34.
167. J. W. Jones, *Law and Legal Theory,* 9.
168. Aristotle *Politics* 3.5.13–15.
169. Aristotle *Politics* 7.14.6, 10, 12.
170. Plato *The Laws* 6.773B, 774.
171. Plato *The Laws* 6.783D–E.
172. Plato *The Laws* 6.784C.
173. On this point see K. J. Dover, *Greek Homosexuality,* 45.
174. Xenophon *Memorabilia* 2.2.4.
175. See Isaeus *On the Estate of Menecles* 3–5 and *On the Estate of Apollodorus* 12, 21.
176. Demosthenes *Against Macartatus* 75.
177. Isaeus *On the Estate of Apollodorus* 30–32.
178. For adultery as a public issue see Hyperides *In Defence of Lycophron* 1.12.13 [cols. 10–13]; Lysias *On the Murder of Eratosthenes* 25–26.
179. *Politics* 4.12.3, 9; 6.5.13. No such term occurs in the *Athenian Constitution.*
180. *Politics* 4.13.9.
181. Aristotle *Politics* 5.9.6.
182. Xenophon *Oeconomicus* 3.15.
183. Xenophon *Oeconomicus* 3.12–4.1.
184. Xenophon *Oeconomicus* 7.3–23, 35–41.
185. Xenophon *Oeconomicus* 10.8.
186. Aristotle *Politics* 1.5.12; Aeschines *Against Timarchus* 6–7.
187. *Oxford Classical Dictionary,* s.v. "Education."
188. Aristotle *Athenian Constitution* 56.6.

189. Demosthenes *Against Timocrates* 103, 105–107. For functions of the *heliaia* see *Oxford Classical Dictionary*, 493.
190. Xenophon *Memorabilia* 2.2.13.
191. Isaeus *On the Estate of Ciron* 32.
192. Isaeus *On the Estate of Cleonymus* 39.
193. Plutarch *Solon* 22.4.
194. Demosthenes *Against Stephanus II* 20.
195. Demosthenes *Against Stephanus II* 18.
196. See MacDowell, *Law in Classical Athens*, 95–98; also Isaeus *On the Estate of Pyrrhus* 64.
197. Plutarch *Solon* 21.2.
198. Demosthenes *Against Stephanus II* 14.
199. Isaeus *On the Estate of Dicaeogenes* 34–35.
200. Demosthenes *Against Macartatus* 51.
201. Isaeus *On the Estate of Philoctemon* 3.
202. Lysias *Against Diogeiton* 1–2.
203. Lysias *Against Alcibiades* 1.24, 30.
204. Lysias *On the Confiscation of the Property of the Brother of Nicias* 7–11.
205. Demosthenes *Against Eubulides* 27.
206. Xenophon *Hellenica* 1.7.21.
207. Xenophon *Memorabilia* 1.2.51–55, 59.
208. Lysias *Against Simon* 6–7, 23. Demosthenes *Against Pantaetus* 45–49 also mentions an instance of intrusion into the women's apartments.
209. Isaeus *On the Estate of Pyrrhus* 14.
210. Demosthenes *Against Aristogeiton I* 88–90.
211. Isaeus *On the Estate of Pyrrhus* 27.
212. Demosthenes *Against Neaera* 22.
213. Lysias *Olive Stump* 16–18.
214. Henderson, *Maculate Muse*, 4, citing Pindar's *Ninth Pythian* 12.
215. Aristotle *Politics* 7.14.
216. Plutarch *Solon* 20.3–4.
217. Xenophon *Memorabilia* 4.4.19–24, esp. 20.
218. Plutarch *Solon* 23.1.
219. Aeschines *Against Timarchus* 119.
220. Demosthenes *Against Neaera* 67.
221. Isaeus *On the Estate of Pyrrhus* 39.
222. Herodotus *History* 3.101.
223. Xenophon *Anabasis* 5.4.33–34. For some additional evidence see Dover, *Greek Popular Morality in the Time of Plato and Aristotle*, 206.
224. Aeschines *Against Timarchus* 90.
225. Demosthenes *Against Neaera* 33.
226. Xenophon *Symposium* 9.3–7.
227. Xenophon *Symposium* 8.21–22.
228. Xenophon *Symposium* 8.34.
229. Plato *Symposium* 183.
230. Plato *Symposium* 182D.
231. Dover, *Greek Homosexuality*, 147, 151.
232. Henderson, *Maculate Muse*, 208–209.

233. For a convenient summary of legislation concerning sexual offenses see MacDowell, *Law in Classical Athens,* 124–126.
234. Aeschines *Against Timarchus* 51–52.
235. Aeschines *Against Timarchus* 137.
236. Aeschines *Against Timarchus* 13–17.
237. Aeschines *Against Timarchus* 119.
238. Aeschines *Against Timarchus* 107–108.
239. Aeschines *Against Timarchus* 138–139.
240. Lysias *Against Simon* 3.
241. Xenophon *Symposium* 2.18.
242. Theophrastus *Characters* 11.1–3.
243. Aristotle *Athenian Constitution* 28.3.
244. Aeschines *Against Timarchus* 22–27, 33–35.
245. Xenophon *Memorabilia* 1.4.6.
246. *The Peace* 99–100. On the terms for privies see Henderson, *Maculate Muse,* 191–192.
247. Henderson, *Maculate Muse,* 35.
248. Alan F. Westin, "Privacy in Western History: From the Age of Pericles to the American Republic," 22–23. See also Oscar Jacob, *Les Esclaves Publics à Athènes,* esp. 13–19.
249. A. W. Lawrence, *Greek Architecture,* 244, 248.
250. Xenophon *Oeconomicus* 9.5.
251. Xenophon *Memorabilia* 3.11.9.
252. Lysias *On a Wound by Premeditation* 16.
253. Demosthenes *Against Neaera* 45–46.
254. Demosthenes *Against Neaera* 41.
255. Demosthenes *Against Neaera* 107–114, esp. 114.
256. Aeschines *Against Timarchus* 42.
257. Xenophon *Memorabilia* 4.5.2–8.
258. Demosthenes *Against Aristogeiton* 1.30.
259. Demosthenes *Against Conon* 22; see also 3–4, 9, 14, 43.
260. Demosthenes *On the Chersonese* 51.
261. *Oxford Classical Dictionary,* s.v. "Prometheus."
262. For an interesting review of this discussion see E. R. Dodds, "The *Prometheus Vinctus* and the Progress of Scholarship," in *The Ancient Concept of Progress,* chap. II.
263. Aristotle *Politics* 1.1.12.
264. Aristotle *Eudemian Ethics* 1.5.12.
265. Aristotle *Eudemian Ethics* 2.2.4–6.
266. George Boas, *Rationalism in Greek Philosophy,* 220.
267. See *Eudemian Ethics* 2.7–9, especially the definition of voluntary action at 2.9.3.; also for a smoother exposition, *Nichomachean Ethics* 3.1–4.
268. Aeschines *Against Ctesiphon* 78.
269. Aeschines *Against Timarchus* 30.
270. Aeschines *Against Timarchus* 28–29.
271. Aeschines *Against Timarchus* 153.
272. Demosthenes *De Corona* 8.
273. Demosthenes *De Corona* 95.
274. *Oxford Classical Dictionary,* s.v. "Dokimasia" and "Atimia."

275. *Oxford Classical Dictionary*, s.v. "Euthyna"; Aristotle *Athenian Constitution* 48.
276. Demosthenes *Second Olynthiac* 19.
277. Aristotle *Politics* 5.7.8.
278. Aristotle *Politics* 5.7.22.
279. See Plutarch *Aristides* 2.4, where the author contrasts him with Themistocles.
280. Demosthenes *Third Olynthiac* 21–26.
281. Aristotle *Nicomachean Ethics* 8.1.3–5; 4.1.
282. For the classification of the forms of friendship see *Nicomachean Ethics* 8.1–3; its perfect form 8.3.6; its exclusive nature, 8.6.2–3. A similar discussion occurs in *Eudemian Ethics* 7.2.9–52.
283. *Eudemian Ethics* 7.7.1–8; 7.10.2–14, 24–30.
284. Xenophon *Oeconomicus* 1.14.
285. Xenophon *Memorabilia* 2.10.4. See also 2.5; 6.1–8.
286. Xenophon *Memorabilia* 2.6.1–16, esp. 12.
287. Xenophon *Memorabilia* 2.4.3.
288. On justice in friendship see *Nicomachean Ethics* 8.9.1–3; 8.12.8.
289. *Nicomachean Ethics* 8.1.4.
290. *Eudemian Ethics* 7.1.4–6.
291. Plato *Laws* 8.837A.
292. Plato *Laws* 5.743C.
293. Plato *Laws* 6.759B.
294. Plato *Laws* 6.776A.
295. Aristotle *Nicomachean Ethics* 9.5.3.
296. Theophrastus *Characters* 7.
297. Xenophon *Symposium* 1.1–8.
298. Plato *Symposium* 172–175.
299. For the latter see Demosthenes *Against Neaera*.
300. Aristophanes *Lysistrata* 15–20.
301. Plato *Laws* 5.729E.

Chapter 3: PRIVACY, PROPHECY, AND POLITICS IN THE OLD TESTAMENT

1. Roland de Vaux, *Histoire ancienne d'Israël*, I, 365–368.
2. For this sketch I have drawn heavily on a recent synthesis by a careful scholar, William H. McNeill, *A World History* (3rd ed., 1979), 69–72. McNeill risks many more dates than the longer account in H. H. Ben-Sasson, editor, *A History of the Jewish People*, 3–182 and Vaux, *Histoire ancienne*, I and II, which I have also consulted.
3. Vaux, *Histoire ancienne*, I, 256, 260–261.
4. Deut. 17:2–6.
5. Exod. 22:20.
6. Deut. 4:24.
7. Deut. 7:2–5.

8. Deut. 20:17.
9. Deut. 28:64.
10. Num. 21:2–3.
11. Exod. 32 entire; passage quoted 32:27–29.
12. Gen. 22.
13. Jer. 48:10.
14. Jer. 17:9–10.
15. Isa. 47:10–11.
16. Isa. 29:15.
17. Deut. 13:12–16.
18. Deut. 13:6–9.
19. Eccles. 8:14 and 9:9–10.
20. Eccles. 12:14.
21. Deut. 31:14–22.
22. Ezek. 20:25–26.
23. Deut. 28:15–68; quotation from verse 63.
24. Exod. 15:22–27; 16 entire.
25. 2 Chron. 6:28.
26. All these themes come together in Ps. 109.
27. Gen. 1:28–29; 2:15.
28. Gen. 9:8–16.
29. Gen. 17:9–15; see also 15:17–21 for the promise of territory.
30. Exod. 19:1–6.
31. Judg. 1:16–36; 2:2–4, 11–15.
32. Vaux, *Histoire ancienne,* I, 224, 227–228.
33. Vaux, *Les Institutions de l'Ancien Testament,* I, 23.
34. Vaux, *Institutions,* I, 39.
35. Vaux, *Institutions,* I, 17.
36. Vaux, *Institutions,* I, 40–41.
37. Exod. 13:13–23.
38. Josh. 1:12–18.
39. Deut. 19:15–21.
40. Judg. 2:16.
41. Judg. 21:25.
42. 1 Sam. 8.
43. 1 Sam. 10:25.
44. 2 Sam. 16:22. The tale of Bathsheba, Uriah the Hittite, and Nathan is in 2 Sam. 11–12; for Absalom see 2 Sam. 13–18.
45. 1 Kings 21.
46. 1 Kings 22:37–40.
47. For a detailed description see Vaux, *Institutions,* I, 103–250; II, 9–88.
48. Vaux, *Institutions,* I, 220.
49. Vaux, *Institutions,* I, 231.
50. Vaux, *Institutions,* I, 235–236.
51. Vaux, *Institutions,* I, 238–239.
52. Vaux, *Institutions,* I, 247–250.
53. Deut. 21:18–21.
54. Ben-Sasson, *History,* 145.
55. Isa. 11:11.

56. Isa. 24:1–3.
57. Isa. 11:6. See also 19:24; 30:23.
58. Isa. 1:11, 17; 2:8.
59. Isa. 13:11.
60. Isa. 14:20–21.
61. Isa. 58:6.
62. Isa. 61:8.
63. Isa. 5:11.
64. Isa. 5:21–23.
65. Isa. 3:16–17.
66. For the political context of his preaching see Ben-Sasson, *History,* 152–157.
67. Jer. 38:4, 6–13.
68. Jer. 15:17.
69. Jer. 20:1–3, 7.
70. Jer. 26: 8–19.
71. Jer. 32:3.
72. Jer. 36:1–26.
73. Jer. 37:15.
74. Jer. 40:4–6.
75. Jer. 6:20.
76. Jer. 6:11.
77. Jer. 12:1–3.
78. Jer. 5:26–28.
79. Jer. 8:10.
80. Jer. 17:11.
81. Jer. 22:13–14.
82. Jer. 5:3–5.
83. Jer. 26:7–11.
84. Jer. 9:4–5.
85. Jer. 2:13, 17; 3:13.
86. Jer. 7:18; see also 7:31 for allegations of human sacrifice.
87. Jer. 31: esp. 10–14, 31–34.
88. For a good historical treatment of military institutions see Vaux, *Institutions,* II, 9–30.
89. Deut. 5:6–21.
90. Deut. 12:8.
91. Lev. 19:23, 27. For the Ten Commandments see 19:2, 3, 4, 5, 12 and others.
92. Lev. 19:9, 11, 12, 13, 14.
93. Lev. 19:15.
94. Ezek. 18:5–9.
95. Vaux, *Institutions,* I, 221–250.
96. Lev. 19:11, 12.
97. Lev. 19:13–14.
98. Lev. 19:17.
99. Lev. 19:18.
100. Lev. 19:32–33.
101. Lev. 19:35–36.

102. Lev. 19:9.
103. Lev. 19:13, 14, 17.
104. Isa. 58:7.
105. Exod. 19:23–24.
106. Lev. 16:2. On the ark and tabernacle see Exod. 25 and 26.
107. Lev. 15:31.
108. Vaux, *Institutions,* I, 38–39.
109. Num. 30.
110. Vaux, *Institutions,* I, 40–41.
111. Vaux, *Institutions,* I, 42–43.
112. Vaux, *Institutions,* I, 45–47.
113. Vaux, *Institutions,* I, 48–49.
114. Vaux, *Institutions,* I, 51.
115. Vaux, *Institutions,* I, 53–54.
116. Deut. 24:5.
117. Vaux, *Institutions,* I, 62–63.
118. Num. 5:11–29.
119. His life may be found in 1 Sam. 17:12 through 1 Kings 2:12 and 1 Chron. 11–29.
120. Lev. 25:25–32; Vaux, *Institutions,* I, 254.
121. Exod. 20:17.
122. Deut. 23:24–25.
123. Exod. 22:5.
124. 1 Sam. 25.
125. 2 Sam. 4.
126. Exod. 12:14–20.
127. Exod. 12:1–13.
128. Exod. 12:43–49.
129. Num. 9:14.
130. Exod. 23:9.
131. Deut. 14:2.
132. See the list in Lev. 11, which is fuller than Deut. 14:3–21.
133. Douglas, *Purity and Danger,* chap. 3.
134. Deut. 23:12.
135. 1 Kings 11:3.
136. Deut. 22:13–21.
137. The list may be found in Lev. 20:10–16.
138. 2 Sam. 13:11–14.
139. Gen. 19:30–38.
140. Lev. 19:19.
141. Douglas, *Purity and Danger,* 53.
142. Lev. 18:19–25.
143. There is a long list in Lev. 15. See also Lev. 12 on childbirth and menstruation; Deut. 23:10 on nocturnal emissions.
144. Gen. 38:7–10.
145. Deut. 25:5–10.
146. Exod. 22:16; Deut. 22:28–29.
147. Deut. 22:25–27.
148. Exod. 21:7–10.

149. Lev. 19:20–22.
150. Lev. 19:29.
151. Lev. 21:9.
152. Vaux, *Institutions*, II, 248, refers to the demolition of the house of sacred prostitutes in the Temple of Yahweh.
153. Gen. 39.
154. Judg. 16.
155. Song of Sol. 3.
156. Song of Sol. 8:1–4; 6–7.
157. Gen. 2:25.
158. Gen. 3:7–8.
159. Gen. 3:21.
160. Gen. 4:8–10.
161. Lev. 18:6–18; 20:17–22.
162. Lev. 18:19–20; 20:18. The latter citation refers only to menstruation.
163. Deut. 22:5.
164. Ezek. 21:24–26.
165. Isa. 3:16–17.
166. Jer. 13:26.
167. Prov. 14:10.
168. Ps. 119:113–120.
169. Prov. 25:17.
170. Jer. 9:4.
171. Prov. 27:10.

Chapter 4: ANCIENT CHINESE CONCEPTIONS OF PUBLIC AND PRIVATE

1. *Mencius*, trans. D. C. Lau, 10.
2. The text I have used is *Hsün Tzu: Basic Writings*, trans. Burton Watson, with a biographical sketch on pp. 1–3.
3. The text used is *Basic Writings of Mo Tzu*, trans. Burton Watson.
4. Burton Watson, *Early Chinese Literature*, 153–154. This book provides an excellent introduction to the documentary sources for ancient Chinese history.
5. See *Lao Tzu: Tao Te Ching*, trans. D. C. Lau, 11–12 and Appendices I and II.
6. The text used is *The Complete Works of Chuang Tzu*, trans. Burton Watson.
7. See *Han Fei Tzu: Basic Writings*, trans. Burton Watson.
8. J.J.L. Duyvendak, *The Book of Lord Shang: A Classic of the Chinese School of Law*.
9. *Han Fei Tzu*, "The Five Vermin," section 49, p. 106. In these and certain other texts I have used a bastard form of citation giving the title of the chapter and the number of the section, as used in the original Chinese, followed by the page number in the Burton Watson translation. This appears to be the only way that would permit reference to other transla-

tions and the original. With other texts it is possible to use the classical form of citation without confusing English readers.

10. *Han Fei Tzu,* "The Five Vermin," section 49, p. 113.
11. *Han Fei Tzu,* "On Having Standards," section 6, p. 22.
12. *Han Fei Tzu,* "The Eight Villainies," section 9, p. 47.
13. *Han Fei Tzu,* "The Five Vermin," section 49, p. 105.
14. *Mencius,* VII B, 7.
15. *Han Fei Tzu,* "The Five Vermin," section 49, p. 111.
16. *Han Fei Tzu,* "Precautions Within the Palace," section 17, p. 87.
17. *Han Fei Tzu,* "Wielding Power," section 8, pp. 40–41; "Mr. Ho," section 13, p. 81; "The Five Vermin," section 49, pp. 104–105, 115–116.
18. *Han Fei Tzu,* "Mr. Ho," section 13, p. 81.
19. Cf. the comments by Watson, *Han Fei Tzu,* 14.
20. *Analects* XIII, 14, 19.
21. *Analects* I, 2.
22. *Analects* XIII, 18.
23. *Analects* II, 21.
24. *Analects* XIII, 14.
25. *Analects* II, 9; cf. V, 15 where the word "public" does not occur in describing the official duties of a gentleman.
26. *Analects* X, 5.
27. *Analects* XII, 14.
28. *Analects* XVII, 12.
29. *Analects* XIX, 23.
30. *Hsün Tzu,* "Improving Yourself," section 2, p. 32.
31. *Hsün Tzu,* "The Regulations of a King," section 9, pp. 42, 49.
32. *Hsün Tzu,* "A Discussion of Heaven," section 17, pp. 84–85.
33. *Hsün Tzu,* "Man's Nature is Evil," section 23, p. 166.
34. Watson, Introduction, *Chuang Tzu,* 13–14.
35. *Lao Tzu,* Book One, VII.
36. See *Chuang Tzu,* chap. 6, "The Great and Venerable Teacher," p. 70 and *Lao Tzu,* Book One, III, XIX, XXIX, XXXVI, XXXVII; Book Two, LXXX, XLIII, XLVIII, LXXVIII.
37. On inaction see *Lao Tzu,* Book One, XXXVII and Book Two, XLIII, LXIII, LXIV. On uselessness see *Chuang Tzu,* chap. 1, "Free and Easy Wandering," pp. 33–34; chap. 4, "In the World of Men," p. 64.
38. Cf. *Mencius,* VII A, 15.
39. *Analects* I, 5.
40. *Analects* XI, 6.
41. *Analects* XII, 9; XX, 2.
42. *Mencius,* I A, 2; I B, 5 expresses a similar sentiment.
43. *Mencius,* II A, 5.
44. *Mencius,* III A, 3.
45. *Mencius,* III B, 8.
46. *Mencius,* I A, 3.
47. *Mencius,* I A, 3; see also I A, 4.
48. *Mencius,* I B, 1–2.
49. *Mencius,* I B, 6; I B, 12; II B, 4.

50. *Mencius*, IV A, 1.
51. *Mencius*, VII A, 23; see also 22.
52. *Mencius*, VI B, 7.
53. *Mencius*, I B, 7.
54. *Hsün Tzu*, "The Regulations of a King," section 9, pp. 36, 37.
55. *Hsün Tzu*, "Debating Military Affairs," section 15, p. 74.
56. *Hsün Tzu*, "The Regulations of a King," section 9, pp. 45–46.
57. *Lao Tzu*, Book Two, LVII.
58. *Lao Tzu*, Book One, XVII.
59. *Lao Tzu*, Book One, XXIX; Book Two, LVIII.
60. *Han Fei Tzu*, "Wielding Power," section 8, p. 39.
61. *Han Fei Tzu*, "The Two Handles," section 7, p. 31; "The Eight Villanies," section 9, pp. 46–47.
62. *Han Fei Tzu*, "Precautions Within the Palace," section 17, p. 87; "The Two Handles," section 7, p. 31.
63. *Han Fei Tzu*, "The Five Vermin," section 49, p. 113.
64. *Han Fei Tzu*, "Mr. Ho," section 13, p. 82.
65. *Han Fei Tzu*, "The Five Vermin," section 49, p. 111.
66. *Han Fei Tzu*, "Facing South," section 18, pp. 93–94. But note "Precautions Within the Palace," section 17, p. 88, where he draws on high antiquity for authority.
67. *Han Fei Tzu*, "The Difficulties of Persuasion," section 12, p. 77; see also "The Ten Faults," section 10, pp. 50, 68.
68. *Han Fei Tzu*, "Eminence in Learning," section 50, pp. 125, 128.
69. *Han Fei Tzu*, "Wielding Power," section 8, p. 40.
70. *Han Fei Tzu*, "Eminence in Learning," section 50, pp. 121–122.
71. Waley, *Book of Songs*, no. 288 [Mao text 224]. The Mao text is named after an early Chinese editor and is the one usually cited. Waley's numbering of the poems differs because he grouped them by topic. According to Watson, *Early Chinese Literature*, these songs were compiled probably around 600 B.C. (p. 202).
72. *Analects* XI, 23.
73. *Mencius*, I A, 3; the same point occurs in the next section I A, 4.
74. *Mencius*, I A, 6.
75. *Mencius*, I A, 7.
76. *Mencius*, II B, 13.
77. *Mencius*, IV A, 20.
78. *Mencius*, IV B, 3.
79. *Mencius*, IV B, 4.
80. *Mencius*, V A, 9.
81. *Mencius*, VI B, 9.
82. *Mencius*, VI B, 14.
83. *Chuang Tzu*, chap. 6, "The Great and Venerable Teacher," p. 79.
84. *Chang Tzu*, chap. 7, "Fit for Emperors and Kings," pp. 92–94.
85. *Mo Tzu*, "Identifying With One's Superior," Part I, section 11, p. 35.
86. *Mo Tzu*, "Against Confucians," Part I, section 39, p. 129.
87. *Han Fei Tzu*, "The Ten Faults," section 10, p. 50.
88. *Han Fei Tzu*, "The Ten Faults," section 10, p. 68.

89. Watson, *Early Chinese Literature,* 91–93; quotation from p. 93. A cangue is a heavy, very large square yoke worn around a prisoner's neck, preventing him from reaching his mouth with food or drink.
90. *Analects* VIII, 9.
91. Waley, "Introduction," *Analects,* 31.
92. See especially *Mencius,* III A, 4; III B, 10.
93. *Analects* VI, 27.
94. *Analects* IV, 11. See XIII, 23, 26 for further contrasts.
95. *Analects* XVI, 9.
96. *Analects* VIII, 10.
97. *Analects* XVII, 25.
98. *Analects* IX, 7.
99. *Analects* VII, 7, 8.
100. *Mencius,* VII B, 14.
101. *Mencius,* V A, 5.
102. *Mencius,* V A, 6.
103. *Mencius,* IV A, 9.
104. *Mencius,* V B, 5.
105. *Mencius,* III B, 9.
106. *Tso chuan,* Duke Hsiang 31 [542 B.C.], as translated in Watson, *Early Chinese Literature,* 63.
107. *Mencius,* VII A, 5.
108. *Mencius,* III A, 4.
109. *Mencius,* IV B, 19.
110. *Mencius,* III A, 3.
111. *Hsün Tzu,* "A Discussion of Rites," section 19, p. 92.
112. *Hsün Tzu,* "The Regulations of a King," section 9, p. 33.
113. *Hsün Tzu,* "Dispelling Obsession," section 21, p. 122.
114. Watson, *Early Chinese Literature,* 159.
115. *Lao Tzu,* Book Two, XLIX, 110.
116. *Lao Tzu,* Book Two, XLIX, 112.
117. *Lao Tzu,* Book One, XX, 47.
118. *Lao Tzu,* Book Two, LXV, 157.
119. *Lao Tzu,* Book Two, LXV, 157.
120. See, e.g., *Lao Tzu,* Book Two, LXXVIII, 187.
121. *Lao Tzu,* Book Two, LXXII, 175.
122. *Lao Tzu,* Book Two, LXXV, 181–181a.
123. E.g., Waley, *Book of Songs,* no. 276 [Mao text 113].
124. Watson, *Chuang Tzu,* 1.
125. Watson, *Early Chinese Literature,* 160.
126. See Watson, *Chuang Tzu,* 13–14 for the translator's comments on the state of the text.
127. *Chuang Tzu,* chap. 2, "Discussion on Making All Things Equal," pp. 38–39.
128. *Chuang Tzu,* chap. 4, "In the World of Men," pp. 62–63.
129. *Chuang Tzu,* chap. 3, "The Secret of Caring for Life," p. 50.
130. *Chuang Tzu,* chap. 2, "Discussion on Making All Things Equal," p. 46.
131. *Mo Tzu,* "Against Music," Part I, section 32, p. 111.
132. *Mo Tzu,* "Against Music," Part I, section 32, pp. 110–111.

133. *Mo Tzu,* "Honoring the Worthy," Part I, section 8, pp. 20–21.
134. *Mo Tzu,* "Honoring the Worthy," Part II, section 9, p. 30.
135. *Mo Tzu,* "The Will of Heaven," Part II, section 27, pp. 85, 88.
136. *Mo Tzu,* "Universal Love," Part III, section 16, pp. 39–40, 44.
137. *Mo Tzu,* "Universal Love," Part III, section 16, pp. 44, 49.
138. *Mo Tzu,* "Against Fatalism," Part I, section 35, pp. 117, 123.
139. *Mo Tzu,* "Explaining Ghosts," Part III, section 31, pp. 104–105.
140. *Mo Tzu,* "Honoring the Worthy," Part I, section 8, pp. 19–20.
141. *Mo Tzu,* "Honoring the Worthy," Part II, section 9, p. 22.
142. *Mo Tzu,* "The Will of Heaven," Part I, section 26, p. 79.
143. *Mo Tzu,* "The Will of Heaven," Part I, section 26, p. 84.
144. *Han Fei Tzu,* "The Eight Villainies," section 9, p. 44.
145. *Han Fei Tzu,* "The Eight Villainies," section 9, p. 45.
146. Jacques Gernet, *La Chine ancienne,* 81.
147. L. S. Vasil'ev, *Agrarnye Otnosheniya i Obshchina v Drevnem Kitaye,* 210–211. There is a brief mention of village elders in Confucius, *Analects* X, 10.
148. Watson, *Early Chinese Literature,* 202, 229.
149. Waley, *Book of Songs,* no. 39 [Mao text 87].
150. Waley, *Book of Songs,* no. 40 [Mao text 30].
151. Waley, *Book of Songs,* no. 46 [Mao text 91].
152. Waley, *Book of Songs,* explanatory n. pp. 34–35 and no. 24 [Mao text 76]. Waley points out the similarity to European courtship customs.
153. *Mencius,* III B, 3.
154. Waley, *Book of Songs,* note on marriage, p. 66.
155. *Analects* I, 13.
156. *Mencius,* V B, 5.
157. *Analects* V, 1.
158. Robert van Gulik, *La Vie sexuelle dans la Chine Ancienne,* trans. from English by Louis Evrard, 42. This edition is preferable to the original English version which contains several pages in Latin.
159. Van Gulik, *Vie sexuelle,* 54–56.
160. Van Gulik, *Vie sexuelle,* 74.
161. Van Gulik, *Vie sexuelle,* 75–76.
162. Van Gulik, *Vie sexuelle,* 77. The author uses the term "sapphic" which strictly speaking is more accurate than the now widely used "Lesbian."
163. Van Gulik, *Vie sexuelle,* 77–78.
164. Van Gulik, *Vie sexuelle,* 78–79.
165. Van Gulik, *Vie sexuelle,* 80.
166. *Analects* IX, 17.
167. *Hsün Tzu,* "A Discussion of Music," section 20, esp. p. 120.
168. *Mo Tzu,* "Against Fatalism," Part I, section 35, p. 121.
169. *Han Fei Tzu,* "The Eight Villainies," section 9, p. 43; "The Difficulties of Persuasion," section 12, p. 78.
170. *Hsün Tzu,* "Man's Nature is Evil," section 23, p. 168.
171. *Han Fei Tzu, loc. cit.*
172. Watson, *Early Chinese Literature,* 85–86.
173. *Mencius,* IV B, 33.
174. For an example see *Han Fei Tzu,* "The Ten Faults," section 10, p. 71.

175. *Han Fei Tzu,* "Wielding Power," section 8, p. 41.
176. *Analects* III, 13, n. 4.
177. *Mo Tzu,* "Explaining Ghosts," Part III, section 31, pp. 108–109.
178. *Analects* II, 5–8.
179. *Analects* IV, 18.
180. *Mencius,* IV A, 19; IV B, 13; V A, 1.
181. *Mencius,* IV A, 11.
182. *Mencius,* VII A, 15.
183. *Analects* IV, 19.
184. *Mencius,* II B, 2.
185. *Mencius,* IV B, 30.
186. *Mencius,* IV A, 18.
187. *Mencius,* IV B, 30.
188. *Analects* XIII, 18.
189. *Han Fei Tzu,* "The Five Vermin," section 49, pp. 105–106.
190. *Chinese Family and Society,* 13.
191. Lang, *Chinese Family,* 19–20.
192. Lang, *Chinese Family,* 20–21.
193. *Analects* VIII, 2.
194. Waley, *Book of Songs,* no. 268 [Mao text 223].
195. See D. C. Lau, *Mencius,* 217, 214, citing the *Lieh nü chuan,* a collection of tales about Mencius, dating from the first century B.C.
196. *Analects* X, 16.
197. Waley, *Book of Songs,* no. 271 [Mao text 256].
198. Waley, *Book of Songs,* no. 266 [Mao text 46].
199. *Mo Tzu,* "The Will of Heaven," section 26, p. 78.
200. *Analects* V, 23.
201. *Analects* III, 7. This emphasis contrasts sharply with the agonistic principle in ancient Greek culture.
202. *Mencius,* V B, 3.
203. *Mencius,* VII B, 31.
204. *Mencius,* VII B, 36.
205. *Analects* I, 4.
206. *Analects* XVII, 14.
207. *Analects* XVI, 4.
208. *Analects* V, 24.
209. Waley, *Book of Songs,* no. 267 [Mao text 220].
210. *Hsün Tzu,* "A Discussion of Music," section 20, pp. 118–120.
211. Waley, "Introduction," *Analects,* 67.
212. Waley, *Analects,* p. 129, n. 6.
213. *Analects* VI, 19.
214. *Analects* XVI, 6.
215. *Mencius,* III B, 7.
216. *Mencius,* III B, 1; V B, 7.
217. *Mencius,* V B, 6.
218. *Hsün Tzu,* "A Discussion of Rites," section 19, p. 90.
219. *Mencius,* VII A, 9.
220. *Mencius,* IV B, 3.

Chapter 5: SOME IMPLICATIONS AND INQUIRIES

1. Fritz Kern, *Gottesgnadentum und Widerstandsrecht im früheren Mittelalter,* 169–173, 285.
2. Kern, *Gottesgnadentum und Widerstandsrecht,* 218, 287, 220.
3. Kern, *Gottesgnadentum und Widerstandsrecht,* 232–234.
4. A convenient brief account is available in "Gregory VII," *Encyclopaedia of the Social Sciences,* Vol. 7 (New York, 1932), 167–168.
5. Kern, *Gottesgnadentum und Widerstandsrecht,* 183–184.
6. Kern, *Gottesgnadentum und Widerstandsrecht,* 190, 195.
7. See Kern, *Gottesgnadentum und Widerstandsrecht,* 290–295.
8. Otto Hintze, "Weltgeschichtliche Bedingungen der Repräsentativverfassung," reprinted in his *Staat und Verfassung,* 146–147.
9. Gianfranco Poggi, *The Development of the Modern State,* 20, 22.
10. Poggi, *Development of the Modern State,* 56.
11. Hintze, "Weltgeschichtliche Bedingungen," 174–175.
12. Henri Pirenne, *Economic and Social History of Medieval Europe,* 57; see also his *History of Europe,* I, 203–204.
13. Henry Charles Lea, *A History of Auricular Confession and Indulgences in the Latin Church,* 3 vols., presents copious evidence on this point; see I, 368–382. Steven E. Ozment, *The Reformation in the Cities,* chaps. 2–3, presents very similar evidence for a later period.
14. Franz Neumann, "Economics and Politics in the Twentieth Century" in *The Democratic and the Authoritarian State,* 260.
15. Adolf Levenstein, *Die Arbeiterfrage,* 176, 178; Ely Chinoy, *Automobile Workers and the American Dream,* 126.
16. Charles Hoffman, *The Chinese Worker,* 51.
17. Thomas G. Rawski, *Economic Growth and Employment in China,* 127, 131; also pp. 34–36.
18. E. B. Vermeer, "Income Differentials in Rural China," *China Quarterly* 32, 89.

BIBLIOGRAPHY

Selected general works (not cited)

Arendt, Hannah, "The Public and the Private Realm," *The Human Condition*. New York, 1958.

Brandeis, Louis and Warren, Samuel D., "The Right to Privacy," *Harvard Law Review* 4(1890): 193–220.

de Grazia, Sebastian, *Of Time, Work, and Leisure*. New York, 1962.

Habermas, Jürgen, *Strukturwandel der Öffentlichkeit: Untersuchungen zu einer Kategorie der bürgerlichen Gesellschaft*. Neuwied am Rhein and Berlin, 1962, 3rd edition, 1968.

Marchand, Donald A., *The Politics of Privacy, Computers, and Criminal Justice Records: Controlling the Social Costs of Technological Change*. Arlington, Va., 1980.

Murphy, Robert M., "Social Distance and the Veil," *American Anthropologist* 66 (1964): 1257–1274.

"Privacy," *International Encyclopedia of the Social Sciences* (New York, 1968), vol. 12, 480–487.

"Privacy as a Behavioral Phenomenon," Stephen T. Margulis, issue editor, *Journal of Social Issues* 33 (1977), no. 3: 1–212.

Schneider, Carl D., *Shame, Exposure, and Privacy*. Boston, 1977.

Schwartz, Barry, "The Social Psychology of Privacy," *American Journal of Sociology* 73 (1968), no. 6: 741–752.

Shils, Edward B., "Privacy: Its Constitution and Vicissitudes," *Law and Contemporary Problems* 31 (1966): 281–306.

Westin, Alan, *Privacy and Freedom*. New York, 1967.

Works cited

The list of works below has the sole purpose of indicating the sources of my information and some of the bases for my views. Except for Chapters 3 and 5 the lists present first the primary sources, followed by works of a more general sort.

CHAPTER 1. ANTHROPOLOGICAL PERSPECTIVES

A. Specific studies

Aberle, David F., "The Psychosocial Analysis of the Hopi Life History" in Robert Hunt, editor, *Personalities and Culture: Readings in Psychological Anthropology*. Garden City, 1967, 79–138.

Balikci, Asen, *The Netsilik Eskimo*. Garden City, 1970.

Barton, R. F., *The Kalingas: Their Institutions and Custom Law*. Chicago, 1949.

Beaglehole, Ernest and Beaglehole, Pearl, "Hopi of the Second Mesa," Memoirs of the American Anthropological Association, no. 44. Menasha, 1935.

Berndt, Ronald M., *Excess and Restraint: Social Control among a New Guinea Mountain People*. Chicago, 1962.

Briggs, Jean L., *Never in Anger: Portrait of an Eskimo Family*. Cambridge, Mass., 1970.

Chagnon, Napoleon A., *Yanomamö: The Fierce People*. New York, 1968.

Dennis, Wayne, *The Hopi Child*. New York, 1940; reprinted, New York, 1972.

Freeman, Derek, *Margaret Mead and Samoa: The Making and Unmaking of an Anthropological Myth*. Cambridge, Mass., 1983.

Goldfrank, Esther, "Socialization, Personality, and the Structure of Pueblo Society," *American Anthropologist* 47 (1945): 516–539.

Gregor, Thomas, *Mehinaku: The Drama of Daily Life in a Brazilian Indian Village*. Chicago, 1977.

Harner, Michael J., *The Jívaro: People of the Sacred Waterfalls*. New York, 1972.

Henry, Jules, *Jungle People*. New York, 1941.

Hoebel, E. Adamson, *The Cheyennes: Indians of the Great Plains*. New York, 1960.

Holmberg, Allan R., *Nomads of the Long Bow: The Siriono of Eastern Bolivia*. Smithsonian Institution, Washington, D.C., 1950; reprinted, Garden City, 1969.

Lee, Richard B. and DeVore, Irven, editors, *Kalahari Hunter-Gatherers: Studies of the !Kung San and Their Neighbors*. Cambridge, Mass., 1976.

Marshall, Lorna, "Sharing, Talking, and Giving: Relief of Social Tensions among the !Kung," in Lee and DeVore, *Kalahari Hunter-Gatherers*, 349–371.

Maybury-Lewis, Daivd, *Akwē-Shavante Society*. New York, 1974.

Morgan, Lewis Henry, *League of the Iroquois*. Rochester, 1851; reprinted, Secaucus, N. J., 1972.

Quain, Buell, "The Iroquois," in Mead, editor, *Cooperation and Competition among Primitive Peoples*. Rev. ed., Boston, 1961.

Redfield, Robert, "Primitive Law," in Bohannan, *Law and Warfare*, 3–24.

Riesman, Paul, *Freedom in Fulani Social Life*. Chicago, 1977.

Savishinsky, Joel S., *The Trail of the Hare: Life and Stress in an Arctic Community*. New York, 1974.

Schebesta, Paul, *Die Bambuti-Pygmäen vom Ituri*. Institut Royal Colonial Belge: Section des Sciences Morales et Politiques, *Mémoires*, II (1938), Chap. VIII, Section 6, "Krieg, Blutrache, Anthropophagie."

———, *Die Bambuti-Pygmäen vom Ituri: Ergebnisse Zweier For-*

schungsreisen zu den Zentralafrikanischen Pygmäen. II. Teil, Fasc. 1 (Brussels, 1941) and Fasc. 2 (Brussels, 1948).

———, "Colin M. Turnbull und die Erforschung der Bambuti-Pygmäen," *Anthropos* 58 (1963), Fasc. 1–2: 214.

Schlegel, Alice, "The Adolescent Socialization of the Hopi Girl," *Ethnology* 12, no. 4 (October 1973): 449–462.

Stirling, M. W., *Historical and Ethnographical Material on the Jívaro Indians.* Smithsonian Institution, Bureau of American Ethnology Bulletin 117. Washington, D.C., 1938.

Thompson, Laura and Joseph, Alice, *The Hopi Way.* Reprint, Chicago, 1947.

Titiev, Mischa, *The Hopi Indians of Old Oraibi: Change and Continuity.* Ann Arbor, 1972.

———, *Old Oraibi: A Study of the Hopi Indians of Third Mesa.* Papers of the Peabody Museum of American Archaeology and Ethnology, Harvard University, vol. 22, no. 1. Cambridge, Mass., 1944.

Turnbull, Colin M., *The Forest People.* New York, 1961.

———, *The Mountain People.* New York, 1972.

———, *Wayward Servants: The Two Worlds of the African Pygmies.* New York, 1965.

Wallace, Anthony F. C., *The Death and Rebirth of the Seneca.* New York, 1969.

B. General works

Altman, Irwin, "Privacy Regulation: Culturally Universal or Culturally Specific?, *Journal of Social Issues* 33, no. 3 (Summer 1977): 66–84.

Bao Ruo-Wang (Jean Pasqualini) and Chelminski, Rudolph, *Prisoner of Mao.* New York, 1973.

Berndt, C. H., summary of note on "Interdependence and Conflict in the Eastern Central Highlands of New Guinea," in Ronald M. Berndt, Royal Anthropological Institute *Proceedings,* nos. 116–117 (July 1955).

Bernstein, Thomas P., "Leadership and Mobilization in the Collectivization of Agriculture in China and Russia: A Comparison." Ph.D. diss., Columbia University, 1970.

Bohannan, Paul, editor, *Law and Warfare: Studies in the Anthropology of Conflict.* New York, 1967.

Bowlby, John, *Attachment.* New York, 1969.

Douglas, Mary, *Natural Symbols.* London, 1970; 2nd ed., New York, 1973.

———. *Purity and Danger: An Analysis of Concepts of Pollution and Taboo.* New York, 1966.

Ford, Clellan S. and Beach, Frank A., *Patterns of Sexual Behavior.* New York, 1951; Colophon ed., New York, 1972.

Fortes, Meyer and Evans-Pritchard, E. E., editors, *African Political Systems.* Oxford, 1940.

Gennep, Arnold van, *The Rites of Passage,* translated by Monika B. Vigedom and Gabrielle L. Caffee. Chicago, 1960.

Genovese, Eugene, *Roll Jordan Roll: The World the Slaves Made.* New York, 1974.

Gluckman, Max, *Custom and Conflict in Africa.* London, 1956.

Haring, Douglas, compiler, *Personal Character and Cultural Milieu: A Collection of Readings.* Revised edition, Syracuse, 1956.

Hippler, Arthur E., book review of Ronald P. Rohner, *They Love Me, They Love Me Not* (HRAF Press, 1975), *Journal of Psychological Anthropology* 1, no. 1 (Winter 1978): 137–140.

Hobhouse, L. T., *Morals in Evolution: A Study in Comparative Ethics.* Edinburgh, 1906; 7th ed., London, 1951.

Hunt, Robert, editor, *Personalities and Culture: Readings in Psychological Anthropology.* Garden City, 1967.

Lee, Richard B. and DeVore, Irven, editors, *Man the Hunter.* Chicago, 1968.

Lewis, W. H., *The Splendid Century: Life in the France of Louis XIV.* New York, 1953; reprinted, New York, 1957.

Macpherson, C. B., *The Political Theory of Possessive Individualism: Hobbes to Locke.* Oxford, 1962.

Mair, Lucy, *Primitive Government: A Study of Traditional Political Systems in Eastern Africa.* Bloomington and London, 1977.

Malinowski, Bronislaw, *The Sexual Life of Savages in North-Western Melanesia.* New York, 1929.

Mead, Margaret, editor, *Cooperation and Competition among Primitive Peoples.* Rev. ed., Boston, 1961.

Moore, Sally F., *Law as Process: An Anthropological Approach.* London, 1978.

Naipaul, V. S., *A House for Mr. Biswas.* London, 1961; Penguin, 1976.

Sayre, Robert, *Solitude in Society: A Sociological Study in French Literature.* Cambridge, Mass., 1978.

Stone, Lawrence, *The Family, Sex and Marriage: In England 1500-1800.* New York, 1977.

Strayer, Joseph R., *On the Medieval Origins of the Modern State.* Princeton, 1970.

Westermarck, Edward A., *The History of Human Marriage.* 3 vols. 5th ed., London, 1921.

———, *The Origin and the Development of the Moral Ideas.* 2 vols. 2nd ed., London, 1912, 1917.

Whiting, John W. M. and Child, Irvin L., *Child Training and Personality: A Cross Cultural Study.* New Haven, 1953.

CHAPTER 2. CLASSICAL ATHENS

A. Primary sources

Except for Homer the texts are from the Loeb Classical Library editions. For the sake of accuracy I have taken the liberty of modifying the translations in a few instances.

Aeschines, Speeches. 1919; reprint, 1958.

Andocides in *Minor Attic Orators.* 2 vols. Vol. I, 1941; reprint, 1968.

Antiphon in *Minor Attic Orators.* 2 vols. Vol I, 1941; reprint, 1968.

Aristophanes, *Plays of Aristophanes.* 3 vols. 1924; reprint, 1931.

Aristotle. 23 vols. *The Athenian Institution, Eudemian Ethics* in Vol. XX; reprint, 1971. *The Nicomachean Ethics* in Vol. XIX; reprint, 1968, *Politics,* 1932; reprint, 1959.

Demosthenes, Orations and Letters. 7 vols. 1930; reprint, 1949.

Dinarchus in *Minor Attic Orators.* Vol. II, 1954; reprint, 1962.

Diogenes Laertius, *Lives of Eminent Philosophers*. 2 vols. London, 1925.

Herodotus, *History*. 4 vols. 1920–24.

Homer, *Iliad* and *Odyssey* in *Homeri Opera*. 3rd ed., 1917; reprint, Oxford, 1954–56.

Hyperides in *Minor Attic Orators*, 2 vols. Vol. II, 1954; reprint, 1962.

Isaeus, Works. 1927; reprint, 1962.

Isocrates, Works. 2 vols. 1928–29.

Lycurgus in *Minor Attic Orators*. 2 vols. Vol. II, 1954; reprint, 1962.

Pindar, The Odes of. 1915; rev. ed., 1937.

Plato, *Apology and Phaedrus* in *Plato in Twelve Volumes*, Vol. I. London, 1914. *Lysis* and *Symposium* in Vol. V; *The Laws* in Vols. X and XI. London, 1926.

Plutarch, *Lives*. 11 vols. 1914.

Sophocles. Two Volumes. 1913.

Theophrastus, The Characters of. 1929.

Thucydides, *History of the Peloponnesian War*. 4 vols. Rev., ed., 1919.

Xenophon, *Anabasis*, 2 vols. 1920–22; *Hellenica*, 2 vols., 1918–20; *Memorabilia, Oeconomicus, Socrates' Defence*, and *Symposium*, 1923.

B. General works

Andreades, Andreas Michael, *A History of Greek Public Finance*. Vol. I, Cambridge, Mass., 1933.

Boas, George, *Rationalism in Greek Philosophy*. Baltimore, 1961.

Beauchet, Ludovic, *Histoire du Droit Privé de la République Athenienne*. 4 vols. Paris, 1897.

Bury, J. and Meiggs, Russel, *A History of Greece*. 4th ed., New York, 1975.

Busolt, Georg and Swoboda, Heinrich, *Griechische Staatskunde*. Munich, 1926.

Derenne, Eudore, *Les Procès d'Impiété intentés aux philosophes à Athenes au Vᵐᵉ et au IVᵐᵉ siècles avant J.-C*. Paris, 1930.

de Romilly, J., *La Loi dans la pensée grecque*. Paris, 1971.

Diels, Hermann and Kranz, Walther, *Die Fragmente der Vorsokratiker*. Griechisch und Deutsch. 3 vols. 10th ed., Berlin, 1960–1961.

Dodds, E. R., *The Ancient Concept of Progress: And Other Essays on Greek Literature and Belief*. Oxford, 1973.

Dover, K. J., *Greek Homosexuality*. Cambridge, Mass., 1978; Vintage Books, 1980.

———, *Greek Popular Morality in the Time of Plato and Aristotle*. Berkeley, 1974.

Duyvendak, J.J.L., *The Book of Lord Shang: A Classic of the Chinese School of Law*. London, 1928.

Finley, M. I., editor, *Slavery in Classical Antiquity*. Cambridge, 1960.

Havelock, Eric A., *The Liberal Temper in Greek Politics*. New Haven, 1957.

Henderson, Jeffrey, *The Maculate Muse: Obscene Language in Attic Comedy*. New Haven, 1975.

Hignett, C., *A History of the Athenian Constitution*. Oxford, 1952.

Hofstadter, Richard, *The Idea of a Party System*. Berkeley, 1970.

Jacob, Oscar, *Les Esclaves Publics à Athènes*. Liège, 1928.

Jones, A.H.M., *Athenian Democracy*. New York, 1958.

Jones, J. Walter, *The Law and Legal Theory of the Greeks*. Oxford, 1956.

Lawrence, A. W., *Greek Architecture*. Baltimore, 1957.

Liddell, H. G. and Scott, R., *A Greek-English Lexicon*. Unabridged. 9th rev. ed., Oxford, 1940; reprinted, Oxford, 1977.

————, *An Intermediate Greek-English Lexicon,* an abridgement of the 1883 ed. of the large *Oxford Greek Lexicon*. Oxford, 1889; reprinted, Oxford, 1955.

MacDowell, Douglas M., *The Law in Classical Athens*. Ithaca, 1978.

Meyer, Johann Jakob, *Das Altindische Buch vom Welt- und Staatsleben: Das Arthaçastra des Kautilya*. Leipzig, 1926.

Polanyi, Karl, *The Livelihood of Man*. Edited by Harry W. Pearson. New York, 1977.

Tawney, R. H., *The Acquisitive Society*. New York, 1920.

Teiwes, Frederick C., *Politics and Purges in China*. White Plains, 1979.

Wechsler, Howard J., *Mirror to the Son of Heaven*. New Haven, 1974.

Westin, Alan F., "Privacy in Western History: From the Age of Pericles to the American Republic." Ph.D. diss., Harvard University, 1965.

CHAPTER 3. THE OLD TESTAMENT

Ben-Sasson, H. H., editor, *A History of the Jewish People*. Cambridge, Mass., 1976.

Clark, Kenneth, *The Nude: A Study in Ideal Form*. New York, 1959.

Douglas, Mary, *Purity and Danger*. London, 1966.

Harvard Medical School Health Letter 6, no. 5 (March 1981).

The Holy Bible: Revised Standard Version, Containing the Old and New Testaments. Translated from the original tongues being the version set forth A.D. 1611. . . . Revised A.D. 1952. New York, 1953.

Interpreter's Dictionary of the Bible. Supplementary Volume, Nashville, 1976.

The New Columbia Encyclopaedia. 4th ed., New York, 1975.

McNeill, William H., *A World History*. 3rd ed., Oxford, 1979.

Nelson's Complete Concordance of the Revised Standard Version Bible. New York, 1957.

Vaux, Roland de, *Histoire ancienne d'Israël: Des origines à l'installation en Canaan*. 2 vols. Paris, 1971.

————, *Les Institutions de l'Ancien Testament*. 2 vols. Paris, 1958–1960.

CHAPTER 4. ANCIENT CHINA

A. Primary sources in translation

The Complete Works of Chuang Tzu. Translated by Burton Watson. New York, 1968.

The Analects of Confucius. Translated and annotated by Arthur Waley. London, 1938; reprinted, New York, n.d.

Han Fei Tzu: Basic Writings. Translated by Burton Watson. New York, 1946.

Hsün Tzu: Basic Writings. Translated by Burton Watson. New York, 1963.

Lao Tzu: Tao Te Ching. Translated with an Introduction by D. C. Lau. Penguin Books, 1963.

Mencius. Translated with Introduction by D. C. Lau. Penguin Books, 1970.

Basic Writings of Mo Tzu. Translated by Burton Watson. New York, 1967.

Duyvendak, J. J. L., *The Book of Lord Shang: A Classic of the Chinese School of Law.* London, 1928.

Tch'ouen ts'iou et Tso tchouan. Edited and translated by S. Couvreur, S. J. 3 vols. Ho Kien Fou, 1914.

Waley, Arthur, *Book of Songs.* Translated from the Chinese. New York, 1937; reprinted, New York, 1978.

B. General works

Gernet Jacques, *La Chine ancienne: des origines à l'empire.* Paris, 1964.

Gulik, Robert van, *La vie sexuelle dans la Chine Ancienne.* Translated by Louis Evrard from *Sexual Life in Ancient China* (Leiden, 1961). Paris, 1971.

Lang, Olga, *Chinese Family and Society.* New Haven, 1946.

Vasil'ev, L. S., *Agrarnye Otnosheniya i Obshchina v Drevnem Kitaye.* Moscow, 1961.

Watson, Burton, *Early Chinese Literature.* New York, 1962.

CHAPTER 5. SOME IMPLICATIONS AND INQUIRIES

Chinoy, Ely, *Automobile Workers and the American Dream.* New York, 1955; reprinted, Boston, 1965.

Hintze, Otto, *Staat und Verfassung: Gesammelte Abhandlungen zur allgemeinen Verfassungsgeschichte.* Edited by Gerhard Oestreich. Vol. 1. 2nd ed., Göttingen, 1962.

Hoffmann, Charles, *The Chinese Worker.* Albany, 1974.

Kern, Fritz, *Gottesgnadentum und Widerstandsrecht im früheren Mitterlalter: Zur Entwicklungsgeschichte der Monarchie.* Leipzig, 1914.

Lea, Henry Charles, *A History of Auricular Confession and Indulgences in the Latin Church. 3 vols. 1896; reprinted, New York, 1968.*

Levenstein, Adolf, *Die Arbeiterfrage.* Munich, 1912.

Neumann, Franz, *The Democratic and the Authoritarian State.* Glencoe, 1957.

Ozment, Steven E., *The Reformation in the Cities: The Appeal of Protestantism to Sixteenth-Century Germany and Switzerland.* New Haven, 1975.

Pirenne, Henri, *Economic and Social History of Medieval Europe.* London, 1936.

————, *History of Europe.* 2 vols. New York, 1958.

Poggi, Gianfranco, *The Development of the Modern State: A Sociological Introduction.* Stanford, 1978.

Rawski, Thomas G., *Economic Growth and Employment in China.* Oxford, 1979.

Schneider, Laurence A., *A Madman of Ch'u: The Chinese Myth of Loyalty and Dissent.* Berkeley, 1980.

Vermeer, E. B., "Income Differentials in Rural China," *China Quarterly* 89 (March 1982): 1–33.

INDEX